ADVANCED QUANTITATIVE RESEARCH METHODS FOR URBAN PLANNERS

Advanced Quantitative Research Methods for Urban Planners provides fundamental knowledge and hands-on techniques about research, such as research topics and key journals in the planning field, advice for technical writing, and advanced quantitative methodologies.

This book aims to provide the reader with a comprehensive and detailed understanding of advanced quantitative methods and to provide guidance on technical writing. Complex material is presented in the simplest and clearest way possible using real-world planning examples and making the theoretical content of each chapter as tangible as possible. Hands-on techniques for a variety of quantitative research studies are covered to provide graduate students, university faculty, and professional researchers with useful guidance and references.

A companion to *Basic Quantitative Research Methods for Urban Planners*, *Advanced Quantitative Research Methods for Urban Planners* is an ideal read for researchers who want to branch out methodologically and for practicing planners who need to conduct advanced analyses with planning data.

Reid Ewing, PhD, is Distinguished Professor of City and Metropolitan Planning at the University of Utah, associate editor of the *Journal of the American Planning Association* and *Cities,* and columnist for *Planning* magazine, writing the column "Research You Can Use." He directs the Metropolitan Research Center at the University. He holds master's degrees in Engineering and City Planning from Harvard University and a PhD in Urban Planning and Transportation Systems from the Massachusetts Institute of Technology. A recent citation analysis found that Ewing, with 24,600 citations, is the sixth most highly cited among 1,100 planning academic planners in North America.

Keunhyun Park, PhD, is an assistant professor in the Department of Landscape Architecture and Environmental Planning at Utah State University. He holds bachelor's and master's degrees in Landscape Architecture from Seoul National University and a PhD in Metropolitan Planning, Policy, Design from the University of Utah. His research interests include technology-driven behavioral research (e.g. drone, VR/AR, sensor, etc.), behavioral outcomes of smart growth, and active living.

ADVANCED QUANTITATIVE RESEARCH METHODS FOR URBAN PLANNERS

Edited by Reid Ewing and Keunhyun Park

Routledge
Taylor & Francis Group

NEW YORK AND LONDON

First published 2020
by Routledge
52 Vanderbilt Avenue, New York, NY 10017

and by Routledge
2 Park Square, Milton Park, Abingdon, Oxon, OX14 4RN

Routledge is an imprint of the Taylor & Francis Group, an informa business

Library of Congress Cataloging-in-Publication Data
A catalog record for this title has been requested

ISBN: 978-0-367-34327-9 (hbk)
ISBN: 978-0-367-34326-2 (pbk)
ISBN: 978-0-429-32503-8 (ebk)

Typeset in Bembo
by Apex CoVantage, LLC

CONTENTS

1

INTRODUCTION

*Divya Chandrasekhar, Fatemeh Kiani, Sadegh Sabouri,
Fariba Siddiq, and Keunhyun Park*

The world is an increasingly complex place, and the tools we use to understand it are also growing in sophistication. There are many reasons for this. Quantitative researchers of today wish to understand the world more holistically—to move away from traditional methods that isolate phenomena in order to study them and to move toward ways of studying phenomena within their broader (but also deeper) context. Researchers of today also desire to push the field of quantitative analysis beyond its historical legacy of *what?* questions to questions of *how?* and *why?*

Researchers in the field of planning are not an exception. With the adoption of rigorous techniques, researchers are seeking to address the complex and multifaceted issues in urban planning. In this, they are aided by the changing nature of the data: More studies are employing mixed methods designs, producing more discrete and categorical data, and doing so in much larger quantities. The advent of *big data* provides tremendous explanatory power to quantitative research, but it also demands methodological innovations that embrace the complexity of data instead of rejecting it.

Changing times need novel ways of thinking, and the purpose of this book is to introduce urban planning researchers to some of these novel, sophisticated ways. This book has two main objectives: *first*, to provide the reader with a comprehensive and detailed understanding of innovative, advanced quantitative methods in urban planning, and *second*, to provide guidance on technical writing since much of scientific advancement is predicated upon effective communication of research findings. To the editors' knowledge, there is no such book with detailed guidance on the use of advanced research methods and their applicability in urban planning research. The audience for this book is primarily doctoral students and early career researchers in urban planning, although those in allied fields such as geography, public administration, public health, and sociology may also find it useful.

The readers of the book are expected to have a basic knowledge of statistics and quantitative research. Descriptive statistics, *t*-test, ANOVA test, correlation, and chi-square have been referred to in different chapters of this book. Particularly, understanding regression analysis is critical because more advanced methods, such as multilevel modeling, Poisson regression, and structural equation modeling, are subject to the same caveats and limitations as linear regression analysis. Violating the assumptions of the model may lead to inefficient and/ or biased parameter estimators. Other problems that can similarly affect nonlinear estimators include multicollinearity of independent variables, omitted variables, misspecification, dependence of cases or observations on one another, and small sample sizes.

Companion Book: *Basic Quantitative Research Methods for Urban Planners*

Readers interested in learning about introductory concepts in quantitative research are directed to the companion book in this series: *Basic Quantitative Research Methods for Urban Planners*. That book is aimed at master's-level students in urban planning and allied fields who wish to enter professional practice. The book introduces the reader to key definitions and concepts in general social science research (Chapter 1), a guide to writing skills and techniques for urban planners (Chapter 2), types of empirical research design (Chapter 3), data types and sources in urban planning research (Chapter 4), and other important concepts in quantitative research including conceptual frameworks (Chapter 5), validity and reliability (Chapter 6), descriptive statistics (Chapter 7), inferential statistics (Chapter 8 to 13), and quasi-experimental design (Chapter 14). Notably, logistic regression analysis and quasi-experimental research techniques are included in *Basic Quantitative Research Methods for Urban Planners* instead of this one. The editors hope to encourage more planning professionals to use these relatively advanced techniques and, in their turn, push the field forward.

Structure of the Advanced Methods Book

This book is laid out in 11 chapters, each coauthored by a leading expert in advanced analytical methods and one or more doctoral students in urban planning—a nod to the importance of our student community in driving methodological innovations. Chapter 2 introduces the basics of technical writing and publication. It is often useful to start research with the end product in mind because it helps select the right frame and tool for the exercise—a bit like outlining a design before coloring in the details. And just like drawing, this is an iterative exercise, often requiring that the outline (i.e., the main argument) or the coloring (i.e., the data analysis) be adjusted to suit each other.

In Chapter 3, Terzano and others describe the journey between completing a manuscript and publishing it. The chapter covers considerations for choosing a journal (such as impact factor, ranking, and topical match) and the peer-review process, and it describes common article topics in planning-related journals. In the latter half of the chapter, the authors analyze the column "Research You Can Use" in *Planning* magazine as a basis for identifying currently common topics of interest in urban planning research, such as methodological issues, climate change and the natural environment, social justice, and sprawl, travel, and the built environment. The authors hope to help the readers understand the lay of the land within these subfields as well as find the best outlet for their own research.

Chapters 4–10 describe specific analytical techniques in detail, including their purpose, historical use, mechanics, and step-by-step instructions on how to execute them using SPSS, AMOS, HLM, and R software. Each chapter also provides examples to demonstrate how these models and techniques have been applied to real-world problems in urban and regional planning. In Chapter 4, Musunuru and others describe Poisson and negative binomial regressions, which are appropriate for studies using count data, a common occurrence in urban and regional planning studies. The authors consider issues of model estimation and fit, overdispersion, equidispersion, underdispersion, and more complex models before outlining a detailed process to execute this technique using SPSS and R. The chapter concludes with examples of how these models have been applied to studies on smart growth policy adoption and crash prediction.

Chapter 5 introduces factor analysis, a technique to reduce complexity in data without losing the benefits of complexity thinking. Two techniques are described, principal component analysis (PCA) and common factor analysis (FA), which is further broken down into explanatory and confirmatory factor analysis (EFA and CFA, respectively). Readers are introduced to critical terminology in the use of these techniques such as multiple forms of variance, communalities, eigenvalues, factor loadings, factor scores, scree plots, and correlation, as well as a step-by-step description of how to execute this technique in SPSS and R. Authors Wheelwright and others conclude with examples of how factor analysis has been used to study the greenness of neighborhoods and land cover patterns.

In Chapter 6, authors Garfinkel-Castro and others introduce cluster analysis, which is used to classify data into a number of *natural groups* based on their attributes. Unlike a typical statistical test, cluster analysis is a data organization technique and can prove invaluable in the exploratory phase of research when hypotheses are still being developed. Readers will find a detailed step-by-step process of applying three cluster analysis methods: hierarchical, k-means, and two-step, as well as examples of how these methods have been used to classify neighborhoods and develop a typology for transit-oriented development (TOD).

Chapter 7 introduces multilevel modeling (MLM), which is an advancement of the linear regression technique and particularly useful to analyze hierarchical, nested data. Multilevel modeling is also sometimes referred to as *mixed-effects modeling* or *random-effects modeling*. Authors Levine and others make a strong case for using MLM techniques when presented with interdependent data, then detail the exact process of executing this technique in HLM, and finally show how it has been used to examine the concept *quality of life*, as well as the relationship between homeownership and poverty.

Chapter 8 introduces structural equation modeling (SEM), which use data to test theoretical models developed from the literature. The strength of SEM lies in its ability to address endogeneity and to explore causal networks and, in turn, to provide explanatory power to quantitative research. Authors Miller and others describe three modeling techniques (path analysis, confirmatory factor analysis, and hybrid models), along with a detailed process to execute SEM using the AMOS and R software. They conclude with examples of how SEMs have been used to test the relationship between the built environment and vehicular miles traveled (VMT) and to examine how sprawl and upward social mobility are related.

Kim and Brewer introduce spatial analysis in Chapter 9, which is used to organize, analyze, and interpret geographical data. Spatial analysis is of fundamental importance to urban planning because it is concerned with matters of physical space. Spatial analysis is also a technique very much *in development* and, as such, provides urban planning researchers with an early opportunity to *advance the field*. For ease of understanding, the authors have split the chapter into two parts: spatial data analysis, which involves identifying spatial patterns from data, and spatial econometrics, which advances the analysis into regression models. Spatial econometrics can be used to test whether changes in space affect changes in other, spatial or nonspatial, aspects of urban planning. The chapter also showcases how spatial analysis has been used to compare urban compactness and sprawl and to show how light rail transit (LRT) affects gentrification over time and space.

The last two chapters of the book deviate from traditional notions of quantitative empirical research. Chapter 10 introduces the increasingly popular meta-analysis and its more novel cousin, meta-regression analysis. A meta-analysis is a *study of studies* that involves synthesizing literature using quantitative techniques. Meta-regression analysis is an extension of this method that researchers can use to explore the heterogeneity of result outcomes within the same set of literature and explain why it is so. Authors Stevens et al. present multiple examples of how these techniques have been used to explore, synthesize, and explain research findings on topics such as compact development, scenario planning, and plan quality. Meta-analysis techniques provide researchers with a powerful yet robust tool for the advancement of theory building.

In the final chapter, Chapter 11, authors Millard-Ball and Kim introduce readers to another increasingly popular research approach: mixed methods research. The power of mixed methods research lies is in its ability to combine the reliability of quantitative inquiry with the more nuanced understanding of qualitative methods. The authors showcase three designs within mixed methods research based on how quantitative and qualitative steps are sequenced: simultaneously (convergent) or one before the other (exploratory and explanatory research). The authors include several examples of the use of mixed methods research in studying a range of planning problems, from gentrification to pedestrian–automobile collisions. This final chapter also indicates the importance for even the most devoted quantitative researcher to expand their skill set to include some qualitative methods.

Techniques Not Included in This Book

The field of quantitative research is ever expanding, and many innovative techniques useful to researchers are not showcased in this book. Obviously, it is impossible to describe all of these methods and techniques. Here, we briefly describe some of the advanced methods used by urban planners beyond those in this book so that interested readers may consider looking into them.

In Chapter 13 of *Basic Quantitative Research Methods for Urban Planners*, we described binary and multinomial logistic regressions. However, discrete choice models are not confined to these two. Ordered logit and nested logit are two other popular discrete-choice models. Ordered logit is used to model choices that have an inherent order to them like neighborhood satisfaction (e.g., satisfied, indifferent, dissatisfied), Likert scale questions (e.g., strongly agree, agree, disagree, and strongly disagree) in many behavioral surveys, and the like.

The nested logit model (also known as nested multinomial logit) is used when groups of alternatives are similar to each other in an unobserved way. In other words, a structure that partitions the alternatives into groups or nests can be specified. Travel mode choice (i.e., walk, bike, transit, and auto) is a good example in which our choices are nested in motorized (transit and auto) and nonmotorized (walk and bike) groups.

In addition to logistic regression, we have probit regression models, which have been used widely, especially in transportation. Both logistic and probit regression models are types of generalized linear models, and both have versions for binary, ordinal, or multinomial categorical outcomes, which we explained for logistic regression. Probit regression is almost the same as logistic regression, and the real difference is the use of different link functions. Logistic regression uses a logit link function (explained in *Basic Quantitative Research Methods for Urban*

Planners), whereas probit regression uses an inverse normal link function. In reality, the differences in the results of the models (e.g., binary logistic versus binary probit) are usually slight to nonexistent. However, the interpretation of the models is different and much easier in the logistic models. This is because in the logistic regression, by simply back-transforming the log-odds, we can acquire the odds ratios, which is an intuitive way to interpret the effects.

In Chapter 4 of this book, we explain Poisson and negative binomial regression models. Other methods can be used to model count data, such as generalized Poisson, quasi-Poisson, and Conway-Maxwell Poisson regression. One of the most important benefits of these models is that they can handle underdispersion (i.e., the variance of the dependent variable is less than the mean) as well. Poisson model is better used when we have equidispersion (i.e., the variance is equal to the mean), and negative binomial is used when the dependent variable is overdispersed (i.e., the variance is greater than the mean).

When there are far more observed zero counts than expected given the mean of the distribution, zero-inflated and hurdle models are two possible models that can be used. Both of these models are described in two stages. The basic idea in the hurdle model is that a Bernoulli probability governs the binary outcome of whether our dependent count variable has a zero or positive value. If the value is positive, the hurdle is crossed, and the conditional distribution of the positives is governed by a truncated-at-zero count data model.

As far as we know, Ewing et al. (2015) used this model for the first time in the planning field. Their first stage was the estimation of logistic regression models to distinguish between households with and without walk, bike, or transit trips. Their second stage was the estimation of negative binomial regression models for the number of trips by these modes for households that have such trips. In zero-inflated models, the count variable is modeled as a mixture of a Bernoulli distribution and a Poisson or negative binomial or any other count distribution supported on non-negative integers. Therefore, in zero-inflated models, counts can still be zero. However, in hurdle models, they must be nonzero (at stage 2).

Generalized linear models with L1 (known as Lasso) or L2 (known as Ridge) regularization are more advanced models used to avoid or reduce the risk of overfitting models by adding a penalty to the model-fitting process. This is achieved by setting the constraint that the sum of the absolute model coefficients ($\sum |\beta j| pj = 1$) must be less than a specified threshold (t). To achieve this constraint, the coefficients of uninformative variables are reduced or shrunk, and if shrunk to zero, this has the effect of removing that covariate from the model. Note that the key difference between L1 and L2 regularization is the penalty term.

In addition to the generalized linear models discussed in the two books, some methods can be used to identify and characterize nonlinear regression effects. These methods are called generalized additive models (GAM). In real life, effects are often not linear, and in GAM, these nonlinear effects are captured using unspecified smooth functions. In other words, GAM has the form $E(Y) = \alpha + f_1(X_1) + f_1(X_2) + \cdots + f_n(X_n)$, where f_i represents the smooth functions for each of the independent (X_i) variables.

To recapitulate, the field of quantitative research is expanding enormously, and there are numerous advanced statistical techniques and methods. The focus of this subsection was to familiarize the readers with some of these techniques and methods beyond those in the book chapters. Interested readers may also consider looking into more advanced analytical techniques, such as Bayesian statistics (as oppose to frequentist statistics, which is the basis of these two books) and machine learning (e.g., Naive Bayes, Random Forest, Neural Network, and Gradient Boosting Algorithms).

Data and Measurements

This section provides a refresher on the fundamental concepts and terminologies of empirical research methods utilized in this book. Empirical research depends on empirical evidence, or observable data, to formulate and test theories and come to conclusions. Data used in research can be described in many ways. First, if you collect the data yourself, it is called *primary data*. It can come from a survey or an interview you create and conduct, from direct observation of human behavior, or from a measurement of the environment such as sidewalk widths or the number of street trees. If you use data that someone else has collected, you are using *secondary data*. The EPA's Air Quality Index is a good example.

Data can be either aggregate or disaggregate. *Disaggregate* data simply means looking at individuals' characteristics such as race, income, or education level, plus individuals' behavior such as fruit and vegetable consumption or minutes of moderate exercise. *Aggregate* data are summaries of disaggregate data, meaning that information on individuals is compiled and aggregated. Examples are average household income, percentage of nonwhite population, and average vehicle miles traveled within a given spatial boundary. Usually, in planning research, disaggregate data are considered as having higher quality but are harder to gather due to privacy issues or cost. Aggregate data raise issues of aggregation bias and the ecological fallacy but may be appropriate if you are interested in differences from place to place (Ewing et al., 2017).

Related to the distinction between aggregate and disaggregate data, an important concept is the unit of analysis. The *unit of analysis* is the entity being analyzed in a study. In social science research, typical units of analysis include individuals, groups, geographical units (e.g., town, Census tract, state), and social organizations. The level of data and the unit of analysis are closely associated with each other: Disaggregate data enable you to analyze at the individual level, and an individual-level analysis requires you to collect disaggregate data.

The *unit of observation* should not be confused with the unit of analysis. For example, a study may have a unit of observation at the individual level but may have the unit of analysis at the neighborhood level, drawing conclusions about neighborhood characteristics from data collected from individuals.

Data can be either cross-sectional or longitudinal according to the temporal dimension. Cross-sectional data are collected at a single point in time. Regardless of the time interval or period (e.g., minutes, days, years), contemporaneous measurements occur within the same period for all variables and all cases. In 2015, the Wasatch Front Regional Council (2018) in Utah put extensive efforts into measuring urban design qualities (including pedestrian counts) for over 1,200 blocks throughout the region. This is an example of cross-sectional and aggregate data.

Longitudinal data are collected over time—you have at least two waves of measurement. An example is the Public Transportation Ridership Report quarterly published by the American Public Transportation Association (APTA). The ridership report contains what is sometimes called time-series data, implying many waves of measurement over time.

A further distinction is made among several types of longitudinal data. Repeated cross-sectional data are collected on the same set of variables for multiple periods but with different cases in each period. For transportation planners—an example is the National Household Travel Survey (NHTS) by the U.S. Department of Transportation (DOT) —data on travel and sociodemographic characteristics of the American public. Surveys under the current name were conducted in 2001, 2009, and 2017 with almost identical questions but for different survey participants.

Another type of longitudinal data is panel data. In *panel data*, both the cases and variables remain the same over time. As an example, the National Crime Victimization Survey (NCVS), administered by the Bureau of Justice Statistics, is a national survey of about 90,000 households on the frequency, characteristics, and consequences of criminal victimization in the United States. The selected households are interviewed seven times (at six-month intervals) over three years. Panel data represent the gold standard for planning research, since the repeated observation of the same cases (individuals or groups) inherently controls for individual and group differences that cannot be measured but can be assumed invariant over time.

Lastly, data can be classified by the scale of measurement. There are four scales of measurement. First, a *nominal scale* categorizes cases with no numerical equivalent (e.g., male/female, introvert/extrovert, city/suburb). Second, an *ordinal measurement* can rank-order the cases, but the distances between attributes have no meaning. For example, five-star hotels are supposed to be *better* than lower-ranked hotels in terms of accommodations and services. However, we do not know if the distance from five-star to four-star is the same as four-star to three-star. A better example for planners is the categorization of people as low income, medium income, or high income. Third, in *interval measurement*, we can assume equal intervals between values. Typical examples include temperature and IQ. When we measure temperature (in Fahrenheit), the distance from 30° to 40° is the same as the distance from 70° to 80°. Note, however, that in interval measurement, ratios don't make any sense, and there is no true zero (0° Celsius does not mean no temperature). Sprawl metrics, developed by Ewing and Hamidi (2014), are measured in terms of standard deviations above and below the mean, but there is no true zero when it comes to compactness or sprawl. Lastly, *ratio measurement* always has a meaningful absolute zero; that is, zero indicates the absence of the variable measured. Weight, age, and frequency of behaviors are examples. It is called a ratio scale since you can construct a meaningful fraction or ratio with its values: Someone can weigh twice as much as another or can walk twice as frequently as another. In contrast to sprawl measures, density is a ratio scale variable.

Variables with nominal or ordinal measurement are called *categorical*, while those with interval or ratio measurement are called *continuous*. Knowing the level of measurement helps you interpret the data and decide on an appropriate analysis method.

Conceptual Framework

What is of interest to planners is causality. For example, a research question could be, "Will more highway construction induce more traffic?"

A *theory* is an explanation of why things occur. In the preceding research question, a theory could be, "If highway capacity increases, people will drive more" (induced demand theory). Derived from theory, a statement that is testable is called a *hypothesis*. A hypothesis that follows from the preceding theory is, "As highway lane miles increase, vehicle miles traveled (VMT) will increase." When confirmed by many tests of related hypotheses, a theory can be deemed a *law* (e.g., the "universal law of traffic congestion" isn't a real law but was incorrectly labeled a law by Anthony Downs in a famous article about highway-induced traffic—highway expansion doesn't always lead to increased driving if there is already free-flowing traffic).

Readers might recognize the different words used in theory and hypothesis, such as capacity versus lane miles and travel versus VMT. In general, a theory consists of constructs or abstract concepts and how they are related to one another. Highway capacity, travel, growth, and sprawl are examples. On the other hand, a hypothesis is phrased in terms of variables, that is, quantities that vary, are measurable, and partially capture constructs. VMT, highway lane miles, population growth, and residential density are examples, respectively corresponding to the preceding constructs (see Chapter 5 of *Basic Quantitative Research Methods for Urban Planners*). They too are ordinarily described by relationships to one another.

A theory or hypothesis or multiple theories or hypotheses can be verbally or visually represented by a conceptual framework (or conceptual model, causal path diagram). A conceptual framework consists of logical relations among concepts or variables that guide your research. Despite the importance of adopting conceptual frameworks, researchers in the planning field have not devoted earnest attention to them (see Chapter 5 of *Basic Quantitative Research Methods for Urban Planners*). A survey of planning articles showed that it is rare for planners to articulate conceptual frameworks and even rarer for them to schematically diagram them.

Two types of variables are defined in most studies. They are independent (or predictor, explanatory, or X) variables and dependent (or response, outcome, or Y) variables. *Dependent variables* represent outcomes or consequences that you try to understand. *Independent variables* are those hypothesized to influence or predict the values of the dependent variables. In causal models, an independent variable represents a cause, and a dependent variable represents an effect.

Correlation refers to a statistical index that describes how strongly variables are related to one another. It simply means that two things happen together: For example, more highway construction is accompanied by more traffic, but we don't know which one is the cause and which one is the effect or whether a third variable is causing both, such as population growth. Please remember that correlation does not imply causation (see Chapters 5 and 9 of *Basic Quantitative Research Methods for Urban Planners*).

Statistics

In a quantitative study, a conceptual framework can be represented as a mathematical model. A *mathematical model* uses mathematical language to describe the behavior of a system. It is composed of mathematical equations representing the functional relationships among variables. Mathematical models can take many forms, including statistical models.

The value of mathematical models may not be evident to many planners. At the core of these statistical approaches is the idea that patterns can be ascertained from our data. For example, without a model, thousands of household travel surveys themselves do not tell us anything about the association between the neighborhood environment and household travel behavior. A *model* allows us to explore relationships that might not be immediately evident from the raw observations themselves (Tolmie, Muijs, & McAteer, 2011).

There are basically two types of statistics in quantitative planning research: descriptive and inferential. *Descriptive statistics* describe a collection of data from a sample or population. They form the basis of virtually every quantitative analysis and are also used in many qualitative studies to describe cases. Examples of descriptive statistics are mean (or average), median, variance, and standard deviation values (see Chapter 7 in Basic Quantitative Research Methods for Urban Planners).

After describing the data, you will usually want to make a decision about the statistical and practical significance of relationships among the variables. *Inferential statistics* involve statistical methods that draw conclusions from data that reach beyond the data as such. Inferential statistics may also be defined as a process of drawing inferences about a population from a sample. Here, a *population* means the full set of people or things with a characteristic one wishes to understand, whereas a *sample* is a subset of individuals from a larger population. Because there is very rarely enough time or money to gather information from everyone or information about everything in a population, the goal becomes finding a representative sample of that population.

Please note that inferential statistics do not prove something to be *true*. It can only give a measure of how confident or certain we are that it is true. Also, it is often easier to consider whether we should accept or reject that nothing happened (*null hypothesis*) than it is to *prove* that something did happen (*alternative hypothesis*). That's why we reject the null hypothesis and accept the alternative hypothesis when the probability that the null hypothesis is true is low (conventionally, when the probability is less than one in 20, or 5%).

A *null model* is a model where coefficients (slopes) for all independent variables are set equal to zero and only the constant term (intercept) is allowed to vary. You can interpret the null model as saying that under the null hypothesis, there is no relationship between independent and dependent variables and that the best estimate of a new observation is the mean of the dependent variable (i.e., the intercept in a regression equation).

A *best-fit model*, or *fitted model*, has just the right number of predictors needed to explain the data well. Fitting a model is a trade-off between parsimony and explanatory power (i.e., the goodness of fit) because high parsimony models (i.e., models with few parameters) tend to produce a worse fit to the data than low parsimony models. Occam's razor, or the so-called law of briefness, states that you should use no more variables than necessary. This means that we want to reduce our model to the simplest form that still does a good job of predicting outcomes. A model that is missing significant variables is called *underspecified* and will likely produce biased coefficient estimates. A model that has excess variables that are not significant is called *overspecified* and will likely produce inefficient (high standard error) coefficient estimates.

A *saturated* model is one in which there are as many estimated parameters as data points. By definition, this will lead to a perfect fit but will be of little use statistically, as you have no data left to estimate variance. In structural equation modeling (see Chapter 8), models are automatically compared to a saturated model (one that allows all variables to intercorrelate), and this comparison allows the analysis to discover missing pathways and thereby reject inconsistent models.

Chapter Structure

Most chapters have a recurring structure to help readers understand each of the methods more easily, albeit varied among chapters—for example, Chapter 1 provides an overview of the book and Chapters 2 (writing) and 3 (planning journals and topics) present specialized topics rather than research methods. Each section answers specific questions.

- **Overview:** What is the essence of the method? What do we need to know before applying the method?
- **Purpose:** How is this method used, and what is it used for?
- **History:** When was it developed? Who developed the method?
- **Mechanics:** What are the components of the method? What assumptions must be met, or under what conditions would you use this method? What are the limitations of the method?
- **Interpreting Results:** How can we understand the results? How can we know if the results are valid and reliable?

- **Step by Step**: How can we utilize the method using SPSS or R (or another appropriate software package)? How can we apply the method to real planning data?
- **Planning Examples**: What two interesting studies from the planning literature use the method?
- **Conclusion**: How can we summarize the method and assess its usefulness?

Actual examples from peer-reviewed journal articles are provided to show how planning scholars have used a particular method to analyze one or more real planning problems. This part makes our book distinguishable from other textbooks in other fields by connecting the methods to our readers.

Datasets

"Step by Step" is another section that makes our two books different from earlier planning texts. These books provide not only theoretical understanding but also seek to foster understanding of how to apply each method using real planning data.

UZA Dataset

One dataset used in this book, the urbanized area (UZA) dataset, allows us to test the theory of induced travel demand (i.e., highways generate their own demand) and also test theories about how the built environment is related to highway demand. The highway data come from the Federal Highway Administration (FHWA)'s *Highway Statistics*. Our transit data come from the National Transit Database. Other data come from other sources. For spatial units, we used FHWA's urbanized area boundaries. We limited our sample to large urbanized areas with populations of 200,000 or more for which all variables in Table 1.1 could be estimated. Of the 173 urbanized areas meeting the population criterion, some cases were lost for lack of other data (e.g., compactness metrics, transit data, or fuel price data). Our final sample consists of 157 urbanized areas. This dataset is used in Chapters 5, 6, and 8.

The variables in our models are defined in Table 1.1. They are as follows:

- **Our dependent variables**: Daily VMT per capita and annual traffic delay per capita;
- **Our independent variables**: The independent variables of primary interest are lane miles of highway capacity per 1,000 population and population density and other measures of compactness. Control variables include population size, per capita income, and metropolitan average fuel price.

All variables are presented both in linear and in logged forms (the latter transformed by taking natural logarithms). The use of logarithms has two advantages. First, it makes relationships among our variables more nearly linear and reduces the influence of outliers (such as New York and Los Angeles). Second, it allows us to interpret parameter estimates as elasticities (the ratio of the percentage change in a dependent variable associated with the percentage change in an independent variable), which summarize relationships in an understandable and transferable form.

This database has been used in three published articles (Ewing et al., 2014; Ewing et al., 2017; Ewing et al., 2018), which relate daily VMT per capita or annual delay per capita for

TABLE 1.1 Variables in UZA database (FHWA urbanized areas in 2010)

Variable	Definition	Source	Mean	Standard Deviation
pop000	Population (in thousands)	U.S. Census	1,124.7	2,072.3
inc000	Income per capita (in thousands)	American Community Survey	26.9	5.2
hhsize	Average household size	U.S. Census	2.6	0.3
veh	Average vehicle ownership per capita	American Community Survey	0.4	0.04
area	land area in square miles	U.S. Census	514.3	597.5
popden	Gross population density in persons per square miles	U.S. Census	1877.6	897.3
lm	Road lane mile per 1000 population	FHWA Highway Statistics NAVTEQ	3.1	0.8
flm	Freeway lane miles per 1000 population	FHWA Highway Statistics	0.7	0.3
olm	Other lane miles per 1000 population	FHWA Highway Statistics NAVTEQ	2.4	0.7
rtden	Transit route density per square mile	National Transit Database	2.4	2.3
tfreq	Transit service frequency	National Transit Database	6,717.0	3,396.9
hrt	Directional route miles of heavy rail lines per 100,000 population*	National Transit Database	9.7	53.1
lrt	Directional route miles of light rail lines per 100,000 population*	National Transit Database	9.2	26.8
tpm	Annual transit passenger miles per capita	National Transit Database	98.9	138.0
fuel	Average metropolitan fuel price	Oil Price Information Service	2.8	0.2
vmt	Daily VMT per capita	FHWA Highway Statistics	23.9	5.3
empden	Gross employment density in employees per square mile	LEHD	863.1	414.0
lt1500	Percentage of the population living at low suburban densities (less than 1500 persons per square mile)	U.S. Census	23.1	12.9
gt12500	Percentage of the population living at medium to high urban densities (greater than 12,500 persons per square mile)	U.S. Census	4.8	8.5
urbden	Net population density of urban lands	U.S. Census, NLCD	3,287.7	1,046.8
denfac	Density factor	Multiple sources—see Ewing and Hamidi (2014)	100.0	25.0
mixfac	Mix factor	multiple sources—see Ewing and Hamidi (2014)	100.0	25.0
cenfac	Centering factor	Multiple sources—see Ewing and Hamidi (2014)	100.0	25.0
strfac	Street factor	Multiple sources—see Ewing and Hamidi (2014)	100.0	25.0
Compact	Compactness index	Multiple sources—see Ewing and Hamidi (2014)	100.0	24.9
Delay	Annual delay per capita in hours	INRIX/TTI congestion data	27.7	9.8
Tti	Travel time index	INRIX/TTI congestion data	1.2	0.1

urbanized areas to regional compactness, highway capacity, transit service, average fuel price, and other covariates. More studies using this database are coming.

Household Dataset

The other dataset used in this book is the household travel dataset, which allows us to test how the built environment is associated with people's travel choices. We have been collecting household travel survey data from metropolitan planning organizations (MPOs) in the United States for many years. Additional GIS data (land use parcels, street network, transit stops, travel time skims, etc.) were also collected from state, county, and local governments to compute built environmental variables. The unit of analysis is the individual household. The spatial unit is the half-mile road network buffer around the household's address.

The full dataset consists of 931,479 trips made by 94,620 households in 34 regions of the United States. For this book, we make available data for a subset of 14,212 households from 10 regions: Seattle, Washington; Kansas City, Missouri; Eugene, Oregon; San Antonio, Texas; Detroit, Michigan; Richmond, Virginia; Charleston, South Carolina; Winston-Salem, North Carolina; Syracuse, New York; and Madison, Wisconsin. Precise *XY* coordinates for households, often provided to us under strict confidentiality requirements, have been replaced with census block group geocodes. In this book, chapters 4, 7, and 9 use "HTS.household.10regions.sav" dataset. For Multilevel Modeling (chapter 7), region-level file ("HTS.region.sav") is also used. For Spatial Econometrics (chapter 9), you need a shapefile for Washington state (tract10. shp) from the online resource page of this book.

The variables in this dataset are defined in Table 1.2. They are as follows:

- **Household-related variables**: Any VMT (a dummy variable for households with any VMT versus those with no VMT), household VMT (for those with VMT), number of auto trips, any walk (again, a dummy variable), number of walk trips (for those with any walk trips), any bike, number of bike trips, any transit, number of transit trips, number of vehicles, household size, number of workers, household income, housing type;
- **Built environment variables within a half-mile of household location**: Activity density, job-population balance, land use entropy, intersection density, percentage of four-way intersections, transit stop density, percentage of regional employment that can be reached within 10, 20, and 30 minutes by auto and in 30 minutes by transit;
- **Regional variables**: Population size, regional average fuel price, compactness indices.

Most variables are presented in linear form. Some variables are logged (transformed by taking natural logarithms). The reason for using logarithms is the same as mentioned previously for the UZA dataset.

The household travel dataset has been used in three published articles (Ewing et al., 2010, 2015; Tian et al., 2015). More studies using this database are coming. The published studies relate the built environment to travel behavior, at the household level or the trip level.

TABLE 1.2 Variables in household database (based on household travel surveys from different years)

Variable	Definition	N	Mean	Sta. Dev.
rhhnum	household ID	14,212	—	—
region	region ID	14,212	—	—
geoid	Census block group FIPS code (only for Seattle region)	3,904	—	—
dependent variables				
anyvmt	any household VMT (1 = yes, 0 = no)	14,199	0.94	0.25
lnvmt	natural log of household VMT (for households with any VMT), adjusted by average vehicle occupancy rate	13,285	3.07	1.02
autotrips	household car trips	14,212	8.49	7.23
anywalk	any household walk trips (1 = yes, 0 = no)	14,212	0.21	0.41
walktrips	household walk trips (for households with any walk trips)	2,960	3.41	2.94
anybike	any household bike trips (1 = yes, 0 = no)	14,212	0.03	0.18
biketrips	household bike trips (for households with any bike trips)	450	3.22	2.69
anytransit	any household transit trips (1 = yes, 0 = no)	14,212	0.07	0.26
transittrips	household transit trips (for households with any transit trips)	1,004	2.68	2.27
Independent variables – household				
veh	number of vehicles	14,212	1.90	1.03
hhsize	household size	14,212	2.38	1.26
hhworker	number of employed household members	14,212	1.16	0.87
htype	housing type (0=other, 1=single-family-detached, 2=single-family-attached, 3=multi-family) (no data in Detroit)	13,249	—	—
sf	housing type (1 = single-family, 0 = other)	13,273	0.81	0.40
hhincome	real household income (in 1000s of 2012 dollars)	13,355	69.10	41.73

(*Continued*)

TABLE 1.2 (Continued)

Variable	Definition	N	Mean	Sta. Dev.
income_cat	household income grouped by three income brackets (1=less than $35K, 2=between $35K and $75K, 3=over $75K)	13,355	2.13	0.76
Independent variables – a half-mile buffer				
actden	activity density within one-half mile (population plus employment per square mile in 1000s)	14,179	5.24	8.69
jobpop[1]	job-population balance within one-half mile	14,151	0.60	0.25
entropy[2]	land use entropy within one-half mile	14,146	0.34	0.27
intden	intersection density (per square mile) within one-half mile	14,179	140.22	123.78
pct4way	percentage 4-way intersections within one-half mile	14,153	29.26	22.29
stopden	transit stop density within one-half mile	14,179	23.55	36.77
emp10a	percentage of regional employment within 10 min by auto	14,212	14.70	17.57
emp20a	percentage of regional employment within 20 min by auto	14,212	45.15	31.34
emp30a	percentage of regional employment within 30 min by auto	14,212	66.63	30.76
emp30t	percentage of regional employment within 30 min by transit	14,212	20.78	20.77
Region variables (HTS.region.10regions.sav)				
region	region ID	10	–	–
date	year of the household travel survey	10	–	–
regname	region name	10	–	–
regpop	population within the region in 1000s	10	1529.39	1524.59
fuel	average regional fuel price	10	2.87	.14

Variable	Definition	N	Mean	Sta. Dev.
compact	measure of regional compactness developed by Ewing and Hamidi (2014); higher values of the index correspond to more compact development, lower values to more sprawling development.	10	104.68	31.59

Note: Variables starting with "ln" represents that the original variable is log-transformed.

1 The job–population index measures balance between employment and resident population within a buffer. Index ranges from 0, where only jobs or residents are present within a buffer, not both, to 1 where the ratio of jobs to residents is optimal from the standpoint of trip generation. Values are intermediate when buffers have both jobs and residents, but one predominates. jobpop = 1 − [ABS(employment − 0.2*population)/(employment + 0.2*population)]. ABS is the absolute value of the expression in parentheses. The value 0.2, representing a balance of employment and population, was found through trial and error to maximize the explanatory power of the variable.

2 The entropy index measures balance between three different land uses. The index ranges from 0, where all land is in a single use, to 1 where land is evenly divided among the three uses. Values are intermediate when buffers have more than one use but one use predominates. The entropy calculation is: entropy = − [residential share*ln(residential share) + commercial share*ln(commercial share) + public share*ln(public share)]/ln(3), where ln is the natural logarithm of the value in parentheses and the shares are measured in terms of total parcel land areas.

Computer Software Used in This Book

The statistical software packages used in the "Step by Step" sections of Chapters 3–8 were chosen for ease of use. In three chapters—Chapters 3–5, the key software of choice is SPSS. Also, we provide R codes for all "Step by Step" sections—Chapters 3–8. SPSS is available on a trial basis, and R is a free software.

Released in 1968, SPSS is a classic, leading software package for quantitative research in the social sciences. Thanks to its user-friendly interface and easy-to-use drop-down menus, it is a useful tool for nonstatisticians as well. One of the advantages in terms of learning is its similarity to Excel, something many students are already familiar with. Other benefits include official support and extensive documentation. Thus, SPSS is by far the most common software used in academic research generally and in planning programs.

In 2018, Robert Muenchen analyzed Google Scholar, a scholarly literature search engine, to see the trend of data analysis software in scholarly use (http://r4stats.com/articles/popularity). The most popular software package in scholarly publications was SPSS, more than twice the second most widely used package, R (Figure 1.1). He attributed this result to the balance between power and ease of use of SPSS.

A survey of planning programs in the United States showed that SPSS is very popular for use in the classroom. At both the graduate and undergraduate levels, professors reported using SPSS nearly three times as often as the next most popular software package, Stata. The similarity between SPSS and Excel was cited as a major reason for using the IBM-produced software. (Indeed, most professors reported using SPSS alongside Excel in the classroom.)

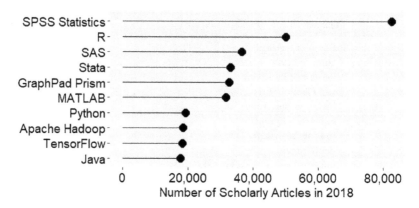

FIGURE 1.1 Number of scholarly articles that use each software package in 2018

Source: Adjusted from http://r4stats.com/articles/popularity/

TABLE 1.3 Frequency of responses by instructors of planning courses to the question, "Which software package(s) do you utilize in the methods course(s) you teach?" (*n*=44)

Software	Frequency of Use (%)
SPSS	52
Stata	20
SAS	7
R	4
All others	17

Results, shown in Table 1.3, are based on a survey of ACSP full member accredited schools. Forty-one of the 107 programs responded, a response rate of 38%. Additionally, one affiliate member school and two corresponding member schools responded to a request for information.

Of course, SPSS is not without limitations. It is commercial (i.e., not free) and may be slower in handling large datasets than other software. It cannot estimate all types of models. For instance, its multinomial logistic regression model is constrained. Emerging open-source, free software such as R or Python can be an alternative to SPSS for urban researchers. While this book sticks to menu-driven software for most chapters, we are forced to use R, command-driven software, in Chapter 9 on spatial econometrics.

In Chapter 7, on multilevel modeling, we use HLM, Hierarchical Linear and Nonlinear Modeling software, available from Scientific Software International, with its easy-to-use menus. In Chapter 8, on structural equation modeling, we use AMOS, an added module of SPSS, with its easy-to-use graphical interface. Both HLM and AMOS are available on a trial basis.

Works Cited

American Public Transportation Association. (2017). *Public transportation ridership report.* Retrieved from www.apta.com/resources/statistics/Pages/ridershipreport.aspx

Bracken, I. (1981). *Urban planning methods: Research and policy analysis.* London: Methuen Publishing.

Contant, C. K., & Forkenbrock, D. J. (1986). Planning methods: An analysis of supply and demand. *Journal of Planning Education and Research, 6*(1), 10–21. https://doi.org/10.1177/07394 56X8600600104

Dickey, J. W., & Watts, T. M. (1978). *Analytic techniques in urban and regional planning.* New York, NY: McGraw-Hill.

Edwards, M. M., & Bates, L. K. (2011). Planning's core curriculum: Knowledge, practice, and implementation. *Journal of Planning Education and Research, 31*(2), 172–183. https://doi.org/10.1177/0739456X11398043

Ewing, R., Greenwald, M., Zhang, M., Walters, J., Feldman, M., Cervero, R., & Thomas, J. (2010). Traffic generated by mixed-use developments: Six-region study using consistent built environmental measures. *Journal of Urban Planning and Development, 137*(3), 248–261. https://doi.org/10.1061/(ASCE) UP.1943-5444.0000068

Ewing, R., & Hamidi, S. (2014). *Measuring urban sprawl and validating sprawl measures.* Washington, DC: National Institutes of Health and Smart Growth America.

Ewing, R., Hamidi, S., Gallivan, F., Nelson, A. C., & Grace, J. B. (2014). Structural equation models of VMT growth in US urbanised areas. *Urban Studies, 51*(14), 3079–3096. https://doi. org/10.1177/0042098013516521

Ewing, R., Hamidi, S., Tian, G., Proffitt, D., Tonin, S., & Fregolent, L. (2017). Testing Newman and Kenworthy's theory of density and automobile dependence. *Journal of Planning Education and Research.* https://doi.org/10.1177/0739456X16688767

Ewing, R., Tian, G., Goates, J. P., Zhang, M., Greenwald, M. J., Joyce, A., . . . Greene, W. (2015). Varying influences of the built environment on household travel in 15 diverse regions of the United States. *Urban Studies, 52*(13), 2330–2348. https://doi.org/10.1177/0042098014560991

Ewing, R., Tian, G., Lyons, T., & Terzano, K. (2018). Does compact development increase or reduce traffic congestion? *Cities, 72,* 94–101.

Ferguson, E. (2014). *Ferguson on quantitative research methods in planning: A comparative assessment of teaching versus practice.* Guest essay on Urban Planning Research blog. Retrieved from http://planning-research.com/ quantitative-research-methods-in-planning-a-comparative-assessment-of-teaching-versus-practice

Gaber, J., & Gaber, S. (2007). *Qualitative analysis for planning & policy: Beyond the numbers.* Chicago, IL: American Planning Association.

Greenlee, A. J., Edwards, M., & Anthony, J. (2015). Planning skills: An examination of supply and local government demand. *Journal of Planning Education and Research, 35*(2), 161–173. https://doi. org/10.1177/0739456X15570321

Guzzetta, J. D., & Bollens, S. A. (2003). Urban planners' skills and competencies: Are we different from other professions? Does context matter? Do we evolve? *Journal of Planning Education and Research, 23*(1), 96–106. https://doi.org/10.1177/0739456X03255426

Muenchen, R. A. (2015). *The popularity of data science software.* Retrieved from http://r4stats.com/ articles/popularity/

Patton, C. V., Sawicki, D. S., & Clark, J. J. (2013). *Basic methods of policy analysis and planning* (3rd ed.). Upper Salle River, NJ: Pearson Education, Inc.

Silva, E. A., Healey, P., Harris, N., & Van den Broeck, P. (Eds.). (2014). *The Routledge handbook of planning research methods.* London: Routledge.

Tian, G., Ewing, R., White, A., Hamidi, S., Walters, J., Goates, J. P., & Joyce, A. (2015). Traffic generated by mixed-use developments: Thirteen-region study using consistent measures of built environment. *Transportation Research Record, 2500,* 116–124. https://doi.org/10.3141/2500-14

Tolmie, A., Muijs, D., & McAteer, E. (2011). *Quantitative methods in educational and social research using SPSS.* London: McGraw-Hill Education.

Tracy, S. J. (2012). *Qualitative research methods: Collecting evidence, crafting analysis, communicating impact.* Hoboken, NJ: John Wiley & Sons.

U.S. Bureau of Justice Statistics. (2016). *National crime victimization survey.* Retrieved from www.bjs.gov/ index.cfm?ty=dcdetail&iid=245

U.S. Census Bureau. (2018). Retrieved from www.census.gov/data.html

U.S. Department of Transportation. (2017). *National household travel survey*. Retrieved from http://nhts. ornl.gov/

U.S. Environmental Protection Agency. (2016). *Air quality index*. Retrieved from https://airnow.gov/ index.cfm?action=aqibasics.aqi

U.S. Federal Highway Administration. (2016). *Highway statistics*. Retrieved from www.fhwa.dot.gov/ policyinformation/statistics.cfm

Wasatch Front Regional Council. (2018). *Walkability and measuring urban street design*. Retrieved from https://wfrcgis.maps.arcgis.com/apps/MapSeries/index.html?appid=7d1b1df5686c41b593d1e5ff5 539d01a

Willemain, T. R. (1980). *Statistical methods for planners*. Cambridge, MA: The MIT Press.

2

TECHNICAL WRITING

Robin Rothfeder and Reid Ewing

Overview

Writing is an essential communication tool for planners. Practitioners use writing to produce plans, ordinances, staff reports, legal documents, consulting reports, and other deliverables. Scholars use writing to situate their research within existing literature, to describe their research methods, to explain their research results, and to apply those results in a practical setting. Whether professional or academic, most final planning products take the form of written communication. Planners, in short, write for a living.

If you read the dry pages of journals and reports, you might be tempted to conclude that great writing by planners is a lost art. We believe otherwise. Classic planning works—Mumford, Jacobs, Appleyard, Whyte, and many others—contain brilliantly insightful and artistic writing. In the following quotation, for instance, Whyte uses just a few simple sentences to highlight an essential planning problem, to provide a specific example of the problem, and to suggest within that example the seed of a solution. In so doing, he indicates many of the essential characteristics of current planning trends, such as Smart Growth and New Urbanism, decades before their time.

> In almost all U.S. cities the bulk of the right-of-way is given to the roadway for vehicles, the least to the sidewalk for pedestrians. New York's Lexington Avenue is a prime example, in particular the four block stretch between Fifty-seventh and Sixty-first streets. It is the reduction ad absurdum of the U.S. city street—and by its very excesses it provides clues for its redemption.
>
> —*William H. Whyte, 1988, p. 69*

Most of us may never write as elegantly as William H. Whyte. But today's planners can and should be able to write prose that is informative and well composed. This chapter presents many of the basic skills and techniques needed to write well. The chapter will:

1. Provide an overview of why planners write;
2. Describe key features of the early writing process, including objectives, scope, and audience;

3. Review the mechanics of writing, from individual word choices to the organization of whole documents;
4. Offer guidance for rewriting and editing;
5. Discuss in detail the standard structure of academic research papers; and
6. Present two very different articles written by planners that exemplify the craft of writing.

Each section of the chapter uses planning examples to highlight important concepts. The emphasis is on technical writing for academic planners. Nevertheless, many of the tools and strategies described herein apply to any writing project, from a poem, to a magazine article, to a staff report. In the end, clear thinking, good writing, and enjoyable reading all go hand in hand (Gopen & Swan, 1990).

Purpose

> Writing well requires more than putting words on paper. Writing is best when it is concise, meaningful, and easily understood.
>
> —*Victor C. Pellegrino, 2003, p. 9*

Planners write for a living. But many planners also have more personal and more fundamental motivations for writing. We want to influence and inspire people. We want to promote positive social and environmental changes. We want to see core values realized in the world around us: health, livability, sustainability, justice, among others. Good writing is one of our most important tools for making these goals a reality.

In terms of substantive content, planners may write for any number of reasons. Here, we consider two broad categories: writing intended primarily for technical or specialized consumption and writing intended primarily for nontechnical or public consumption.

Technical Writing

Writing for technical or specialized communication includes both professional planning practice and academic planning research. According to the American Planning Association (APA): "Professional planners help create a broad vision for the community. They also research, design, and develop programs; lead public processes; effect social change; perform technical analyses; manage; and educate" (APA, 2013). Associated technical writing products typically include plans, zoning and subdivision ordinances, staff reports, legal deliberations, and consulting agency reports.

Plans take stock of a local municipality and craft a future vision for that place (e.g., City of Portland, 2011). Zoning and subdivision ordinances establish regulations for land use, density, building envelope, site development, public infrastructure, and other planning issues (e.g., Salt Lake City, 2019). Staff reports make recommendations about project applications and record the details of decision-making processes (e.g., City of Berkeley, 2019). Consulting agency reports may have a variety of purposes, including informing decision makers, educating the public, arguing for or against planning activities, solving planning problems, translating planning research results for nontechnical audiences, and/or synthesizing the results of a public engagement process (e.g., Blueprint Jordan River, 2008).

Academic planning researchers may share many of the same motivations as practicing professional planners. In addition, according to the *Journal of the American Planning Association* (*JAPA*, 2019), planning scholars typically:

> do at least one of the following:
> - contribute to the theoretical and conceptual foundation of planning;
> - improve the link between planning and successful policy implementation;
> - advance the methods used in planning practice and planning research;
> - explain empirical relationships important to planning;
> - interpret noteworthy physical, economic, and social phenomena that have spatial dimensions; or
> - analyze significant consequences of planning approaches, processes, and contexts.

Myers and Ryu exemplify many of these goals in their award-winning 2009 *JAPA* article, "Aging Baby Boomers and the Generational Housing Bubble." This article is an excellent example of clear, important research coupled with clear, effective writing. The authors explain their work with succinct but entertaining prose:

> We aim to identify the point at which boomers will begin to offer more homes for sale than they buy. . . . We project when this will occur in all 50 states. . . (and) we discuss the planning implications of these possible futures.
> —*Myers and Ryu, 2008, p. 18*

Along with such peer-reviewed journal articles, other scholarly writing products for technical or specialized communication include books, conference papers, and chapters in edited volumes. This book contains dozens of relevant examples.

Public Scholarship

Some planners participate in research and practice simultaneously, through processes of public scholarship. One example is Bent Flyvbjerg, who developed and employed the phronetic research method to explain transportation planning in Denmark and to promote political, institutional, and environmental changes. Flyvbjerg's work in Denmark led to peer-reviewed articles (Flyvbjerg, Holm, & Buhl, 2002; Flyvbjerg, Skamris Holm, & Buhl, 2004), chapters in edited volumes (Burchell, Mandelbaum, & Mazza, 1996; Allmendinger & Tewdwr-Jones, 2002; Campbell & Fainstein, 2003), and complete books (Flyvbjerg, 1998, 2001). Eventually, his writing extended to multimedia communication, including radio, print, and television. Ultimately, Flyvbjerg's public scholarship led to substantive changes in local planning documents and public engagement processes.

When we read work by Bent Flyvbjerg, we can understand why he has had such a profound impact. His writing is incisive and evocative. Consider these lines, from his 2002 *JPER* article "Bringing Power to Planning Research":

> First, I would choose to work with problems that are considered problems not only in the academy but also in the rest of society. Second, I would deliberately and actively feed the results of my research back into the political, administrative, and social processes that I studied.
>
> —Bent Flyvbjerg, 2002, p. 362

In this chapter, we will return to Bent Flvybjerg as we highlight key writing concepts and strategies.

Technical Versus Nontechnical Writing

As you might assume, the difference between technical and nontechnical writing is more of a spectrum, or sliding scale, than a black-and-white distinction. For instance, while the preceding quotation comes from a highly regarded and rigorously peer-reviewed journal, some academic planners may find the language overly personal or subjective. Indeed, public scholarship like Flyvbjerg's frequently falls into the gray area between technical and nontechnical writing.

One very common strategy that blurs the line between technical and nontechnical writing is storytelling. Stories play a variety of roles in planning research and practice (Sandercock, 2003; Throgmorton, 2003). Even in quantitative empirical work, stories are important for engaging the reader and for leading them through a sea of complicated information (Bem, 2002). Flyvbjerg demonstrates how storytelling can set the stage for decades of research and practice. In the following quote, he begins the story of the now infamous Aalborg Project. The details of this very first meeting remain relevant throughout all of the articles, books, interviews, and public policies that Flyvbjerg ultimately produced.

> In Aalborg, Denmark, on an autumn day in the late 1970s, a group of high-level city officials gather for a meeting. Only one item is on the agenda: initiation of what will eventually become an award-winning project recommended by the OECD for international adoption, on how to integrate environmental and social concerns in city politics and planning, including how to deal with the car in the city. From the very outset the stakes are high. Making the car adapt to the city in the scale now envisioned is something never before tried in Denmark.
>
> —Bent Flyvbjerg, 1998, p. 9

While the line between technical and nontechnical writing can be blurry, it is nevertheless useful to make certain distinctions. One difference concerns the logic and chronology of the narrative structure. Nontechnical writing may employ a complex chronology or obscure logic, but technical writing never will. As Daryl Bem explains in *Writing the Empirical Journal Article*: "It is not a novel with subplots, flashbacks, and literary allusions, but a short story with a single linear narrative line" (2002, p. 4).

Another difference concerns tone. Nontechnical writing may employ colorful imagery and emotionally charged language. On the other hand, even if the author is a strong advocate of certain ideals, technical writing "aims to be clean, clear, and unemotional" (Katz, 2009, p. 3). Flyvbjerg may be an advocate for change, but he advances his position through his rigorous research and willingness to engage potentially confrontational dialogues without aggression— and not through allusion or through emotional appeal.

A third difference concerns evidentiary standards. Peer-reviewed journal articles, in particular, must show extensive evidence in support of their arguments (Katz, 2009). Nontechnical writing, on the other hand, does not have set standards for what constitutes appropriate evidence. This does not mean, however, that nontechnical writing is incapable of presenting rigorous evidence.

Finally, good technical writing involves layers of expertise. Bem states that a person who is "intelligent . . . [but] with no expertise . . . should be able to comprehend the broad outlines" of technical writing (2002, p. 4). At the same time, "specialized audiences who share a common background" should be able to gain a much deeper understanding of the same project. Nontechnical writing, on the other end, is generally intended to inform and inspire a non-expert audience (Bem, 2002).

With these considerations in mind, we can see that some written products, including peer-reviewed articles, ordinances, and legal documents, require mostly technical writing. Other written products, such as poetry and fiction, require mostly nontechnical writing. Still other written products—such as plans, reports, and newspaper or magazine articles—may involve a mix of technical and nontechnical writing.

Public scholar Nan Ellin employs this mixed approach to writing. She translates complex ideas for a lay audience, seeking to give her work a broader reach and a wider impact than it would have strictly within the academy. Consider this passage from Ellin's book *Good Urbanism*. Here, she draws the reader in with a simple and accessible metaphor, which at the same time captures a subtle and insightful observation about cities. In this way, Ellin uses colorful, nontechnical writing to set the stage for the more technical case studies that follow.

> A house I once lived in came with a potted grape ivy. I watered the plant regularly but oddly, it never grew. It didn't die, but during the two years I lived there, it never changed shape nor sprouted a leaf. Leaving this grape ivy behind for the next inhabitants, it became emblematic for me of so many places that, while they may be surviving, are clearly not thriving.
>
> —*Nan Ellin, 2013, p. 1*

Planning and JAPA

In considering technical and nontechnical writing for planners, it is interesting to compare the writing guidelines provided by *Planning* magazine with the instructions for authors provided by the scholarly *Journal of the American Planning Association*. Both are products of the American Planning Association.

Planning is intended for popular consumption by professionals and interested laypeople (Tait, 2012). *Planning's* guidelines are brief, requesting "a straightforward, nontechnical style" with "a minimum of elaboration." *JAPA* is a leading academic planning journal (Goldstein & Maier, 2010), although it is also targeted at a *professional* audience. *JAPA*'s guidelines are extensive, with several pages of requirements and instructions for authors. The journal wants "vivid and direct writing in the active voice," with as much detail and elaboration as needed to establish "significant research news."

These guidelines differ substantially. *Planning* magazine prefers brevity and overall clarity to rigorous specificity—a nontechnical writing style. *JAPA* also wants clarity but at a much higher level of detail and for a much more specialized audience—a more technical writing style. Both publications seek to provide lessons for practicing planners, but lessons are central to *Planning* magazine while they act as a conclusion to *JAPA* articles. Unlike many academic journals, to remain accessible to readers, the most technically challenging sections of *JAPA* articles are relegated to appendices.

Research You Can Use

The two styles of writing come together in a bimonthly column written for *Planning* magazine by the second author of this chapter, titled "Research You Can Use." The column has been appearing since 2006 and has covered at one time or another almost every type of research method in language intended to be accessible to the practicing planner (see Chapter 3). A few simple writing principles underlie these columns:

1. Tell readers something they don't already know in almost every paragraph, only occasionally state the obvious, and never dwell on the obvious.
2. Strive to make technically challenging material seem simple and familiar (creating a series of aha moments).
3. Write in terms of concepts and examples, always describing the forest (a concept) before exploring the trees (examples). People don't learn well with one or the other but not both.
4. Wherever possible, add graphic illustrations to clarify text, break up text, and create interest. It is the reason why planning reports and books are almost always illustrated.
5. Whenever possible, present the material as a story. People like stories. It is the reason newspaper articles often start with a human interest story, politicians often tell stories to illustrate their larger points, and many of us read stories for entertainment.
6. Circle back to earlier ideas, particularly at the very end, as familiarity is the key to understanding.
7. Remember that more (volume of writing) is usually less, and less is usually more. The columns were initially a single page but have spilled over to a second page in recent years. They are seldom much more than 1,000 words.

One of the columns follows in order to illustrate the preceding concepts with concrete examples (following all seven rules). The column is a story of discovery. It is short and contains a high density of information. It has one big concept and several examples. It simplifies complex technical information to the extent possible. It contains a graphic illustration. It circles back to the lead sentence at the end. These concepts are evident in all the "Research You Can Use" columns, which now number more than 70 (mrc.cap.utah.edu/publications/research-you-can-use).

This column originally ran in *Planning* magazine, and permission has been granted by the American Planning Association to reprint here.

RESEARCH YOU CAN USE

A "New" (250-Year-Old) Way of Thinking about Statistics

My last column (October) was critical of a recent *JAPA* article by Echenique et al., which, in my view, neglected mountains of evidence in order to make the case that changes in urban form would have little effect on regional sustainability. This month, I will pivot to two more publication-worthy articles coming up in *JAPA* and *JPER*, and promise never again to return to the offending study. But first I want to make one more point.

an event has taken place that provides evidence to the contrary. In short, a single event isn't likely to dramatically change the odds because the probability after the event depends not only on the event but on prior probabilities, or "priors."

Another characteristic of Bayesian statistics is that predictions are constantly being refined as new events occur, new data become available, and prior probabilities change. In our times, presidential election odds change with new polls, new economic news, and new debate performances. Thus, Silver had to repeatedly revise his priors and his election predictions.

Moving on (let it go, Reid), let's look at two recent articles that, while well-constructed and admirable in many ways, illustrate a non-Baysian view of probability. The *JAPA* article, by Bernadette Hanlon,

> Bayes's theory is concerned with conditional probability . . . that a hypothesis is still true even after an event has taken place that provides evidence to the contrary.

Marie Howland, and Michael McGuire, evaluates Maryland's smart growth program. Using conventional statistics in the manner of R.A. Fisher (another English statistician who was a critic of Bayes), they model farmland conversion under the state's program and then use the model to "predict" conversions. They conclude that "Maryland's incentive-based strategy is not completely effective at preventing sprawl."

The *JPER* article, by Aaron Golub, Subhrajit Guhathakurta, and Bharath Sollapuram, addresses the effects on property values of light-rail transit in Phoenix. Using Fisher's approach, they develop a hedonic price model that also passes a conventional significance test. They then create price profiles and confirm "the value of proximity" to light-rail stations. Mind you, I am not suggesting that these conclusions are wrong. I suspect they are right. I am just saying that they ignore prior probabilities in making statistical inferences.

According to Silver, hypothesis testing without regard to prior research is on the way out. "Some professions," he writes, "have considered banning Fisher's hypothesis test from their journals. In fact, if you read what's been written in the past ten years, it's hard to find anything that does not advocate a Bayesian approach." But you wouldn't know that from reading planning journals. Why are planners the last to know? ∎

Reid Ewing

Ewing is a professor of city and metropolitan planning at the University of Utah and an associate editor of *JAPA*. Past columns are available at www.arch.utah.edu/dgi-bin

BAYES'S THEOREM APPLIED TO URBAN FORM

Prior probability that urban form matters		
· Initial estimate of likelihood	x	95%
New simulation concludes that urban form does not matter		
· Probability of simulation result if it matters	y	20%
· Probability of simulation result if it does not matter	z	100%
· Posterior probability that urban form matters		
· Revised estimate of likelihood that urban form matters, $\frac{xy}{xy+z(1-x)}$ in light of simulation	$xy+z(1-x)$	79%

Reid Ewing

When I wrote the October column, I was unaware that I was arguing for a Bayesian approach to planning research. Bayesian theory and its inventor are the subjects of a best-selling book by Nate Silver called *The Signal and the Noise: Why So Many Predictions Fail—but Some Don't*. The book describes the work of a statistician named Thomas Bayes, who lived in 18th century England and who came up with a dramatically new way of thinking about probability. After hearing Silver on NPR and the *Daily Show* talking about the odds of victory for the two candidates in last month's presidential election, I ran out and bought the book. But it wasn't until I read it that I realized that there is an alternative to the conventional way of testing research hypotheses.

Bayes's theory is concerned with conditional probability—the probability that a hypothesis is still true even after

Now check out typical quantitative studies published today. The only nod to prior research—or to any sort of context—is found in an article's literature review or, occasionally, in its conclusion. In the table above, I have applied Bayes's theorem to the urban form question. The prior probability that urban form matters is very high. Considering more than 200 land-use travel studies and 100 regional scenario studies, I set the prior probability at 95 percent. Then along came a simulation and a *JAPA* article that concluded the opposite.

Under reasonable assumptions, Bayes's theorem tells us that, even after the simulation, there is still a 79 percent chance that urban form matters. This kind of probabilistic thinking is entirely absent from the Echenique article. Instead, its authors make sweeping conclusions about the inconsequence of urban form ("overconfident conclusions," Silver would say).

FIGURE 2.0 Research You Can Use

Source: with permission from American Planning Association

Preliminaries

Understanding why you are writing helps you determine for whom to write, what to write, and what your specific goals for writing should be. Budinski suggests that, after identifying your underlying reasons for writing, your initial plan of action should include three basic elements: identify your audience, determine the scope of your document, and specify your particular objectives (2001, p. 56). We would add a fourth: Learn everything practical about your subject before you start writing.

Audience

Planners must write to meet the needs and expectations of their audience. These will vary from situation to situation. If you are writing a general plan, your audience will be the residents, politicians, and other planners who will work with the general plan. If you are preparing a traffic impact analysis, your audience may include traffic engineers, a developer, and a planning commission. If you are writing a grant for a research or design project, your audience will be the sponsoring agency's selection committee. If you are writing for scholarly publication, your initial audience will be a journal editor and a panel of reviewers, and your eventual audience may include the journal's entire readership.

Whatever the context, it is crucial to clearly identify the person, group, or organization that you are writing for. Your audience will determine the style, tone, and structural format of your document, including word choices, length and complexity of sentences and paragraphs, and overall organization (Katz, 2009).

Scope

Scope refers to boundaries on the technical depth, the level of detail, and the number of ideas/cases/subjects in your written document (Budinski, 2001, p. 60). How much time do you have to complete the project? Is the project relevant to just one place, or will it be applicable on a larger scale? Does your audience expect a succinct summary or an extensive, detailed analysis?

Answering these questions will help you identify what needs to be included in your document and what does not. Both the writer and the reader will benefit when the scope of the writing is focused and refined.

Objectives

Identifying your audience and setting your scope will paint a clear picture of the style, organizational structure, and range of ideas covered in your document. The other crucial component is a list of goals and objectives: the particular outcomes your writing will produce.

As Budinski explains, specific project objectives (outcomes) are different from the overall purpose (intention) for writing (2001, p. 63). If you are writing a plan, as previously described, the purpose is to take stock of the community and to craft a future vision. Goals and objectives might be to increase transit-oriented development, to improve access to open space, to reduce water pollution, and the like. If you are writing for scholarly publication, your purpose is to complete a research article that adds to a body of disciplinary knowledge. Goals and objectives might be to model the influences on transit ridership, to explain the relationship between open space and mental health, or to test a green infrastructure design for its ability to decontaminate storm water runoff. Along with the scope and audience, your specific objectives will determine the substantive content of your writing—the words you choose and the way you put them together.

Learn Everything Practical

Read and research your subject thoroughly before starting to write. The authors of this chapter copy and paste significant points from earlier writings on a subject into a Word file. Another approach is taking written notes. A third is highlighting key points on a PDF or hard copy. It is amazing how quickly one can become relatively expert on a subject just by reading widely and conscientiously.

In the experience of the authors of this chapter, when writing on a subject is fuzzy, it is usually because the thinking on the subject is fuzzy, and the way to clarify is to learn more about the subject. When writing is blocked or sluggish, it is usually because the writer doesn't have enough information about the subject. Go back and learn more, and the writing block will likely disappear.

Example

Before moving to the mechanics of writing, let us return to the example of Bent Flyvbjerg, reflecting on audience, scope, and objectives. For the 2002 article, we know that his initial audience was a *JPER* editor and a panel of reviewers and that his extended audience eventually included the entire *JPER* readership. Regarding scope and objectives, Flyvbjerg's article is wonderfully succinct and clear.

> I decided to study how rationality and power shape planning in the town where I live and work, Aalborg, Denmark.
>
> —*Bent Flyvbjerg, 2002, p. 355*

Flyvbjerg could be certain that his specialized audience would have a complex understanding of the words "rationality" and "power." For a social scientist versed in critical theory, these terms have specific meanings that clearly express the author's objectives. This is an article about the underlying, structural elements of public policy. What reasons do planners and politicians use to legitimate or justify their decisions? How do the dynamics of unequal power relationships impact those decisions and related decision-making processes? Specifically, how do these issues come to bear in the town of Aalborg, Denmark? With one simple sentence, Flyvbjerg alerts his expert *JPER* audience as to exactly what his article's scope and objectives will be. His knowledge of place was unquestionable—wide and deep—since he was a long-time resident and student of Aalborg.

Writing this well is a tall order. Even crafting clear, simple sentences is more difficult than it may seem. But the process is not a mystery. If you understand and practice the basic mechanics of writing, you will learn to write well.

Mechanics

Whether your written document is a general plan, a research article, a grant application, or a staff report, the fundamental tools of writing remain the same. Understanding writing mechanics means knowing how to make structural choices at each scale of your document: words, sentences, paragraphs, and whole document organization. This section focuses on these basic building blocks of writing.

Words

First and foremost are the words we choose. As previously demonstrated, single words (i.e., rationality, power) can convey large amounts of information, especially in technical writing for a specialized audience. In these circumstances, it is important to avoid ambiguous terms, loaded language, slang, and colloquialisms (Rubens, 2002). In addition, much of scientific and technical writing relies on writers and readers sharing a common language (id.). Therefore, it is important to use familiar terminology for your audience in an accepted and consistent manner (id.). Writers must realize that many technical terms are not known to everybody, even in a specialized audience (Budinski, 2001). A good technical paper should explain terminology in words understandable to the reader and should provide definitions if necessary. Acronyms are particularly common in planning and need to be defined when first used.

No matter the audience, word choices determine and are determined by grammar, including punctuation, number (singular or plural), tense (past, present, or future), and perspective (first, second, or third person) (Kolln & Gray, 2009). In general, it is important to keep a consistent, or parallel, tense and perspective throughout a written document (id., p. 84).

Together, tense and perspective also influence whether your writing is in active voice or passive voice. As the name implies, writing in the *active voice* connects a clear subject with a clear action. The preceding Flyvbjerg quote—"I decided to study how rationality and power shape planning"—is a good active sentence.

Suppose that Flyvbjerg had wished to obscure his role in the research process. In this case, he might have written, "The influence of rationality and power on planning was the subject studied." In this *passive* sentence, the active transitive verb phrase ("decided to study") has become a past participle combined with the verb "to be" ("was studied"). The object of the active sentence ("how rationality and power shape planning") has become the subject of the passive sentence ("the influence of rationality and power on planning"). And, most importantly, the subject of the active sentence—Bent Flyvbjerg, the person who will actually conduct the study—has disappeared entirely.

Bem explains that, traditionally, technical writers "used the passive voice almost exclusively" (2002, p. 20). The idea was to make research seem perfectly neutral and objective by eliminating any reference to the subjective role of the researcher. However, as Bem asserts, "This practice produces lifeless prose and is no longer the norm" (id.). As noted, *JAPA* now specifically requests writing in the active voice. Most publishers in most contexts, technical and nontechnical, now do the same.

Ultimately, word choices will constitute the structure of your sentences, paragraphs, and completed documents. Words are the basic components of rhetorical grammar and the building blocks of sophisticated, precise communication. As Kolln and Gray argue, there is a crucial difference between choosing a word that approximately expresses your thoughts versus choosing a word that conveys your exact meaning. That difference often boils down to whether you get what you want—a scholarship, a job, a published article—or not.

Word choices are quite deliberate in the "Research You Can Use" column previously reproduced. From the title ["A *'New' (250-Year-Old)* Way of Thinking about Statistics"] to the body ("promise *never again* to return to the *offending* study") to the final sentence ("Why are planners the *last to know*"), the words and phrases are meant to convey drama and controversy.

Sentences

Sentences consist of words, phrases, clauses, and punctuation. A sentence must have a subject (generally a noun or noun phrase) and a predicate (generally a verb or verb phrase) and should follow grammatical conventions, unless there is a particular reason for doing otherwise (Kolln & Gray, 2009, p. 21). *Rhetorical Grammar* is an excellent resource on grammatical conventions, as are Strunk, White, and Kalman (2007) and Zinsser (2001).

A good sentence should state one or two ideas clearly and simply. Here are a few tips for writing strong sentences:

- Use short, simple sentences (Rubens, 2002).
- Ordinarily, place a verb immediately after a grammatical subject. When the subject is separated from the verb, the reader is challenged to understand what the sentence is all about (Gopen & Swan, 1990).
- Use repetition and parallel construction, within and between sentences, to improve flow, cohesion, precision, and understanding (Kolln & Gray, 2009).
- Scrutinize every word. Can you substitute or remove words to make a sentence convey the same meaning more swiftly? (Ross-Larson, 1999). Especially in technical writing, sentences stripped to their "cleanest components" will generally serve you best (Zinsser, 2001, p. 7).

When crafting sentences, sometimes emulation is an efficient strategy. As writer Bruce Ross-Larson (1999, p. 18) observes:

> It was only when I began trying to identify what was unusual about a sentence—a dramatic flourish, an elegant repetition, a conversational injection—that I began to see the patterns [in sentences]. So to move from the common to the stunning, begin to look for patterns in good writing that you can emulate.

This is good advice. Let us look to a great planning author for inspiration.

Kevin Lynch is a highly esteemed planning scholar and writer. In his classic 1984 book *Good City Form*, he demonstrates a wide variety of sentence styles and structures. Here is a short, *declarative* statement: "When values lie unexamined, they are dangerous" (1984, p. 1). This is an important premise for Lynch's entire book. Planners must examine the underlying values of city form, he says, in order to avoid the dangerous mistakes of the past and to plan desirable futures. Such short, declarative sentences can create clear and powerful writing. However, these assertions must be accompanied by strong evidence and insightful analysis. Otherwise, the audience may perceive that the author lacks credibility.

Lynch immediately establishes credibility in *Good City Form* by illustrating how human values have influenced urban form throughout time. He then offers a long *descriptive* sentence, summarizing his observations:

> But some general themes are evident, even in the few examples cited: such persistent motives among city builders as symbolic stability and order; the control of others and the expression of power; access and exclusion; efficient economic function; and the ability to control resources.
>
> *(1984, p. 36)*

This sentence involves sophisticated grammar, punctuation, and structural composition. Lynch establishes a parallel internal phrase scheme—stability *and* order, control *and* expression, access *and* exclusion—before purposefully abandoning that pattern, giving added weight to the final two items on his list. This long descriptive sentence is more complex than the short declarative sentence. It is also more specific and more detailed, improving Lynch's position as an authority on city form.

In addition to declarative and descriptive statements, Lynch (1984) also uses *analytical* sentences. Consider this series of insights about the organic metaphor for city form:

> The central difficulty is the analogy itself. Cities are not organisms, any more than they are machines, and perhaps even less so. They do not grow or change of themselves, or reproduce or repair themselves. They are not autonomous entities, nor do they run through life cycles, or become infected. They do not have clearly differentiated functional parts, like the organs of animals.
>
> *(p. 95)*

These sentences analyze the proposition that "a city is a living organism." Lynch (1984) acknowledges that certain elements of this metaphor can be useful, but he takes issue when the model is generalized to all aspects of all cities. He specifically demonstrates how and where the problematic comparison breaks down, concluding that planning actions should be based on reasons "other than 'organic' ones" (p. 95).

These analytical sentences represent a good balance of length and complexity: long enough to form focused arguments, simple enough to enable easy reading. Each sentence is strong and effective in its own right. In addition, considering all of the sentences together, we learn much about the flow between sentences in a cohesive paragraph. We will return to this example in the following section. Before doing so, however, let us consider one more sentence style exemplified by Lynch (1984): the *artful summary*.

> Once we can accept that the city is as natural as the farm and as susceptible of conservation and improvement, we work free of those false dichotomies of city and country, artificial and natural, man versus other living things.
>
> *(p. 257)*

This sentence does more than communicate effectively. The prose is rhythmic. It evokes an emotional response. It inspires the reader to agree with Lynch's conclusion and with all the ideas that led him there. Such is the power of truly excellent writing.

Paragraphs

Sentences combine to form paragraphs. Paragraphs are the building blocks of insightful ideas and sophisticated arguments. They provide the substance and proof of your claims, theses, and opinions (Sova, 2004). Pellegrino (2003) compares a paragraph to an orange, where "an orange has several distinct sections connected to each other to form a whole fruit" (p. 19). Try to make each paragraph have one main point (the fruit), with each sentence (the orange slices) building the overall argument.

The authors of this chapter try to keep their paragraphs short, typically covering no more than one subject. The first sentence of a paragraph is the topic sentence. The *topic sentence* states the main point of the paragraph. Writing simple and clear topic sentences is extremely important to good writing because topic sentences tell the reader what the paragraph is about as well as define the scope and size of the paragraph (Pellegrino, 2003). The rest of the sentences in the paragraph support the topic sentence.

In the preceding example, Kevin Lynch's paragraph has a very clear topic sentence. The second sentence clarifies and expands upon this topic sentence: "The central difficulty is the analogy itself. Cities are not organisms." The next three sentences in the paragraph highlight specific difficulties with the analogy. All three sentences have a parallel structure, with the same subject and nearly identical punctuation and grammar. Additional sentences, not quoted, provide even more specific explanations of why cities are not organisms. The concluding sentence then summarizes the same point as the topic sentence, while also serving as a transition to the topic sentence of the next paragraph.

As with sentences, paragraphs may have a variety of structures and styles. Victor Pellegrino (2003) describes several paragraph types that bear repeating here.

A *narrative paragraph* tells a story that the reader can relate to. Generally, it is written in chronological sequence and can contain dialogue. A planner may use a narrative paragraph to describe the general vision for a town or city, using a story to establish the goals and values of the residents.

The previously quoted paragraph by Bent Flyvbjerg (1998, p. 9) is a good example of a narrative paragraph. The story in this paragraph—the genesis of the Aalborg Project—underlies an entire body of work, including large-scale public policies and a fully articulated research paradigm. Notice how Flyvbjerg's writing style is simultaneously entertaining and informative. Narrative paragraphs are very useful for this dual purpose.

A *comparison paragraph* focuses on developing the similarities between subjects. Writing a comparison paragraph is straightforward. Decide which aspects of the subjects to compare, and write down how each of these aspects is similar.

The previously quoted paragraph by Nan Ellin (2013, p. 1) is a good example of a comparison paragraph. Ellin highlights a fascinating similarity, likening a plant that neither dies nor thrives to cities that suffer the same fate. This unusual comparison helps the reader reflect on the health of urban places from a completely new perspective.

Comparison paragraphs pair nicely with contrast paragraphs. For Ellin, the contrast is obvious: cities that do not die and do not merely survive but that grow and thrive. In fact, this contrasting idea provides the title of her book, *Good Urbanism*.

A *contrast paragraph*, as opposed to a comparison paragraph, details the difference between two topics. These paragraphs are particularly effective when writing to persuade or to describe. The contrast can help the reader understand that the differences between two subjects are significant and important.

Nan Ellin uses a brief contrast paragraph to summarize the purpose of *Good Urbanism*:

> We have, to some extent, buried our instinctual capacity to create habitats that support us most fully, places where we may thrive. This book asks what exactly has been lost and describes a path for uncovering this buried urban instinct, dusting it off, and updating it to serve us today.
>
> *(p. 3)*

Good urbanism, then, is all about contrast: what city-makers have done before, what they are doing now, and what they might do differently in the future, including strategies both old (buried) and new (updated).

The paragraph by Kevin Lynch (1984, p. 95) is another good example of a contrast paragraph. Here, Lynch contrasts certain characteristics of cities with the properties of living organisms, demonstrating that the organic metaphor is an inadequate model of urban form. This contrasting paragraph supports Lynch's ensuing argument: that the ecosystem is a better model of urban form than the machine or the living organism.

Narrative, comparison, and contrast paragraphs are all useful writing tools. Try using each of these paragraph types to add variety and interest to your writing. For 27 more ways to organize and write effective paragraphs, see Pellegrino's (2003) *A Writer's Guide to Powerful Paragraphs*.

Cohesion Within and Between Paragraphs

Good writing requires cohesion—"the connection of sentences to one another . . . the flow of a text"—and the way the individual sentences and paragraphs of that text combine to form "a unified whole" (Kolln & Gray, 2009, p. 84).

Kolln and Gray suggest three key strategies for cohesive writing. First, repeat important words and phrases, so that the reader is frequently reminded of your central subject matter. Second, employ the "known-new" strategy: Make sure that each sentence (or paragraph) contains some known information, establishing a logical connection with the preceding sentence (or paragraph), and some new information, keeping the writing active and avoiding the mistake of redundancy (Kolln & Gray, 2009, p. 84). Third, use parallelism: "the repetition of structures of the same form for purposes of clarity and emphasis" (id.).

All of the authors just quoted—Flyvbjerg, Ellin, and Lynch—provide excellent examples of cohesion between sentences. Their writing shows clear evidence of repetition, the known-new strategy, and parallelism. Along with this cohesion between sentences, it is also important to create cohesion between the paragraphs of a whole document. In the following list, we have listed each successive topic sentence from the "Introduction" section of John Forrester's seminal *JAPA* article, "Critical Theory and Planning Practice." Notice how each topic sentence—the main idea of each paragraph—informs and flows into the next topic sentence of the next paragraph.

- "This paper introduces *critical theory* for use in planning contexts . . ." (p. 275)
- "This work is based on eighteen months of regular observation of a metropolitan city planning department's office of environmental review . . ." (p. 275)
- "In a nutshell, the argument is as follows: critical theory gives us a new way of understanding action, or what a planner does, as attention-shaping

(communicative action), rather than more narrowly as a means to a particular end (instrumental action) . . ." (p. 275)

- "Such a view leads us to ask a more specific set of questions of the planner than the ones we've always asked before about whose ends or interests are being served." (p. 276)

—John Forester, 1980

Tone and Voice

Good writing conveys the author's unique identity. Just as each person has an individual and recognizable speaking voice, so does our written voice convey a particular persona. In Zinsser's words: "Ultimately the product that any writer has to sell is not the subject being written about, but who he or she is" (2001, p. 5).

Tone expresses the author's relationship with and attitude toward the subject matter: critical or supportive, participant or observer, ignorant or informed. *Voice*, on the other hand, expresses who the author is. Writing experts stress that the underlying voice of a written document must be authentic: The identity expressed must be consistent with the author's actual mode of communication (Zinsser, 2001; Kolln & Gray, 2009). This still leaves many options available. You have one voice when speaking with family and friends, another when speaking with colleagues, a third when speaking with your boss. All three voices are genuine representations of yourself, but you select different words for each voice to suit the appropriate context.

Writing tone and voice should be determined by your audience and objectives. You want to choose words, sentences, and paragraphs that will express a trustworthy, convincing, and authentic persona. This is the power of mastering written mechanics and rhetorical grammar. With practice, you gain the ability to choose exactly how you communicate, tailoring each writing product to your specific readership and your particular goals. The second author of this chapter uses an entirely different tone and voice when writing the "Research You Can Use" column as opposed to writing a technical paper for a scholarly journal.

Another great example of different tone and voice is the contrast between articles on induced traffic written by Robert Cervero, one for popular consumption in the magazine/journal *Access* and titled "Are Induced Travel Studies Inducing Bad Investments," the other for professional planners and academics in the *Journal of the American Planning Association* and titled "Road Expansion, Urban Growth, and Induced Travel: A Path Analysis." As a class exercise in our doctoral technical writing course at the University of Utah, we encourage students to compare the two, paragraph by paragraph, section by section.

The popular piece summarizes induced demand results as follows:

> The path analysis showed that for every 100 percent increase in capacity there'd be an eighty percent increase in travel, reflecting increased travel speeds and land use shifts along improved corridors. However, only around half the increases in speed and growth in building permits was due to the added capacity. Factors like employment and income growth accounted for the other half.
>
> (Cervero, 2003a, p. 26)

The technical piece says the same thing differently:

> Overall, the estimated longer-term path model, summarized in Figure 2.4, performed fairly well in accounting for VMT growth along sampled California freeway segments. Evidence

of "induced travel," "induced growth," and "induced investment" was uncovered. Elasticity estimates of induced travel, however, were lower than that found in most previous studies, including those focused on California freeways. An estimated 80% of California's freeway capacity additions were absorbed by traffic spurred by faster speeds and land use shifts; however, less than half (39%) of this absorption can be attributed to lane–mile expansions.

(Cervero, 2003a, p. 158)

Even the graphics used to depict relationships between highway expansion and VMT differ between the two articles (compare Figures 2.1 and 2.2). The technical graphic provides more details but ultimately not a lot more information.

Organization

In addition to structuring sentences and paragraphs, it is important to properly organize your whole document. Select the organizational approach that best fits your audience and objectives. If you are writing a scholarly article, adhere to the guidelines of scholarly writing. The organization is relatively standardized. After the introduction, there is a literature review, then a methods section, a results section, and a discussion/conclusion section. If you are writing a professional report, use examples as models for your writing. Study the organization of articles in professional journals, general plans, and transportation analyses. If you are aware of the

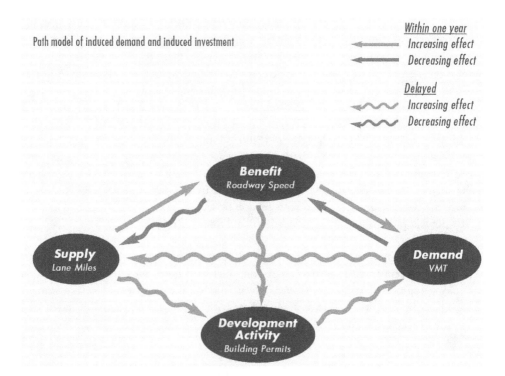

FIGURE 2.1   Popular graphic of induced demand and induced investment

Source: Cervero, 2003a

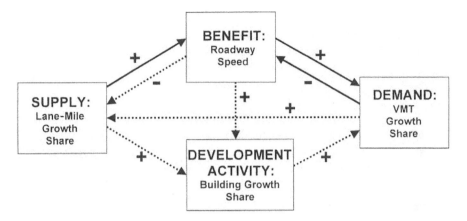

FIGURE 2.2 Technical graphic of induced demand and induced investment

Source: Cervero, 2003b; copyright © The American Planning Association, www.planning.org, reprinted by permission of Taylor & Francis Ltd, http://www.tandfonline.com on behalf of The American Planning Association.

structure of your writing in advance, you can save time and effort writing your manuscript and ensure you meet the expectations of your readers.

> Unity is the anchor of good writing. . . . [I]t satisfies the readers' subconscious need for order.
>
> —*Zinsser, 2001, p. 50*

The next step is to write your first draft. Get your main points on paper, and reorder those points for logical flow. Use headers and subheaders to help organize information. We cannot stress enough the use of headers and subheaders as an organizing device. Strive for clarity, coherent paragraphs, and logical organization (Zinsser, 2001). It is more important to complete a draft rather than to get stuck struggling over small details. Later on, your work will be revised several times. However, the better your first draft is, the fewer revisions you will need, so strive for a balance between speed and perfection.

Katz (2009) provides several useful suggestions for how to organize a written document:

- Use outlines.
- Start by blocking out general ideas, and arrange them in a simple linear order.
- Collect information from outside resources.
- Form rough sentences about the general ideas.
- Arrange the sentences into more specific themes.
- Shape your themed lists into rough paragraphs.
- Sculpt the "rough chunks," assembling one specific paragraph for each specific theme.
- Shape a working draft, moving incrementally toward finer levels of detail.
- Focus on precise wording only at the very end.

Katz cautions us to remember that while the writing *product* may be linear, beginning with an introduction and ending with a conclusion, the writing *process* is frequently nonlinear. In a scholarly article, one may often begin by writing a literature review, a description of research methods, and an overview of the results before constructing parallel introduction and conclusion sections, which frame what has already been written (Bem, 2002).

Rewriting, Editing, and Polishing

> Writing improves in direct ratio to the number of things we can keep out of it that shouldn't be there. . . . Most first drafts can be cut by as much as 50 percent without losing any information or losing the author's voice.
>
> —*Zinsser, 2001, p. 17*

Write, rewrite, and rewrite again. Good writing is good revising, and it behooves you to conduct several rounds of review before your document is complete. In fact, the process of "rewriting is the essence of writing well" (Zinsser, 2001, p. 84). Just because all the sections of the paper have been composed does not mean that the draft is ready for submission. Almost without exception, the first draft is nowhere near completion. The next essential step is editing and revising. The authors of this chapter find that many of their students (not all) rush to finish and submit a first draft, and they never spend the necessary time on second and third drafts.

This section presents some useful revision strategies and skills, that you will need to develop (Rubens, 2002). The first round of revision should include an analysis of audience, purpose, and organization. Does the paper meet the expectations and organization of the intended audience? Have you clearly stated the purpose of the research? Does the information presented in the paper appear in the correct sections? These questions will help ensure that the paper meets the expectations of the audience, states a clear purpose, and is organized according to accepted conventions. The use of headings and subheadings is important because that will tip you off to when content is misplaced.

As an author, you may be exhausted after producing a draft. So take a break and come back with fresh eyes. In addition, gain a new perspective by enlisting others as reviewers and editors. Send your first draft to several people for revisions. Pick at least one person who is unfamiliar with the technical specifics of your work—perhaps your spouse or partner—and have them read the document. If your document is written clearly and concisely, even an uninitiated reader should comprehend what you are trying to say. The readers who are familiar with your topic will provide the necessary technical revisions.

Incorporate these revisions into your draft. Manage negative feedback with grace and without defensiveness, and thank your reviewers for their time (Rudenstam & Newton, 2007). In our responses to review comments, any positive comment elicits a thank you. If you think a reviewer is incorrect (they certainly can be), use evidence and persuasion rather than emotion to make your point. A good review is invaluable, and they are doing you a favor. The authors of this chapter have always marveled at the value of peer reviews, provided at no cost, simply by submitting an academic paper to a peer-reviewed journal.

As you review, it is most important to ensure that the whole manuscript tells a story or makes a tight-knit argument. Then check the flow of logic from one paragraph to the next. You will almost always find that reordering paragraphs leads to a more logical flow. Finally check that each sentence relates to the ones before and after (Gopen & Swan, 1990).

After you've reviewed the style and organization of your paragraphs and sentences, you should double-check that you've cited all your sources correctly. An in-text citation, or *author-date citation*, acknowledges a reference immediately after it appears. Place the citation in parentheses and a period after the parenthesis (Rubens, 2002). Then ensure that all your works cited in the text appear in your works cited section and vice versa. Knowing where to find your sources is important for your readers.

Sometimes it is possible that a writer can know too much about a topic to write about it clearly (Rubens, 2002). If this is the case, these writers make inappropriate assumptions about audience knowledge—unless they can remember the needs of the intended audience (Rubens, 2002). To avoid this mistake, have a nonexpert friend or family member read your work aloud. And read your work out loud to yourself to gain a better sense of how the writing flows.

Your document will improve during the process of revision and rewriting. Sometimes it will take several rounds of revisions until the final product emerges. Keep in mind, however, the importance of completing a work on time (Budinski, 2001). Reports should be completed when action is needed; proposals for funding must obviously meet any submission deadline.

The trick is to find the balance between taking enough time to put your work through several rounds of revision and submission. Academics are notorious for getting things in late. Consultants get things in on time but may sacrifice rigor or completeness. One leading planning academic (who will remain nameless) was known for submitting great reports a year or even two years late, and it eventually cost him in competitions for grants and contracts. Another academic planner (who will also remain nameless) is well-known for both quality and timeliness and has had a successful consulting career, as well as a very successful academic career.

Katz suggests a succinct, step-by-step process for rewriting, editing, and polishing. Try to follow his advice as you refine your written documents (2009, pp. 25–28):

- Rework the entire draft, paragraph by paragraph. Create cohesion and flow within and between paragraphs.
- Then, cut, trim, and simplify, sentence by sentence. Fix specific types of problems— "Don't read for overall meaning. Don't pay attention to the global features. Instead, concentrate on sentences and words, and pick a single task each time you sit down" (p. 25).
- Replace passive verbs with active verbs.
- Replace vague descriptions with precise adjectives.
- Stop writing when you come to the end of your ability, and seek outside help.

Literature Reviews

We now focus on a critical section of all academic products and many practice documents. Planning academics and practitioners have one research practice in common: conducting literature reviews. You may think of this as an inherently academic exercise (all academic articles include a literature review right after the introduction or as part of the introduction, identifying gaps in the literature). But we would wager that most technical memos written by planners begin with Google searches aimed at finding relevant literature. This section is meant to help both academics and practitioners conduct literature reviews. As a template, we will refer to the publication criteria used by the *Journal of Planning Literature* (*JPL*) and as an example of a solid literature review, we will draw on the *JPL* article, "Urban Form and Residential Energy Use: A Review of Design Principles and Research Findings," by Yekang Ko of the University of Texas at Arlington.

Style

Is the paper well written, in the active voice? Does it have a cogent statement of purpose? Is it clear, convincingly argued, and logically organized? It's the last of these—the lack of organization—that bothers us most in reviewing academic papers. Thoughts do not flow logically, and extraneous or tangential matters find their way into sections where they don't belong.

Headings and subheadings can help. They serve as signposts for readers and instill discipline in authors, who are less likely to stray from their topic when it is neatly labeled. Ko's review organizes the relevant literature under four headings (housing type and size, density, community layout, and planting and surface coverage) with three subheadings under each (statistical studies, simulation studies, and experiments). The review doesn't stray from the topic at hand.

Scope

Does the article cover the literature on the topic comprehensively, focusing on the most important work and citing additional material? The trick to ensuring that a literature review is "systematic" (to use the term of art) is to search bibliographic databases. Academics have access to many excellent databases through their universities, but everyone can make use of Google Scholar. As a test, type in the keywords "residential energy" and "urban planning." Google Scholar comes up with a whopping 1,160 choices and tells you just how often the source article has been cited. How can you possibly be "comprehensive" when faced with so many articles? There are three tricks. First, relegate lesser studies to tables. Ko summarizes 17 articles in one efficient table. Second, limit narrative summaries of individual articles to the most important and synthesize the rest—e.g., "Several authors agree on. . . ." Finally, limit the scope of the review. Ko lists both the topics that will be covered in her review and those that will not be.

Accuracy

Does the author describe and interpret the literature accurately and explain technical items at an appropriate level of detail? Authors tend to present other scholars' findings through the lens of their own thesis. In another paper, the second author of this chapter reviewed for *JPL*, the authors summed up five articles by saying that the authors "all concluded that people living in low-density suburbs are more likely to be overweight, use an automobile more often and for shorter trips, ride bikes and walk less, and have a higher risk of obesity-related illnesses than their more urban counterparts." Not even close to true.

The main findings of articles are usually contained in the abstract, the conclusion, or the results section. When it comes to quantitative studies, we recommend that you also look at the tables. They tell the whole story.

Analysis

Two other *JPL* review criteria, in our experience, are problematic. To save space, we offer one cautionary note for each. The first is analysis: Articles should be more than a simple presentation of what has been published, avoiding the tendency to uncritically report what Smith or Jones says. We reviewed a paper on sprawl recently for the journal *Sustainability* that, in the first two drafts, recounted the findings of the now infamous Echenique article without acknowledging the controversy surrounding it (see "Research You Can Use," October 2012).

Connection to Planning

This is another tricky criterion: The question here is whether the discussion is useful for the planning profession and the practice of planning. Literature reviews and research studies often overreach, going beyond the available evidence to draw broader conclusions that support the author's biases. A paper the second author of this chapter reviewed for *Environment and Planning* recommended streetscape improvements based on a project's Walk Score. But Walk Scores do not measure streetscape quality.

Planning Examples

For this section, we have selected award-winning papers in prominent planning journals to use as our case studies of excellent writing.

JPER *Winner*

Professor Donald Shoup was awarded the Chester Rapkin Award for the Best Paper in the *Journal of Planning Education and Research (JEPR)* in 2009. The award is named after Professor Rapkin who was a distinguished educator, who mentored 70 doctoral and numerous master students at the University of Pennsylvania, Columbia University, and Princeton University. According to the awards committee, Shoup's article "presents a potentially very important innovation in zoning, which could have significant application in practice." Beyond its practical utility, the "paper is a model for how to write an academic paper within a professional domain," and "it is persuasive, elegant, and economical" (UCLA, 2012).

The premise of Shoup's (2008) article is that it is difficult to assemble sites that are large enough to redevelop at high densities, especially in city centers. As a result, regeneration in city centers is impeded, and suburban sprawl spreads onto large sites already in single ownership. He suggests a new planning strategy to encourage voluntary land assembly: graduated density zoning. This strategy can increase the incentive for landowners to cooperate and participate in land assembly so that they can obtain a valuable economic opportunity, rather than hold out and miss the opportunity to combine contiguous properties to trigger higher-density economic benefits.

Shoup demonstrates how to craft an effective introduction. The introduction begins by detailing the traditional approach that cities have used to keep private land-owners from holding out in land assemblage. He illustrates the controversy surrounding eminent domain by using examples of cities taking land from private landowners. These examples are strengthened by powerful quotations: "No one should be forced to sell just because a city says a neighborhood isn't rich enough to stay" (Huffstutter, 2006). By the time the readers reach the end of the introduction, Shoup has clearly demonstrated that eminent domain is a problem and something new is needed. Stating why the research is needed is one of the primary purposes of the introduction.

Also included in the introduction are his research questions, which appear directly after the point is made that this is an important research topic. Shoup asks, "Can cities assemble land for infill development without resorting to eminent domain?" Following this research question, Shoup suggests his hypothesis that graduated density zoning may be a promising strategy, and then he outlines how the rest of the paper will proceed. This is a very good example of an effective introduction.

Shoup uses informative headings to organize his information within the paper. While he does not explicitly label his sections as methods or results, the information flows logically and is presented in the standard structure of scholarly articles.

An effective technique that Shoup uses liberally is pairing concepts with examples. For example, he uses concepts and examples to guide a reader through a complex section describing graduated density zoning. This concept will not be familiar to all readers, but after his description of the concept and use of an example, readers should have a very clear understanding of how it works.

He writes about an example of a city and a rail transit line. The city wants to increase density around the stations, and transit-oriented development would require sites larger than the existing parcels. The existing properties are small and in poor condition, but many owners either oppose higher density or are holding out for higher prices. Eminent domain is not an attractive option for the city either. Again, Shoup sets the stage to describe the concept of graduated density zoning, and the example is made real to the reader.

The awards committee commented that the Shoup uses "ingenious figures to make its message clear." These ingenious figures illustrate his concepts and research questions. For example, in order to demonstrate that large single lots gain more square footage than two single lots, Shoup shows the contrasting floor plans (Figure 2.3). Clearly the single lot gains more square footage by reclaiming the setback between the buildings. Furthermore, as Shoup explains, a land assembly of larger lots leads to better urban design, cost savings, and an increase in density.

Overall, Shoup's article demonstrates effective writing. It is clear, concise, and meaningful. One of the "Research You Can Use" columns takes issue with Shoup's methodology but not with his writing (Ewing, August–September 2008).

JAPA *Winner*

Another award-winning article that demonstrates a significant original contribution to the field of planning and serves as a model to be emulated by other researchers is Dowell Myers and SungHo Ryu's 2008 article, "Aging Baby Boomers and the Generational Housing Bubble: Foresight and Mitigation of an Epic Transition." Each year, the *Journal of the American Planning Association* honors the authors of excellent *JAPA* articles with the Best Article award. According to the selection criteria, the award goes to an article that communicates its content in a clear, logical, and comprehensible manner and that appeals to a wide audience. This article does just that and received the award in 2008.

Myers and Ryu investigated the impact that the 78 million baby boomers will have on the housing market when they sell off their high-priced homes to relatively less advantaged generations who are fewer in number. Using a long-run projection of annual home buying and selling by age groups in the 50 states, the authors consider implications for communities of the anticipated downturn in demand.

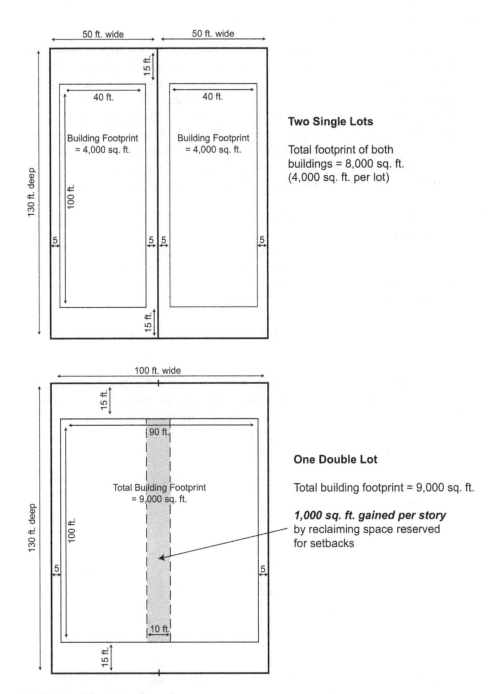

FIGURE 2.3 Contrasting floor plans

Source: Shoup, 2008; The American Planning Association, www.planning.org, reprinted by permission of Taylor & Francis Ltd, http://www.tandfonline.com on behalf of The American Planning Association.

Let us take a look at how the two coauthors have crafted an introduction that grabs the reader, as well as clearly indicating their contribution to the field:

> The giant baby boom generation born between 1946 and 1964 has been a dominant force in the housing market for decades. This group has always provided the largest age cohorts, and has created a surge in demand as it passed through each stage of the life cycle. As its members entered into home buying in the 1970s, gentrification in cities and construction of starter homes in suburbs increased. Their subsequent march into middle age was accompanied by rising earnings and larger expenditures for move-up housing. Looking ahead to the coming decade, the boomers will retire, relocate, and eventually withdraw from the housing market. Given the potential effects of so many of these changes happening in a limited period of time, communities should consider how best to plan this transition.

This single paragraph is focused and interesting, and it leads the reader directly to why this research is important. Great paragraph.

Following their introduction, the authors review the literature on baby boomers, demographic changes, and changes in the housing market. The literature review is well researched: Over 30 articles are cited. Despite the wealth of research, the authors clearly indicate that their research is filling a gap, the raison d'etre of a literature review:

> What have not been recognized to date are the grave impacts of the growing age imbalance in the housing market.

The methods section of this paper is complete and easy to follow. The authors describe their databases, the size of the sample, and what measures they will use. The steps in their statistical analysis are also detailed. All in all, this is what a methods section should look like.

Their results section is not an exception either: It clearly presents the results. The use of illustrative figures helps tell the story (see Figure 2.4).

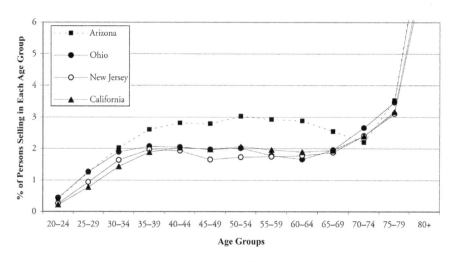

FIGURE 2.4 Average annual percentage of persons selling homes in each age group

They conclude their paper with implications for local planning and open doors to future research.

> Planners must adjust their thinking for a new era that reverses many longstanding assumptions. Though planners in many urban areas have been struggling against gentrification, they may now need to stave off urban decline. Whereas decline once occurred in the central city, it may now be concentrated in suburbs with surpluses of large-lot single-family housing. Whereas residential development once focused on single-family homes, many states may swing toward denser developments clustered near amenities. Whereas the major housing problem was once affordability, it could now be homeowners' dashed expectations after lifelong investment in home equity. The new challenge may be how to sustain municipal services in the face of declining property values. All of these reversals result from the aging of the baby boomers. By using foresight, planners have a better chance of leading their communities through the difficult transition ahead.

Conclusion

This chapter offers guidance for technical writing, including the purpose of writing in planning, key features of the writing process, its mechanics from individual word choices to the organization of whole documents, guidance for rewriting and editing, and two noteworthy academic papers in top planning journals. In sum, technical writing, applicable to most documents that planners produce, should have a story with a clear, logical narrative line (i.e., argument), be supported by evidence, and involve layers of expertise.

Like any advanced skill, writing must be developed through systematic instruction and practice. However, writing is hard and frustrating for everyone. "If you find that writing is hard," wrote William Zinsser (2001, p. 12), "it's because it *is* hard." Interestingly, books about writing suggest that the only cure is writing itself. Simply allotting (not finding) time to write and sticking to the schedule should make you a productive writer (Boice, 1990; Silvia, 2007; Zinsser, 2001). We look forward to reading more well written papers and reports in planning. There are many "good things still to be written" (Saroyan, 1952, p. 2).

Works Cited

Allmendinger, P., & Tewdwr-Jones, M. (Eds.). (2002). *Planning futures: New directions for planning theory*. New York, NY: Psychology Press.

American Planning Association. (2013). *What is planning?* Retrieved from www.planning.org/aboutplanning/

Appleyard, D. (1981). *Livable streets*. Berkeley, CA: University of California Press.

Bem, D. J. (2002). Writing the empirical journal article. In J. M. Darley, M. P. Zanna, & H. L. Roediger III (Eds.), *The complete academic: A career guide*. Washington, DC: American Psychological Association.

Blueprint Jordan River. (2008). *Blueprint Jordan River*. Retrieved from http://jordanrivercommission.com/wp-content/uploads/BlueprintJordanRiver_LowRes3.pdf (accessed on December 5, 2019)

Boice, R. (1990). *Professors as writers: A self-help guide to productive writing*. Stillwater, OK: New Forums Press.

Budinski, K. G. (2001). *Engineers' guide to technical writing*. Materials Park, OH: ASM International.

Burchell, R. W., Mandelbaum, S. J., & Mazza, L. (Eds.). (1996). *Explorations in planning theory*. Piscataway, NJ: Transaction Publishers.

Campbell, S., & Fainstein, S. S. (2003). *Readings in planning theory (Studies in Urban & Social Change)*. Malden, MA: Wiley & Sons, Ltd.

Cargill, M., & O'Conner, P. (2009). *Writing scientific research articles: Strategy and steps*. West Sussex, UK: Wiley Blackwell.

Cervero, R (2002). Induced travel demand: Research design, empirical evidence, and normative policies. *Journal of Planning Literature, 17*(1), 3–20. https://doi.org/10.1177/088122017001001

Cervero, R. (2003a). Are induced travel studies inducing bad investments? *Access, 22*, 22–27.

Cervero, R. (2003b). Road expansion, urban growth, and induced travel: A path analysis. *Journal of the American Planning Association, 69*(2), 145–163.

City of Berkeley. (2019). *2019 agendas and minutes*. Retrieved from https://www.cityofberkeley.info/Clerk/Commissions/Commissions__Planning_Commission_Homepage.aspx (accessed on December 5, 2019)

City of Portland. (2011). *Comprehensive plan goals and policies*. Retrieved from https://www.portlandonline.com/bps/Comp_Plan_Nov2011.pdf (accessed on December 5, 2019)

Ellin, N. (2013). *Good urbanism: Six steps to creating prosperous places*. Washington, DC: Island Press.

Ewing, R. (2008, August–September). Graduated density zoning—The danger of generalizing from a sample of one. *Planning*, p. 62.

Flyvbjerg, B. (1998). *Rationality and power: Democracy in practice*. Chicago, IL: University of Chicago Press.

Flyvbjerg, B. (2001). *Making social science matter: Why social inquiry fails and how it can succeed again*. Cambridge: Cambridge University Press.

Flyvbjerg, B. (2002). Bringing power to planning research: One researcher's praxis story. *Journal of Planning Education and Research, 21*(4), 353–366.

Flyvbjerg, B., Holm, M. S., & Buhl, S. (2002). Underestimating costs in public works projects: Error or lie? *Journal of the American Planning Association, 68*(3), 279–295.

Flyvbjerg, B., Skamris Holm, M. K., & Buhl, S. L. (2004). What causes cost overrun in transport infrastructure projects? *Transport Reviews, 24*(1), 3–18.

Forester, J. (1980). Critical theory and planning practice. *Journal of the American Planning Association, 46*(3), 275–286.

Goldstein, H., & Maier, G. (2010). The use and valuation of journals in planning scholarship: Peer assessment versus impact factors. *Journal of Planning Education and Research, 30*(1), 66–75.

Gopen, G. D., & Swan, J. (1990). *The science of scientific writing*. Retrieved from https://cseweb.ucsd.edu/~swanson/papers/science-of-writing.pdf

Holtzclaw, J. (2000). Smart growth—As seen from the air. Convenient neighborhood, skip the car. *Sierra Club*. Retrieved from http://vault.sierraclub.org/sprawl/transportation/holtzclaw-awma.pdf

Huffstutter, P. J. (2006, July 27). Ohio landowners win eminent domain case. *Los Angeles Times*. Retrieved from https://www.latimes.com/archives/la-xpm-2006-jul-27-na-eminent27-story.html

Jayaprakash, S. (2008). *Technical writing*. Mumbai, IN: Global Media.

Journal of the American Planning Association (JAPA). (2019). *Aims and scope*. Retrieved from https://www.tandfonline.com/action/journalInformation?show=aimsScope&journalCode=rjpa20 (accessed on December 5, 2019)

Katz, M. J. (2009). *From research to manuscript: A guide to scientific writing*. Cleveland, OH: Springer Science and Business Media.

Kolln, M., & Gray, L. S. (2009). *Rhetorical grammar*. Harlow, UK: Longman.

Lebrun, J. (2007). *Scientific writing: A reader and writer's guide*. River Edge, NJ: World Scientific.

Lester, T., Kaza, N., & Kirk, S. (2014). Making room for manufacturing: Understanding industrial land conversion in cities. *Journal of the American Planning Association, 79*(4), 295–313. https://doi.org/10.1080/01944363.2014.915369

Lindsay, D. (2010). *Scientific writing: Thinking in words*. Collingwood, AU: CSIRO Publishing.

Lynch, K. (1984). *Good city form*. Cambridge, MA: MIT press.

Myers, D., & Ryu, S. (2008). Aging baby boomers and the generational housing bubble: Foresight and mitigation of an epic transition. *Journal of the American Planning Association, 74*(1), 17–33. https://doi.org/10.1080/01944360701802006

Nelson, A. C. (2006). Leadership in a new era: Comment on planning leadership in a new era. *Journal of the American Planning Association*, *72*(4), 393–409. https://doi.org/10.1080/01944360608976762

Pellegrino, V. C. (2003). *A writer's guide to powerful paragraphs*. Wailuku, HI: Maui'ar Thoughts Company.

Pitt, D., & Bassett, E. (2014). Collaborative planning for clean energy initiatives in small to mid-sized cities. *Journal of the American Planning Association*, *79*(4), 280–294. https://doi.org/10.1080/01944363.2014.914846

Ross-Larson, B. C. (1999). *Effective writing*. New York, NY: WW Norton & Company.

Rubens, P. (2002). *Science & technical writing*. New York, NY: Routledge.

Rudenstam, K. E., & Newton, R. R. (2007). *Surviving your dissertation* (3rd ed.). Thousand Oaks, CA: Sage Publications.

Ryberg-Webster, S. (2014). Preserving downtown America: Federal rehabilitation tax credits and the transformation of U.S. cities. *Journal of the American Planning Association*, *79*(4), 266–279. https://doi.org/10.1080/01944363.2014.903749

Salt Lake City. (2019). *Salt Lake City, Utah City Code*. Retrieved from https://www.sterlingcodifiers.com/codebook/index.php?book_id=672 (accessed on December 5, 2019)

Sandercock, L. (2003). Out of the closet: The importance of stories and storytelling in planning practice. *Planning Theory & Practice*, *4*(1), 11–28.

Saroyan, W. (1952). *The bicycle rider in Beverly Hills*. New York, NY: Charles Scribner's Sons.

Shoup, D. (2008). Graduated density zoning. *Journal of Planning Education and Research*, *28*(2), 161–179. https://doi.org/10.1177/0739456X08321734

Silvia, P. J. (2007). *How to write a lot: A practical guide to productive academic writing*. Washington, DC: American Psychological Association.

Sova, D. B. (2004). *Writing clearly: A self-teaching guide*. Hoboken, NJ: John Wiley and Sons.

Strunk, W., White, E. B., & Kalman, M. (2007). *The elements of style (illustrated)*. London: Penguin.

Tait, M. (2012). Building trust in planning professionals: Understanding the contested legitimacy of a planning decision. *Town Planning Review*, *83*(5), 597–618.

Throgmorton, J. A. (2003). Planning as persuasive storytelling in a global-scale web of relationships. *Planning Theory*, *2*(2), 125–151.

UCLA. (2012). *Shoup receives his second Rapkin Award for best article in JPER*. Retrieved from http://publicaffairs.ucla.edu/news/transportation/shoup-receives-his-second-rapkin-award-best-article-jper

Whyte, W. H. (1988). *City: Rediscovering the center*. New York, NY: Doubleday.

Zinsser, W. (2001). *On writing well: 25th anniversary edition*. New York, NY: HarperCollins.

3

PLANNING JOURNALS AND TOPICS

Kathryn Terzano, David Proffitt, Fariba Siddiq, and Reid Ewing

Overview

Most readers of this book will have heard the phrase "publish or perish." Academics of all stripes—planners included—face intense pressure to publish new research if they want to keep their jobs and advance in the profession. Publishing also has value beyond job security, though. Science, practice, and indeed all human knowledge advances only when people share their ideas, findings, and questions. These days, this means publishing articles in peer-reviewed academic journals. But how do you go about doing this?

Knowing how to navigate the path from the completed study to published study is invaluable for researchers. It also is helpful for planning practitioners. Academic journals publish the newest ideas and evidence for all kinds of planning issues, which means that all kinds of planners could benefit from understanding planning journals and how they approach topics in the field.

Planning is such a broad field that it can be difficult to figure out where one area of interest ends and the next begins. Subfields such as transportation, housing, smart growth, economic development, public health, disaster planning and recovery, and natural resource and environmental planning obviously have a lot of overlap. These intersections can make it difficult to find the best outlet for your work and can make it hard to figure out what direction to take when conducting research. Reviewing some of the topics covered in "Research You Can Use," a regular column in *Planning* magazine, is a helpful exercise for finding your bearings in the sometimes tangled paths of planning research.

"Research You Use Can Use," authored by Reid Ewing, the fourth author of this chapter, has appeared as a column in *Planning* magazine since November of 2006. Directed at planning practitioners and interested members of the public who read the magazine and increasingly at other academics who conduct the research that informs practice, the column has sought to distill the takeaway messages from select academic research studies that have the potential to be useful in planning practice.

Planning is published by the American Planning Association (APA), which is the professional association for planning practitioners in the United States and is undoubtedly the best known publication among professional planners, who receive the monthly magazine as part of their membership in APA. Since the column's inception, more than 70 columns have been published in an attempt to bridge the gap between planning academia and planning practice.

These columns discuss more than 100 publications (and occasionally, in-press work), most of which are academic journal articles but several of which are key books in the planning field and at least two of which are reports prepared by planning practitioners. Although the majority of the columns focus on informing the readership about the work of planning researchers, on occasion, the columns instead present exemplary work by practitioners.

The rest of this chapter provides an overview of planning journals and research topics by highlighting studies discussed in "Research You Can Use" columns. All past columns are available online for free at http://mrc.cap.utah.edu/publications/research-you-can-use/.

Planning Journals

Finding the best publication outlet for your research is only getting more challenging as the planning field diversifies. The good news is that there has never been more opportunity to publish in a range of high-quality journals. The bad news is that the path to publication can be confusing for novice researchers.

The two main considerations when choosing a journal are the topics it covers and its ranking. Topic, the first consideration, should be obvious. Some journals are interdisciplinary, while others focus on a limited range of subjects. You do not want to waste time submitting your work someplace that will not be interested. The journals *Transportation*, *Economic Development Quarterly*, and *Housing Policy Debate* have obvious foci. The *Journal of the American Planning Association* (*JAPA*) and the *Journal of Planning Education and Research* (*JPER*) are interdisciplinary, yet even these two journals are distinct. *JAPA* expects its articles to have takeaways for planning practice, while *JPER* has more of an academic bent.

The second consideration, ranking, also requires a little research and planning. "Research You Can Use" has frequently referred to two sets of journal rankings:

- Reputational rankings based on an online survey of academic planners published in *JPER* by Goldstein and Maier back in 2010
- Journal impact factor rankings (for 2018 at the time of this writing) as published in the *Journal of Citation Reports* (Impact factors measure the average number of citations for recent articles in a journal and are often deemed to reflect the importance of a journal.)

Academic planners are encouraged to consider each set of rankings when they choose outlets for their research (see Table 3.1.). Goldstein and Maier reported the interesting fact that reputation rankings and impact factors were essentially uncorrelated. That is still the case today when we array the journals for which we have both sets of rankings and have computed a Spearman correlation coefficient. Of course, 2007, the year Goldman and Maier conducted their survey, was a while ago, and reputation rankings may have changed.

Arguably, *JAPA* remains the most prominent journal in the planning field by reputation. It is also the most frequently featured journal in the "Research You Can Use" column. *JPER* is in second place, both in reputation and frequency of appearance in the column. Other journals featured in the column include *Journal of Planning Literature* (*JPL*), *Journal of Urban Design* (*JUD*), *Journal of Transport & Health* (*JTH*), *Landscape and Urban Planning* (*LAND*), and *Cities*. The August–September 2014 column ("Hot Journal, Hotter Cities") discussed the journal *LAND* in comparison to *JAPA*, *JPER*, and *JPL*, while *Cities* was featured in the April 2018 column ("Multiple Lessons from a Single Paper on Urban Sprawl"). In their 2018 two-year impact factors, *LAND* ranked number one and *Cities* ranked number two among journals

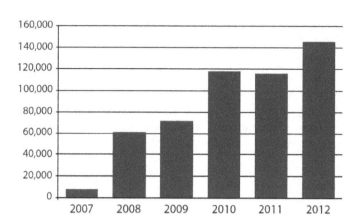

FIGURE 3.1 *JAPA* downloads

Source: Ewing, July 2013a, p. 45; with permission from The American Planning Association

in the Urban Studies category. Both are more international in their coverage than *JAPA* or *JPER*. So they present a real choice for planning scholars.

The December 2013 column ("Costs of Sprawl Revisited") predicts a trend toward more open-access journals within the urban planning field. Bev Wilson and Arnab Chakraborty chose the open-access journal *Sustainability* as the outlet for their international review of the sprawl literature. Open-access journals are free to readers but not authors, who pay a publication charge. Being free to readers, they have the potential to reach a larger audience than paid subscription journals. However, they have yet to achieve the reputation or impact of subscription journals in the planning field. Many subscription journals now offer authors the option of making their articles open access, which would seem to represent the best of both worlds.

Impact Factors

Impact factors are a measure of how frequently the *average* article in a journal is cited in subsequent articles, even in other journals. Impact factors are calculated by dividing the number of times articles published in previous years were cited by the total number of citable items the journal published in the years under study. (Citable items typically include articles, reviews, proceedings, and notes but not editorials or letters to the editor.) The February 2010 column, "A Bonanza of Journal Articles," defines impact factors and relates their importance. The column also praises *JAPA* for increasing its impact factor after seeing several years of decline.

A new study (Stevens et al., 2019) seeks to update Goldman and Maier's findings on the importance of journal reputation versus impact factor. For hundreds of published planning articles, Mark Stevens, Keunhyun Park, Guang Tian, Keuntae Kim, and Reid Ewing have modeled which article, journal, and author characteristics are associated with higher citation counts. Citations are a good indicator of how widely the article is disseminated and how many people find it interesting and useful. Stevens et al. find that articles published in higher-impact journals are cited more often than articles in lower-impact journals, while journal reputation matters much less. This may provide further guidance on the selection of journals as outlets for planners' work. Interestingly, the study also finds that, all else being equal, planning articles by multiple authors include a high number of citations to other articles, and feature titles phrased in the form of a question are cited more often than those that are not.

TABLE 3.1 Planning journal rankings

Journal Name	5-Year Impact Factor (2016)	Reputation*
American Journal of Sociology	6.10	3
Landscape and Urban Planning	5.02	12
Progress in Planning	4.83	N/A
Journal of Policy Analysis and Management	3.54	4
Land Use Policy	3.53	4
Transportation Research Part A—Policy and Practice	3.49	9
World Development	3.35	6
Regional Studies	3.30	9
Journal of Planning Literature	3.25	26
Transportation	2.98	5
Journal of Urban Economics	2.93	8
Cities	2.80	N/A
International Journal of Urban and Regional Research	2.76	15
Journal of Urban Technology	2.71	N/A
Journal of Regional Science	2.63	5
Habitat International	2.59	N/A
Urban Studies	2.56	39
Planning Theory	2.54	8
Journal of Planning Education and Research	2.45	106
Environment and Planning D	2.44	3
Land Economics	2.38	4
Journal of the American Planning Association	2.34	124
Environmental Management	2.21	4
Environment and Planning A	2.18	24
Urban Geography	1.90	N/A
Journal of Environmental Planning and Management	1.87	18
Housing Studies	1.82	8
Urban Affairs Review	1.82	20
Environment and Planning B	1.75	15
Regional Science and Urban Economics	1.75	N/A
Natural Hazards Review	1.69	4
Society & Natural Resources	1.63	N/A
Journal of Urban Affairs	1.60	29
International Regional Science Review	1.57	N/A
Journal of Urban Planning and Development	1.55	N/A
Journal of Housing Economics	1.52	N/A
Housing Policy Debate	1.49	126
Disasters	1.44	N/A
Journal of Housing and the Built Environment	1.19	N/A
Economic Development Quarterly	1.08	21
Transportation Research Record	0.87	4
Journal of Architectural and Planning Research	0.41	9

* Respondents each chose five the most important journals (Goldstein and Maier, 2010). Weights applied to five top choices (most valued = 5, second most valued = 4, etc.). Weighted number of times mentioned summed over all respondents.

Peer Review

One of the major differences between academic journals and other types of publishing is the former's use of peer review. Peer review is just what it sounds like: the evaluation of studies by others working in the same field, that is, your peers. After you submit your manuscript to a journal, the editor or associate editor will send it out for review to several academics (typically three or four) who have done similar work. (Most journals use a *double-blind* review process wherein both reviewers and authors are kept anonymous, though editors sometimes will ask authors of studies cited in the manuscript to review it, to be sure to keep critiques of previous work fair and collegial!)

The reviewers' job is to ensure your manuscript addresses an important issue in the field, uses appropriate methods correctly, and is generally of high quality. All the reviewers will provide comments on your manuscript and make a recommendation to the editor or associate editor as to whether it should be published. The editor then decides, based on the reviewer comments, whether to accept your manuscript as is, send it back to you with a request that it be revised and resubmitted, or reject it outright. Articles are rarely accepted as is, making "revise and resubmit" or "provisional acceptance" a more common response. Rejection is, sadly, also a possibility. It is also not uncommon that the editor rejects your paper before sending it out for review, an outcome called "desk reject." But whatever the editor's decision, you should read the reviewers' and editor's comments carefully and use them to improve your work. Getting free advice from established researchers is a rare privilege. It means that the next time around, probably with a different journal, the reviews are likely to be more favorable. Whatever you do, don't give up on a publication simply because you get one rejection.

A number of "Research You Can Use" columns center on journals and peer review. "Peer Review Clarifies Lots of Things, Including the Relationship of Sprawl and Air Pollution" (July 2010) describes the process and benefits of academic peer review, stating that "the fundamental truth about peer review is that it makes good papers better, often much better." "Reviewing the Reviews" (October 2013) explains the process of peer review in more detail, citing the criteria used by the *Journal of Planning Literature* (*JPL*).

Perhaps the column that has garnered the most attention, "Brouhaha over *JAPA* Article: Is Flawed Peer Review to Blame?" (October 2012), discusses an article that sparked controversy

Database	How Often Cited
Academic Search/Premier	3
Dissertation and Theses/Full Text	169
Energy Citations/Database	49
Google Scholar	1,160
JSTOR	28
Pais International	2
Proquest	183
Scopus	26
Sociological Abstracts	3
Web of Knowledge	0

Keywords: "residential energy" and "urban planning"

FIGURE 3.2 Use of database

Source: Ewing, October 2013b, p. 46; with permission from The American Planning Association

and the possibility that inadequate peer review allowed the article, which is argued to be sub-par, to be published in a well-regarded journal.

Overview of Planning Topics

The "Research You Can Use" column has by no means exhausted the list of interesting and impactful planning topics, but it has certainly covered a lot of them. The column on "Edgy Planning Issues" (October 2015) included an inventory of planning topics that appeared in *JAPA* and *JPER* from 2001 to 2014 (see Table 3.2).

We advise planning students to find topics that are well represented in the literature (so someone will be interested in your work) but not oversubscribed (so it is difficult to get papers published). We also advise students to catch topics on the *way up* in the general interest level, not on the way down. Interest in topics tends to go in cycles, and you do not want to be the last one to the party.

The rest of this chapter presents examples of planning research topics that have been covered in "Research You Can Use."

Methodological Issues

Methodological issues are a common topic in planning research. In fact, entire journals are dedicated to explorations of methodological questions. Planning-related journals covering methodology include *Environment and Planning B: Urban Analytics and City Science* and *Transportation Research Part B: Methodological*, among others.

A perennial debate in planning research (and indeed all the social sciences) concerns the best uses of quantitative and qualitative methods. The column "When Qualitative Research Trumps Quantitative—Cultural Economy and Smart Growth" (October 2007) features two

TABLE 3.2 *JAPA* and *JPER* article topics (2001–2014)

Topic	Number	%
Methods, tools, and new technology	28	4.49
Economic development	31	4.98
Environment, resource management, energy, disasters	76	12.2
Diversity in planning (gender, minority)	26	4.17
Housing and community development	74	11.88
Land use policy and governance	40	6.42
Food systems, health, safety	38	6.1
Planning education and pedagogy	38	6.1
The planning process, administration, law and dispute resolution	66	10.59
Planning theory	28	4.49
Regional and intergovernmental planning, growth management	41	6.58
Transportation and infrastructure, travel behavior	59	9.47
Urban design and preservation	18	2.89
International planning	40	6.42
New urbanism	11	1.77
Planning history	9	1.44

academic journal articles that use qualitative methods to provide unique insights where quantitative work would have been found lacking. "When Quantitative Research Trumps Qualitative—What Makes Transfer of Development Rights Work?" (January 2009) takes a different tack in critiquing a qualitative study that would have made a stronger contribution to the literature if the authors had also employed quantitative methods. The column further discusses how such a quantitative or mixed-methods study could have been carried out.

"Mixing Methods for Clearer Results" (February 2013) more directly addresses three ways that quantitative and qualitative data can be combined in a mixed-method design: merging the data, connecting the data, and embedding the data (see Figure 3.3).

An additional column, "Observation as a Research Method (and the Importance of Public Seating)" (February 2014), highlights observational methods of research and focuses on a dissertation-turned-book (Mehta, 2013) that used observation in the same vein as William H. Whyte, Allan Jacobs, and others, with the addition of a quantitative analysis of the observations. Finally, "Finding Happiness in Public–Private Partnerships: The Case for Case Studies" (January 2007) advocates for the qualitative research method of case studies for in-depth analysis. The examples in the January 2007 column come from Lynn Sagalyn's *JAPA* article (Winter 2007) on public–private partnerships.

Other columns review (or, depending on the reader, introduce) quantitative methods. Most of these columns use existing studies as examples to illustrate or critique a given method, but several columns delve into the method directly. Regression, in its various forms, is probably the most common analytical method used in planning. "Not Your Grandparents' Regression Analysis" (April 2014) provides an introduction to how regression analysis functions and its common pitfalls, including spatial autocorrelation. The column also strikes a cautionary note about the need to consult experts for the advanced analyses required by today's standards. (See Figure 3.4.)

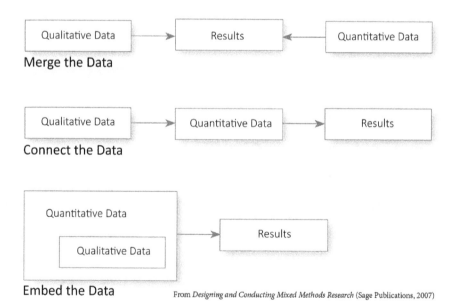

From *Designing and Conducting Mixed Methods Research* (Sage Publications, 2007)

FIGURE 3.3 Three ways of mixing quantitative and qualitative data

Source: Based on Creswell & Plano Clark, 2018

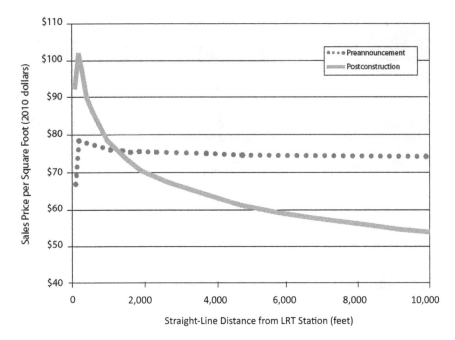

FIGURE 3.4   Capitalization effect based on proximity to LRT using regression model

Source: Golub, Guhathakurta, & Sollapuram, 2012

"Different Models of Metropolitan Economic Performance" (June 2008) discusses the relative merits of structural equation modeling over simple linear regression analysis through the example of an academic study that used multiple regression analysis when structural equation modeling would have been a better approach (Figure 3.5).

"Compact Development and Good Outcomes—Environmental Determinism, Self-Selection, or Some of Both?" (July 2009) reopens the discussion of ordinary least squares regression, negative binomial regression, and structural equation modeling, within the context of a larger discussion of the effects of self-selection on study outcomes (see Figure 3.6). "Using Safe Streets as a Research Priority" (May 2009) introduces the reader to Poisson regression and negative binomial regression as possible options when the dependent variable is a count variable with many zero values, as it is with traffic crash frequencies.

One other quantitative method, propensity score matching, is highlighted in a January 2015 column, "Assessing BIDs Using Propensity Score Matching." This column praises the use of propensity score matching specifically because it resembles randomized experiments when the random assignment of research subjects is almost always impossible in planning research. The importance of choosing the right method, such as propensity score matching, is discussed since the wrong method could lead to the wrong conclusions.

Meta-analysis as a research method is discussed in two columns. The earlier column, "Regional Scenario Plans and Meta-Analysis" (March 2007), defines meta-analysis and goes on to highlight Keith Bartholomew's meta-analysis of 80 regional scenario plans, based on Bartholomew's article in *Transportation*, "Land Use-Transportation Scenario Planning: Promise and Reality" (Bartholomew, 2007; see Figure 3.7). Meta-analysis was (and still is) rare

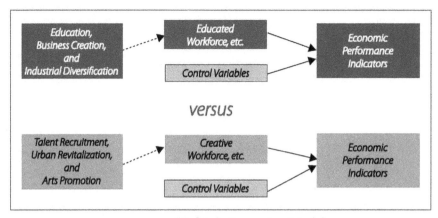

versus

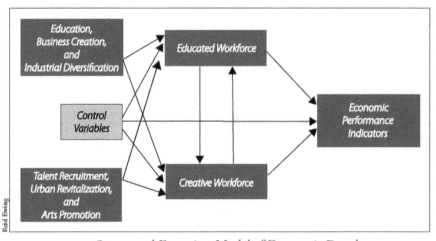

Multiple Regression Model

Structural Equation Model of Economic Development

FIGURE 3.5 Different models of Metropolitan Economic Performance

Source: Ewing, June 2008a, p. 52; with permission from The American Planning Association

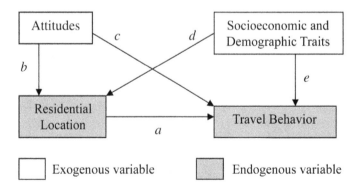

FIGURE 3.6 Effects of the built environment on travel behavior

Source: Reprinted from Mokhtarian, P. L., & Cao, X. (2008). Examining the impacts of residential self-selection on travel behavior: A focus on methodologies. Transportation Research Part B: Methodological, 42(3), 204–228.with permission from Elsevier

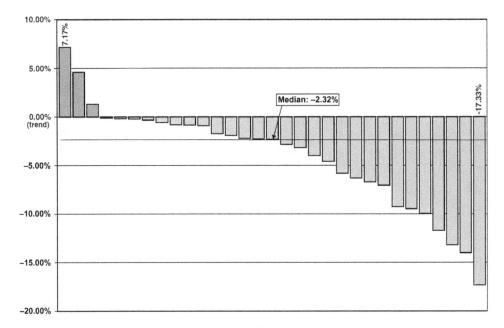

FIGURE 3.7 Range of maximum variation in VMT compared to trend scenario (planning horizons standardized to 20 years)

Source: Bartholomew, 2007; Reprinted by permission from: Springer, Transportation, Land use-transportation scenario planning: promise and reality, Keith Bartholomew, Copyright: Springer Science+Business Media B.V. 2006

in planning; as of the March 2009 column, "Meta-Analysis of Plan Quality—More Than a Literature Review," only about 10 meta-analyses had appeared in the planning literature. This latter column provides a more detailed description of meta-analysis than the earlier column and also encourages scholars to think beyond traditional literature reviews to instead use meta-analysis to summarize and examine the existing literature.

Other columns examine the theoretical underpinnings for research studies in planning. "Make Way for a New Theory" (February 2011) summarizes the argument that planning does not have its own theoretical basis but rather borrows theory from cognate fields. An exception to the rule of borrowing from other fields has historically been rational planning continues with an explanation of the theory of collaborative rationality, another theory with its origins in planning (see Figure 3.8). Other theories are also discussed in different columns.

The topic of sociology-based grounded theory is introduced in "Toward a Grounded Theory of Sustainable Zoning" (May of 2015). Grounded theory has been applied to study concepts in diverse fields, and this column reviews Edward Jepson and Anna Haines' "Zoning for Sustainability: A Review and Analysis of the Zoning Ordinances of 32 Cities in the United States" (2014) to describe how grounded theory can be applied to zoning. Another column in the same year, "A Physicist Tries to Solve the City" (December 2015), points out flaws in urban scaling theory, an approach developed by physicists that has proved problematic in its actual application to urban phenomena.

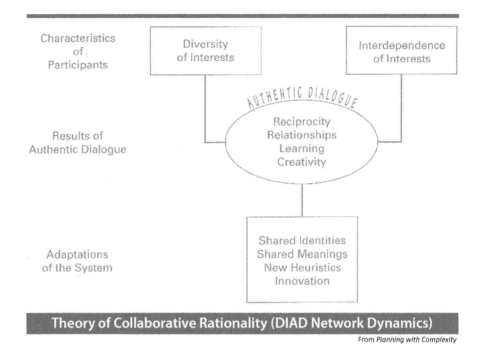

FIGURE 3.8 Theory of collaborative rationality

Source: Innes, J. E., & Booher, D. E. (2010); Planning with complexity: An introduction to collaborative rationality for public policy. copyright © The American Planning Association, www.planning.org, reprinted by permission of Taylor & Francis Ltd, http://www.tandfonline.com on behalf of The American Planning Association.

Climate Change and the Natural Environment

The number of publications on climate change has ebbed and flowed along with public interest in the topic, but we believe it is once again on the way up. In fact, a November 2008 column ("First Look at Climate Action Planners—So Much More to Be Done") states that "climate change will be the defining issue for urban planners in the 21st century." This prediction was based on, among other things, Stephen Wheeler's Autumn 2008 *JAPA* article ("State and Municipal Climate Change Plans: The First Generation"; see Figure 3.9) and the then-recent passage of California's Sustainable Communities and Climate Protection Act of 2008 (SB 375), a regional planning act aimed at encouraging metropolitan planning organizations to reduce carbon dioxide emissions from driving through more compact development.

Governmental and organizational responses to climate change—known as climate action planning—constitute another topic likely to grow in importance over the next few years due to the lack of a national-level action in the United States. A column on climate change, "Is Anyone Listening as Climate Change Speeds Up?" (December 2011), addresses this important issue. Climate action plans are again discussed in "Mixing Methods for Clearer Results" (February 2013), which describes two studies by Adam Millard-Ball, one quantitative and the other qualitative. Millard-Ball finds little evidence for a causal relationship between climate action planning and emission-reduction measures. (See Figure 3.10.)

Two climate-related planning issues, urban heat islands and ecological planning, are discussed in the August–September 2014 column ("Hot Journal, Hotter Cities"; see Figure 3.11).

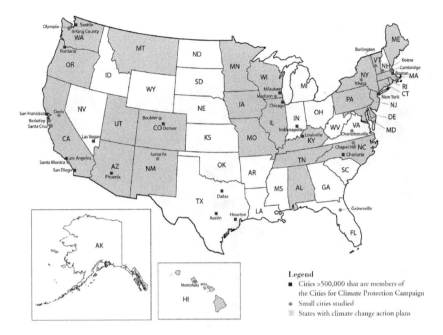

FIGURE 3.9 States and cities with climate action plans

Source: Wheeler, S. M. (2008). State and municipal climate change plans: The first generation. Journal of the American Planning Association, 74(4), 481–496. copyright © The American Planning Association, www.planning.org, reprinted by permission of Taylor & Francis Ltd, http://www.tandfonline.com on behalf of The American Planning Association.

Approved Regional Greenhouse Gas Emission Reduction Targets		
	Targets	
MPO Region	2020	2035
Southern California Association of Governments	−8	−13
Metropolitan Transportation Commission	−7	−15
San Diego Association of Governments	−7	−13
Sacramento Area Council of Governments	−7	−16
San Joaquin Valley MPOs (there are 8)	−5	−10
6 Other MPOs:		
Tahoe	−7	−5
Shasta	0	0
Butte	+1	+1
San Luis Obispo	−8	−8
Santa Barbara	0	0
Monterey Bay	0	−5

California Air Resources Board, http://www.arb.ca.gov/cc/sb375/final_targets.pdf

Courtesy Reid Ewing

Targets are expressed as percent change in per capital greenhouse gas emissions relative to 2005.

FIGURE 3.10 Approved regional greenhouse gas reduction targets

Source: Ewing, December 2011b, p. 41

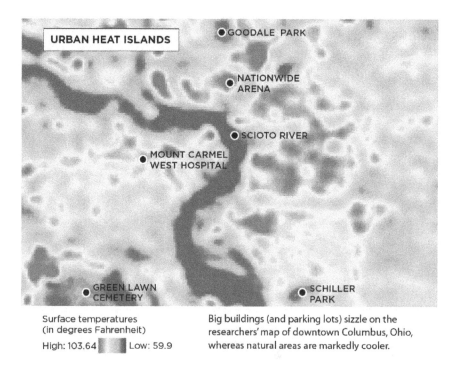

Surface temperatures
(in degrees Fahrenheit)

High: 103.64 ▮ ▯ Low: 59.9

Big buildings (and parking lots) sizzle on the
researchers' map of downtown Columbus, Ohio,
whereas natural areas are markedly cooler.

FIGURE 3.11   Urban heat islands in Columbus, Ohio

Source: Reprinted from Chun, B., & Guldmann, J. M. (2014). Spatial statistical analysis and simulation of the urban heat island in high-density central cities. Landscape and urban planning, 125, 76–88. with permission from Elsevier

The article at the center of the July 2010 column ("Peer Review Clarifies Lots of Things, Including the Relationship of Sprawl and Air Pollution") takes a close look at the relationship between compact metropolitan regions and ozone concentrations. The article's authors, Lisa Schweitzer and Jiangpin Zhou, find that compact metropolitan areas have lower ozone concentrations than sprawling metropolitan areas but that ozone exposures are greater in these same compact areas because population is concentrated in areas with the highest ozone levels (see Figure 3.12). The relationship between regional planning and air quality is also discussed in the April 2013 column, "Coordinating Land Use and Transportation in Sacramento."

Social Justice Issues

Planners have long had a concern with social justice. A good example is a study of upward mobility conducted by a team from Harvard and University of California–Berkeley, which found that intergenerational mobility varies across geographic areas of the United States. The column "Mapping Mobility" (June 2014) reviews the study and links it to a University of Utah study, which found that a cost of sprawl is a lack of upward mobility: Children born into lower-economic-status families were found to be less likely to achieve upward mobility if they lived in sprawling areas as compared to compact areas. The likely reason is the relatively limited access to employment opportunities available in sprawling areas.

In April 2018, sprawl was linked directly to income inequality in the column "Multiple Lessons from a Single Paper on Urban Sprawl." The paper upon which this column

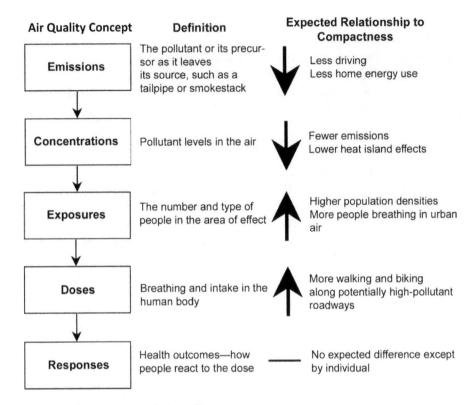

FIGURE 3.12 Compactness and air quality

Source: Schweitzer, L., & Zhou, J. (2010). Neighborhood air quality, respiratory health, and vulnerable populations in compact and sprawled regions. Journal of the American Planning Association, 76(3), 363–371. copyright © The American Planning Association, www.planning.org, reprinted by permission of Taylor & Francis Ltd, http://www. tandfonline.com on behalf of The American Planning Association.

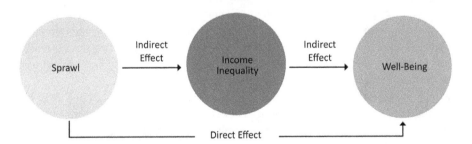

FIGURE 3.13 Sprawl's negative direct and indirect impacts

Source: Reprinted from Lee, W. H., Ambrey, C., & Pojani, D. (2018). How do sprawl and inequality affect well-being in American cities?. Cities, 79, 70–77. with permission from Elsevier

is based, published in the journal *Cities*, finds that consistent with a priori expectations, lower levels of sprawl are, on average, associated with lower levels of income inequality. Additionally, lower levels of income inequality are linked to higher levels of perceived financial well-being. Sprawl thus has both direct and indirect effects on well-being (see Figure 3.13).

In December 2017, the column addressed the issue of gentrification in "A Mixed Picture of Gentrification." We argued that gentrification has benefits for the residents of gentrifying neighborhoods and that gentrification should not be equated to residential displacement. A case study of multifamily development along a light rail line in Salt Lake City, replacing vacant lots, abandoned commercial centers, and parking lots, was used to illustrate the distinction between gentrification and displacement.

Land Use and Development Regulations

Land use and development regulations are, in many ways, the heart of planning. Not surprisingly, the use of regulatory tools such as zoning to push specific development patterns is of fundamental interest to planning researchers. (See Figure 3.14.)

One example of this is a comparative study of land readjustment practices around the world. The study, "An Examination for the Efficient Applicability of the Land Readjustment Method in the International Context," appeared in the February 2008 issue of the *Journal of Planning Literature*. A concurrent "Research You Can Use" column, "Land Readjustment— Learning from International Research," promotes the technique of land readjustment, where property owners in a given area allow a third party to replace (and sometimes rezone) the property in a way that enhances its value and makes for more efficient use of the land overall. The column notes how land readjustment had its origins in Germany but is well used in planning throughout the developed world, except for the United States and the UK.

The very first column in the series, "Does Growth Management Work? Program Evaluation at Its Best" (November 2006), introduces the then-forthcoming *JAPA* article by John Landis, "Growth Management Revisited: A Reassessment of Its Efficacy, Price Effects, and Impacts on Metropolitan Growth Patterns," in which three growth management techniques are found to be successful in their aim, and two growth management techniques are found to be ineffective. An update of Landis's work on growth management effectiveness, "Growth Management Revisited—Again," appears in the February 2018 issue of *Planning* magazine. Once again, the evidence of effectiveness is mixed. (See Figure 3.15.)

The August–September 2008 column ("Graduated Density Zoning—The Danger of Generalizing from a Sample of One") introduces graduated density zoning and critiques it as a potential method for creating higher-density development by promoting site assembly. The column discusses two Maryland counties that used site assembly-density bonuses and recommends exercising caution in adopting graduated density zoning by itself.

Taking a nongovernmental approach, Rebecca Retzlaff's *JPER* article, "The Use of LEED in Planning and Development Regulation," is described in the September–October 2009 column ("What Planners Need to Know About Evaluating LEED"), along with a second article ("Sustainable by Design? Insights from U.S. LEED-ND Pilot Projects" by Ajay Garde, *JAPA*) that was much more critical of LEED. (See Figure 3.16.)

Sprawl, Travel, and the Built Environment

The relationship between travel and the built environment is one of the most studied topics in urban planning. Hundreds of published articles examine how decisions about the location and form of urban infrastructure and land uses affect the way we build and get around our cities. Often, this discussion is framed as *sprawl* versus compactness. But academic planners tend to

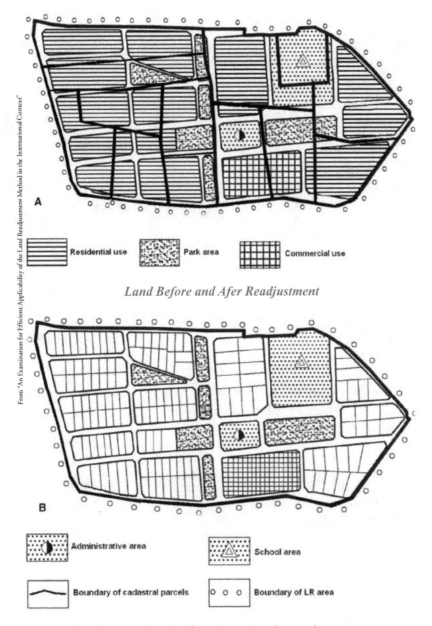

Land Before and Afer Readjustment

FIGURE 3.14 Land readjustment: learning from international research

Source: Turk, 2008

use a more nuanced vocabulary, describing the built environment in terms of the so-called *D variables*: development density, land use diversity, street design, destination accessibility, distance to transit, and demographics.

One of the main criticisms of sprawling development patterns is the long-term costs it entails. The December 2013 column "Costs of Sprawl Revisited" reviews three articles:

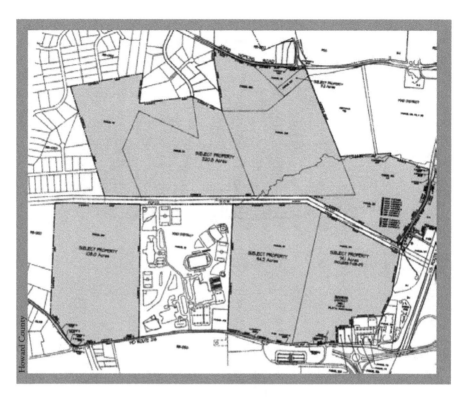

FIGURE 3.15 Howard County used mixed use overlay zoning to develop the new urbanist community of Maple Lawn Farms

Source: Ewing, August–September 2008b, p. 62

Rating System	Approximate Number
New construction (NC)	14,780
Core and shell (CS)	2,835
Commercial interiors (CI)	2,432
Retail (NC and CI)	100
Existing buildings: Operations and maintenance	3,484
Schools	907
Homes	17,081
Neighborhood development	238

FIGURE 3.16 Registered LEED projects for rating system

Source: Ewing, October 2009, p. 43; with permission from The American Planning Association

one that examines the loss of agricultural land as a result of sprawl, a second that looks at transportation-related costs of sprawl in the United States, and a third that finds the impacts of sprawl on air, energy, land, and water.

More recent columns covered an emerging regional planning paradigm in the United States: polycentric development connected by high-quality transit. The first column highlights the work on polycentricity by a rising scholar, Shima Hamidi, an assistant professor at the University of Texas at Arlington (May 2017). The follow-up highlights related but more real estate–focused research on vibrant centers by Emil Malizia, a professor of planning at University of North Carolina–Chapel Hill (July 2017). The bottom-line: Office properties in vibrant, compact, mixed-use suburban centers outperform typical single-use suburban office space on nearly all metrics.

One of the central questions concerning smart growth is whether Americans actually prefer sprawling, automobile-centric development over compact, walkable neighborhoods. After all, U.S. cities continue to grow outward, and sprawl sells. However, some research suggests that sprawl is less popular among home buyers than real estate developers. The December 2007 column ("The Demand for Smart Growth: What Survey Research Tells Us") discusses the 2004 National Survey on Communities carried out for a nonprofit organization, Smart Growth America. The survey found evidence of latent demand for the kind of compact, walkable neighborhoods that are the antithesis of sprawl and are encouraged through smart growth policies. (See Figure 3.17.)

The February 2010 column ("A Bonanza of Journal Articles") discusses an article by Paul Lewis and Mark Baldassare, "The Complexity of Public Attitudes Toward Compact Development: Survey Evidence from Five States," that finds at least half of all Americans at the time

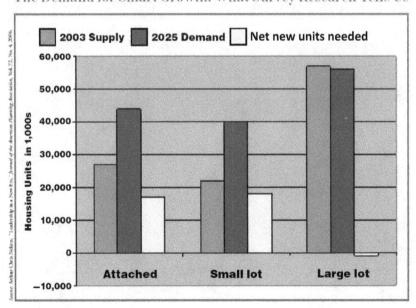

FIGURE 3.17 2025 demand for different housing types

Source: Nelson, 2006

of their study would consider living in a compact, mixed-use neighborhood. These results reinforce the idea that latent demand exists for the development of this kind.

In December 2009, the column "Top Academics vs. Top Thinkers" critiques a National Academy of Sciences report on the relationship between driving and the built environment, specifically on different scenarios of energy use, which in turn are based on differing assumptions about the intensity of residential development. The column further critiques the NAS report's consideration of residential development alone, when compact commercial development also reduces energy consumption and greenhouse gas emissions.

The April 2011 column ("Traffic Generated by MXD: New Prediction Methods Ahead") returns to the subject of traffic and its relationship to smart growth, or at least one significant feature of smart growth: mixed-use development. The column explains how mixed-use developments (MXDs) create favorable conditions within the MXD area for walking, biking, and taking transit and thus reduce the number of external car trips. The column then introduces research by a team (Michael Greenwald, Ming Zhang, Robert Cervero, Jerry Walters, Mark Feldman, Larry Frank, and John Thomas) whose article was slated for publication in the *Journal of Urban Planning and Development*. In their then-forthcoming article, the researchers report on their study of 239 MXDs and their findings that the internalization of trips in these MXDs is related to the MXD's land area, employment, the balance of jobs and population, and intersection density. (See Figure 3.18.)

Transportation is such a huge subfield of planning that it has its own sub-subfields. Traffic safety, street design, and active travel modes are all important topics within transportation.

FIGURE 3.18   RiverPlace MXD

Source: Ewing, April 2011a, p. 48

Eric Dumbaugh and Robert Rae's 2009 *JAPA* article, "Safe Urban Form: Revisiting the Relationship Between Community Design and Traffic Safety," points out that the significant body of work on the relationship between the built environment and household travel has tended to overlook the relationship between the built environment and traffic safety. The May 2009 column "Using Safe Streets as a Research Priority" discusses their finding that neighborhoods with traditional street design features such as pedestrian-oriented retail uses and interconnected streets tend to suffer fewer automobile crashes (even after controlling for vehicle miles traveled). The bad guys when it comes to crashes? Arterial streets and big-box stores. (See Figure 3.19.)

The March 2015 column ("Golden Age of Street Design") optimistically predicts the dawning of a golden age of street design based on the rise of the complete streets movement, which advocates for streets that accommodate pedestrians, bicyclists, and transit riders in addition to automobile users. The column makes the connection between poor street design and overly conservative geometric standards, road widening as a solution to congestion, lack of investment in street trees and special materials, and other factors but notes that we are already seeing streets being redesigned through road diets, the installation of curb-separated protected bike lanes, and centerline medians designed for pedestrian comfort and safety.

Performance metrics for transportation get a close examination in the 2012 *JAPA* article, "Does Accessibility Require Density or Speed? A Comparison of Fast Versus Close in Getting Where You Want to Go in U.S. Metropolitan Regions," by Jonathan Levine, Joe Grengs, Qingyun Shen, and Qing Shen. The July 2012 column "Accessibility vs. Mobility: The Right Methodology" summarizes the study's argument (that accessibility is more important than mobility) and the authors' methods (structural equation modeling), praising both. (See Figure 3.20.)

Eric Dumbaugh

FIGURE 3.19 From 2004 to 2006, San Antonio's historic King William District consisted of three intersecting arterials, with six injurious crashes and no traffic fatalities

Source: Based on Dumbaugh & Rae, 2009

The April 2016 column "*JAPA*, A Year in Review" highlights three transportation-related articles published by *JAPA* in 2015. The first article mentioned, Noreen McDonald's "Are Millennials Really the 'Go-Nowhere' Generation?" presents evidence that younger people travel fewer miles than previous generations at comparable ages. The second article ("How Differences in Roadways Affect School Travel Safety" by Chia-Yuan Yu) describes school travel–related crash data in Austin, Texas. The third article ("Parking Infrastructure: A Constraint on or Opportunity for Urban Redevelopment? A Study of Los Angeles County Parking Supply and Growth" by Mikhail Chester et al.) estimates how parking affects travel and urban form. (See Figure 3.21.)

Active transportation, aside from how it is discussed in connection with compact development in a number of columns, is at the forefront of planning research. The May 2007 column, "The Perils of Causal Inference: Bicycling in Davis, California," critiques a study in which the author makes a bold causal assertion that is not sufficiently supported by empirical evidence. Specifically, certain city policies are credited with one of the nation's highest bike mode shares, when many other factors are also at work. "A 'Natural Experiment'— Closing Broadway" (April 2010) presents more solid evidence that pedestrian malls, under the right circumstances, may produce substantial benefits with minimal disruption to traffic. Bicycling to School and Safe Routes to School programs are briefly mentioned in the October 2011 column ("Another Bonanza") and more expansively in the November 2014 column ["Correlation Does Not Imply Causation (When It Comes to Childhood Obesity)"]. The latter column highlights four *JPER* articles about healthy schools. Finally, the August–September 2016 column ("Active Living: A Planning Subfield Comes of Age") describes the origin and immense growth of active living research as a planning subfield. (See Figure 3.22.)

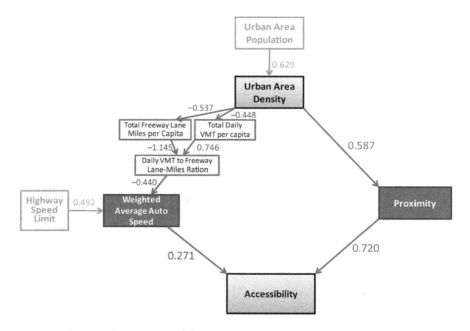

FIGURE 3.20 Structural equation model

Source: Levine, J., Grengs, J., Shen, Q., & Shen, Q. (2012). Does accessibility require density or speed? A comparison of fast versus close in getting where you want to go in US metropolitan regions. Journal of the American Planning Association, 78(2), 157–172. copyright © The American Planning Association, www.planning.org, reprinted by permission of Taylor & Francis Ltd, http://www.tandfonline.com on behalf of The American Planning Association.

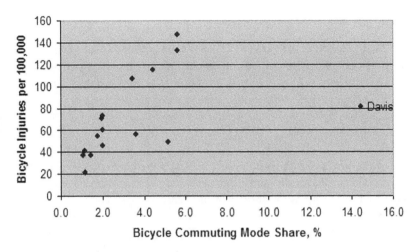

FIGURE 3.21 Bicycle injuries per capita versus mode share in 16 California cities

Source: Based on Garrick, 2005

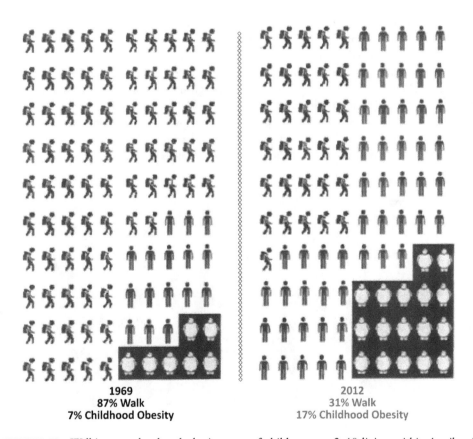

FIGURE 3.22 Walking to school and obesity rates of children ages 2–19 living within 1 mile of school

Source: Botchwey, Trowbridge, & Fisher, 2014

Urban Design

The July 2011 column "Urban Design vs. Urban Planning: A Distinction with a Difference" argues that urban design is distinct from urban planning but just as important. Where planning focuses on the regional, city, and neighborhood scales, urban design tends to focus on the street, park, or transit stop. Similarly, the orientation of the fields falls at opposite ends of a spectrum, with urban design showing a greater concern for aesthetics and planning showing a greater concern for functionality. Finally, planning is customarily a two-dimensional activity, with plans represented in plan view, not model, elevation, or section. Urban design is three-dimensional, with the vertical dimension just as critical as the horizontal ones. It is the vertical dimension of buildings that creates the great streets and public spaces of great cities.

The D variable of design is the subject of the February 2016 column, "Contribution of Urban Design Qualities to Pedestrian Activity," which delves into ways of measuring urban design. The column begins with a discussion of a 2009 *Journal of Urban Design* article ("Measuring the Unmeasurable: Urban Design Qualities Related to Walkability" by Reid Ewing and Susan Handy), which operationalized imageability, enclosure, human scale, transparency, and complexity to create a link to walkability. The column reports on a later study that found transparency (measured by the proportion of first-floor façade with windows, the proportion of active uses at street levels, and the proportion of continuous building frontage) was the most significant influence on pedestrian activity. Finally, the column summarizes the findings of a third study, again from the *Journal of Urban Design* (Ameli, Hamidi, Garfinkel-Castro, & Ewing, 2015) that also examined urban design and walkability and that found both transparency and imageability to be highly correlated with pedestrian counts.

Other columns touch on the issue of urban design in different ways. For example, the July 2007 column ("Security of Public Spaces: New Measures Are Reliable, But Are They Valid?") presented a then-forthcoming *JAPA* article ("Toward a Methodology for Measuring Security in Publicly Accessible Spaces" by Jeremy Nemeth and Stephan Schmidt) that, in part, linked the physical design of public spaces to issues of security and natural surveillance.

FIGURE 3.23 Transparency of ground-floor building facades along streets in downtown Salt Lake City has been found to significantly impact levels of pedestrian activity

Source: Ewing, February 2016, p. 50

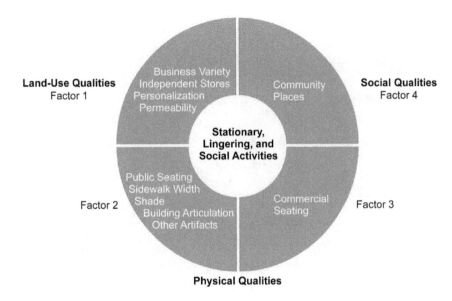

FIGURE 3.24 Important street characteristics

Source: Mehta, 2013

The February 2014 column ["Observation as a Research Method (and the Importance of Public Seating)"] describes how observational methods are often appropriate for urban design research—particularly when it comes to what makes an active and successful street, plaza, or park—using examples of well-known observers such as Jane Jacobs, Donald Appleyard, and William H. Whyte. The column continues by describing the work of Vikas Mehta, whose 2013 book *The Street: A Quintessential Social Public Space* combines observational work with quantitative analysis. Mehta's findings include the idea that social activity is strongly correlated with public seating, an idea that harkens back to William H. Whyte. (See Figure 3.24.)

Other Topics

Other topics have cropped up in articles highlighted by "Research You Can Use" columns less frequently but are no less important. Discussions of public–private partnerships, for instance, appear in two columns, years apart ["Finding Happiness in Public–Private Partnerships: The Case for Case Studies" (January 2007) and "A Bonanza of Journal Articles" (February 2010)].

A new public health tool, Health Impact Assessments (HIAs), is introduced to planners in the October 2010 column ("Translational Research: The Next New Thing"). (See Figure 3.25.)

The April 2012 column ["Great Topic (Urban Agriculture) and Good Start (to Academic Career)"] introduces urban agriculture as a trending research topic, Livability, specifically AARP's Livability Index, is discussed in the July 2015 column ("Measuring Livability"). (See Figure 3.26.)

The October 2015 column ("Edgy Planning Issues") provides summaries of articles on three very different yet *edgy* topics: property rights challenges to regional planning, the relationship between travel behavior and social connections in neighborhoods with a large share

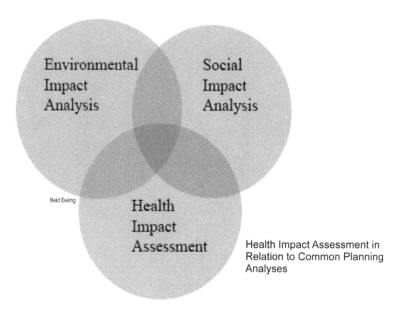

Reid Ewing

Health Impact Assessment in
Relation to Common Planning
Analyses

FIGURE 3.25   Health impact assessment in relation to common planning analyses

Source: Ewing, October 2010, p. 40

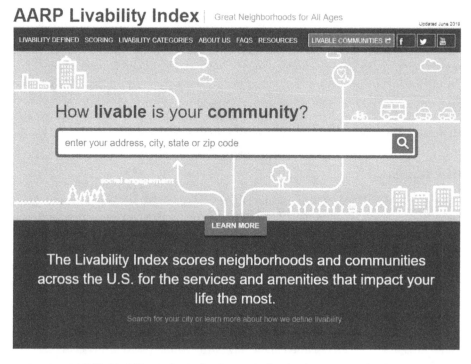

FIGURE 3.26   AARP's Livability Index is the first tool of its kind to measure livability down to the
neighborhood level for the entire country

Source: Ewing, July 2015, p. 42

of gay and lesbian residents, and land use issues related to medical marijuana dispensaries. The possible birth of a new planning subfield also comes up in the November 2016 column, "Fire-Resilient Community Design: A New Planning Subfield?"

Finally, two columns discuss the importance of translational research, or research that provides a ready application of basic findings into practice. The first half of the October 2010 column, "Translational Research: The Next New Thing," is devoted to explaining what translational research is. The next column, "Translational Research in Action" (December 2010), summarizes six planning tools that exemplify translational research.

Conclusion

Successfully navigating the maze of academic publishing is an important skill for any researcher, particularly for people in applied fields such as planning where academics want to convey their findings to practitioners. Knowing which journals are out there to publish your work, understanding the peer-review process, and keeping up with the latest works in several subfields of interest are almost as important as basic research skills.

The "Research You Can Use" column will undoubtedly continue to pick out the most important and groundbreaking new research to share with the readers of *Planning* magazine. As new research directions arise, new topics are written about, and new methods are developed, the column will highlight the research that planners should know about.

Works Cited

Ameli, S. H., Hamidi, S., Garfinkel-Castro, A., & Ewing, R. (2015). Do better urban design qualities lead to more walking in Salt Lake City, Utah? *Journal of Urban Design, 20*(3), 393–410. https://doi.org/1 0.1080/13574809.2015.1041894

Bartholomew, K. (2007). Land use-transportation scenario planning: Promise and reality. *Transportation, 34*(4), 397–412. http://doi.org/10.1007/s111116-006-9108-2

Botchwey, N. D., Trowbridge, M., & Fisher, T. (2014). Green health: Urban planning and the development of healthy and sustainable neighborhoods and schools. *Journal of Planning Education and Research, 34*(2), 113–122.

Chester, M., Fraser, A., Matute, J., Flower, C., & Pendyala, R. (2015). Parking infrastructure: A constraint on or opportunity for urban redevelopment? A study of Los Angeles County parking supply and growth. *Journal of the American Planning Association, 81*(4), 268–286. https://doi.org/10.1080/01944 363.2015.1092879

Chun, B., & Guldmann, J. M. (2014). Spatial statistical analysis and simulation of the urban heat Island in high-density central cities. *Landscape and Urban Planning, 125,* 76–88. https://doi.org/10.1016/j. landurbplan.2014.01.016

Creswell, J. W., & Plano Clark, V. L. (2018). *Designing and conducting mixed methods research* (3rd ed.). Thousand Oaks, CA: Sage Publications.

Dumbaugh, E., & Rae, R. (2009). Safe urban form: Revisiting the relationship between community design and traffic safety. *Journal of the American Planning Association, 75*(3), 309–329. http://doi. org/10.1080/01944360902950349

Ewing, R. (2008a, June). Different models of metropolitan economic performance. *Planning,* p. 52.

Ewing, R. (2008b, August–September). Graduated density zoning—The danger of generalizing from a sample of one. *Planning,* p. 62.

Ewing, R. (2009, October). What planners need to know about evaluating LEED. *Planning,* p. 43.

Ewing, R. (2010, October). Translational research: The next new thing. *Planning,* p. 40.

Ewing, R. (2011a, April). Traffic generated by MXD: New prediction methods ahead. *Planning,* pp. 48–49.

Ewing, R. (2011b, December). Is anyone listening as climate change speeds up? *Planning*, p. 41.

Ewing, R. (2013a, July). Come home to *JAPA*. *Planning*, p. 45.

Ewing, R. (2013b, October). Reviewing the reviews. *Planning*, p. 46.

Ewing, R. (2015, July). Measuring livability. *Planning*, p. 42.

Ewing, R. (2016, February). Contribution of urban design qualities to pedestrian activity. *Planning*, p. 50.

Ewing, R., & Greene, W. (2003). *Travel and environmental implications of school siting*. Washington, DC: US Environmental Protection Agency.

Ewing, R., Greenwald, M., Zhang, M., Walters, J., Feldman, M., Cervero, R., . . . Thomas, J. (2010). Traffic generated by mixed-use developments—six-region study using consistent built environmental measures. *Journal of Urban Planning and Development*, *137*(3), 248–261. https://doi.org/10.1061/(ASCE) UP.1943-5444.0000068

Ewing, R., & Handy, S. (2009). Measuring the unmeasurable: Urban design qualities related to walkability. *Journal of Urban Design*, *14*(1), 65–84. https://doi.org/10.1080/13574800802451155

Garde, A. (2009). Sustainable by design? insights from US LEED-ND pilot projects. *Journal of the American Planning Association*, *75*(4), 424–440. https://doi.org/10.1080/01944360903148174

Garrick, N. W. (2005). Land use planning and transportation network design in a bicycle friendly American city. In *84th TRB Annual Meeting [C/CD]*. Washington, DC: TRB.

Goldstein, H., & Maier, G. (2010). The use and valuation of journals in planning scholarship: Peer assessment versus impact factors. *Journal of Planning Education and Research*, *30*(1), 66–75. http://doi.org/10.1177/0739456X10375944

Golub, A., Guhathakurta, S., & Sollapuram, B. (2012). Spatial and temporal capitalization effects of light rail in Phoenix: From conception, planning, and construction to operation. *Journal of Planning Education and Research*, *32*(4), 415–429. https://doi.org/10.1177/0739456X12455523

Hamidi, S., & Ewing, R. (2014). A longitudinal study of changes in urban sprawl between 2000 and 2010 in the United States. *Landscape and Urban Planning*, *128*, 72–82. https://doi.org/10.1016/j.landurbplan.2014.04.021

Innes, J. E., & Booher, D. E. (2010). *Planning with complexity: An introduction to collaborative rationality for public policy*. Abingdon, Oxon: Routledge.

Jacobs, A. B. (1995). *Great streets*. Cambridge, MA: MIT Press.

Jepson, E. J., & Haines, A. L. (2014). Zoning for sustainability: A review and analysis of the zoning ordinances of 32 cities in the United States. *Journal of the American Planning Association*, *80*(3), 239–252. http://doi.org/10.1080/01944363.2014.981200

Landis, J. D., Deng, L., & Reilly, M. (2002). *Growth management revisited: A reassessment of its efficacy, price effects, and impacts on metropolitan growth patterns*. University of California Institute of Urban and Regional Development, Working paper 2002–02. Retrieved from https://escholarship.org/content/qt26r5p50j/qt26r5p50j.pdf (accessed on December 6, 2019)

Lee, W. H., Ambrey, C., & Pojani, D. (2018). How do sprawl and inequality affect well-being in American cities? *Cities*, *79*, 70–77. https://doi.org/10.1016/j.cities.2018.02.023

Levine, J., Grengs, J., Shen, Q., & Shen, Q. (2012). Does accessibility require density or speed? A comparison of fast versus close in getting where you want to go in US metropolitan regions. *Journal of the American Planning Association*, *78*(2), 157–172. http://doi.org/10.1080/01944363.2012.677119

Lewis, P. G., & Baldassare, M. (2010). The complexity of public attitudes toward compact development: Survey evidence from five states. *Journal of the American Planning Association*, *76*(2), 219–237. https://doi.org/10.1080/01944361003646471

Malizia, E. (2014). *Preferred office locations: Comparing location preferences and performance of office space in CBDs, suburban vibrant centers and suburban areas*. NAIOP Research Foundation. Retrieved from https://www.naiop.org/-/media/Research/Research/Research-Reports/Preferred-Office-Locations/Preferred-Office-Locations-Final-Report.ashx (accessed on December 6, 2019)

McDonald, N. C. (2015). Are millennials really the "go-nowhere" generation? *Journal of the American Planning Association*, *81*(2), 90–103. https://doi.org/10.1080/01944363.2015.1057196

Mehta, V. (2013). *The street: A quintessential social public space*. Abingdon, Oxon: Routledge.

Millard-Ball, A. (2012). Do city climate plans reduce emissions? *Journal of Urban Economics*, *71*(3), 289–311. https://doi.org/10.1016/j.jue.2011.12.004

Mokhtarian, P. L., & Cao, X. (2008). Examining the impacts of residential self-selection on travel behavior: A focus on methodologies. *Transportation Research Part B: Methodological, 42*(3), 204–228.

Nelson, A. C. (2006). Leadership in a new era: Comment on "Planning leadership in a new era". *Journal of the American Planning Association, 72*(4), 393–409. https://doi.org/10.1080/01944360608976762

Németh, J., & Schmidt, S. (2007). Toward a methodology for measuring the security of publicly accessible spaces. *Journal of the American Planning Association, 73*(3), 283–297. https://doi.org/10.1080/01944360708977978

Retzlaff, R. C. (2009). The use of LEED in planning and development regulation: An exploratory analysis. *Journal of Planning Education and Research, 29*(1), 67–77.

Sagalyn, L. B. (2007). Public/private development: Lessons from history, research, and practice. *Journal of the American Planning Association, 73*(1), 7–22. https://doi.org/10.1080/01944360708976133

Schweitzer, L., & Zhou, J. (2010). Neighborhood air quality, respiratory health, and vulnerable populations in compact and sprawled regions. *Journal of the American Planning Association, 76*(3), 363–371.

Stevens, M. R., Park, K., Tian, G., Kim, K., & Ewing, R. (2019). Why do some articles in planning journals get cited more than others? *Journal of Planning Education and Research.* https://doi.org/10.1177/0739456X19827083

Taylor & Francis. (n.d.). *JAPA downloads.*

Turk, S. S. (2008). An examination for efficient applicability of the land readjustment method at the international context. *Journal of Planning Literature, 22*(3), 229–242.

U.S. Green Building Council. (n.d.). *Registered LEED projects for rating system.*

Wheeler, S. M. (2008). State and municipal climate change plans: The first generation. *Journal of the American Planning Association, 74*(4), 481–496. http://doi.org/10.1080/01944360802377973

Whyte, W. H. (1980). *The social life of small urban spaces.* New York, NY: Project for Public Spaces.

Wilson, B., & Chakraborty, A. (2013). The environmental impacts of sprawl: Emergent themes from the past decade of planning research. *Sustainability, 5*(8), 3302–3327.

Yu, C. Y. (2015). How differences in roadways affect school travel safety. *Journal of the American Planning Association, 81*(3), 203–220. https://doi.org/10.1080/01944363.2015.10805

4

POISSON AND NEGATIVE BINOMIAL REGRESSION ANALYSIS

Anusha Musunuru, David Proffitt, Reid Ewing, and William H. Greene

Method	Dependent Variable	Independent Variables	Test Statistics
Chi-Square	Categorical	Categorical	Chi-square statistic
Difference of Means	Continuous	Categorical (two categories)	t-statistic
ANOVA	Continuous	Categorical (multiple categories)	F-statistic
Linear Regression	Continuous	Continuous (though can represent categorical)	t-statistic R2 statistic
Logistic Regression	Categorical (Dichtomous)	Continuous (though can represent categorical)	Asymptotic t-statistic Pseudo-R2 statistic
Poisson/Negative Binomial Regression	Count	Continuous (though can represent categorical)	Wald statistic Pseudo-R2 statistic

FIGURE 4.0 Poisson and negative binomial regression

Overview

The word "count" is typically used as a verb meaning to itemize or to indicate by units, or items so as to find the total number of units involved. A great amount of data collected by urban planners, medical statisticians, and economists takes the form of counts, used as a noun; that is, they are non-negative integers. For instance, the number of individuals who die on a highway, the number of smart growth policies in an area, and the number of red blood cells on a microscope slide are all count data.

Two regression methods are ordinarily used to model count data: Poisson regression and negative binomial regression. This chapter covers the purpose, history, mechanics, and interpretation of these models. Step-by-step instructions explain how to conduct the analysis in

SPSS and R. Case study examples are used to demonstrate the applicability of count models to the real world of urban and regional planning. For further reading, see the publications cited in this chapter.

Purpose

Many parametric statistical models are based on underlying probability distributions (Hilbe, 2014). For example, linear regression models, which are widely used by urban planners, are based on a normal probability distribution.

Linear regression models are not appropriate for count data primarily because a linear model might lead to the prediction of negative counts. Counts are discrete non-negative integers. A regression model with a count response variable measures the likelihood of an event happening in a given period of time. Poisson and negative binomial regression analyses are used to estimate the parameters of probability distributions that best fit common count data (Hilbe, 2014).

History

The French mathematician Simeon-Denis Poisson developed the Poisson distribution in his 1837 exploration of jury verdicts, *Research on the Probability of Criminal and Civil Verdicts* (Editors of Encyclopedia Britannica, 2017). While his conclusion that jury trials should be decided by simple majority decisions did not garner much attention then or since, the Poisson distribution has won enduring acceptance.

Since Poisson's time, subsequent investigations have found the distribution to accurately predict the frequency of low-probability events in a surprisingly wide range of situations. In one of the first applications in the late nineteenth century, the German statistician von Bortkiewicz used the Poisson distribution to model the number of deaths from horse kicks in the Prussian Army. In the 1930s, the statistician Gosset—who was employed by the Guinness brewery at the time—found that it described the distribution of yeast cells suspended in beer (Brooks, 2004). Since then, Poisson probability has been used to develop theories of queuing (Brooks, 2004) and in the analysis of traffic, radioactivity, and the random occurrence of events in time or space (Editors of Encyclopedia Britannica, 2017).

G. Udny Yule (1910) is generally credited with formulating the first negative binomial distribution by dealing with the number of deaths that would occur as a result of being exposed to a disease. During the 1940s, most of the original work on count models came from George Beall (1942), F. J. Anscombe (1949), and Maurice Bartlett (1947). Particularly, Bartlett (1947) proposed an analysis of square root transforms on Poisson data by examining variance-stabilizing transformations for overdispersed data. Leroy Simon (1961), following his seminal work differentiating the Poisson and negative binomial models (1960), was the first to publish a maximum likelihood algorithm for fitting the negative binomial. It was not until the 1980s that people became able to use a computer to estimate the Poisson and negative binomial models as parts of generalized linear models (GLM) (Hilbe, 2011).

After the first development of William Greene's LIMDEP in 1987, the negative binomial models became available in most commercial software packages, including SPSS, Stata, SAS, R, MATLAB, among others.

Mechanics

Poisson Regression

The Poisson distribution is fundamental to the modeling of count data. Let y be the number of events that occur in a unit of space or time, and λ be the rate, or the expected number of occurrences during the fixed interval. Then x will have a Poisson distribution with parameter λ:

$$p(y) = \frac{\lambda^y e^{-\lambda}}{y!}$$

where
$y = 0, 1, 2, \ldots$, and
λ is the mean and variance of y.

This distribution is a one-parameter distribution defined entirely by the mean λ. The variance is identical to the mean, so the variance/mean ratio is equal to one. As the mean value of the distribution increases, so does the variability of the data. This feature is referred to as *equidispersion* (Hilbe, 2014).

Figure 4.1 shows examples of the Poisson distribution with different mean values.

The Poisson regression assumes that the logarithm of the expected count value can be modeled by a linear combination of the independent variables.

$$\ln \text{ (expected count)} = b_o + b_1 X_1 + b_2 X_2 + \ldots$$

where
b is the regression coefficient, and
X is the independent variable.

The observations (cases) are usually assumed to be independent.

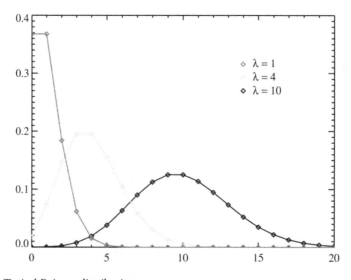

FIGURE 4.1 Typical Poisson distributions

Source: Glen, 2013

The negative binomial regression model allows modeling of a far wider range of variability than the Poisson regression model. The negative binomial model makes the same distributional assumptions as the Poisson distribution, with the exception that it has a second parameter σ: the dispersion parameter (Hilbe, 2014). It can therefore be used to model distributions that are flatter than the Poisson distribution.

There are two primary forms of the negative binomial distribution: NB1 and NB2. Both models have a mean of λ and a variance that is affected by the mean λ and the dispersion parameter σ. For the standard parameterization, NB2, the variance is $\lambda(1 + \sigma\lambda)$. The other parametrization, NB1 has a variance of $\lambda(1 + \sigma)$. In both cases, the distribution reverts to the Poisson when σ equals zero.

Like the Poisson regression, the negative binomial (NB) regression assumes that the logarithm of the expected count value can be modeled by a linear combination of the independent variables and a disturbance term that has a *log-gamma* distribution. The formula for the logarithm contains an extra parameter σ:

$$\ln(\text{expected count}) = b_0 + b_1 X_1 + b_2 X_2 + \ldots + \sigma * e$$

where
e is the error, and
$\sigma * e$ corrects for overdispersion.
When e is integrated out of the conditional Poisson distribution, the NB model results.

Model Estimation and Assessment of Fit

Poisson and negative binomial models are estimated with a maximum likelihood algorithm. This technique calculates regression coefficients that make the observed values of the dependent variable most likely to have occurred (Piza, 2012).

A commonly used fit measure used with count models, especially Poisson regression, is called the deviance goodness-of-fit statistic. The deviance is defined as two times the difference between the log likelihood of the saturated model and the log-likelihood of the fitted model (see Chapter 1). The deviance follows a chi-square distribution. If the resulting chi-square p-value is less than 0.05, the model is considered well fit.

Testing for Overdispersion

To identify whether data are overdispersed, first compute the mean and variance of the count variable being modeled. If the variance is roughly equal to the mean, the data are equidispersed and may be fitted with a Poisson model. If the variance of the data is less than the mean, the data are *Poisson underdispersed*. Similarly, if the variance of the data is greater than the mean, the data are *Poisson overdispersed*. It turns out that most count data are Poisson overdispersed (see Figure 4.2).

The next step to identify overdispersion is to check the values of two dispersion statistics—the deviance divided by the degrees of freedom or the Pearson chi-square divided by the degrees of freedom (Rodriguez, 2013; Hilbe, 2014). Equidispersion is indicated when the dispersion statistic has a value of 1. If a Poisson model has a dispersion statistic value less than or greater than 1, the data are said to be underdispersed or overdispersed, respectively.

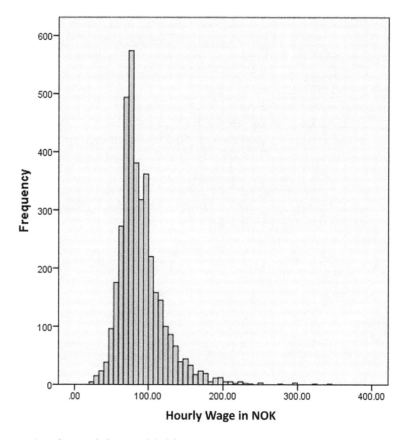

FIGURE 4.2 Overdispersed data modeled by Poisson distribution (note: NOK referred to Norwegian Currency)

After identifying overdispersion, the next step is determining the most likely reason for it. Overdispersion is caused by a positive correlation between responses or by an excess of variation between counts (Hilbe, 2014). To deal with the former, try adding independent variables, transforming independent variables, modeling interactions among independent variables, or dropping outlying values from the dataset (see Chapter 12 of *Basic Quantitative Research Methods for Urban Planners*). If these strategies do not reduce the dispersion statistics to values near 1, you will want to use negative binomial regression to model overdispersed data.

Handling Excess Zeros: Zero-Inflated Models

A variety of count data situations can be modeled using either Poisson or negative binomial regression. If there are far more observed zero counts than expected given the mean of the distribution, a zero-inflated Poisson (ZIP) or a zero-inflated negative binomial (ZINB) model is used.

Zero-inflation models can be thought of in terms of two regime mixture models, with the first always generating zeroes and the second generating the full range of counts.

Underdispersed Count Data

As mentioned, in a Poisson distribution, the variance of the data equals the mean. In rare situations, the variance of the data is less than the mean, which is known as underdispersed data. These types of data are lumped more tightly together than would be expected based on Poisson or negative binomial distributional assumptions (Hilbe, 2014). Underdispersed data can result in the standard errors being overestimated with the Poisson model. This means that the coefficients of the model are seen to be not significant, when in fact they are significant.

Several models for underdispersed data include generalized Poisson regression (Consul & Famoye, 1992), double Poisson regression (Efron, 1986), Conway-Maxwell Poisson regression (Shmueli, Minka, Kadane, Borle, & Boatwright, 2005), and quasi-Poisson regression (Giuffrè, Grana, Giuffrè, & Marino, 2013; Hüls et al., 2017; Ribeiro, Zeviani, Bonat, Demetrio, & Hinde, 2018).

More Complex Models

In addition to the traditional Poisson, NB2, NB1, and generalized Poisson models, two-step mixture models, longitudinal data count models, and some Bayesian treatments of count data are becoming popular. These models are based on the nature and type of count data, such as highly skewed, truncated, and bifurcated data. A majority of these complex models are estimated using the standard maximum likelihood algorithm and goodness-of-fit tests. These analyses are done using statistical software such as SPSS, STATA, SAS, and R. We'd also note that many of the exotic versions of count models appear in LIMDEP and not the others, including (a) censored and truncated Poisson and NB, (b) latent class Poisson and NB, (c) NB-P, (d) gamma, (e) all manner of panel data models including fixed and random effects, random parameters, and more.

Interpreting Results

The most important results of a Poisson or negative binomial regression model are the goodness-of-fit statistics and the regression coefficients. It is a good idea to check the model's goodness of fit first because these statistics can reveal problems that invalidate the regression coefficients. Always remember that "a model is only as good as the results of its fit statistics."

Three goodness-of-fit tests have been traditionally used with count models (Hilbe, 2014): pseudo-R-squared statistics, deviance statistics, and the likelihood ratio (LR) test statistics, all of which can be used only for a relative comparison between models. The pseudo-R-squared measures a relative log likelihood between the fitted model and the null (intercept-only) model. As discussed in the Logistic Regression chapter (Chapter 13) of *Basic Quantitative Research Methods for Urban Planners*, we cannot interpret the pseudo-R-squared as a proportion of variance explained by the model, unlike the R-squared in linear regression. Both deviance test (previously discussed) and LR test are comparative statistics between two different models. They are especially useful when deciding whether to add a predictor (or a set of predictors) to a model (i.e., between two models, one of which is nested within the other).

More contemporary statistics for the purpose of assessing comparative model fit are the Akaike Information Criterion (AIC) and Bayesian Information Criterion (BIC). While there are multiple ways to formulate them, Hilbe (2011) provides that the consistent parameterizations of AIC and BIC are:

$$\text{AIC} = \frac{-2(\mathcal{L} - k)}{n}$$

$$\text{BIC} = \frac{-2(\mathcal{L} - k \times \ln(k))}{n}$$

where
$\mathcal{L}$ is the model log likelihood,
k is the number of predictors including the intercept, and
n represents the number of model observations.
The inclusion of k shows that AIC and BIC are adjusted for the model complexity (i.e., the number of predictors).

Step by Step

For the purpose of illustration, the household travel dataset ("HTS.household.10regions.sav") is used here. Let's assume that you want to model the number of automobile trips made by a household (*autotrips*) in terms of household and built environment characteristics.

The first step is to load the data into SPSS and look at descriptive statistics of the outcome variable. This histogram is especially useful in deciding whether to use Poisson or negative binomial regression. Go to "Graphs" → "Legacy Dialogs" → "Histogram" and add *autotrips* to the variable list while checking "Display normal curve."

The histogram shows an overdispersed distribution (i.e., right skewed) (See Figure 4.3). The average number of cars per household is 8.49, and the standard deviation is 7.226. Because the variance, the square of the standard deviation, is 52.2 and much larger than the mean, we can assume that negative binomial is an appropriate model. But this needs to be confirmed with dispersion statistics.

To run a generalized linear model including Poisson and negative binomial, go to "Analyze" → "Generalized Linear Models" and select "Generalized Linear Models." (See Figure 4.4.)

A dialog box appears. The first and default tab is Type of Model. Note that you can actually run multiple types of regression, even including linear regression and binary logistic regression. Under the "Counts" section, select "Poisson loglinear." Then move to the next tab, "Response." (See Figure 4.5.)

The Response tab is where the dependent variable for the model is specified. In this case, add *autotrips*, the number of trips made by automobile in a household. (See Figure 4.6.)

Then the next tab is "Predictors" in which the independent variables are specified. Select the variables that are likely to explain the number of auto trips. In this example, we will include *hhsize, hhworker, hhincome, actden, stopden,* and *emp30t*. Add them to the "Covariates" box. Note that the "Factors" box is for categorical independent variables, while the "Covariates" box is for continuous independent variables. (See Figure 4.7.)

Then move to the next tab, "Model." Add all independent variables in the left box to the "Model" box by clicking the arrow button. We will keep default settings for other tabs such as "Estimation" and "Statistics." Click "OK" to run a model. (See Figure 4.8.)

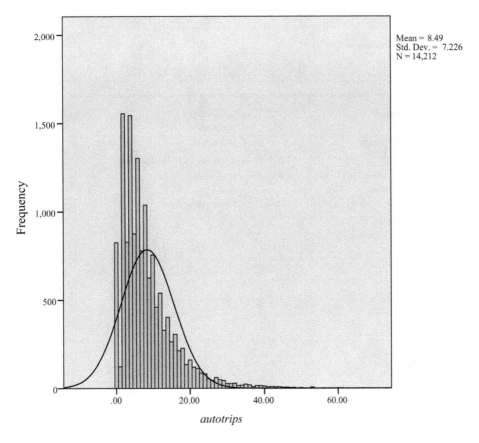

FIGURE 4.3 Histogram of the auto trips variable

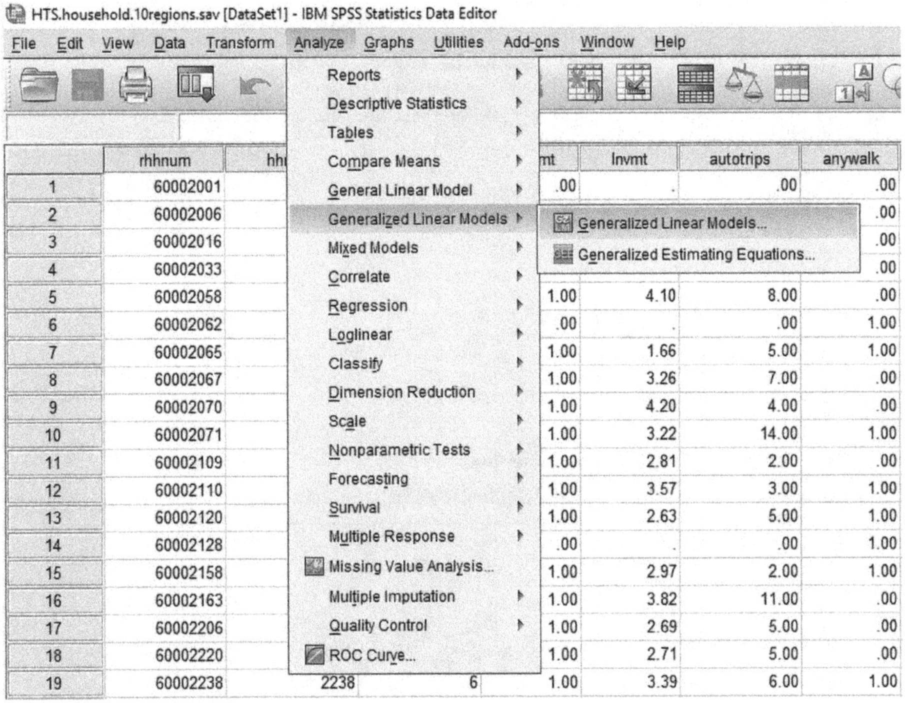

FIGURE 4.4 Selecting generalized linear models in SPSS

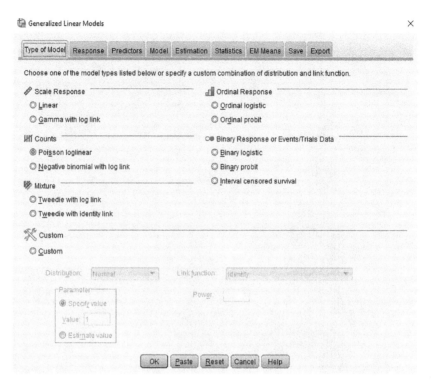

FIGURE 4.5 Generalized linear models window: Type of Model tab

FIGURE 4.6 Generalized linear models window: Response tab

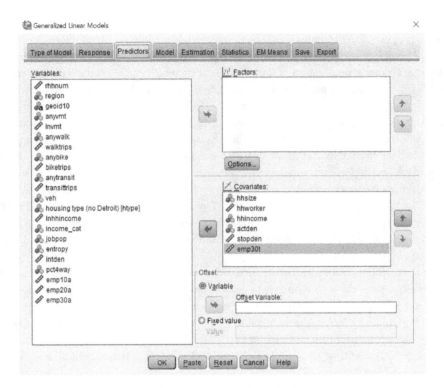

FIGURE 4.7   Generalized linear models window: "Predictors" tab

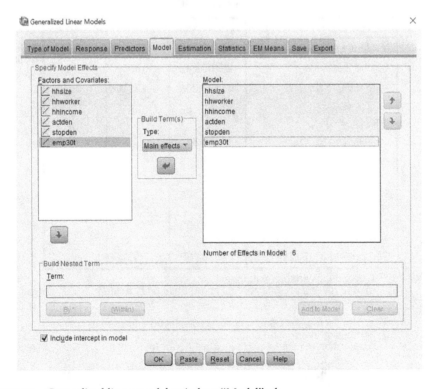

FIGURE 4.8   Generalized linear models window: "Model" tab

SPSS provides many output tables. The first three tables contain general information about the model, number of cases, and descriptive statistics of the variables. Figure 4.9 is a Goodness of Fit table presenting several indices of the goodness of fit, which can be used to compare models. The table also provides dispersion statistics. Remember that the dispersion statistics can be calculated in two ways: the deviance divided by the degrees of freedom or the Pearson chi-square divided by the degrees of freedom (Rodriguez, 2013; Hilbe, 2014). SPSS provides two statistics in the Value/df column (3.511 and 3.539 in our case). Because both values are much greater than 1.0 and the histogram of the *autotrips* variable showed a right-skewed distribution, we confirm that the overdispersion is real, and thus the negative binomial model is more appropriate.

To run negative binomial regression, go back to the "Generalized Linear Models" window and choose "Negative binomial with log link." Figure 4.10 shows the Goodness of Fit table from the negative binomial model. The dispersion statistics are now less than 1.0. Also, we can see that both AIC and BIC statistics decrease from the Poisson regression, indicating an improved goodness of fit of the model.

The tables in Figure 4.11 provide tests of the model as a whole. In the Omnibus Test table, the likelihood ratio chi-square provides a test of the overall model, comparing this model to a null model without any predictors. We can see that our model is a significant improvement over such a model by looking at the *p*-value of this test. The Tests of Model Effects table displays the statistical significance of each of the independent variables in the Sig. column. This table is especially useful when having categorical independent variables because it is the only table that considers their overall effect.

Goodness of Fit[b]

	Value	df	Value/df
Deviance	46765.842	13319	3.511
Scaled Deviance	46765.842	13319	
Pearson Chi-Square	47137.058	13319	3.539
Scaled Pearson Chi-Square	47137.058	13319	
Log Likelihood[a]	-47242.307		
Akaike's Information Criterion (AIC)	94498.613		
Finite Sample Corrected AIC (AICC)	94498.621		
Bayesian Information Criterion (BIC)	94551.095		
Consistent AIC (CAIC)	94558.095		

Dependent Variable: autotrips
Model: (Intercept), hhsize, hhworker, hhincome, actden, stopden, emp30t

a. The full log likelihood function is displayed and used in computing information criteria.
b. Information criteria are in small-is-better form.

FIGURE 4.9 Goodness of fit measures and dispersion statistics for the Poisson model

Goodness of Fit [b]

	Value	df	Value/df
Deviance	6714.633	13319	.504
Scaled Deviance	6714.633	13319	
Pearson Chi-Square	5202.444	13319	.391
Scaled Pearson Chi-Square	5202.444	13319	
Log Likelihood[a]	-41257.860		
Akaike's Information Criterion (AIC)	82529.720		
Finite Sample Corrected AIC (AICC)	82529.728		
Bayesian Information Criterion (BIC)	82582.202		
Consistent AIC (CAIC)	82589.202		

Dependent Variable: autotrips
Model: (Intercept), hhsize, hhworker, hhincome, actden, stopden, emp30t

a. The full log likelihood function is displayed and used in computing information criteria.
b. Information criteria are in small-is-better form.

FIGURE 4.10   Goodness of fit measures and dispersion statistics for the negative binomial model

Omnibus Test[a]

Likelihood Ratio Chi-Square	df	Sig.
2850.632	6	.000

Dependent Variable: autotrips
Model: (Intercept), hhsize, hhworker, hhincome, actden, stopden, emp30t

a. Compares the fitted model against the intercept-only model.

Tests of Model Effects

	Type III		
Source	Wald Chi-Square	df	Sig.
(Intercept)	1688.697	1	.000
hhsize	1398.776	1	.000
hhworker	22.330	1	.000
hhincome	101.405	1	.000
actden	40.752	1	.000
stopden	7.355	1	.007
emp30t	7.658	1	.006

Dependent Variable: autotrips
Model: (Intercept), hhsize, hhworker, hhincome, actden, stopden, emp30t

FIGURE 4.11   Model fit outputs

The Parameter Estimates table in Figure 4.12 contains the coefficients for each of the predictor variables along with their standard errors, Wald chi-square values, p-values, and 95% confidence intervals. All variables are significant, as presented in the previous table, and have expected signs: The number of auto trips is positively associated with bigger household size, more workers, and higher income and is negatively associated with the D variables.

Because the dependent variable in both Poisson and negative binomial regression is log-transformed, the exponentiated values are usually easier to interpret. For categorical independent variables, the exponentiated regression coefficient shows the proportion of increase or decrease in the count of one group versus another (the reference group). For continuous independent variables, the exponentiated regression coefficient shows the proportion of increase or decrease in the count associated with a one-unit increase in the independent variable.

For our example, one more person in a household (*hhsize*) increases the expected log count of auto trips by 0.318. If you exponentiate the coefficient 0.318, you get 1.37. So one more person means a 37% increase in the expected number of auto trips by a household. Likewise, the exponentiated coefficient for *actden* is 0.992. Thus, for each one-unit increase on activity density, the expected number of auto trips decreases by 0.8%.

In R

Figures 4.13 through 4.15 show an R script to run Poisson and negative binomial regression models. After reading the SPSS data file, you may first examine the distribution of the dependent variable—the number of auto trips, in this case. Figure 4.14 shows codes for Poisson regression and an overdispersion test (*AER* package). The test result suggests an overdispersion ($p<.01$) and thus, negative binomial as a more appropriate modeling approach. Then we run the final model (*glm.nb* function in *MASS* package) in Figure 4.15. ANOVA test confirms that our model is better than the null negative binomial model, based on the likelihood ratio test.

Parameter Estimates

| Parameter | B | Std. Error | 95% Wald Confidence Interval | | Hypothesis Test | | |
			Lower	Upper	Wald Chi-Square	df	Sig.
(Intercept)	1.116	.0271	1.062	1.169	1688.697	1	.000
hhsize	.318	.0085	.301	.335	1398.776	1	.000
hhworker	.059	.0125	.035	.084	22.330	1	.000
hhincome	.002	.0002	.002	.003	101.405	1	.000
actden	-.008	.0013	-.011	-.006	40.752	1	.000
stopden	-.001	.0003	-.001	.000	7.355	1	.007
emp30t	-.001	.0005	-.002	.000	7.658	1	.006
(Scale)	1[a]						
(Negative binomial)	1						

Dependent Variable: autotrips

Model: (Intercept), hhsize, hhworker, hhincome, actden, stopden, emp30t

a. Fixed at the displayed value.

FIGURE 4.12 Negative binomial regression model output

```
#POISSON AND NEGATIVE BINOMIAL REGRESSION ANALYSIS
library("foreign")
hts<-read.spss("HTS.household.10regions.sav",to.data.frame=TRU
E)

hist(hts$autotrips,freq=F,xlab="auto trips",main="Histogram of
auto trips")
lines(density(hts$autotrips,adjust=3),col="red")
```

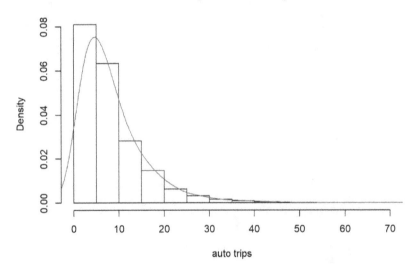

Histogram of auto trips

FIGURE 4.13   Reading SPSS data and generating a histogram: R script and outputs

Planning Examples

Smart Growth Policy Adoption

Smart growth, according to the American Planning Association, can be defined as having two main thrusts: promoting denser development and protecting agricultural and wild land from development. For the smart growth phenomenon to be successful, its goals must be advanced by supporters at the state and local levels. However, since each locality is different, there is no uniformity in the policies adopted to promote smart growth.

To research how local municipalities have implemented smart growth policies, O'Connell (2009) chose eight policies commonly referenced by smart growth advocates:

1. An urban growth boundary;
2. A program for the purchase of development rights;
3. A program for the transfer of development rights;
4. Zoning policies designed to encourage smaller lot size;

```
glm2<-glm(autotrips~hhsize+hhworker+hhincome+actden+stopden+em
p30t,data=hts,family=poisson(link = "log"))
summary(glm2)
```

```
##
## Call:
## glm(formula = autotrips ~ hhsize + hhworker + hhincome + ac
tden +
##       stopden + emp30t, family = poisson(link = "log"), data
= hts)
##
## Deviance Residuals:
##      Min        1Q    Median        3Q       Max
## -10.6827   -1.4101   -0.3374    0.8605    9.3564
##
## Coefficients:
##               Estimate Std. Error z value Pr(>|z|)
## (Intercept)  1.234e+00  9.153e-03 134.828  < 2e-16 ***
## hhsize       2.804e-01  2.158e-03 129.957  < 2e-16 ***
## hhworker     5.751e-02  3.760e-03  15.296  < 2e-16 ***
## hhincome     2.399e-03  7.424e-05  32.317  < 2e-16 ***
## actden      -8.844e-03  6.833e-04 -12.943  < 2e-16 ***
## stopden     -8.151e-04  1.290e-04  -6.317 2.67e-10 ***
## emp30t      -1.618e-03  1.613e-04 -10.033  < 2e-16 ***
## ---
## Signif. codes:  0 '***' 0.001 '**' 0.01 '*' 0.05 '.' 0.1 '
' 1
##
## (Dispersion parameter for poisson family taken to be 1)
##
##     Null deviance: 73095  on 13325  degrees of freedom
## Residual deviance: 46766  on 13319  degrees of freedom
##   (886 observations deleted due to missingness)
## AIC: 94499
##
## Number of Fisher Scoring iterations: 5
```

```
library(AER)
dispersiontest(glm2)
```

```
##
##  Overdispersion test
##
## data:  glm2
## z = 37.13, p-value < 2.2e-16
## alternative hypothesis: true dispersion is greater than 1
## sample estimates:
## dispersion
##   3.548427
```

FIGURE 4.14   Running a Poisson regression and a dispersion test: R script and outputs

5. Policies designed to encourage transit-oriented development;
6. Policies to encourage infill or brownfield development;
7. Policies to encourage reinvesting in or rehabilitation of existing buildings; and
8. Zoning policies to permit mixed-use development.

The author surveyed planning and development officials in 202 cities to understand in detail the factors that lead to the adoption of local smart growth policies. Surveys were sent to officials of 13 cities with at least 50,000 population that were found to have comprehensive land

```
library(MASS)
glm.nb1<-glm.nb(autotrips~hhsize+hhworker+hhincome+actden+stop
den+emp30t,data=hts)
summary(glm.nb1)
```

```
##
## Call:
## glm.nb(formula = autotrips ~ hhsize + hhworker + hhincome +
actden +
##     stopden + emp30t, data = hts, init.theta = 3.347672462,
link = log)
##
## Deviance Residuals:
##     Min      1Q   Median      3Q     Max
## -4.5578  -0.8315  -0.1753   0.4718   4.9385
##
## Coefficients:
##               Estimate Std. Error z value Pr(>|z|)
## (Intercept)  1.1379669  0.0168016  67.730  < 2e-16 ***
## hhsize       0.3116775  0.0048560  64.185  < 2e-16 ***
## hhworker     0.0597395  0.0076980   7.760 8.47e-15 ***
## hhincome     0.0024375  0.0001487  16.393  < 2e-16 ***
## actden      -0.0086908  0.0010220  -8.504  < 2e-16 ***
## stopden     -0.0008658  0.0002217  -3.905 9.41e-05 ***
## emp30t      -0.0013094  0.0002997  -4.369 1.25e-05 ***
## ---
## Signif. codes:  0 '***' 0.001 '**' 0.01 '*' 0.05 '.' 0.1 '
 ' 1
##
## (Dispersion parameter for Negative Binomial(3.3477) family
taken to be 1)
##
##     Null deviance: 22529  on 13325  degrees of freedom
## Residual deviance: 14994  on 13319  degrees of freedom
##   (886 observations deleted due to missingness)
## AIC: 77944
##
## Number of Fisher Scoring iterations: 1
##
##
##             Theta:  3.3477
##         Std. Err.:  0.0614
##
##  2 x log-likelihood:  -77927.6020
```

```
glm.nb0<-glm.nb(autotrips~1,data=hts)
anova(glm.nb1,glm.nb0)
```

```
## Likelihood ratio tests of Negative Binomial Models
##
## Response: autotrips
##                                                       Model
theta
## 1                                                         1
1.823113
## 2 hhsize + hhworker + hhincome + actden + stopden + emp30t
3.347672
##   Resid. df   2 x log-lik.   Test   df LR stat. Pr(Chi)
## 1     14211       -89170.64
## 2     13319       -77927.60 1 vs 2  892 11243.04       0
```

FIGURE 4.15   Running a negative binomial regression and an ANOVA test with a null model: R script and outputs

use policies at the local level. Surveys were also sent to cities that had the same population requirement but that did not meet the comprehensive land use policy requirement.

The dependent variables were the eight smart growth policies previously mentioned, which were separated into two main groups: land-preserving policies and inner-city redevelopment policies. This gave the author three dependent variables: number of smart growth policies, number of land-preserving policies, and number of redevelopment policies.

Independent variables were based on survey questions and their responses, as well as on census data. The independent variables were population growth, population with a college degree, family income, number of supporters, number of opponents, and whether a comprehensive plan was required.

Models were estimated for the three dependent variables with Poisson regression (see Figure 4.16). Only the models for total number of policies and number of land-preserving policies reached statistical significance.

Most of the hypotheses were supported by the count models, except for the hypothesis that smart growth policies are adopted to slow growth and racial change. The effects of these variables were in the expected direction but were not significant.

Overall, it was found that more supporters of smart growth policies leads to more smart growth policies being adopted, that supporters of smart growth have more leverage in adopting land-preserving policies than they do with redevelopment policies, and that having a state-mandated comprehensive plan leads to the adoption of more smart growth policies.

Independent Variables	Model 1: Predicting Total Number of Smart Growth Policies[a]			Model 2: Predicting Number of Land Preserving Policies[b] Only			Model 3: Predicting Number of Inner-City Redevelopment Policies[c] Only		
	Coeff.	S.E.	z	Coeff.	S.E.	z	Coeff.	S.E.	z
Constant	0.964	0.285	3.38***	−0.955	0.45	−2.15*	1. 201	0.373	3.23
1990 population (millions)	0.496	0.245	2.02*	0.827	0.36	2. 36*	0..211	0.345	0.61
1980–1992 % population growth	0.001	0.001	0.05	−0.001	0.040	−0.04	−0.001	0.000	−0.07
1990% population with college degree	0.011	0.005	2.12*	0.018	0.007	2.45*	0.004	0.007	0.67
1989 median family income ($ thousands)	−0.014	0.006	−2.32*	−0.022	0.009	−2.43*	−0.007	0.008	−0.89
1990% housing units owner occupied	0.004	0.005	0.75	0.014	0.008	1.80	−0.004	0.006	−0.69
1990% White	0.162	0.201	0.81	0.450	0.321	1.40	−0.060	0.258	−0.23
Number of types of opponents	−0.003	0.026	−0.10	−0.012	0.001	−0.30	−0.007	0.034	0.21
Number of types of supporters	0.066	0.018	3.61***	0.104	0.027	3.81***	0.044	0.025	1.40
Comprehensive planning required (1) or not required (0) by 1992	0.207	0.087	2.37*	0.543	0.14	3.94***	−0.039	0.115	−0.34
N		190			190			190	
Likelihood ratio χ^2		44.75			59.89			9.90	
p of χ^2		<0.001			<0.001			0.359	
Pseudo R^2		.058			.096			.017	

Notes:
All coefficient estimates are unstandardized.
[a.] Cities could have from 0 to 8 smart growth policies.
[b.] Cities could have from 0 to 5 land preserving policies.
[c.] Cities could have from 0 to 3 inner-city redevelopment policies.

* $P < 0.05$ ** $P < 0.01$ *** $P < 0.001$

FIGURE 4.16 Poisson regression models predicting number of adopted smart growth policies in surveyed cities

Source: O'Connell, L. (2009). The impact of local supporters on smart growth policy adoption, Journal of the American Planning Association, 75(3), 281–29. copyright © The American Planning Association, www.planning.org, reprinted by permission of Taylor & Francis Ltd, http://www.tandfonline.com on behalf of The American Planning Association.

Crash Prediction

A study in Tucson, Arizona, used crash data to gauge the feasibility of using crash models at the regional planning level to predict future safety conditions (Ladron de Guevara, Washington, & Oh, 2004). For this study, the negative binomial distribution was chosen over Poisson because the mean and variance were not equal, the data being overdispersed.

The dependent variables were the numbers of crashes by type: fatal, injury, and property damage only (PDO) crashes. The independent variables included economic, demographic, and road network variables. Models were run for each of the three dependent variables. (See Figure 4.17.)

The fatal crash frequency was modeled with three independent variables: population density, people of age 17 years or younger, and intersection density. All three were significant at the 0.05% significance level.

Of the three variables, only one variable increased the number of fatal crashes—population density. This finding can be explained by the fact that, as the number of people in an area increases, car trips increase, and hence crashes increase. It is also interesting to note that intersection density decreases the number of fatal crashes, perhaps because high intersection density lowers car travel speeds.

The injury crash model had six independent variables: population density, number of employees, intersection density, and three different road classifications as respective percentages of the overall street network. These variables were found to be statistically significant in the model. (See Figure 4.18.)

Log Likelihood: −394.8815			
Parameter	**Estimate**	**Std Error**	**T-Statistic**
Popden	0.05078290568	0.0299586547	1.6951
Pmin or pop	−5.1819400372	0.60288247573	−8.5953
Intden	−4.8164757002	1.3908559352	−3.4630
Alpha 1	2.7587593688	0.71727782129	3.8462

NOTE: Standard error based on numerical Hessian

FIGURE 4.17 Estimation results for fatal crash model

Log Likelihood: −2748.9182			
Parameter	**Estimate**	**Std Error**	**T-Statistic**
Popden	0.10474820918	0.01869781132	5.6022
Total_Emp	0.04979218698	0.00412343184	12.0754
Intden	6.4856359666	0.83426075467	7.7741
cla3st	4.4337925363	0.94892812674	4.6724
cla4st	4.9236609811	0.77657660279	6.3402
cla7st	3.1058281681	0.79507463581	3.9063
Alpha 1	2.1783925513	0.11306661148	19.2665

NOTE: Standard error based on numerical Hessian

FIGURE 4.18 Estimation results for injury crash model

Log Likelihood: −3188.4297			
Parameter	**Estimate**	**Std Error**	***T*-Statistics**
Popden	0.07091453781	0.01937735337	3.6597
Total_Emp	0.07201810667	0.00479834494	15.0089
Intden	8.4305142797	0.93760743508	8.9915
cla3st	5.2809619076	1.0948686179	4.8234
cla4st	7.1494492381	0.94006421114	7.6053
cla7st	4.1105878474	0.89162172542	4.6102
Alpha 1	2.6955229994	0.12874121901	20.9375

NOTE: Standard error based on numerical Hessian

FIGURE 4.19 Estimation results for property damage crash model

All the independent variables had a positive relation to the number of injury crashes. For the road variable, increasing the percentage of arterial roads, minor arterials, and urban collectors increases injury crashes.

The property damage crash model used the same six independent variables as the injury crash model. The results were similar to the injury crash model but with higher coefficients for the independent variables. (See Figure 4.19.)

Conclusion

Studies exploring how the counts correlate with other characteristics require the use of Poisson or negative binomial regression. The Poisson model is the traditional count response model. While a central assumption of the Poisson distribution is the equivalence of the mean and variance, this assumption is rarely met with real data, especially in the planning field.

When the variance is greater than the mean, you have overdispersion of the dependent variable. This is rather common in planning research: for example, the number of crashes (Wei & Lovegrove, 2013), number of pedestrians (Ameli, Hamidi, Garfinkel-Castro, & Ewing, 2015), number of walk trips (Cao, Handy, & Mokhtarian, 2006), and number of vehicle trips (Tian, Park, & Ewing, 2018). In such cases, the negative binomial model is more appropriate than the Poisson model.

While the negative binomial model is the norm to model overdispersed count data, there are variations and extensions of that model. For example, when overdispersion results from excessive zero counts, a zero-inflated model can be used (Zuur, Ieno, Walker, Saveliev, & Smith, 2009). If there is an excess number of zero values and a zero value is qualitatively different from a positive value, a hurdle model may be appropriate (Mullahy, 1986; Ewing et al., 2014). On the other hand, when there is no possibility of a zero count, a zero-truncated model is an alternative (Zuur et al., 2009). In contrast, when the data is underdispersed, appropriate models include generalized Poisson (Consul & Famoye, 1992) and Conway-Maxwell Poisson (Shmueli et al., 2005). Recently, Bayesian approaches are also being incorporated into count models (Gelman et al., 2013). For comprehensive treatments of count models, we recommend two books: Hilbe (2011, 2014).

Works Cited

Ameli, S. H., Hamidi, S., Garfinkel-Castro, A., & Ewing, R. (2015). Do better urban design qualities lead to more walking in Salt Lake City, Utah? *Journal of Urban Design, 20*(3), 393–410.

Anscombe, F. J. (1949). The statistical analysis of insect counts based on the negative binomial distribution. *Biometrics, 5*(2), 165–173.

Bartlett, M. S. (1947). The use of transformations. *Biometrics, 3*(1), 39–52.

Beall, G. (1942). The transformation of data from entomological field experiments so that the analysis of variance becomes applicable. *Biometrika, 32*(3/4), 243–262.

Brooks, E. B. (2004). *Siméon-Denis Poisson, tales of statisticians*. Retrieved from www.umass.edu/wsp/resources/tales/poisson.html

Cao, X., Handy, S. L., & Mokhtarian, P. L. (2006). The influences of the built environment and residential self-selection on pedestrian behavior: Evidence from Austin, TX. *Transportation, 33*(1), 1–20.

Consul, P. C., & Famoye, F. (1992). Generalized Poisson regression model. *Communications in Statistics-Theory and Methods, 21*(1), 89–109.

The Editors. (2017). Simeon-Denis Poisson. In *The Britannica encyclopedia*. Retrieved from www.britannica.com/biography/Simeon-Denis-Poisson

Efron, B. (1986). Double exponential families and their use in generalized linear regression. *Journal of the American Statistical Association, 81*(395), 709–721.

Ewing, R. (2012). Useful concepts with examples. In class material, *Advanced statistics for planners*, CMP 7960-001.

Ewing, R., Tian, G., Goates, J. P., Zhang, M., Greenwald, M. J., Joyce, A., . . . Greene, W. (2014). Varying influences of the built environment on household travel in 15 diverse regions of the United States. *Urban Studies, 52*(13), 2330–2348.

Gelman, A., Carlin, J. B., Stern, H. S., Dunson, D. B., Vehtari, A., & Rubin, D. B. (2013). *Bayesian data analysis* (3rd ed.). Boca Raton, FL: Chapman and Hall/CRC.

Giuffrè, O., Grana, A., Giuffrè, T., & Marino, R. (2013). Accounting for dispersion and correlation in estimating safety performance functions. *An Overview Starting from a Case Study, Modern Applied Science, 7*(2), 11–23.

Glen, S. (2013). *Poisson distribution/poisson curve: Simple definition*. Retrieved from https://www.statisticshowto.datasciencecentral.com/poisson-regression/ (accessed on December 5, 2019)

Greene, W. H. (2012). *Econometric analysis*. New York, NY: Prentice Hall.

Hilbe, J. M. (2011). *Negative binomial regression*. Cambridge: Cambridge University Press.

Hilbe, J. M. (2014). *Modeling count data*. Cambridge, UK: Cambridge University Press.

Hüls, A., Frömke, C., Ickstadt, K., Hille, K., Hering, J., Von Münchhausen, C., . . . Kreienbrock, L. (2017). Antibiotic resistances in livestock: A comparative approach to identify an appropriate regression model for count data. *Frontiers in Veterinary Science, 4*, Article 71.

Ladron de Guevara, F., Washington, S., & Oh, J. (2004). Forecasting crashes at the planning level: Simultaneous negative binomial crash model applied in Tucson, Arizona. *Transportation Research Record: Journal of the Transportation Research Board* (1897), 191–199. https://doi.org/10.3141/1897-25

Mullahy, J. (1986). Specification and testing of some modified count data models. *Journal of Econometrics, 33*(3), 341–365.

O'Connell, L. (2009). The impact of local supporters on smart growth policy adoption. *Journal of the American Planning Association, 75*(3), 281–229. https://doi.org/10.1080/01944360902885495

Piza, E. L. (2012). *Using Poisson and negative binomial regression models to measure the influence of risk on crime incident counts*. Rutgers Center on Public Security.

Poisson Distribution. (n.d.). Retrieved February 19, 2018, from Wikipedia https://en.wikipedia.org/wiki/Poisson_distribution

Ribeiro Jr, E. E., Zeviani, W. M., Bonat, W. H, Demetrio, C. G. B., & Hinde, J. (2018). Reparametrization of COM-Poisson regression models with application in the analysis of experimental data, arXiv:1801.09795

Rodriguez, G. (2013). *Models for count data with over-dispersion*. Retrieved from http://data.princeton. edu/wws509/notes/c4a.pdf

Shmueli, G., Minka, T. P., Kadane, J. B., Borle, S., & Boatwright, P. (2005). A useful distribution for fitting discrete data: Revival of the Conway—Maxwell—Poisson distribution. *Journal of the Royal Statistical Society: Series C (Applied Statistics)*, *54*(1), 127–142.

Simon, L. J. (1960). The negative binomial and Poisson distributions compared. *Proceedings of the Casualty Actuarial Society*, *47*, 20–24.

Simon, L. J. (1961). Fitting negative binomial distributions by the method of maximum likelihood. *Proceedings of the Casualty Actuarial Society*, *48*, 45–53.

Tian, G., Park, K., & Ewing, R. (2018). Trip and parking generation rates for different housing types: Effects of compact development. *Urban Studies*, *56*(8), 1554–1575.

Wei, F., & Lovegrove, G. (2013). An empirical tool to evaluate the safety of cyclists: Community based, macro-level collision prediction models using negative binomial regression. *Accident Analysis & Prevention*, *61*, 129–137.

Yule, G. U. (1910). On the distribution of deaths with age when the causes of death act cumulatively, and similar frequency distributions. *Journal of the Royal Statistical Society*, *73*(1), 26–38.

Zuur, A. F., Ieno, E. N., Walker, N. J., Saveliev, A. A., & Smith, G. M. (2009). Zero-truncated and zero-inflated models for count data. In *Mixed effects models and extensions in ecology with R* (pp. 261–293). New York, NY: Springer.

5

PRINCIPAL COMPONENT AND FACTOR ANALYSIS

Matt Wheelwright, Zacharia Levine, Andrea Garfinkel-Castro, Tracey Bushman, and Simon C. Brewer

Overview

Advances in computer technology and statistical software packages have afforded incredible capacity to analyze large datasets with many variables. Even a moderately sized dataset can appear daunting and incomprehensible, particularly as the number of variables increases. Many methods exist to tackle the exploration and analysis of multivariate data, and these may be broadly split into two groups: *ordination methods*, that seek to organize data in some way so that similar observations are close together and dissimilar observations are far apart; and *classification methods*, that aim to group similar observations into groups or classes. The underlying goal of both approaches is *data reduction*, that is, the simplification of the dataset, while retaining the greatest amount of information possible. In this way, these methods have much in common with data compression algorithms used in image and video storage.

In this chapter, we discuss the use of two of the most common ordination approaches—principal component analysis (PCA) and common factor analysis (FA)—both of which seek to reduce a larger number of observed variables to a smaller number of derived, uncorrelated variables but without much loss of information. These two approaches are often grouped together under the umbrella term of factor analysis (Figure 5.1; Fayyad, Piatetsky-Shapiro, & Smyth, 1996) as the underlying mathematics are similar and they share much of the same terminology. PCA and FA are similar enough that several researchers cite the use of one method when they are really using the other (Jackson, 2003), and some statistical software packages only distinguish PCA as an extraction method in FA. There are, however, important differences conceptually and in their application that we attempt to clarify here.

Purpose

The process of data reduction, or simplification, can reveal the true underlying structure of a set of interrelated variables (Child, 2006). As previously described, both PCA and FA attempt to do this by creating new, uncorrelated variables. The major difference between these methods is that PCA simply finds the optimal way of combining these variables, with no model of the underlying factors, whereas FA tries to identify and measure these constructs directly.

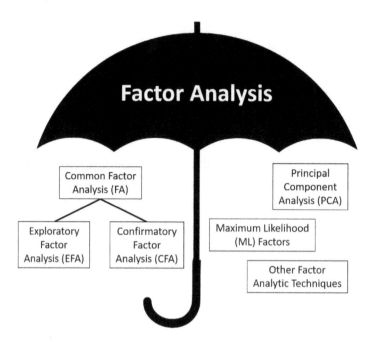

FIGURE 5.1 Various methods within factor analysis

One might wish to reduce variables in this way for a number of reasons. First, as noted in the chapter on linear regression (Chapter 12) of *Basic Quantitative Research Methods for Urban Planners*, using highly correlated *independent variables* in a single regression equation will create the issue of multicollinearity and produce inefficient parameter estimates. PCA or FA can finesse such issues by reducing many highly correlated variables to a few uncorrelated variables that still capture most of the variance in the original dataset. This also makes it possible to work with large-p/low-n datasets, in which the number of variables is larger than observations and for which least squares estimates cannot be used without having to make arbitrary decisions about which variables to retain and which to omit.

Second, the variable of interest, or underlying *construct*, may not be directly measurable; instead we have several variables that are more or less related to it (Figure 5.2). The Venn diagram shows that (1) individual observed variables do not completely represent the underlying construct, (2) the observed variables may represent unrelated constructs or simple measurement error as well as the construct of interest, and (3) where the observed variables intersect (their common variance) is most likely to fall within the bounds of the construct. For example, Hamidi, Ewing, Preuss, and Dodds (2015) tested eight measures of density but were unable to choose among them since they all had face and construct validity. So instead of choosing among them, a *density factor* was derived through PCA and used in subsequent analysis of metropolitan commuting patterns. Used well, these methods can help improve the signal and reduce the noise in data.

Readers should be aware that factor analysis is used for both exploratory and confirmatory analysis. Whereas exploratory factor analysis (EFA) is used to create hypotheses about the underlying structure of multivariate data, confirmatory factor analysis (CFA) is used to test or confirm hypotheses. EFA approaches do not impose any preconceived relationships on data,

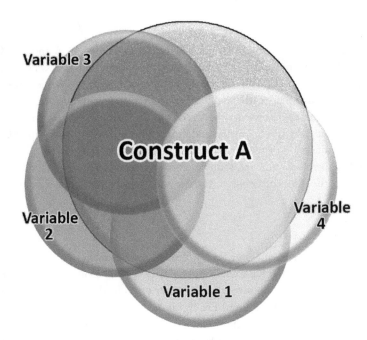

FIGURE 5.2   Venn diagram relating observed variables to underlying construct

whereas CFA evaluates how well a given set of data adheres to a hypothesized structure. This chapter deals exclusively with EFA. For more information on CFA, as a special case of structural equation modeling (SEM), see Brown (2014), Harrington (2009), and Thompson (2015).

History

The origin of factor analysis is generally ascribed to Charles Spearman. His monumental work in developing a psychological theory (Spearman, 1904) involved a single general factor and a number of specific factors. Although the method of principal axes was actually published by Karl Pearson (1901) before Spearman, Spearman is regarded as a father of the subject for his devotion of career to the development of factor analysis. Generally speaking, Spearman sought factors that explained all variance, while Pearson sought components that explained only shared variance (Kim, 2008).

A considerable amount of work on the psychological theories and mathematical foundations of factor analysis followed in the next 20 years. Other than Spearman and Pearson, the principal contributors included Cyril Burt, Godfrey H. Thomson, J. C. Maxwell Garnett, and Karl Holzinger, many of whom were psychologists (Harman, 1976). As the Spearman's Two-Factor Theory was not always adequate to describe psychological tests, some follow-up work explored the possibility of extracting several factors directly from a correlation matrix— the concept of multiple-factor analysis (Holzinger, 1935; Thurstone, 1933, 1947). Particularly, Thurston's technique, known as the *centroid* method, is still widely used today (Vincent, 1953).

Applications of factor analysis to other fields (e.g., medicine, political science, taxonomy, archaeology, economics, and regional science) have become popular since 1950, following the increased availability of computers (Harman, 1976).

Mechanics

In this section, we give a brief review of the mechanics underlying PCA and FA. We start by describing basic but key concepts that underlie these methods, then discuss PCA as it is conceptually slightly simpler, and finally describe the differences with FA. While intimate understanding of the foundational mathematics is unnecessary, interpreting the results depends on an elementary working knowledge. Much of the discussion will focus on the geometric representation of data, which is the easiest and most common way of describing PCA and FA. If this is already understood or feels overwhelming, skip to the "Step by Step" section.

Variance: The spread of numbers around a central tendency. Formally defined as the squared difference between the values of a random variable and its mean, the sample variance is given by:

$$s^2 = \frac{\Sigma(x - \bar{x})^2}{n - 1}$$

Covariance/correlation: A measure of the strength of the relationship between two random variables. If positive, then the values of both variables will tend to increase (or decrease) together. If negative, then as one increases, the other tends to decrease. Covariance and correlation are the foundation of PCA and FA, and in general, we look for correlation between our observed variables and with some unknown, unmeasured components or factors. Correlation (discussed in Chapter 9 of *Basic Quantitative Research Methods for Urban Planners*) scales the covariance by the pooled variance of the two variables, which standardizes the estimate, making it insensitive to the units of the variables. Pearson's sample correlation is given by:

$$r_{xy} = \frac{\Sigma(x_i - \bar{x})(y_i - \bar{y})}{\sqrt{\Sigma(x_i - \bar{x})^2}\sqrt{\Sigma(y - \bar{y})^2}}$$

Variance–covariance matrix: A symmetric matrix of size p (the number of variables), with the variance of each variable on the diagonal and the covariance between each pair of variables on the off-diagonal. A *correlation matrix* has the same form, with ones on the diagonal and pairwise correlations on the off-diagonal.

Principal Component Analysis

In principal component analysis, our main goal is to find a way to aggregate the set of observed variables into a smaller set of *components* (somewhat confusingly, these are also called *factors*). These components are simply a linear combination of the observed variables (Figure 5.3). Note that all variables are used; as there is no underlying model for the component, this avoids having to arbitrarily select which variables to combine. For a set of original variables $(x_1, x_2, \ldots, x_p)$, we get p components:

$$PC_1 = w_{11}x_1 + w_{12}x_2 + \ldots + w_{2p}x_p$$
$$PC_2 = w_{21}x_1 + w_{22}x_2 + \ldots + w_{2p}x_p$$

$$\vdots$$

$$PC_p = w_{p1}x_1 + w_{p2}x_2 + \ldots + w_{pp}x_p$$

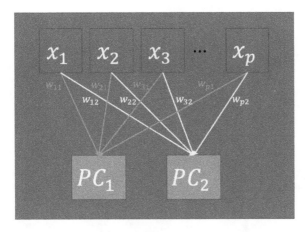

FIGURE 5.3 Relationship between variables and components in principal component analysis

The goal of any PCA algorithm is then to choose these weights $(w_{11}, w_{12}, \ldots, w_{pp})$. In order to achieve the preceding goals, these need to meet two criteria. First, these components should be *orthogonal*, or uncorrelated with each other. This prevents redundancy; Each component describes a separate and independent part of the variance in the dataset. The second criterion is that of *maximum variance*. This states that the first component (PC_1) should represent as much of the variance of all original variables as possible. Each subsequent component should then account for the maximum amount of variance not explained by any preceding components. This helps ensure that most of the information in the data is accounted for by the first few components, and later components represent low variance, random noise.

These weights are derived from the variance–covariance matrix if all variables are on the same scale or using the correlation matrix if not. In practice, these are estimated either by eigen decomposition of this matrix or by using singular value decomposition. A relatively straightforward explanation of what this decomposition is achieving can be obtained by considering a geometric representation of data. Imagine we are trying to identify a small set of factors that describe neighborhood forms, as in Song, Popkin, and Gordon-Larsen (2013). We collect measurement data for neighborhood form metrics from neighborhoods across the country, such as density, number of parks, street network design, land use diversity, and development area. The hypothetical geometric relationship among four of these variables is shown in Figure 5.4. Correlation values are represented by the angles between these observed vectors, with acute angles (less than 90 degrees) representing positive correlation values and obtuse angles (greater than 90 degrees) representing negative correlation values. In this example, the correlation between density and area is the cosine of angle theta, and the correlation between number of parks and area is the cosine of angle phi. Diversity and area are perfectly negatively correlated. The example in Figure 5.4 is simplified to only two dimensions but in reality, has the same number of dimensions as variables.

We now illustrate how these correlations are converted to components based on data used to develop a sprawl index (Ewing & Hamadi, 2014). To keep this simple, we use only two highly correlated variables: log population size and log area (r = 0.896). A scatterplot between the two shows the effect of this correlation (Figure 5.5a). The data are first centered by subtracting the mean from each variable, then the first component (Figure 5.5b, solid line)

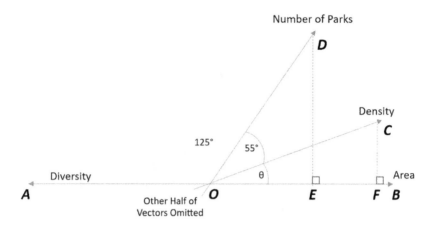

FIGURE 5.4   Correlation among selected observed vectors

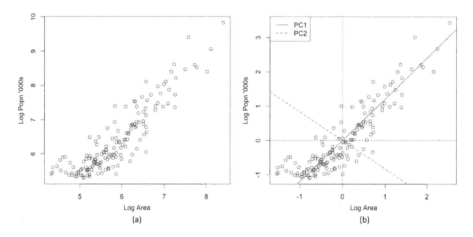

FIGURE 5.5   (a) Uncentered scatterplot of urban area versus population size (both log transformed); (b) centered scatterplot with principal component 1 and 2 overlain

is simply the best fit line through the scatter of points, as this maximizes the variance (i.e., spreads the data out as far as possible). To return to the preceding geometric representation of correlation, the first component is located such that it bisects the angle between both observed vectors (Thurstone, 1947). This component consists of two parts:

- **The eigenvector or *loadings*:** This is a set of p coordinates indicating the direction that the component follows from the origin (Table 5.1). The vector is scaled to have a magnitude of exactly 1. Note that these loadings reflect the correlation between the original variable and the new component, and are very useful in interpretation
- **A set of *scores*:** This is a set of n values giving the projection of each observation onto the new component

Once fitted, the second component is added (dashed line). As previously described, this is constrained to be at a right angle (orthogonal) to the first. If more variables exist, this is then

TABLE 5.1 Loadings, communalities, and eigenvalues for the two-variable urban example

Variable	Factor Vector 1	Factor Vector 2	Communality (h^2)
Log area	−0.707	0.707	1.000
Log population	−0.707	−0.707	1.000
Eigenvalue			
SD	1.376	0.323	
Variance	1.896	0.104	2.000
%. variance	0.948	0.052	1.000

rotated until it explains the maximum amount of the remaining variance. Here, with two variables, this second axis has explained all remaining variance.

Finally, each returned component has an associated eigenvalue. For a correlation matrix, this is usually in standard deviation units and can therefore be used to assess how much of the variance in the dataset was explained by the components. For this highly correlated example, the first component explains approximately 95% of the variance of the two variables. In Table 5.1, an eigenvalue of 1.896 indicates that component 1 explains as much variance as ~1.9 observed variables (out of two).

Factor Analysis

In factor analysis, the goal is to identify one or more underlying, latent *factors* that are related to the set of observed variables. Unlike the simple aggregation of variables in PCA, here we assume that there is some process that explains some part of the variance in each variable. Compared with PCA, this effectively reverses the relationship between components (here termed factors) and variables (Figure 5.6). We now assume that each variable is a linear combination of the set of factors, but notably we do not assume that the relationship is perfect and there will be some residual, unexplained variance (the ϵ term in Figure 5.6). For a set of observed variables $(x_1, x_2, \ldots, x_p)$, each variable is modeled as follows:

$$x_1 = a_{11}f_1 + a_{12}f + \ldots + a_{2p}f_p + \epsilon$$
$$x_2 = a_{21}f_1 + a_{22}f_2 + \ldots + a_{2p}f_p + \epsilon$$

$$\cdot$$
$$\cdot$$
$$\cdot$$

$$x_p = a_{p1}f_1 + a_{p2}f_2 + \ldots + a_{pp}f_p + \epsilon$$

Conceptually then, this is quite different from the PCA approach previously detailed. It is particularly useful when working with a set of variables that are representative of some underlying but unmeasurable construct, such as well-being or resilience. For example, FA is frequently used with survey data where sets of questions are asked all relating to the same construct.

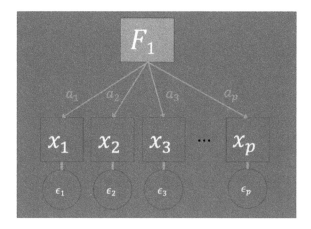

FIGURE 5.6   Relationship between variables and components in factor analysis

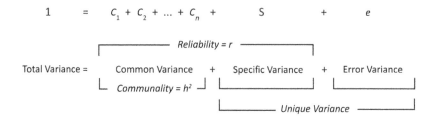

FIGURE 5.7   Sources of variance in observed variables

As we are now interested in factors that influence multiple variables, we need a way to identify this shared contribution. To do this, the variance of each variable can be decomposed into common, unique, and error variance (Figure 5.7). Common variance is shared across all variables and represents the underlying factor. Unique variance is the remaining variance and can be further split into specific variance (the component of unique variance that is reliable but not explained by common factors) and error variance (the unreliable and inexplicable variation in a variable).

To estimate these factors, we use a *reduced* correlation matrix. This replaces the ones on the diagonal of the correlation matrix with an estimate of the communality (h^2). This is a standardized estimate of the proportion of total variance that is common. It is estimated as the value of r obtained regressing each variable against all the others. The analysis then follows the same steps as PCA, by performing eigen decomposition or singular value decomposition of this matrix to obtain factors, loadings, and scores.

Requirements for PCA and FA

As with all quantitative methods, several data assumptions must be met for analytic solutions to be valid. Samples must be randomly collected, and a well accepted rule for sample size is at least 5 observations per variable and at least 100 observations total. Larger sample sizes tend to produce more stable estimates, especially when there are at least 10 observations per variable

(Child, 2006). Each variable is expected to have a normal distribution, and multiple variables have linear relationships.

A major goal of PCA and FA is to represent relationships among sets of variables parsimoniously yet keeping components meaningful. A good solution is both *simple* and *interpretable* that will then yield new insights. From the loadings, you should be able to intuit the nature of the underlying construct represented by each factor. Simple loadings (high correlations with some variables, low with others) are preferred to complex loadings (moderate loadings with many variables) due to ease of interpretation.

SPSS includes two formal tests that indicate the appropriateness of using factor analytic techniques. The first is the Kaiser-Meyer-Olkin (KMO) Measure of Sampling Adequacy, which indicates whether a dataset contains enough observations and variables to merit PCA or FA. The accepted minimum value for KMO is 0.6. Bartlett's Test of Sphericity indicates whether the data are sufficiently correlated and whether common, or shared, variance can be explained by components or factors. Usable data will generate significance levels below 0.05 ($p < .05$).

Interpreting Results

The correlation values between observed vectors and eigenvectors (loadings) lead an analyst directly to the ultimate goal: data reduction. Component or factor vectors extracted represent the underlying structure of a multivariate dataset. However, PCA and FA require the researcher to make judgments about how and why certain observed variables group together (principal components) and what causes (factors) certain observed variables to vary together.

The first principal component is the combination that accounts for the largest amount of variance in the sample (first extracted factor). The second principal component accounts for the next largest amount of variance and is uncorrelated with the first (second extracted factor). Successive components explain progressively smaller portions of the total sample variance, and all are uncorrelated with one another. A scree plot helps depict this relationship (see the "Step by Step" section), showing the eigenvalue for each component.

By convention, principal components or common factors are retained only if they have eigenvalues greater than 1.0. This means that they account for more of the variance in the dataset than a single observed variable alone. Since the purpose of factor analysis is to reduce the number of observed variables to a smaller number of common factors, it would be counterproductive to retain factors with smaller eigenvalues. In addition, factors are retained only up to the point where the scree plot levels off and additional factors capture relatively little additional variance in the original dataset. This point is sometimes referred to as the *elbow* of the scree plot.

In some instances, the results obtained directly from the data collected will not yield simple interpretations of component or factor structure. Under this common scenario, analysts will use a technique called rotation. *Rotation* can take one of two forms: orthogonal rotation or oblique rotation. Orthogonal rotation simply rotates orthogonally extracted factors to better capture the variance of observed variables (Figure 5.8).

Orthogonal rotation leads to different factor loadings because it changes the correlation between factor vectors and observed vectors. Oblique rotation, however, attempts to capture the maximum amount of variance by rotating extracted factors independently in such a way that they are eventually situated in nonorthogonal positions (Figure 5.9). It also changes the

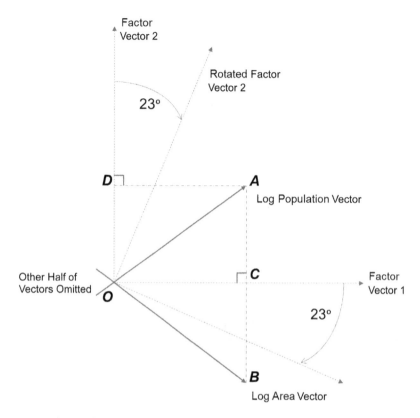

FIGURE 5.8   Orthogonal rotation of factor vectors

correlation between factor vectors to nonzero values. For more information on factor rotation, see Child (2006).

Step by Step

We proceed with step-by-step instructions on how to perform principal component analysis
and factor analysis in real research using SPSS and R.

As introduced multiple times throughout this book, Reid Ewing and his team have
developed and refined sprawl indices for the United States (Ewing, Pendall, & Chen, 2002,
2003; Ewing, Meakins, Hamidi, & Nelson, 2014; Hamidi & Ewing, 2014). Relating to such
indices, sprawl has been linked to physical inactivity, obesity, traffic fatalities, poor air quality, residential energy use, emergency response times, teenage driving, lack of social capital,
and private vehicle commute distances and times (see Ewing & Hamidi, 2015 for a review
paper).

In 2014, Ewing and Hamidi develop refined versions of the sprawl index that incorporate
more measures of the built environment. The refined indices capture four distinct dimensions
of sprawl: development density, land use mix, population and employment centering, and
street accessibility. They developed the indices at four different geographical scales: County,
Metropolitan Statistical Area (MSA), Urbanized Area (UZA), and Census Tract (Ewing &
Hamidi, 2014).

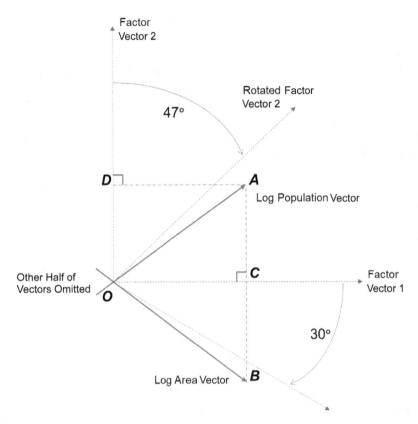

FIGURE 5.9 Oblique rotation of factor vectors

In this exercise, we will replicate their work using our urbanized area data ("UZA.sav"), focusing on one of the four factors: development density. The density factor covers five individual variables: gross density of population (*popden*), gross density of employment (*empden*), percentage of the population living at low suburban densities (*pct1500*), percentage of the population living at medium to high urban densities (*pct12500*), and urban density based on the National Land Cover Database (*urbden*).

We want to combine the five variables into one component representing the degree of development density within each UZA. Principal component analysis can help us take a large number of correlated variables and extract a small number of factors that embody the common variance in the original dataset. The more highly correlated the original variables, the more variance is captured by a single principal component.

An overall procedure of a principal component analysis follows four steps:

1. Compute the correlation matrix for all variables.
2. Complete component extraction and make a decision about the number of underlying components.
3. Complete rotation (optional—not done by Ewing and Hamidi because they were interested in the single principal component that captured the largest share of variance in the five density variables).
4. Calculate principal component scores for further analyses.

Note that for SPSS, both PCA and FA are run from the same menu. To begin with, open "UZA.sav," go to "Analyze" menu and select "Dimension Reduction" → "Factor." (See Figure 5.10).

The "Factor Analysis" window (Figure 5.11) will pop up. Add five density-related variables (*popden, empden, pct1500, pct12500,* and *urbden*) to the "Variables" box.

Click on the "Descriptives" button, and check several options (see Figure 5.12). The "Univariate descriptives" option provides means and standard deviations for each variable. The "Coefficients" option produces a correlation matrix between variables. "KMO and Bartlett's test of sphericity" produces the Kaiser-Meyer-Olkin measure of sampling adequacy and Bartlett's test, which were previously explained. "Anti-image" option produces more outputs for testing sampling adequacy. Click on "Continue" to return to the main dialog box, and click on "OK" to run the analysis.

The first table in the output window will be descriptive statistics. Following is a "Correlation Matrix." (See Figure 5.13.) It contains the Pearson correlation coefficient between all pairs of variables. If you selected "Significance levels" in the "Descriptives" window, the associated p-value will appear at the bottom half of the table. In order to obtain useful results, we need to have variables that correlate fairly well. The coefficients vary from -0.388 (between *pct1500* and *pct12500*) to 0.890 (between *popden* and *urbden*). As a rule of thumb, every correlation coefficient should be above 0.30 or below -0.30. If not, you need to consider excluding the variable(s).

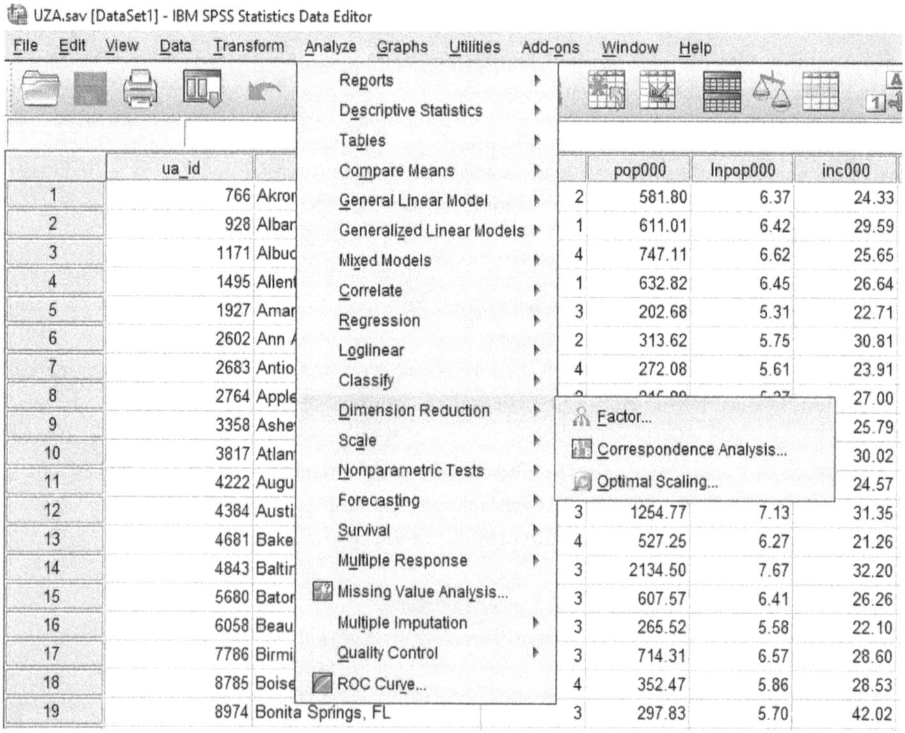

FIGURE 5.10 Selecting the correlation matrix in SPSS

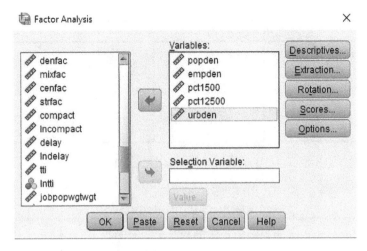

FIGURE 5.11   Adding five density variables in the "Factor Analysis" window

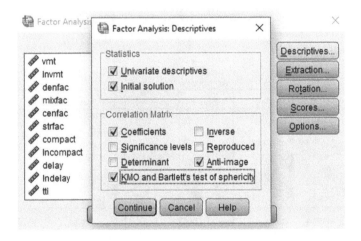

FIGURE 5.12   Factor analysis: "Descriptive" window

The next table (Figure 5.14) is "KMO and Bartlett's Test." The measure of adequacy on the KMO test must be above 0.50. Bartlett's must be lower than the level of significance (e.g., $p < .05$). Bartlett's measure tests whether the correlation matrix is an identity matrix (i.e., all correlation coefficients are zero) or not. Our results meet both requirements, and thus PCA is appropriate.

The diagonal in "Anti-image Matrices" provides the KMO statistics for individual variables (Figure 5.15). The diagonal elements of the anti-image correlation matrix should be 0.5 or higher, while the off-diagonal elements (the partial correlation between variables) need to be small (the smaller, the better). In our example, the minimum diagonal element is 0.739, and the maximum off-diagonal element is −0.658. If you find any variables with values below 0.5 in the diagonal elements, then you need to consider excluding them.

Correlation Matrix

		popden	empden	pct1500	pct12500	urbden
Correlation	popden	1.000	.873	-.784	.670	.890
	empden	.873	1.000	-.671	.639	.737
	pct1500	-.784	-.671	1.000	-.388	-.743
	pct12500	.670	.639	-.388	1.000	.742
	urbden	.890	.737	-.743	.742	1.000

FIGURE 5.13 Correlation matrix between density-related variables

KMO and Bartlett's Test

Kaiser-Meyer-Olkin Measure of Sampling Adequacy.		.768
Bartlett's Test of Sphericity	Approx. Chi-Square	780.133
	df	10
	Sig.	.000

FIGURE 5.14 KMO and Bartlett's Test results

Anti-image Matrices

		popden	empden	pct1500	pct12500	urbden
Anti-image Covariance	popden	.094	-.093	.046	.005	-.065
	empden	-.093	.212	.026	-.074	.050
	pct1500	.046	.026	.309	-.137	.071
	pct12500	.005	-.074	-.137	.346	-.119
	urbden	-.065	.050	.071	-.119	.138
Anti-image Correlation	popden	.760[a]	-.658	.268	.030	-.566
	empden	-.658	.782[a]	.100	-.274	.292
	pct1500	.268	.100	.824[a]	-.419	.345
	pct12500	.030	-.274	-.419	.739[a]	-.545
	urbden	-.566	.292	.345	-.545	.748[a]

a. Measures of Sampling Adequacy(MSA)

FIGURE 5.15 Anti-image matrices result

The next step is component extraction. Go back to the "Factor Analysis" window ("Analyze" → "Dimension Reduction" → "Factor"), and click on the "Extraction" box. (See Figure 5.16). Multiple methods are available, and we will use "Principal components." The "Correlation matrix" is a default option, which takes the standardized form of the matrix. This means that different units in variables will not affect the analysis. Click on both "Unrotated

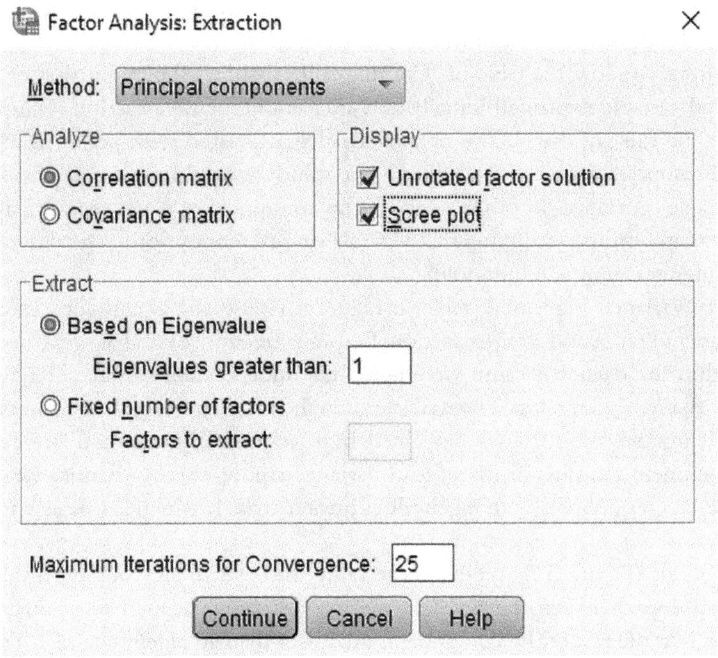

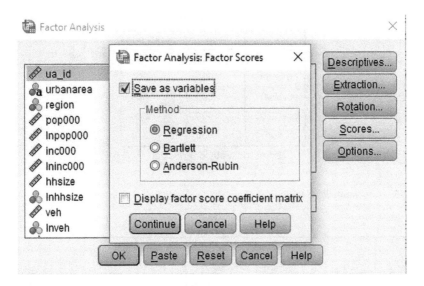

FIGURE 5.16 Factor analysis: "Extraction" window

FIGURE 5.17 Factor analysis: "Factor Scores" window

factor solution" and "Scree plot." As a rule of thumb, the eigenvalue of 1 is the default for a component selection.

Before running the analysis, click on the "Score" box in the main "Factor Analysis" dialog window (Figure 5.17). This allows you to save scores for each case or observation. SPSS creates a new column of the score for each component extracted. There are three methods for obtaining these scores; choose the "Regression" method. With only one extracted factor, as in our example, this option does not make any difference.

In the output window, the table of "Communalities" shows the proportion of variance in each observed variable explained initially and after component extraction (Figure 5.18). So, for example, we can say that 93.0% of the variance associated with *popden* is explained by the retained component. As a rule of thumb, the solution should explain at least half of each original variable's variance. In other words, if the communality is less than 0.5 after extraction, you need to consider dropping that variable or different options (e.g., different rotation method, changing eigenvalue threshold).

The "Total Variance Explained" table in Figure 5.19 lists the eigenvalues associated with each component before and after extraction. Before extraction, SPSS has identified five components within the dataset because we entered five independent variables. Remember that there are as many eigenvectors as variables, though not all of which are important. Each eigenvalue represents the variance explained by that particular component—for example, the first component explains 77.6% of total variance among the five density variables. SPSS then extracts all components with eigenvalues greater than 1, which leaves us with only one component.

The scree plot (Figure 5.20) conveys the same idea as the previous Eigenvalue table. It shows a steep slope between the first and the second components. The gradual trailing off (scree) shows that the rest of the components are lower than an eigenvalue of 1. This supports our decision to select only one component.

Communalities

	Initial	Extraction
popden	1.000	.930
empden	1.000	.801
pct1500	1.000	.669
pct12500	1.000	.600
urbden	1.000	.879

Extraction Method: Principal Component Analysis.

FIGURE 5.18   Communalities table

Total Variance Explained

Component	Initial Eigenvalues			Extraction Sums of Squared Loadings		
	Total	% of Variance	Cumulative %	Total	% of Variance	Cumulative %
1	3.879	77.579	77.579	3.879	77.579	77.579
2	.621	12.412	89.991			
3	.297	5.945	95.936			
4	.142	2.844	98.780			
5	.061	1.220	100.000			

Extraction Method: Principal Component Analysis.

FIGURE 5.19   "Total variance explained" result table

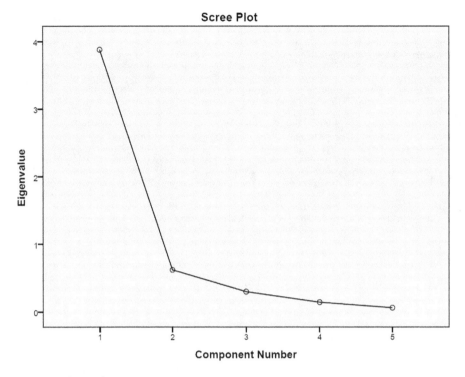

FIGURE 5.20   Scree plot

There is no widely-accepted objective way to decide how many principal components are enough. But the three that are popular are:

1. Eigenvalue of greater than 1.
2. The total variance explained by the PCs or factors. As a rule of thumb, if 70% of the total variance is explained, then there is no need to extract more components.
3. Retain components before the *elbow* of a scree plot.

You will face this problem usually when you have many variables (e.g., a questionnaire with 40–50 questions), and as a result, you will have potentially a large number of components with eigenvalues greater than 1, and choosing which to retain can be difficult.

Back to our "Step by Step" example. Check the dataset. You now have a final column FAC1_1 with scores (Figure 5.21). Sort by this variable in descending order. Los Angeles has the highest density factor score, followed by San Francisco and New York. Scores are scaled such that the mean value is 0, and the standard deviation is 1. The score for Los Angeles, 4.52, means that the density (as a composite measure) in Los Angeles is 4.52 standard deviations above the mean for the urbanized areas in the dataset. Ewing and Hamidi (2017) converted these scores into a more intuitive metric with a mean value of 100 and a standard deviation of 25 (modeled after IQ scores).

If you generate multiple components, you could add up the scores to obtain a single score for each case [Ewing and Hamidi's (2017) Compactness Index is a good example of this]. Also,

avgblk	pctsmlblk	intden	pct4way	FAC1_1	var
.0301	59.4973	44.73	27.47	-.60609	
.0354	61.2879	41.30	19.05	-.14193	
.0298	57.9584	51.49	28.95	.13271	
.0164	77.7518	80.27	34.87	.34722	
.0292	67.9326	42.60	45.50	-.41330	
.0409	50.4812	40.40	17.86	-.24931	
.0200	62.2748	91.99	26.30	.85487	
.0230	60.5347	51.44	31.34	-.16280	
.0399	56.0517	42.73	12.96	-1.70135	
.0527	46.8166	35.51	13.96	-.50130	

FIGURE 5.21 Component scores in descending order

the scores can be used in regression models when groups of independent variables highly correlate with one another (i.e., multicollinearity) (e.g., Ewing et al., 2018).

To replicate what Ewing and his colleagues did to calculate the sprawl index, you need to transform the scores to have a mean of 100 and a standard deviation of 25. This was done for the sake of consistency and ease of understanding (Ewing & Hamidi, 2014). For this step, go to "Transform" → "Compute Variable." In the new window, enter the name of the new variable (e.g., *density_factor*) under the "Target Variable" box. Then enter a formula, FAC1_1*25 + 100 (note that you do not necessarily have to type the variable name; just double-click the extracted component in the variable list to add it into the "Numeric Expression" box). (See Figure 5.22.)

The *density_factor* variable is created (Figure 5.23). Los Angeles now scores 213.03 on the density component. There are actually four components and a combined sprawl index in our dataset; see *denfac*, *mixfac*, *cenfac*, *strfac*, and *compact*. Make sure that the new variable is identical to *denfac*. If you want to replicate other components and sum them to get the composite compactness index, use *entropywgt* and *jobpopwgt* variables for the "Mix" component, *varpop*, *varemp*, *pctempcen*, and *pctpopcen* variables for the "Centers" component, and *avgblk*, *pctsmlblk*, *intden*, and *pct4way* variables for the "Streets" component. Then, the four components are summed and transformed into an index with a mean of 100 and a standard deviation of 25 (Ewing & Hamidi, 2017).

The next optional step is component rotation. Ewing and Hamidi (2017) did not rotate for the reason already noted (a single-component case), but for illustrative purposes, we will rotate. Go back to the "Factor Analysis" window ("Analyze" → "Dimension Reduction" → "Factor"), and click on the "Rotation" box (Figure 5.24). As previously explained, rotation maximizes the loading of each variable on one of the extracted components while minimizing the loading on all other components. The choice of rotation depends on whether or not you think that the underlying components should be related. If there are theoretical grounds to think that the components are independent, then the varimax method, the most common of the orthogonal rotation methods, is recommended. Varimax attempts to minimize

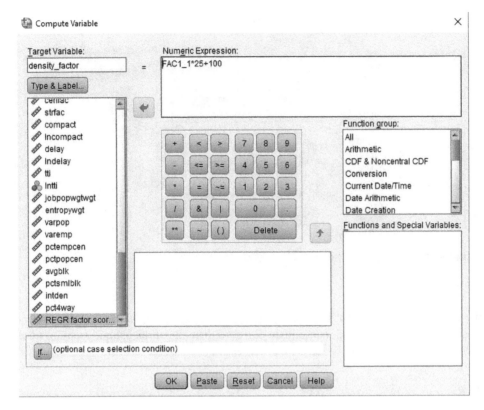

FIGURE 5.22   Calculating new density component scores

pctsmlblk	intden	pct4way	FAC1_1	density_factor	var
59.4973	44.73	27.47	-.60609	84.85	
61.2879	41.30	19.05	-.14193	96.45	
57.9584	51.49	28.95	.13271	103.32	
77.7518	80.27	34.87	.34722	108.68	
67.9326	42.60	45.50	-.41330	89.67	
50.4812	40.40	17.86	-.24931	93.77	
62.2748	91.99	26.30	.85487	121.37	
60.5347	51.44	31.34	-.16280	95.93	
56.0517	42.73	12.96	-1.70135	57.47	
46.8166	35.51	13.96	-.50130	87.47	

FIGURE 5.23   Final density component scores with a mean of 100 and a standard deviation of 25

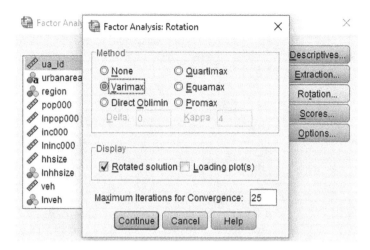

FIGURE 5.24   Factor analysis: "Rotation" window

the number of variables that have high loadings on a single component. This may enhance interpretability. If your components might correlate, then one of the oblique rotations (direct oblimin or promax) should be selected. In this example, we select varimax.

In R

Figures 5.25 through 5.27 show an R script to replicate the principal component analysis we did to extract a density factor in SPSS. First, *cor, KMO, cortest.bartlett* functions (in *psych* package) generate a correlation matrix, KMO test, and Bartlett's test, respectively (Figure 5.25). The results suggest that PCA is appropriate. The *fa.parallel* function provides a scree plot to help with determining the number of factors you extract (Figure 5.26). Then you may run *principal* function with *nfactors=1* option (the number of factors; Figure 5.26). The output displays the component loadings (from the pattern matrix), the h2 (communalities), the u2 (the uniquenesses) for each variable, as well as other information—for example, 78% of variance is explained by the principal component (PC1). Finally, you can compute a factor score (*$scores*) and convert it to a density factor (with a mean of 100 and a standard deviation of 25; Figure 5.27). The results should be identical to those from SPSS.

Planning Examples

Measuring Greenness of Neighborhoods

In 2010, an article in *Landscape and Urban Planning* (Leslie, Sugiyama, Ierodiaconou, & Kremer, 2010) utilized PCA to measure neighborhood greenness. This study aimed to examine agreement between the perceived greenness of neighborhoods and an objective measure of greenness using a normalized vegetation index (NDVI). As a measure of greenness, the NDVI is obtained from visible incident energy absorbed and near-infrared incident energy reflected by plants (Cohen & Goward, 2004).

```
# FACTOR ANALYSIS
library("foreign")
uza<-read.spss("UZA.sav",to.data.frame=TRUE)

uza_den<-uza[,c("popden","empden","pct1500","pct12500","urbden")]

library(psych)
cor(uza_den)
```

```
##                popden      empden     pct1500     pct12500     urbden
## popden      1.0000000  0.8731787  -0.7843783   0.6695744  0.8898776
## empden      0.8731787  1.0000000  -0.6713275   0.6389633  0.7366135
## pct1500    -0.7843783 -0.6713275   1.0000000  -0.3884130 -0.7427047
## pct12500    0.6695744  0.6389633  -0.3884130   1.0000000  0.7416003
## urbden      0.8898776  0.7366135  -0.7427047   0.7416003  1.0000000
```

```
KMO(uza_den)
```

```
## Kaiser-Meyer-Olkin factor adequacy
## Call: KMO(r = uza_den)
## Overall MSA =  0.77
## MSA for each item =
##    popden   empden  pct1500 pct12500   urbden
##      0.76     0.78     0.82     0.74     0.75
```

```
cortest.bartlett(uza_den)
```

```
## $chisq
## [1] 780.1332
##
## $p.value
## [1] 3.846219e-161
##
## $df
## [1] 10
```

FIGURE 5.25   Reading SPSS data ("UZA.sav"), selecting a set of variables, and running correlation matric, KMO test, and Bartlett's test: R script and outputs

An initial list of 17 perceived measures of greenness was compiled from a survey of adults (N = 94) living in Warrnambool, Australia. All items were scaled from 1 to 4 (1 = strongly disagree to 4 = strongly agree), with higher scores indicating a higher perceived greenness value for the characteristic.

Then a PCA with oblique rotation was performed on these items. The PCA result identified four dimensions (58% explained variance) based on the scree plot and interpretability of

```
fa.parallel(uza_den, fa="pc", n.iter=100,
           show.legend=FALSE, main="Scree plot with parallel analy
sis")
```

Scree plot with parallel analysis

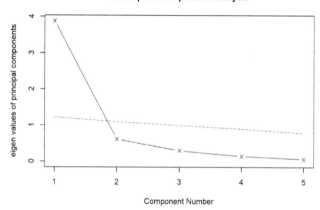

```
## Parallel analysis suggests that the number of factors =  NA   and
the number of components =  1
```

```
pc <- principal(uza_den, nfactors=1, score=T)
pc
```

```
## Principal Components Analysis
## Call: principal(r = uza_den, nfactors = 1, scores = T)
## Standardized loadings (pattern matrix) based upon correlation ma
trix
##             PC1   h2   u2 com
## popden     0.96 0.93 0.07   1
## empden     0.90 0.80 0.20   1
## pct1500   -0.82 0.67 0.33   1
## pct12500   0.77 0.60 0.40   1
## urbden     0.94 0.88 0.12   1
##
##                  PC1
## SS loadings     3.88
## Proportion Var  0.78
##
## Mean item complexity =  1
## Test of the hypothesis that 1 component is sufficient.
##
## The root mean square of the residuals (RMSR) is  0.09
##   with the empirical chi square  26.5  with prob <  7.1e-05
##
## Fit based upon off diagonal values = 0.98
```

FIGURE 5.26   Creating a scree plot and running a PCA: R script and outputs

```
head(pc$scores)
```

```
##                 PC1
## [1,] -0.6060883
## [2,] -0.1419290
## [3,]  0.1327117
## [4,]  0.3472172
## [5,] -0.4133020
## [6,] -0.2493127
```

```
uza.pc<-cbind(uza,pc$scores)
uza.pc$density_factor<-uza.pc$PC1*25+100
print(head(uza.pc[,c("urbanarea","PC1","density_factor")]))
```

```
##                 urbanarea          PC1 density_factor
## 1 Akron, OH             -0.6060883       84.84779
## 2 Albany, NY            -0.1419290       96.45178
## 3 Albuquerque, NM        0.1327117      103.31779
## 4 Allentown, PA-NJ       0.3472172      108.68043
## 5 Amarillo, TX          -0.4133020       89.66745
## 6 Ann Arbor, MI         -0.2493127       93.76718
```

FIGURE 5.27   Computing component scores: R script and outputs

components. Table 5.2 shows component loadings, explained variance, and internal consistency (Cronbach's alpha). These dimensions were interpreted as (1) street greenness, (2) green expanse, (3) sport facilities, and (4) green amenity, respectively. Five of the individual items did not load heavily on any of these four dimensions. Finally, the sum of item scores was calculated for each component and used as component scores.

The greenness score was used to examine correspondence between perceived and objective measures of greenness. Component scores for each of the PCA-derived dimensions were dichotomized using a median split and assessed against the high/low NDVI categories. Then the agreement between two different measures was assessed using the kappa statistic. This process was repeated for those living close to and far from the city center.

Results indicate that there was a lack of agreement between the perceived and objective measures of greenness, suggesting that these measures are capturing different aspects of neighborhood landscaping.

Land Cover Patterns

Cain, Riitters, and Orvis (1997) used common factor analysis to determine underlying factors that caused variations in land cover patterns. The study aimed to aggregate and decipher indicators established in previous research. The indicators came from satellite imagery throughout

TABLE 5.2 Principal component analysis on perceived items of neighborhood greenness (Leslie et al., 2010)

Item	1	2	3	4
Tree cover or canopy along footpaths	0.74			
Many street trees in my local area	0.72			
Many roadside plantings of trees/shrubs	0.70			
Many large trees in my local area	0.61			
Lots of green median strips	0.52			
Views of nature from my home		−0.83		
Pockets of natural bushland or coastal vegetation		−0.63		
Sports fields nearby			0.84	
School grounds with grassed areas nearby			0.73	
Lots of greenery around my local area				0.83
Local park or reserve close to where I live				0.72
Pleasant natural features				0.67
Mean (SD)	14.1	5.8	6.4	10.2
	(3.2)	(1.8)	(1.7)	(2.0)
% variance	28.3	12.9	8.3	7.3
Cronbach's alpha	0.75	0.52	0.60	0.69

Source: Reprinted from Leslie, E., Sugiyama, T., Ierodiaconou, D., & Kremer, P. (2010). Perceived and objectively measured greenness of neighbourhoods: are they measuring the same thing? Landscape and Urban Planning, 95(1), 28–33. with permission from Elsevier

the Tennessee River and Chesapeake Bay watersheds. Pixels of a single-scaled map were assigned an attribute class, or type of land cover. The raster-based GIS models included 28 indicators of the landscape ecological pattern (Table 5.3). Factor analysis revealed that six dimensions could explain the majority of shared variance among the 28 indicators. Cain et al. (1997) conducted the analysis at various geographic scales to determine how reliable the six common factors were in explaining land cover variation.

The authors found that their six newly identified factors helped to explain land cover variation better than previously defined factors. However, satellite imagery and land cover classification systems, especially at low resolution, could not truly account for all ecological complexity. As a result, the authors caution against the use of pattern metrics in land cover analysis without biological justification of indicators.

Conclusion

Principal component and factor analysis are data-reduction techniques that replace a large number of correlated variables with a small number of uncorrelated assumptions, simplifying the analyses. There are several stages to the analysis: Check some initial issues (e.g., sample size adequacy); compute the correlation matrix for all variables; complete factor extraction and make a decision about the number of underlying factors; complete factor rotation; and calculate factor scores for further analyses.

As the complexity of the information increases, so does the need for data–reduction techniques. Also, as a social science, planning research deals with many latent variables, which cannot be measured simply and directly (e.g., sprawl, resilience, vitality). As a result, PCA and FA can also contribute to theory development.

As a final note, we acknowledge that PCA and FA often do not provide clean, easily interpretable results. Different extraction methods can lead to different solution sets. There is an art

TABLE 5.3 Land cover measurements and resulting causal common factors

Indicators:
NTYP: Number of types
PMAX: Maximum attribute class proportion
SIDI: Simpson diversity of attribute classes
SIEV: Simpson evenness of attribute classes
SHDI: Shannon diversity of attribute classes
SHEV: Shannon evenness of attribute classes
SUMD Sum of diagonal elements of adjacency matrix, A
SIDA: Simpson diversity of adjacency matrix
SICO Simpson contagion
SHDA: Shannon diversity of adjacency matrix
SHCO: Shannon contagion
FDDA: Area-weighted average of fractal dimension from density-area scaling
NPAT: Number of patches
LPAT: Largest patch
PSIZ: Average patch size
P005: Proportion of area in which patches are greater than five pixels
PA-1: Average perimeter-area ratio
PA-2: Average adjusted perimeter-area ratio
DSTA: Average adjusted perimeter-area ratio using gardner's d-statistic
NASQ: Average normalized area, square model
RGYR: Average radius of gyration
PTRD: Average patch topology ratio dimension
ABRR: Average bounding rectangle ratio
ABSR: Average area boxside ratio
ACCR: Average circumscribing circle ratio
ALAR: Average area-by-longest axis ratio
OCFC: Perimeter-area scaling-pixels
OEFC: Perimeter-area scaling-edges

Common Factors:
Diversity
Texture
Fractal dimension
Patch perimeter complexity
Patch shape
Patch compaction dimension

Source: Reprinted by permission from: Springer Nature, Landscape Ecology, A multi-scale analysis of landscape statistics, Douglas H. Cain, Kurt Riitters, Kenneth Orvis, Copyright:1997 Kluwer Academic Publishers

to quantitative analytical work. The set of methods discussed here can take years of experience to perfect and understand on an intuitive level. We feel confident that this chapter has provided a sufficient introduction for elementary analysis, but we refer you to the further readings throughout the chapter for more in-depth coverage of the subject (see Works Cited section).

Works Cited

Brown, T. A. (2014). *Confirmatory factor analysis for applied research* (2nd ed.). New York: Guilford Publications.

Cain, D. H., Riitters, K., & Orvis, K. (1997). A multi-scale analysis of landscape statistics. *Landscape Ecology, 12*(4), 199–212. https://doi.org/10.1023/A:1007938619068

Child, D. (2006). *The essentials of factor analysis* (3rd ed.). London: A&C Black.

Cohen, W. B., & Goward, S. N. (2004). Landsat's role in ecological applications of remote sensing. *AIBS Bulletin, 54*(6), 535–545. https://doi.org/10.1641/0006-3568(2004)054[0535:LRIEAO]2.0.CO;2

Ewing, R., & Hamidi, S. (2014). Measuring urban sprawl and validating sprawl measures. Washington, DC: National Institutes of Health and Smart Growth America.

Ewing, R., & Hamidi, S. (2015). Compactness versus sprawl: A review of recent evidence from the United States. *Journal of Planning Literature, 30*(4), 413–432. http://doi.org/10.1177/0885412215595439

Ewing, R., & Hamidi, S. (2017). *Costs of sprawl.* New York: Routledge.

Ewing, R., Hamidi, S., Tian, G., Proffitt, D., Tonin, S., & Fregolent, L. (2018). Testing Newman and Kenworthy's theory of density and automobile dependence. *Journal of Planning Education and Research, 38*(2), 167–182.

Ewing, R., Meakins, G., Hamidi, S., & Nelson, A. C. (2014). Relationship between urban sprawl and physical activity, obesity, and morbidity—Update and refinement. *Health & Place, 26*, 118–126. http://doi.org/10.1016/j.healthplace.2013.12.008

Ewing, R., Pendall, R., & Chen, D. (2002). *Measuring sprawl and its impact.* Retrieved from www.smart growthamerica.org/sprawlindex/sprawlreport.html

Ewing, R., Pendall, R., & Chen, D. (2003). Measuring sprawl and its transportation impacts. *Transportation Research Record: Journal of the Transportation Research Board* (1831), 175–183.

Fayyad, U., Piatetsky-Shapiro, G., & Smyth, P. (1996). *Knowledge discovery and data mining: Towards a unifying framework.* Retrieved from www.aaai.org/Papers/KDD/1996/KDD96-014.pdf

Hamidi, S., & Ewing, R. (2014). A longitudinal study of changes in urban sprawl between 2000 and 2010 in the United States. *Landscape and Urban Planning, 128*, 72–82. https://doi.org/10.1016/j.landurbplan.2014.04.021

Hamidi, S., Ewing, R., Preuss, I., & Dodds, A. (2015). Measuring sprawl and its impacts: An update. *Journal of Planning Education and Research, 35*(1), 35–50.

Harman, H. H. (1976). *Modern factor analysis.* Chicago, IL: University of Chicago Press.

Harrington, D. (2009). *Confirmatory factor analysis.* Oxford: Oxford University Press.

Holzinger, K. J. (1935). *Preliminary report on Spearman-Holzinger unitary trait study. No. 5. Introduction to Bi-factor theory.* Chicago, IL: Chicago of University Press.

Jackson, J. E. (2003). *A user's guide to principal components.* Hoboken, NJ: Wiley Series in Probability and Statistics.

Kim, H. J. (2008). Common factor analysis versus principal component analysis: Choice for symptom cluster research. *Asian Nursing Research, 2*(1), 17–24. https://doi.org/10.1016/S1976-1317(08)60025-0

Leslie, E., Sugiyama, T., Ierodiaconou, D., & Kremer, P. (2010). Perceived and objectively measured greenness of neighbourhoods: Are they measuring the same thing? *Landscape and Urban Planning, 95*(1), 28–33. https://doi.org/10.1016/j.landurbplan.2009.11.002

Nichol, J., & Wong, M. S. (2009). Mapping urban environmental quality using satellite data and multiple parameters. *Environment and Planning B: Planning and Design, 36*(1), 170–185.

Pearson, K. (1901). On lines and planes of closest fit to systems of points in space. *The London, Edinburgh, and Dublin Philosophical Magazine and Journal of Science, 2*(11), 559–572. https://doi.org/10.1080/14786440109462720

Song, Y., Popkin, B., & Gordon-Larsen, P. (2013). A national-level analysis of neighborhood form metrics. *Landscape and Urban Planning, 116*, 73–85. https://doi.org/10.1016/j.landurbplan.2013.04.002

Spearman, C. (1904). "General intelligence," Objectively determined and measured. *The American Journal of Psychology, 15*(2), 201–292.

Thompson, B. (2004). *Exploratory and confirmatory factor analysis: Understanding concepts and applications.* Washington, DC: American Psychological Association.

Thurstone, L. L. (1933). *A simplified multiple-factor method.* Chicago, IL: Chicago of University Press.

Thurstone, L. L. (1947). *Multiple factor analysis: A development and expansion of vectors of the mind.* Chicago, IL: Chicago of University Press.

Velicer, W. F., & Jackson, D. N. (1990). Component analysis versus common factor analysis: Some issues in selecting an appropriate procedure. *Multivariate Behavioral Research, 25*(1), 1–28. https://doi.org/10.1207/s15327906mbr2501_1

Vincent, D. F. (1953). The origin and development of factor analysis. *Applied Statistics*, 107–117.

6

CLUSTER ANALYSIS

Andrea Garfinkel-Castro, Tracey Bushman, Sadegh Sabouri, Simon C. Brewer, Yu Song, and Keunhyun Park

Overview

Cluster analysis (CA) is one of a suite of methods used for the classification of multivariate data. Unlike the ordination methods discussed in the previous chapter, here the goal is to classify subjects into a set of groups based on how similar they are to one another.

As an organizational approach, CA can be understood intuitively. Cases are grouped together based on the greatest similarity (within the set of variables) and move toward ever more specific levels of similarity. An example familiar to many is that of a supermarket (Burns & Burns, 2009). Imagine you want to buy some oranges. In a market, you expect to find that foods are grouped first according to their most basic type. For example, canned goods are kept together while fresh produce is similarly grouped. But if this was the extent of the clustering, it could take a long time to find oranges. So markets organize at a more detailed level. Citrus are arranged together, different apple types are placed together, and bananas can be found next to plantains. Oranges are a type of citrus, and this is where you will most likely find them, next to the lemons and limes. You might even find different types of oranges to choose from, such as Valencia, navels, or tangelos, which you'd also expect to find grouped together.

CA provides a means to organize multivariate data. An elegant way to think of CA is to see it as "the art of finding groups in data" (Kaufman & Rousseeuw, 1990, p. 1). A central concept in CA is the assumption that the groups or clusters that are formed are homogeneous: similar within clusters yet different between clusters, with remaining variation within a cluster considered noise. To continue the supermarket metaphor, while some oranges may be larger or smaller than the average, they are all found in the same section. This concept underlies both methodological considerations and applications of CA.

In this chapter, we start by discussing the goals of CA and some of the history of the method. We then detail basic terms and concepts used, before describing three of the most widely applied clustering algorithms. This is followed by instructions of how to carry out CA and visualize the results in SPSS and R and finally by a brief overview of how clustering has been used in planning studies.

Purpose

CA is an exploratory approach that provides researchers with an opportunity to develop greater familiarity with the structure of their data. It does this by exploring relationships between individual observations in a *parameter space*, a multidimensional space defined by the available attributes. It is an unsupervised form of classification (i.e., no *a priori* information on grouping is used), so it excels at uncovering unknown groupings within datasets. This leads to one of the main assumptions of CA, which is that the observations are clustered within this space, not evenly and continuously distributed. This is an important assumption, as many clustering algorithms will work even if this underlying structure is not present. Visualization of the observations through paired scatterplots or ordination biplots, for example non-metric multidimensional scaling (NMDS), can help assess whether this assumption holds for a dataset.

As previously described, CA aims to both group and separate data using the notion of *similarity*: Individual observations are grouped into clusters if the value of their attributes is comparable; clusters of cases are separated based on differences. In practice, dissimilarity or distance metrics (e.g., multivariate Euclidean distance) are used, and the optimum clustering solution is therefore the one that minimizes the dissimilarity of the observations within each cluster and maximizes the dissimilarity between the clusters. The choice of attributes or variables used to calculate dissimilarity is therefore important in determining the final set of clusters. Using the supermarket analogy again, canned oranges will typically be shelved near other canned fruit rather than near fresh oranges, but it would be possible to group all types of oranges together, if packaging attributes were ignored. CA allows researchers flexibility.

As the example of oranges demonstrates, defining characteristics is subjective but important. There may be instances when being canned is a more important characteristic for grouping than being fruit, or vice versa. Weighting, or allowing a variable to be scaled in a manner that increases its importance, may be of interest, such as with a residential preference survey. In other instances, it may be preferable to equalize values so as to more evenly distribute the influence of variables, such as in neighborhood typologies (see Song & Knaap, 2007, discussed later in the chapter). The relative ease and speed of the cluster algorithms in software such as SPSS and R make CA an attractive approach to exploring underlying, subtle, and obscure patterns in data. Data management methods such as CA gain in value as datasets grow in terms of size and complexity. CA is suitable for class-, index-, or group-level analysis and fits into research methods at varying stages, as demonstrated by the articles highlighted in the Planning Examples section of this chapter.

Like principal component analysis, CA is also a data reduction method. In general, the goal is to produce homogeneous clusters of observations from one large, undifferentiated set, rather than aggregating variables into a smaller set of factors. This is called Q-mode analysis and is based on the dissimilarity between pairs of observations. A second approach (R-mode) is more analogous to PCA. This is based on pairwise dissimilarities between variables and can be used to reduce many variables into groups (Burns & Burns, 2009; Norušis, 2008).

History

Classification is fundamental to most branches of science. In biology, for example, the theory and practice of classifying organisms is generally known as *taxonomy*. Building on Aristotle's classification of animals and Theophrastos's classification of plants, Carl Linnaeus published his work *Genera Plantarum* in 1737, in which he said, "All the real knowledge which we possess, depends on methods by which we distinguish the similar from the dissimilar" (as cited in Everitt, Landau, Leese, & Stahl, 2011, p. 2). In addition to biology, classification has also played a central role in the developments of other fields of science, like the periodic table in chemistry and the classification of stars in astronomy.

Clustering was originated in psychology by Zubin (1938) and Tryon (1939) and in anthropology by Driver and Kroeber (1932). Computational difficulties retarded its development until the late 1950s, when computerization resulted in a proliferation of clustering techniques (Bailey, 1975). Since then, much significant work on the application of cluster analysis has been done in the field of biology (Sokal & Sneath, 1963; Sneath & Sokal, 1973). Clustering methods have received attention from researchers in many other disciplines as well, including economics (Fisher, 1969), mathematics (Jardine & Sibson, 1971), geography (Ray & Berry, 1965), market research (Green, Frank, & Robinson, 1967), psychiatry (Pilowsky, Levine, & Boulton, 1969), and urbanization (Wingo, 1967). The past few years have seen a renewal of interest in CA methods, as it forms a key branch of unsupervised machine learning.

Some of the early attempts to apply cluster analysis are introduced here. For marketing research, Green et al. (1967) classified cities into a small number of groups on the basis of 14 variables including city size, newspaper circulation, and per capita income. In psychiatry, Pilowsky et al. (1969) clustered patients on the basis of their responses to a depression questionnaire, together with their personal characteristics, and found a significant cluster related to depression. In archaeology, Hodson (1966) used a clustering technique to construct a taxonomy of hand axes found in the British Isles.

Terminology differs from one field to another (Scoltock, 1982). In biology, the term "numerical taxonomy" is frequently used as a substitute for cluster analysis. In pattern recognition, the terms are generally "clustering" or "classification," while in machine learning, the term "unsupervised learning" is often found. Geographers use the term "regionalization." Other terms that are frequently used in most fields are "classification," "grouping," "clumping," "typology," and "Q-analysis."

Terminology

This section presents basic vocabulary used for CA and an overview of cluster and data typologies (Gan et al., 2007). Frequently overlooked, it is included here to facilitate the learning of and access to the CA process. Not all the terms included in the vocabulary section are used within this chapter. Similarly, not all terms used elsewhere in other sources are included in this section. Its purpose is to serve as a reference or starting point when navigating through this chapter, and when performing the CA process.

Clusters: Cluster, group, class. These all refer to clusters regardless of size or shape/pattern. Clusters are made up of data. Also see Cluster typology later in this list.

Centroid: The center point of a cluster, usually defined as the set of average attribute values based on the observations in that cluster.

Data: Data point, observation, object, record, or case. These terms and others are found in the literature and refer to the individual item to which variables are attributed.

Distances: Dissimilarity, measure or coefficient of similarity or dissimilarity, distance between pairs of data points or clusters (also referred to as *proximity*, Gan et al., 2007). All CA processes are dependent on some kind of measure of dissimilarity between observations, frequently presented as an $n \times n$ distance matrix containing all pairwise distances between observations. Because CA is most frequently used with numeric data, the distance referred to is literal and mappable. Multivariate Euclidean distances (the *ordinary* distance between two points in multidimensional space) are most frequently used, but many other measures of distance exist (see Gan et al., 2007), including measures for categorical data. Distance matrices can be easily generated by most software programs, including SPSS and R.

Cluster typology: In general, there are two basic patterns to clusters: compact, or center-based clusters, and chained clusters (Gan et al., 2007) (see Figure 6.1).

Scale conversion (alternately, standardization): As the scales used to measure data may not be the same, it may be necessary to standardize the data. The decision of whether to standardize or not depends on the objectives of the analysis as well as on the data involved. For example, Norušis (2008) points out, "Variables that are measured in large numbers will contribute to the distance more than variables recorded in smaller numbers" (p. 366). If standardization is desired, Gan et al. (2007) note that "any scale can be converted to any other scale"

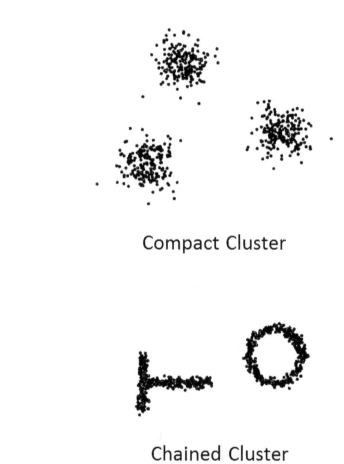

Compact Cluster

Chained Cluster

FIGURE 6.1 Cluster types are compact, or center-based, and chained

Source: Gan et al., 2007, p. 7

(p. 25). There are three basic approaches to take when clustering objects measured in different scales (Gan et al., 2007, p. 25):

1. Use a distance measure that can incorporate information from different types of variable (e.g., z-score distance).
2. Carry out separate analyses of the same set of objects, with each analysis calculating the distance between variables of a single type only, and then synthesize the results.
3. Standardize the variables in the same way (e.g., z-scores), and use a basic distance measure (e.g., Euclidean).

Methodology

There are a large number of algorithms for CA, and these can largely be differentiated by the type of cluster they produce:

- **Hierarchical versus partitioning**: Hierarchical methods work iteratively, allowing existing clusters to be merged (bottom up) or divided (top down). This results in a tree structure that provides information about the relationship between clusters (i.e., similar clusters will be close together on the tree). Partitioning methods work by simply partitioning the space into a set of clusters directly, then iterating to find the optimum solution.
- **Exclusive versus fuzzy**: Exclusive methods place each observation into one of the possible clusters. With fuzzy methods, all observations belong to all clusters but with a value between 0 and 1 that determines the *strength* of membership.
- **Complete versus partial**: With complete methods, all observations have to be placed in a cluster. Partial methods exclude any observations that do not form part of a natural cluster.

In this next section, we give a brief description of the algorithm behind two commonly used cluster methods: hierarchical cluster analysis and k-means cluster analysis. We focus on these as they are conceptually straightforward and easy to implement. Although simple, both methods have options that can change the behavior of the algorithm, and we include a description of the most important of these.

Hierarchical Cluster Analysis

Hierarchical clustering is described as "one of the most straightforward methods" (Norušis, 2008, p. 363) and is ideal if you have a small dataset and want to easily examine solutions with increasing numbers of clusters. This can be run as an agglomerative or divisive approach, and the basic algorithm for agglomerative clustering is as follows:

1. Consider each observation as a cluster.
2. Calculate the distance matrix between all pairs of clusters.
3. Merge the two clusters with the smallest distances into a single cluster.
4. Recalculate the attributes of this cluster (based on the observations it contains).
5. Update the distance matrix to reflect this new cluster.
6. Repeat until only one cluster remains.

The divisive approach is essentially the reverse of this: Start with a single cluster containing all observations and recursively split it using the largest intercluster distances until each cluster contains only a single observation. While the method is computationally simple, it is worth noting that the memory requirements scale quadratically with the size of the dataset, making hierarchical clustering difficult with larger datasets.

The results are generally visualized as a dendrogram (see Figure 6.12 for an example), where each split in the tree represents a single merge (or split) of the existing clusters. Note that the method does not provide a single solution with a set number of clusters but instead provides solutions for any number of clusters between 1 and n. It is up to the analyst to make the final decision of how many clusters to retain.

The most important parameter in the algorithm controls how the distances between clusters are calculated. Assuming that Euclidean distances are used, if we have two clusters (A and B), each containing only one observation, then the intercluster distance is the same as the distance between observations. As clusters increase in size, then a choice must be made of how to calculate the attribute to use in the distance calculation (the preceding step 4). Some standard options are:

- **Average**: The average of all the pairwise distances between observations in A and observations in B
- **Minimum distance (single link)**: The smallest pairwise distance between observations in A and observations in B
- **Maximum distance (complete link)**: The largest pairwise distance between observations in A and observations in B
- **Ward's method**: Calculation of the centroid (the average value of all attributes) for A and B, then of the distance between centroids

The minimum and maximum distances are affected by outliers but work well when the cluster topology is not spherical and well distinguished. Ward's method and the average distance are less susceptible to outliers and tend to produce compact, spherical clusters.

k-means Cluster Analysis

In contrast to the hierarchical methods, k-means cluster analysis is a partitioning method. As it no longer requires a full distance matrix to be calculated, it can be used with much larger datasets. However, the method requires that the number of clusters be specified in advance. Some tools to help with this are discussed next. The basic algorithm is as follows:

1. Randomly choose k initial centroids (usually by randomly selecting k observations to represent the initial centroids).
2. Assign each observation to the nearest centroid based on a distance metric.
3. Recalculate the centroid for each cluster as the average attribute values of all points currently assigned to it.
4. Repeat from step 2 until the cluster solution stabilizes.

The algorithm will continually update centroids and reassign observations until some stopping rule is reached. Usually this is based on minimizing the sum-of-squares of the difference between the cluster centroid and the assigned observations, summed across all clusters:

$$SS_C = \sum_{i=1}^{k} \sum_{j=i}^{x \in C_i} D\left(m_i, x_j\right)$$

In general, only small set of iterations are required to reach an optimal solution. Nonconvergence or a large number of iterations may suggest that the underlying data do not form easily identified clusters.

It is also important to note that the final cluster solution depends on the choice of initial centroids. As these are chosen randomly, running *k*-means twice with the same data will give different results. Further, if these initial centroids are poorly chosen, the algorithm may converge to a stable but less than optimal solution. To limit the impact of these problems, the algorithm may be run several times, and the solution with the lowest sum-of-squares selected. Alternatively, the initial centroids can be chosen by other methods, for example, by running a hierarchical method and estimating centroids from the corresponding *k* clusters obtained.

Two-Step Cluster Analysis

Although the *k*-means method has less memory requirements than hierarchical clustering, neither of these methods scale well with very large datasets. Two-step clustering was introduced as a way to tackle this limitation. This first classifies observations into a set of smaller subclusters, then groups these subclusters together using a traditional method (Zhang, Ramakrishnon, & Livny, 1996). Computational efficiencies come from (1) the use of a simple, fast method in the first step and (2) the reduction in the number of cases in the second step from *n* observations to *m* subclusters.

In the SPSS implementation of two-step clustering, the first step uses a sequential clustering algorithm, which iterates once across every sample in the dataset. One sample is chosen to form a subcluster. The next sample is compared to this, and if the distance is less than some prespecified threshold, it is added to that subcluster. If not, it forms a new subcluster. Each subsequent sample is then compared to the current list of subclusters and, similarly, either added to one or used to form a new subcluster. In the second step, agglomerative hierarchical clustering is used to form a set of *k* clusters from the subclusters, using cluster centroids to calculate distances.

This method offers two further advantages. First, a likelihood-based distance metric can be used to compare observations in the first step, which allows a greater flexibility in clustering mixed data types, which allows a combination of continuous and categorical variables to be used. Second, the number of clusters can be automatically selected, based on a combination of a Bayesian information criterion and the distance metric. However, the use of a simpler method for the first step may introduce inaccuracies in the clustering. While this can be limited by selecting a higher number of subclusters, this will increase the computational time in the second step. The choice of the threshold is therefore a key parameter in this method and represents a trade-off between speed and accuracy.

Assessing Cluster Solutions

A large and somewhat overwhelming number of metrics exist to assess the solution obtained by a given cluster algorithm (e.g. Calinski & Harabasz, 1974), and a full discussion of these is outside the scope of this chapter. Here, we focus on a single metric, the silhouette index (Rousseeuw, 1987), as it is one of the most flexible approaches, allowing assessment of the solution for individual observations, individual clusters, or the full solution.

For each observation (x_i), calculate two values:

1. a_i: average distance to all other points in the same cluster
2. b_i: average distance to all points in the next nearest cluster

The silhouette index for point i is then:

$$s_i = \frac{b_i - a_i}{\max\left(a_i, b_i\right)}$$

Values close to 1 suggest that the observation is well assigned to this cluster, and -1 suggests that it is poorly assigned (i.e., closer to a different cluster, as a results of the overlap between them). A value close to 0 indicates that this observation falls on the boundary between two clusters. The average value of s_i for any cluster indicates how well this is seperated from the other clusters and can be used, for example, to test different values of k for k-means clustering, or the cutoff for agglomerative clustering.

Step by Step

In this section, we demonstrate the use of cluster analysis in SPSS, applying three clustering methods: hierarchical, k-means, and two-step. Each clustering method has different analytical processes, steps, and outputs. Because there is no *right answer* when conducting a cluster analysis, it is recommended to explore the data through multiple analyses, each using a different method.

A cluster analysis has multiple steps and choices. Each decision can affect the quality and usefulness of the results.

1. Choose appropriate variables.
2. Scale the data and screen for outliers.
3. Calculate distances using an appropriate measure.
4. Select and run a clustering algorithm.
5. Determine the number of clusters.
6. Interpret the clusters and validate the results.

The first (and perhaps most important) step is to select variables upon which we base our clusters, and the choice depends on the study aims. For example, if we are interested in classifying the urbanized areas (UZAs) in terms of their demographic and built environment conditions, we might wish to include the following variables: total population, median household income, total area, freeway lane miles, transit passenger miles, and the compactness index. We might, however, exclude variables such as air quality measurements or health indices, as we may subsequently wish to explore the link between our clusters and these variables. In this example, we will use the following variables from the UZA data set: *pop000, inc000, area, flm, tpm,* and *compact.*

The second step is to ensure that the variables are comparable. As the original values are measure on quite different scales, the results of the cluster analysis will be biased towards larger magnitude variables. Here, we standardize all variables to *z*-scores, by subtracting the mean and dividing by the standard deviation.

In the SPSS menu, go to "Analyze" → "Descriptive Statistics" → "Descriptives." Then add six variables: *pop, inc, area, flm, tpm* and compact. Check on "Save standardized values as variables" and click "OK" (Figure 6.2). This option will add the *z*-scores as new variables.

You will be able to see six new variables added to the right end of the table: *Zpop000, Zinc000, Zarea, Zflm, Ztpm* and Zcompact (Figure 6.3).

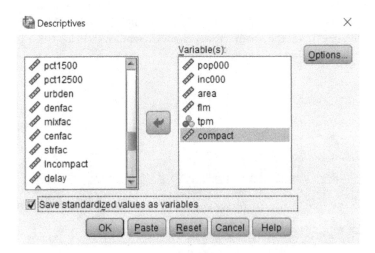

FIGURE 6.2 Adding standardized values as new variables in the UZA dataset

pct4way	Zpop000	Zinc000	Zarea	Zflm	Ztpm	Zcompact
27.47	-.26198	-.49750	-.22690	.31309	-.42612	-.39790
19.05	-.24789	.52071	-.14798	1.27679	-.11115	.19223
28.95	-.18221	-.24019	-.07315	-.80255	.17614	-.62992
34.87	-.23736	-.04946	-.32027	-.03977	-.39419	1.84218
45.50	-.44492	-.81035	-.58764	1.00281	-.65981	.09080
17.86	-.39139	.75819	-.51219	.60152	.24408	-.84097
26.30	-.41144	-.57803	-.73054	-1.16123	1.15668	1.21099
31.34	-.43855	.01947	-.65493	.37896	-.56435	.58432
12.96	-.40492	-.21390	-.24529	2.92474	-.53155	.10366
13.96	1.61388	.60566	4.20841	-.38422	.80820	-1.67178
22.90	-.35210	-.45071	.00100	-.64946	-.66028	-1.00048
23.42	.06276	.86183	.33916	-.03937	.18127	.38976
29.51	-.28830	-1.09001	-.48544	-1.05615	-.35264	-.05698
27.06	.48727	1.02589	.23160	.23288	1.02732	1.27048
22.26	-.24955	-.12320	.17944	-.74309	-.52582	-1.69849
39.34	-.41460	-.92876	-.45453	.93443	-.63893	.98903

FIGURE 6.3 Six new variables standardized as *z*-scores

The following steps—from step 3 (calculating distances) to step 6 (interpreting the clusters)—need to be separately conducted for each of the clustering methods in SPSS.

Hierarchical Clustering

Hierarchical cluster analysis follows three basic steps: (1) calculate the distances, (2) link the clusters, and (3) choose a solution by selecting the right number of clusters.

First, we have to select the variables upon which we base our clusters. Go to "Analyze" → "Classify" → "Hierarchical Cluster" (Figure 6.4). Then select the six variables that we will use for the clustering: *Zpop000, Zinc000, Zarea, Zflm, Ztpm,* and *Zcompact* (Figure 6.5). Click on "Statistics," and check "Proximity matrix." This option will generate a matrix of distances between all UZA pairs (Figure 6.6).

In the main cluster analysis window, click on "Plots" and check "Dendrogram" (Figure 6.7)

Next, go to the "Method" option to select parameters (Figure 6.8). We select "Ward's method" to calculate cluster attributes. Leave the default option for "Measure" ("Squared Euclidean Distance"). In the main cluster analysis window, click "OK" to run a the algorithm.

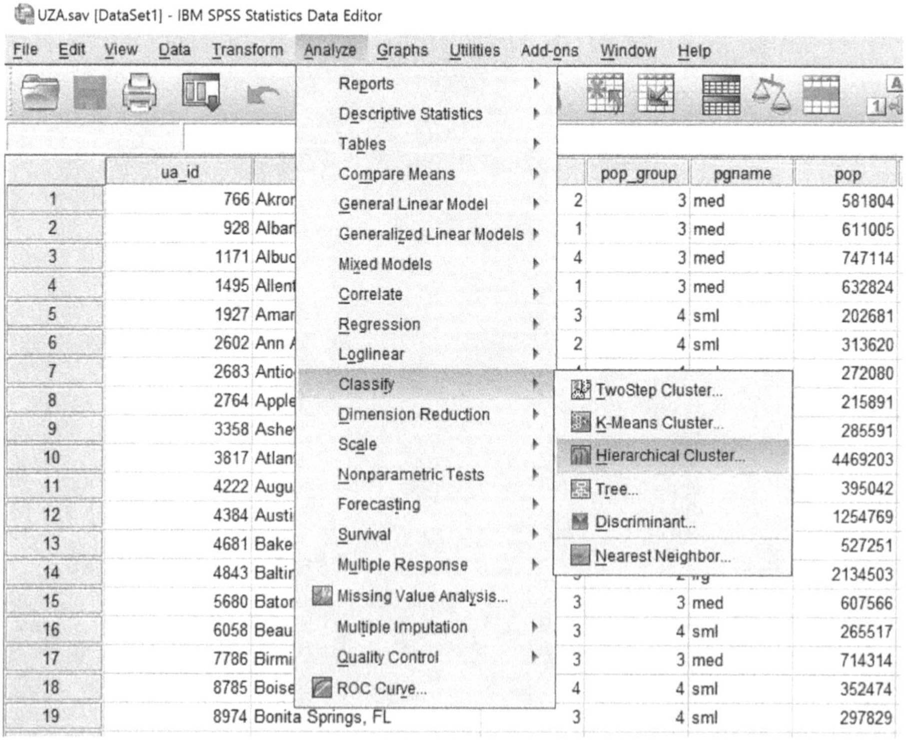

FIGURE 6.4 Initiating a hierarchical cluster analysis in SPSS

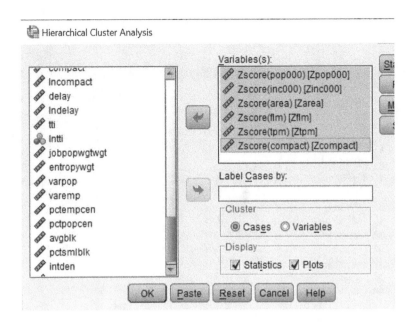

FIGURE 6.5 Adding variables for a hierarchical cluster analysis

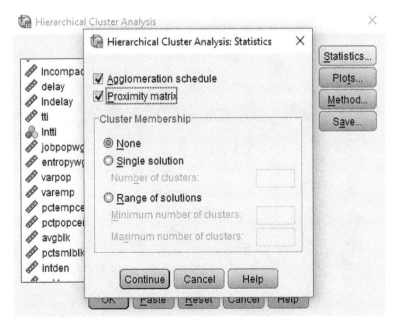

FIGURE 6.6 Adding a proximity matrix in the "Statistics" option

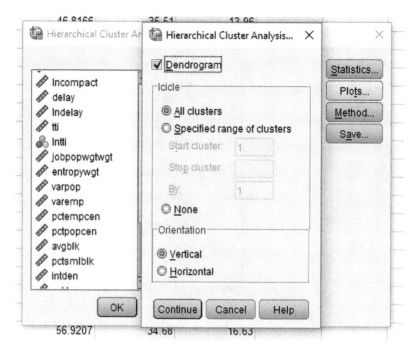

FIGURE 6.7 Adding a dendrogram in the "Plots" option

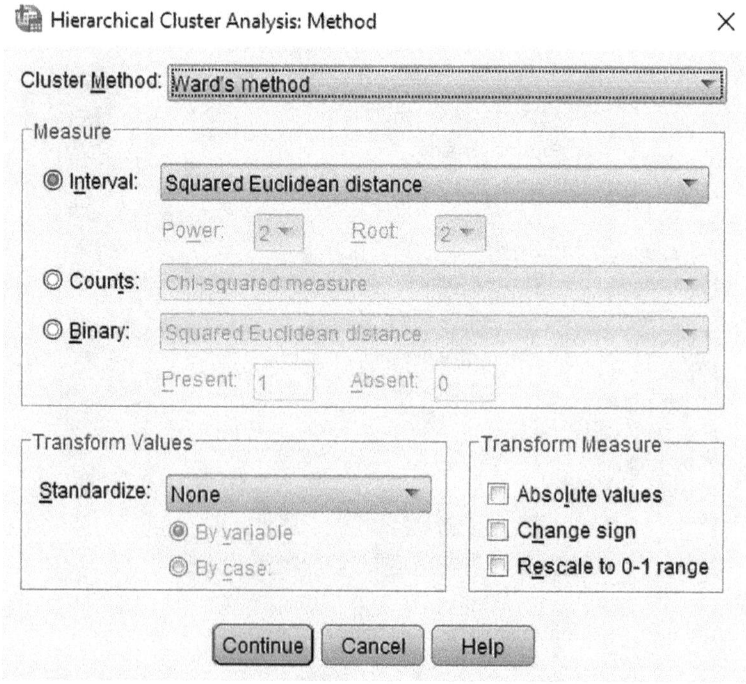

Hierarchical Cluster Analysis: Method ✕

Cluster Method: Ward's method ▼

Measure

◉ Interval: Squared Euclidean distance ▼

Power: 2 ▼   Root: 2 ▼

○ Counts: Chi-squared measure ▼

○ Binary: Squared Euclidean distance ▼

Present: 1   Absent: 0

Transform Values

Standardize: None ▼

◉ By variable

◉ By case:

Transform Measure

☐ Absolute values

☐ Change sign

☐ Rescale to 0-1 range

Continue   Cancel   Help

FIGURE 6.8 Choosing a clustering method

Interpreting Hierarchical CA Output Tables

The table, case processing summary, simply reports the number of cases in the dataset considered valid and missing. All 157 UZAs are valid in our analysis. (See Figure 6.9.)

The next output, the "Agglomeration Schedule," provides a summary description of the clustering process (Figure 6.10). Each row is read from left to right. The first column tells us the clustering stage. The next two columns tell us the two clusters being merged, and the center column (Coefficients) gives the squared Euclidean distance between them. The next two columns report the stage at which each cluster was clustered. The far-right column indicates when the cluster in the Cluster 1 column (second column from the left) will combine with another case or cluster. There is no Next Stage for the final cluster. Note that you will just see the first 100 cases in the output table of SPSS. To see the remaining cases (from 101 to 156), simply double-click on the table; then a new window, "Pivot Table Agglomeration Schedule," will pop up.

The next output is an icicle plot; a graphic representation of agglomeration schedule. Each column represent a single original observation, and the rows represent different numbers of clusters. The length of the column between two observations indicates the point in the clustering process that those two observations were merged. Here we can see that observation 100

Case Processing Summary[a]

	Cases					
Valid		Missing		Total		
N	Percent	N	Percent	N	Percent	
157	100.0	0	.0	157	100.0	

a. Ward Linkage

FIGURE 6.9 Output: Case processing summary

Agglomeration Schedule

	Cluster Combined			Stage Cluster First Appears		
Stage	Cluster 1	Cluster 2	Coefficients	Cluster 1	Cluster 2	Next Stage
1	1	55	.022	0	0	40
2	16	141	.045	0	0	9
3	74	103	.073	0	0	17
4	23	121	.116	0	0	32
5	58	147	.166	0	0	37
6	50	139	.222	0	0	12
7	32	96	.294	0	0	38
8	39	102	.368	0	0	29
9	16	136	.448	2	0	112
10	69	123	.529	0	0	54

FIGURE 6.10 Output: agglomeration schedule

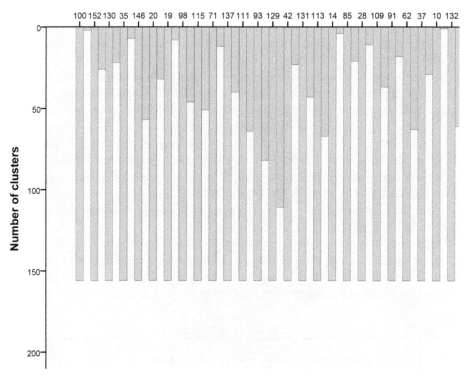

FIGURE 6.11 Output: icicle plot

and 152 were merged when there were approximately 5 clusters (i.e., later in the agglomeration), whereas 129 and 42 were merged earlier. (See Figure 6.11).

The final output is a dendrogram, where represents the full set of clusters in a tree-like structure (Figure 6.12). Here, the vertical axis displays the observations, but ordered now by their similarity. The horizontal axis shows the dissimilarity between clusters as they are merged (this is normalized to $[0, 25]$). Reading from left to right, it is possible to see how the observations are recursively merged together. The scale here obscures the smaller differences on the left hand side, but we can see approximately 25 observations merged into a top cluster, about 7 in the next cluster, 15 in the third, 6 in the fourth and 17 in the fifth. The second and third clusters are then merged together, then this is merged with the first. Note that this is only part of the output, and there will be other observations and clusters not shown here. If we draw an imaginary vertical line at any point on the horizontal axis, then any branch of the dendrogram this intersects with will become a cluster, containing all observations linked to the left. If we place a line at about 1.5, this would result in the five clusters just described. If we move this to about 3.5, this would result in two clusters.

The important question is, where do we put our line to identify the number of clusters? The length of the branches can be used to help here; longer branches represent greater dissimilarity and therefore separation between clusters. Here there is a better separation for two clusters than for three. There are a number of indices that can help assess this (e.g., the silhouette index just described). We note, however, that these are only guides, and using professional judgment to assess and interpret the resulting clusters is as important.

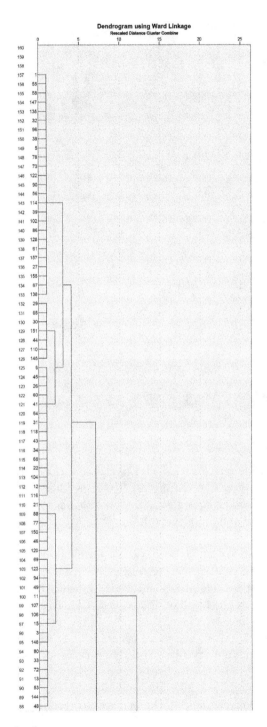

FIGURE 6.12 Output: dendrogram

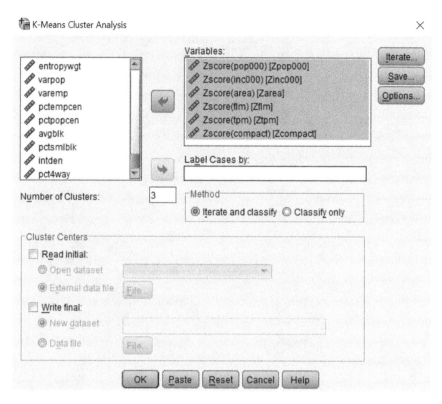

FIGURE 6.13 "*k*-means Cluster Analysis" window

k-means Clustering

We now demonstrate a *k*-means cluster analysis with the same data set (Figure 6.13).To conduct a *k*-means CA, go to "Analyze" → "Classify" → "K-Means Cluster Analysis."Then, select the six variables: *Zpop000, Zinc000, Zarea, Zflm, Ztpm*, and *Zcompact*.

You can specify several options (Figure 6.13).

1. **Label cases by**: Optional; use to label cases.We leave it blank here.
2. **Number of clusters**: Set the number of clusters here. In our example, we use three clusters.
3. **Method**:The two options are "Iterate and classify," in which the cluster centroid is recalculated each time a case is added or deleted, and "Classify only," in which cluster centroids are calculated once with initial clustering.We use the default option.
4. **Cluster centers**: This allows the initial centroids to be read from a file from a file (the "Read initial" option) or to save final cluster centroids (the "Write final" option) (Figure 6.14).

Click on the "Options" box (Figure 6.14).The "Initial cluster centers" option generates an output table of the variable means for each cluster at stage 1.The "ANOVA table" option will run an *F*-test for each variable used against the final cluster solution.This can be helpful in identifying which attributes are the most important in grouping the observations.The "Cluster information for each case" option ensures that the output includes the final cluster location and the Euclidean

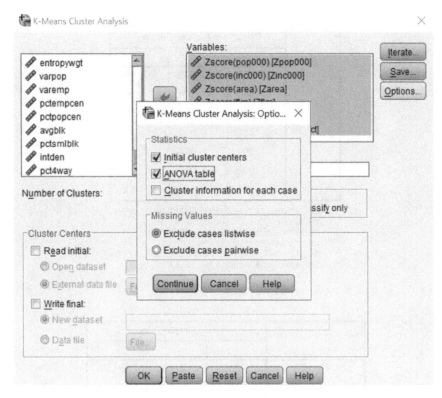

FIGURE 6.14   "*k*-means Cluster Analysis": "Options" window

distance for each observation and its cluster centroid. Lastly, the "Missing Values" option determines the basis for excluding data from analysis. Make sure the "Initial cluster centers" and "ANOVA table" options are selected. Then click on "Continue" → "OK" to run a *k*-means CA.

Interpreting k-means CA Output Tables

The first output is the Initial Cluster Centers table, which shows the mean values for the clusters based on the initial centroids. This can be a useful diagnostic, as the algorithm may struggle to find an optimal set of clusters if these initial centers are too similar. The next output is the Iteration History table (Figure 6.15); this shows the number of iterations required for the solution to converge (here, 8 iterations). The change in centroid values is given for all three requested clusters. If this remains high, the algorithm failed to converge, and it may be necessary to increase the number of iterations in the "Iterate" option in the main "*k*-means Cluster Analysis" window, or provide better starting values for the centroids.

The "Final Cluster Centers" table (Figure 6.16) presents clusters and their mean values of attributes. In our example, cluster one has the highest population, the smallest land area, the shortest freeway lane-miles, the highest transit passenger miles, and is the most compact. In contrast, cluster two has larger area, higher freeway miles and lower transit and compactness. So we might label cluster 1 as compact regions, cluster two as sprawling regions, and cluster three as hybrid regions.

The next output shows the results of the ANOVA tests on the cluster attributes (Figure 6.17). These show significant differences ($p < .05$) for all attributes except freeway lane miles

Iteration History[a]

	Change in Cluster Centers		
Iteration	1	2	3
1	3.497	2.835	2.864
2	1.665	.101	.544
3	.000	.085	.527
4	.000	.047	.242
5	.000	.024	.119
6	.000	.017	.081
7	.000	.000	.000

a. Convergence achieved due to no or small change in cluster centers. The maximum absolute coordinate change for any center is .000. The current iteration is 7. The minimum distance between initial centers is 7.962.

FIGURE 6.15   Output: iteration history

	Cluster		
	1	2	3
Zscore(pop000)	5.78825	-.27630	.69238
Zscore(inc000)	.77686	-.27836	1.28076
Zscore(area)	4.55002	-.29450	.92484
Zscore(flm)	-.98717	.05154	-.13982
Zscore(tpm)	3.63801	-.29545	1.03473
Zscore(compact)	1.45927	-.05765	-.01641

FIGURE 6.16   Output: "Final Cluster Centers"

(flm). Post-hoc tests can be run to perform pairwise comparisons between clusters (see the Chapter 11, "Analysis of Variance (ANOVA)" in *Basic Quantitative Research Methods for Urban Planners*).

The final output table, "Number of Cases in Each Cluster," shows the distribution of observations across clusters (Figure 6.18). This provides information on the relative balance (even or uneven) of cases among clusters, and may be used to identify outliers. In our example, cluster two (sprawling regions) is the biggest since it contains 128 cases, followed by cluster three (hybrid regions; $n = 26$) and cluster one (compact regions; $n = 3$).

At this stage, we recommend to examine cluster solutions, particularly changing the requested number of clusters. Once you have the best solution, click on the "Save" option in the main "*k*-means Cluster Analysis" window, and then check the "Cluster Membership" (Figure 6.19).

	Cluster		Error			
	Mean Square	df	Mean Square	df	F	Sig.
Zscore(pop000)	61.374	2	.216	154	284.232	.000
Zscore(inc000)	27.189	2	.660	154	41.202	.000
Zscore(area)	47.724	2	.393	154	121.375	.000
Zscore(flm)	1.886	2	.988	154	1.908	.152
Zscore(tpm)	39.358	2	.502	154	78.426	.000
Zscore(compact)	3.373	2	.910	154	3.706	.027

The F tests should be used only for descriptive purposes because the clusters have been chosen to maximize the differences among cases in different clusters. The observed significance levels are not corrected for this and thus cannot be interpreted as tests of the hypothesis that the cluster means are equal.

FIGURE 6.17 Output: ANOVA

Number of Cases in each Cluster

Cluster	1	3.000
	2	128.000
	3	26.000
Valid		157.000
Missing		.000

FIGURE 6.18 Output: "Number of Cases in Each Cluster"

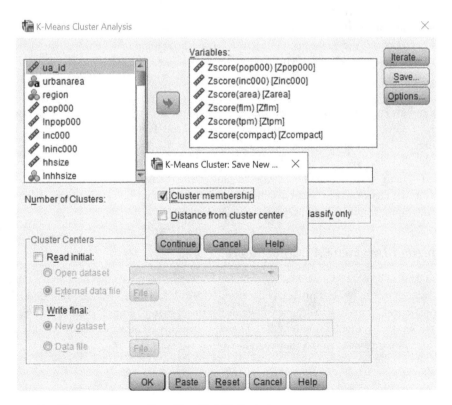

FIGURE 6.19 "k-means Cluster: Save New Variable" window

Now, in our dataset, a new column is added with the title of "QCL_1". This column shows which urbanized areas are in cluster 1, 2, or 3.

Two-Step Clustering

In this section, we walk through a two-step clustering algorithm with the UZA dataset. Start the Two-Step CA by going to "Analyze" → "Classify" → "TwoStep Cluster." Then select the six variables to include in your analysis: *Zpop000, Zinc000, Zarea, Zflm, Ztpm, Zcompact*. Note that the input variables are all continuous; make sure that these are entered in the "Continuous Variables" box.

This dialog box (Figure 6.20) also includes:

- **Distance measure**: Selection here is dependent on the type of data used. If the data used are a mix of continuous and categorical, "Log-likelihood" is the only option. If the data are only continuous, "Euclidean" distances may be chosen instead. In this exercise, we select "Log-likelihood."
- **Count of continuous variables**: This provides the option not to standardize continuous variables (continuous variables are standardized by default). Our variables are already standardized.
- **Clustering criterion**: The two options are "BIC" (Schwarz Bayesian Criterion) and "AIC" (Akaike Information Criterion). Both approaches seek a best fit model; "AIC" has been found to perform better with smaller datasets while "BIC" has performed better with larger datasets (Schwarz, 2014/2011; Acquah, 2010). Since we have 157 cases, we check the AIC Criterion.
- **Number of clusters**: This provides the option to select a specific number of clusters. If not selected, the program will identify an optimal number of clusters based on the criterion selected—BIC or AIC. Otherwise, we can set a fixed number. Here, we check "Determine Automatically."

Then click on "Options" to select the outlier treatment option, which creates a separate cluster for cases that don't fit well into any other cluster (Figure 6.21). Check "Use noise handling," and keep the default percentage 25.

Lastly, click on "Output" and make sure that "Charts and tables (in Model Viewer)" is checked (Figure 6.22). Also, check "Create cluster membership variable" to create a new variable at the right end of the dataset showing which cluster each urbanized area belongs to. Then click on "Continue" and "OK" to run a two-step CA.

Interpreting Two-Step CA Output Tables

The outputs of TwoStep Cluster Analysis include a Model Summary in the output window and a new cluster membership variable (named "TSC_1"), which is at the right end of the data spreadsheet. The Model Summary table shows the two-step CA generated with two clusters from six input variables (Figure 6.23). The cluster quality is measured using the Silhouette index and an index value of 0.5 (between fair and good ranges)..

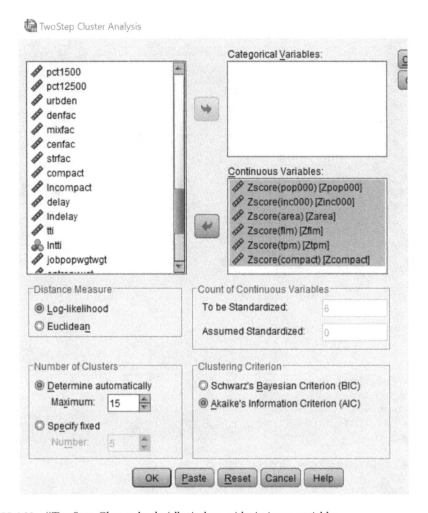

FIGURE 6.20 "TwoStep Cluster Analysis" window with six input variables

Further information about the cluster analysis results is available in a "Model Viewer" window (Figure 6.24). Double-click the output, and a "Model Viewer" will pop out. We can check several types of summaries by choosing different selections from the "View" menu bars at the bottom (both in left and right).

From the cluster sizes view, you can see that the urbanized areas have been classified into two clusters, with the sizes of 14.7% (23 UZAs) and 85.3% (133 UZAs), respectively (Figure 6.24).

From the "Predictor Importance" chart (select on the "View" menu bar at the bottom right), you can find that the most important predictors that have the most influence on the cluster classification are *Ztpm* and *Zpop000* (Figure 6.26). The *Zflm* and *Zcompact* variables have the least importance.

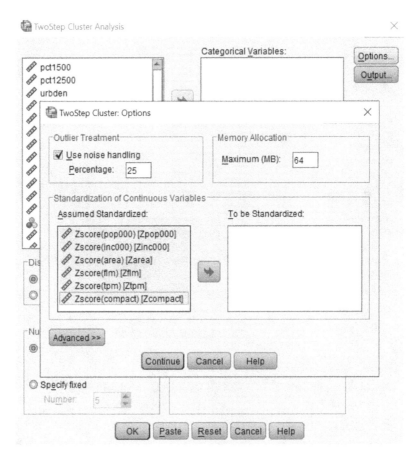

FIGURE 6.21 "TwoStep Cluster: Options" window

The "Clusters" view (click on the "View" menu bar at bottom left) provides the overview of the cluster analysis results (Figure 6.26). It visualizes cluster size, predictor importance, and mean values of the input variables for each cluster. From this result, we might consider cluster 1 as sprawling regions and cluster 2 as compact regions.

You can further explore the distribution of each input variable by cluster type. The icons at the left side of the "Display" button are for displaying the absolute or relative distribution of each variable. Also, when you click any cell in the table (for example, $Ztpm$ in cluster 1), the distribution of the selected attribute in the chosen cluster—either relative or absolute distribution based on your selection on the left side—appears on the right side of the model viewer (Figure 6.26). This information helps you interpret the clusters.

In R

Figures 6.27 through 6.29 show an R script to run a cluster analysis of UZA typology. After reading the SPSS data in R, we create a subset of the six variables and use the scale function

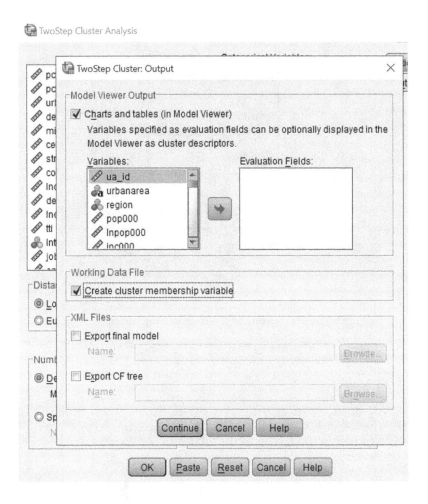

FIGURE 6.22   "TwoStep Cluster: Output" window

to standardize them (Figure 6.27). Hierarchical cluster analysis can be run in R using the *hclust* function. Note that this function requires a dissimilarity matrix as input, not the original data frame. This dissimilarity matrix can be created using the *dist* function. While this requires an extra step, this allows for some flexibility in the choice of the distance or dissimilarity measure used. The *hclust* function has several parameters of interest; the method parameter controls the calculation of cluster attributes (e.g., "ward.D," "single," "complete," "average"). Once run, we use the *cutree* function to divide the data into a set of 4 clusters, and store the cluster numbers. Finally, we plot the dendrogram obtained, and overlay a rectangle showing the selected clusters (note that one cluster only contains a single outlying observation).

R has several add-on packages that extend the basic cluster functionality. Here we use the *NbClust* function (from the *NbClust* package) to estimate the optimal number of clusters using 23 different indices (Figure 6.28). For this example, six indices proposed three as the best number of clusters, followed by two or six. Finally, we run *k*-means using the *kmeans* function, specifying the original data frame ("d") and setting the number of groups to 3 (Figure 6.29). This creates a 'kmeans' object, containing information about the clusters, and we can use this

Model Summary

Algorithm	TwoStep
Inputs	6
Clusters	2

Cluster Quality

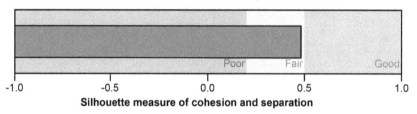

FIGURE 6.23   Output: "Model Summary" and "Cluster Quality"

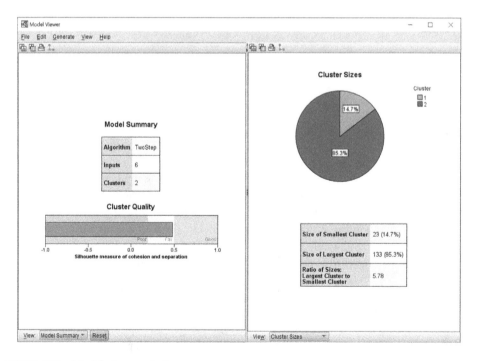

FIGURE 6.24   Model viewer window

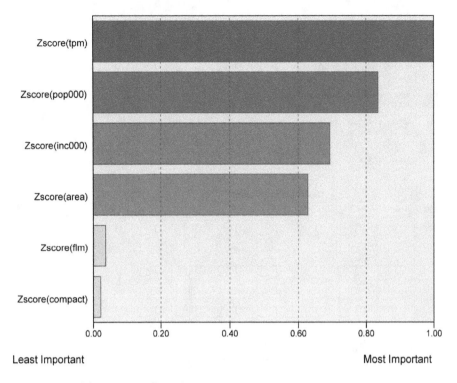

FIGURE 6.25   Model viewer: predictor importance

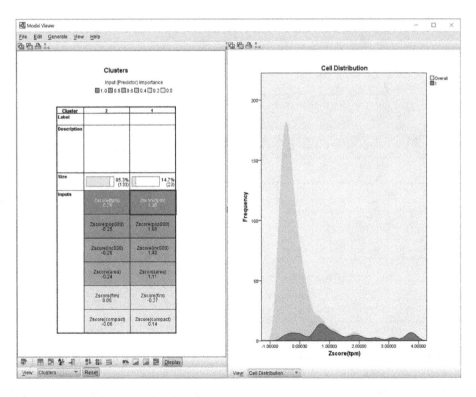

FIGURE 6.26   Model viewer: clusters summary

```
library(foreign)
uza <- read.spss("UZA.sav", to.data.frame = TRUE)
options("scipen" = 100, digits = 4)

uza_cl <- data.frame(scale(uza[,c("pop000", "inc000", "area", "flm", "tpm", "compact")]))
d <- dist(uza_cl)

uza_hc <- hclust(d, method = "ward.D2")
uza$hc_clust <- cutree(uza_hc, 4)

plot(uza_hc, cex = 0.5)
rect.hclust(uza_hc, k = 4)
```

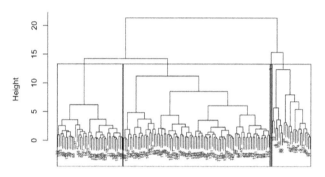

Cluster Dendrogram

FIGURE 6.27 Reading SPSS data ("UZA.sav"), selecting a set of variables, and running a hierarchical clustering: R script and outputs

```
library(NbClust)
uza_nbclust <- NbClust(uza_cl, distance = "euclidean",
                        min.nc = 2, max.nc = 10, method = "ward.D2")

## *** : The Hubert index is a graphical method of determining the number of clusters.
##                 In the plot of Hubert index, we seek a significant knee that corresponds to a
##                 significant increase of the value of the measure i.e the significant peak in Hubert
##                 index second differences plot.
##

## *** : The D index is a graphical method of determining the number of clusters.
##                 In the plot of D index, we seek a significant knee (the significant peak in Dindex
##                 second differences plot) that corresponds to a significant increase of the value of
##                 the measure.
##
## *******************************************************************
## * Among all indices:
## * 5 proposed 2 as the best number of clusters
## * 6 proposed 3 as the best number of clusters
## * 2 proposed 4 as the best number of clusters
## * 2 proposed 5 as the best number of clusters
## * 5 proposed 6 as the best number of clusters
## * 1 proposed 9 as the best number of clusters
## * 2 proposed 10 as the best number of clusters
##
##                       ***** Conclusion *****
##
## * According to the majority rule, the best number of clusters is   3
##
##
## *******************************************************************
```

FIGURE 6.28 Finding an optional number of clusters using Nbclust function: R script and outputs

Source: Charrad et al., 2014

Note: "NbClust" function provides 26 validation indices of clustering such as Calinski and Harabasz index and Silhouette index.

```
set.seed(1234)
uza_km <- kmeans(uza_cl, 3, nstart = 10)
```

```
uza_km$size
```

```
## [1] 66 12 79
```

```
uza_km$centers
```

```
##      pop000  inc000     area     flm     tpm compact
## 1 -0.2856 -0.3581 -0.4310 -0.6641 -0.2184  0.5558
## 2  2.5166  1.2692  2.4635 -0.5333  2.2874  0.6651
## 3 -0.1437  0.1063 -0.0141  0.6358 -0.1650 -0.5654
```

```
uza_cl$kmeans <- uza_km$cluster
head(uza_cl)
```

```
##    pop000 inc000     area     flm     tpm compact kmeans
## 1 5.3194 0.2002  2.3920 -0.7588 1.2530  1.8256      2
## 2 1.0665 2.4619  0.3450 -0.3240 3.7237  3.0299      2
## 3 8.4022 1.4064  6.5682 -1.0245 7.1120  1.8709      2
## 4 0.2419 2.3162 -0.2855 -0.4229 0.6716  1.0212      1
## 5 1.5949 3.1699  1.3004 -0.7309 3.8603  0.6827      2
## 6 2.1149 0.1641  1.4458 -0.9961 0.4827  0.7910      2
```

FIGURE 6.29   Running a *k*-means clustering and assigning a cluster membership to data: R script and outputs

to add the cluster membership back to the original data. One useful piece of information is contained in the object *centers*. This is the centroid values for each cluster, and can help interpretation. Here, the first and second cluster represent dense, compact areas, but where cluster one represent small, low population areas, and two highly populated large areas. Cluster three has low values for the compact index, and can be considered to represent sprawling regions.

Planning Examples

Classification of Neighborhoods

In their 2007 article for the *Journal of Urban Design*, Song and Knaap systematically developed a neighborhood typology using cluster analysis (CA). They then used their neighborhood typology to track the locations of all new single-family homes built within the Portland, Oregon, metro boundary for the year 2000—a total of 6,788 homes. They added to the discussion of urban growth boundary efficacy and policy implications by being able to track new home development relative to neighborhood typology location rather than by census or zip code boundaries. As the authors succinctly note, "[C]lassification facilitates understanding. Human cognition is improved when complex ideas and multiple attributes are organized and structured in a few well-defined constructs" (p. 1).

The authors began by identifying 21 urban form measures (such as lot size) and reducing these down to eight factors (or dimensions) using factor analysis. From these eight factors, six neighborhood types were identified using cluster analysis (see Figure 6.30). A bar graph depicts values for each of the eight factors typical of each of the six neighborhood types. The neighborhood types range from "Sporadic Rural Developments" (Cluster 1) to "Outer Ring Suburbs" (Cluster 3) to "Downtown, Inner and Middle Ring Suburban Redevelopments/

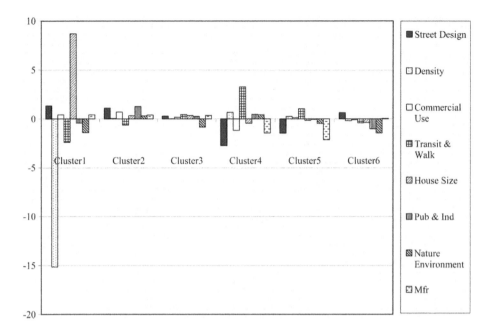

FIGURE 6.30   Eight measures (legend on the right of the graph) result in six clusters or neighbor-hood types. Values shown are for cluster centroids.

Source: Song, Y., & Knaap, G. (2007). Quantitative classifi cation of neighbourhoods: The neighbourhoods of new single-family homes in the Portland metropolitan area. Journal of Urban Design, 12(1), 1–24. copyright © The American Planning Association, www.planning.org, reprinted by permission of Taylor & Francis Ltd, http://www.tandfonline.com on behalf of The American Planning Association

Infill" (Cluster 4). The authors then used these clusters to assign each new single-family home to one of six distinct neighborhood settings, without having to rely on arbitrary administrative boundaries.

While the authors note limitations, such as the use of only physical characteristics (while excluding other important variables such as socioeconomic dimensions), they nonetheless provide a clear framework for further analysis. The authors further provide a detailed discussion of each neighborhood type, emphasizing the need for clear expert interpretation of cluster analysis results.

Transit-Oriented Development (TOD) Typology

In 2014, an article in *Journal of Transport Geography* (Kamruzzaman, Baker, Washington, & Turrell, 2014) utilized cluster analysis to classify neighborhoods based on transit-oriented development (TOD) attributes. In this article, TOD is defined as "moderate to high density development with diverse land use patterns and well connected street networks centered around high frequency transit stops (bus and rail)" (p. 54).

This research utilizes data from census collection districts (CCDs) (average population of about 500) in Brisbane, Australia, with different sets of TOD attributes measured across six objectively quantified built environmental indicators: net employment density, net residential density, land use diversity, intersection density, cul-de-sac density, and public transport accessibility (PTAL). A distinctive feature of this study is that, unlike previous research studies that predominantly focused on transit stations to define neighborhood boundaries (e.g., half mile from stations), it included whole CCDs in Brisbane in order to include potential *development-oriented transit* sites in the analysis.

Using these measures, a two-step cluster analysis was conducted to identify natural groupings of the CCDs with similar profiles. The analysis resulted in four unique TOD clusters: (1) non-TODs, (2) activity center TODs, (3) potential TODs, and (4) residential TODs (Figure 6.31). The cluster quality, measured by the Silhouette Index (Rousseeuw, 1987), was in the *Fair* range. Net employment density was found to have greater influence in forming the clusters followed by net residential density, and PTALs (Figure 6.31). Figure 6.32 presents the spatial distribution of the four clusters in Brisbane.

Input (predictor) importance

◼ 1.0 ◼ 0.8 ◼ 0.6 ▢ 0.4 ▢ 0.2 ▢ 0.0

Cluster	1	2	3	4
Label	Non-TOD	Activity Centre TOD	Potential TOD	Residential TOD
Size	28.7% (497)	9.9% (171)	46.7% (809)	14.8% (257)
Inputs	Employment density 2.66	Employment density 64.85	Employment density 3.63	Employment density 7.48
	Residential density 12.67	Residential density 32.72	Residential density 17.67	Residential density 35.44
	PTALs 1.65	PTALs 7.62	PTALs 3.84	PTALs 8.72
	Cul-de-sac density 0.22	Cul-de-sac density 0.16	Cul-de-sac density 0.09	Cul-de-sac density 0.13
	Land use diversity 0.32	Land use diversity 0.57	Land use diversity 0.47	Land use diversity 0.55
	Intersection density 0.52	Intersection density 0.74	Intersection density 0.64	Intersection density 0.77

FIGURE 6.31   Cluster analysis results showing the types of neighborhoods in Brisbane

Source: Reprinted from Kamruzzaman, M., Shatu, F. M., Hine, J., & Turrell, G. (2015). Commuting mode choice in transit oriented development: Disentangling the effects of competitive neighbourhoods, travel attitudes, and self-selection. Transport Policy, 42, 187–196. with permission from Elsevier

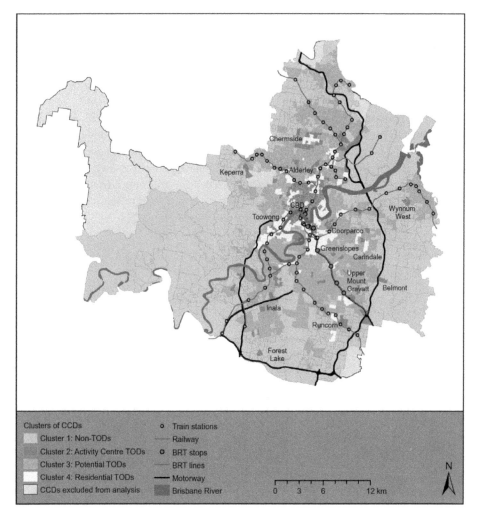

FIGURE 6.32 Spatial distribution of clusters in Brisbane

Source: Reprinted from Kamruzzaman, M., Shatu, F. M., Hine, J., & Turrell, G. (2015). Commuting mode choice in transit oriented development: Disentangling the effects of competitive neighbourhoods, travel attitudes, and self-selection. Transport Policy, 42, 187–196. with permission from Elsevier

Automobile mode share was highest in the non-TOD group (88.6%), followed by potential TODs (81.5%), activity center TODs (74.0%), and residential TODs (68.6%). On the contrary, transit share was highest in residential TODs (18.7%), and the mode share of walking and biking were high similarly in both types of TODs (12.4% in activity center TODs and 11.8% in residential TODs), while being lowest in non-TODs (2.3%).

The authors then used multinomial logistic regression to investigate the choice of 10,013 individuals living in the TOD typologies. Results indicated that, in comparison to people living in residential TODs, people who reside in non-TOD clusters were significantly less likely to use public transport (1.4 times) and active transport (4 times). People living in areas classified as potential TODs were 1.3 times less likely to use transit and 2.5 times less likely to use active transport. Only a little difference in mode choice was evident between residential TODs and activity center TODs.

Another paper by the lead author (Kamruzzaman, Shatu, Hine, & Turrell, 2015) used the same clustering approach and finds that urban TODs enhance the use of public transit and reduce car usage while there was no significant difference in the commuting behavior between traditional suburbs and TADs (transit-adjacent developments, the *evil-twin* of TODs). These studies demonstrate that a typology of TODs (or any urban form) could be developed based on their profile and performance matrices using cluster analysis. These typologies are data-driven but have the advantage of being independent of decisions made in defining administrative boundaries.

Conclusion

Cluster analysis determines how many *natural* groups there are in the data. These typologies are data-driven but have the advantage of being independent of decisions made in defining administrative boundaries.

Applying the methods in practice, however, requires considerable care. Different clustering approaches (e.g., hierarchical versus *k*-means) or different similarity rules (e.g., complete versus average linkage) will generate different results, and it is important to understand the impact of these choices. Often, testing a variety of different methods may improve your interpretation and help chose the best solution. Tools exist to help in this comparison step but must be coupled with a theoretical understanding of the dataset in question.

For example, significant differences between clusters can be examined with ANOVA testing.

Works Cited

Acquah, H. D. G. (2010). Comparison of Akaike information criterion (AIC) and Bayesian information criterion (BIC) in selection of an asymmetric price relationship. *Journal of Development and Agricultural Economics, 2*(1), 1–6.

Anderberg, M. R. (1973). *Cluster analysis for applications.* London: Academic Press.

Anglim, J. (2007). *Cluster analysis and factor analysis* [PowerPoint slides]. Retrieved from http://jeromya nglim.blogspot.com/2009/09/teaching-resources.html

Bailey, K. D. (1975). Extending closed plane curves to immersions of the disk with *n* handles. *Transactions of the American Mathematical Society, 206,* 1–24. https://doi.org/10.1090/S0002-9947-1975-0370621-3

Burns, R. P., & Burns, R. (2009). Cluster analysis. In *Business research methods statistics using SPSS.* Los Angeles, CA: Sage Publications.

Calinski, T., & Harabasz, J. (1974). A dendrite method for cluster analysis. *Communications in Statistics— Theory and Methods, 3*(1), 1–27.

Charrad, M., Ghazzali, N., Boiteau, V., Niknafs, A., & Charrad, M. M. (2014). Package 'nbclust'. *Journal of Statistical Software, 61,* 1–36.

Cole, A. J. (1969). *Numerical taxonomy.* London: Academic Press.

Driver, H. E., & Kroeber, A. L. (1932). Quantitative expression of cultural relationships. *University of California Publications in American Archaeology and Ethnology, 31,* 211–256.

Everitt, B. S. (1974). *Cluster analysis*. London: Heinemann Education Books.

Everitt, B. S., Landau, S., Leese, M., & Stahl, D. (2011). *Cluster analysis* (5th ed.). New York, NY: Oxford University Press.

Fayyad, U., Piatetsky-Shapiro, G., & Smyth, P. (1996). *Knowledge discovery and data mining: Towards a unifying framework*. Retrieved from www.aaai.org/Papers/KDD/1996/KDD96-014.pdf

Fisher, W. D. (1969). *Clustering and aggregation in economics*. Baltimore, MD: John Hopkins.

Gan, G., Ma, C., & Wu, J. (2007). *Data clustering: Theory, Algorithms, and applications*. Philadelphia, PA: Society for industrial and applied mathematics (SIAM).

Green, P. E., Frank, R. E., & Robinson, P. J. (1967). Cluster analysis in test market selection. *Management Science, 13*(8), B387–B400. https://doi.org/10.1287/mnsc.13.8.B387

Hodson, F. R., Sneath, P. H. A., & Doran, J. E. (1966). Some experiments in the numerical analysis of archaeological data. *Biometrika, 53*(3–4), 311–324.

Jardine, N., & Sibson, R. (1971). *Mathematical taxonomy*. New York, NY: John Wiley & Sons.

Kamruzzaman, M., Baker, D., Washington, S., & Turrell, G. (2014). Advanced transit oriented development typology: Case study in Brisbane, Australia. *Journal of Transport Geography, 34*, 54–70.

Kamruzzaman, M., Shatu, F. M., Hine, J., & Turrell, G. (2015). Commuting mode choice in transit oriented development: Disentangling the effects of competitive neighbourhoods, travel attitudes, and self-selection. *Transport Policy, 42*, 187–196.

Kaufman, L., & Rousseeuw, P. J. (1990). *Finding groups in data: An introduction to cluster analysis*. New York, NY: John Wiley & Sons.

Maguire, E. (2011). *Taxonomy in biology and visualization*. Retrieved from files.figshare.com/96920/taxonomy.pdf

Norušis, M. J. (2008). Cluster analysis. In *SPSS 17.0 statistical procedures companion*. Upper Saddle River, NJ: Prentice Hall. Retrieved from www.norusis.com/pdf/SPC_v13.pdf

Odell, P. L., & Duran, B. S. (1974). Comparison of some classification techniques. *IEEE Transactions on Computers, 100*(6), 591–596. https://doi.org/10.1109/T-C.1974.223999

Pilowsky, I., Levine, S., & Boulton, D. M. (1969). The classification of depression by numerical taxonomy. *British Journal of Psychiatry, 115*(525), 937–945. https://doi.org/10.1192/bjp.115.525.937

Ray, D. M., & Berry, B. J. (1965). Multivariate socioeconomic regionalization: A pilot study in central Canada. *Regional Statistical Studies*, 1–48.

Rousseeuw, P. J. (1987). Silhouettes: A graphical aid to the interpretation and validation of cluster analysis. *Journal of Computational and Applied Mathematics, 20*, 53–65. https://doi.org/10.1016/0377-0427(87)90125-7

Schwarz, J. (2014/2011). *Research methodology: Tools, Applied data analysis (with SPSS)*; Lecture 03/04: Cluster analysis. Retrieved from www.schwarzpartners.ch/Applied_Data_Analysis/Lecture%2003_EN_2014%20Cluster%20Analysis.pdf

Scoltock, J. (1982). A survey of the literature of cluster analysis. *The Computer Journal, 25*(1), 130–134. https://doi.org/10.1093/comjnl/25.1.130

Sneath, P. H. A., & Sokal, R. R. (1973). *Numerical taxonomy*. San Francisco, CA: Freeman.

Sokal, R. R., & Sneath, P. H. A. (1963). *Principles of numerical taxonomy*. San Francisco, CA: Freeman.

Song, Y., & Knaap, G. (2007). Quantitative classification of neighbourhoods: The neighbourhoods of new single-family homes in the Portland metropolitan area. *Journal of Urban Design, 12*(1), 1–24. https://doi.org/10.1080/13574800601072640

Tryon, R. C. (1939). *Cluster analysis: Correlation profile and orthometric (factor) analysis for the isolation of unities in mind and personality*. Ann Arbor, MI: Edwards Brothers.

Tryon, R. C., & Bailey, D. E. (1970). *Cluster analysis*. New York, NY: McGraw-Hill.

UNT (University of Northern Texas). (2013). *Information research and analysis lab*. Retrieved from http://txcdk.unt.edu/iralab/cluster-analysis

Wingo, L. (1967). Recent patterns of urbanization among Latin American countries. *Urban Affairs Quarterly, 2*(3), 81–109. https://doi.org/10.1177/107808746700200304

Zhang, T., Ramakrishnon, R., & Livny, M. (1996). *BIRCH: An efficient data clustering method for very large databases*. Proceedings of the ACM SIGMOD Conference on Management of Data, Montreal, Canada, pp. 103–114.

Zubin, J. A. (1938). A technique for measuring like-mindedness. *Journal of Abnormal and Social Psychology, 33*.

7

MULTILEVEL MODELING

*Zacharia Levine, Robert Young, Roger Child,
Brian Baucom, Reid Ewing, and John Kircher*

Overview

In this chapter, you will learn about a special class of regression techniques. *Multilevel modeling*
(MLM) builds upon the theory and procedures of linear regression (see Chapter 12 of *Basic*
Quantitative Research Methods for Urban Planners). However, MLM provides even greater flexibility when working with the general linear model. Before heading into this more sophisticated case of regression analysis, make sure you are comfortable with regression analysis
generally.

Researchers use MLM to analyze data that have nested structures and, as a result, violate
the assumption of independence of observations (cases) in standard regression models. Units
at lower levels of organization share (depend on) characteristics of higher levels of organization, which creates this dependence. A classic case is household travel. It depends not only on
characteristics of the household, such as size and income level, but on characteristics of the
neighborhood and region. Individual households in the same neighborhood share characteristics of the neighborhood, such as density. Neighborhoods in the same region share characteristics of the region, such as fuel price. Variables at all three levels may affect household travel,
but relationships are complicated by the nesting structure.

This chapter explains when to use MLM, why nested data require MLM, how common
models work, how to interpret output from MLM software packages, and how MLM has
been applied in planning studies.

We emphasize the application of statistical analysis and inference to planning. The underlying mathematics are of less importance to planners primarily interested in factors that affect
community planning, but we still need to understand them. Familiarizing yourself with the
mathematics will ensure appropriate usage of MLM and improve your ability to interpret
effects and to diagnose problems and irregularities. We refer planners who need additional
background and technical information to the Works Cited at the end of this chapter, especially Singer and Willet (2003) for conceptual background, and Raudenbush and Bryk (2002),
de Leeuw, Meijer, and Goldstein (2008), or Hox and Roberts (2011) for mathematical and
technical background.

Researchers refer to multilevel modeling by various names. Multilevel modeling, mixed-effects modeling, random-effects modeling, random coefficients regression, covariance component modeling, and hierarchical linear modeling all refer to the same set of statistical methods. Choose the term that follows the convention in your discipline or that makes the most sense to your target audience. We prefer multilevel modeling (MLM).

While many statistical software packages contain multilevel modeling tools, we hereafter refer to a specific software package, Hierarchical linear and nonlinear modeling (HLM) v7.00 (Raudenbush, Bryk, & Congdon, 2011). HLM provides a good environment in which to learn MLM because the series of equations it uses to build a model makes it easy to illustrate many of the important concepts we cover here. As presented in previous chapters, we also use SPSS for data management. An R script is also provided. Other programs that can handle multilevel models include aML, EGRET, GENSTAT, GLLAMM, MIXREG, MLwiN, MPlus, R, SAS, S-Plus, SPSS, STATA, SYSTAT, and WINBUGS. Each has its own merits, and they all accurately estimate model outcomes. For more information on these programs, visit the University of Bristol's Centre for Multilevel Modeling at www.bristol.ac.uk/cmm/learning/mmsoftware/.

Purpose

Multilevel modeling has gained popularity in the urban planning literature because of its ability to account for the structure of data. In research on urban planning, data often possess nested structures. Nesting occurs when scores from individuals within a group are more similar to one another than they are to scores from individuals in other groups. The subject of interest may be individual behavior, but each individual belongs to a larger group in the linear model of an individual's score, and the group mean contributes to the score for the individual. Random differences among group means are called *random effects*. Differences among groups explained by the model are called *fixed effects*. For example, the mean age of members of a group could partly explain why some groups outperform others.

In general, differences among group means, whether they are fixed or random, explain why observations within the same group are more similar to each other than observations sampled from different groups. The greater the variance among group means, the more distant the scores for one group will be from those of other groups, and, relatively speaking, the more similar the scores within each group will be to one another.

MLMs sometimes represent data structures where each group belongs to an even higher unit of organization: one *level* of data is *nested* within another *level* of data. When there is significant variance among higher-order units, characteristics of those units, such as size, diversity, climate, and the like could be used by MLM to explain that higher-order variance.

To characterize a level, a variable must describe a population from which you can draw samples. For instance, a state could serve as a level of nesting because counties within states can be sampled; a country could serve as a level of nesting because states within countries can be sampled; a continent could serve as a higher level of nesting because countries within continents can be sampled. Beyond continent, we have no options for even higher levels of nesting. Earth would not serve as an appropriate level of nesting because there is only one Earth, and its lower levels of nesting (e.g., continent, country, and state) could not be compared to similar levels on another Earth. As researchers go to ever higher levels of data organization, the number of observations at each level diminishes. Maas and Hox (2005) offer an in-depth presentation of sample sizes and what constitutes a level in MLM.

Schweitzer and Zhou (2010) illustrate the concept of hierarchical nesting. This study examined the relationship between air quality, respiratory health, and urban development patterns. The researchers employed a multilevel model where individuals were nested within neighborhoods, which were nested within regions. By collecting air quality information from monitoring stations scattered throughout 80 regions and 539 neighborhoods, Schweitzer and Zhou showed that compact development tends to reduce ozone *concentrations*. However, they also found that compact development tends to increase ozone *exposures* for everyone, including those at risk of respiratory health problems.

When we attune our minds to nested data structures, we begin to see them in many contexts: Residents are nested within cities, counties are nested within metropolitan areas, transit stops are nested within transportation corridors, and open spaces are nested within green infrastructure networks. For example, Ewing et al. (2010) used MLM to investigate individual trip making and specifically whether trips stayed in the same area or left it and, if they left it, whether their mode of travel was by transit, walking, or automobile. Trips were nested within mixed-use developments (MXDs), and MXDs were nested within regions (Figure 7.1). Consistent built environment measures characterized the MXDs and regions and explained reductions in external automobile trips.

We can easily expand our view beyond physical or geographical nesting. Repeated measures studies can create hierarchical structures. If we collect information about individuals over time, then the repeated measurements on an individual are grouped under that individual. Alcock, White, Wheeler, Fleming, and Depledge (2014) uses longitudinal data to explore mental health impacts of moving to greener or less green urban environments. The authors tracked individual responses to the UK's General Health Questionnaire over a five-year time period and limited their study to individuals who moved residences between years two and three. The responses at each time point were nested within individuals. Alcock et al. (2014) tested three response hypotheses (see Figure 7.2):

1. An immediate improvement to mental health following a move to a greener area, followed by a return to normalcy (e.g., *adaptation*),
2. An immediate improvement followed by a plateau (e.g., *shifting baseline*), and
3. An improvement in mental health after a period of time following the move (e.g., *sensitization*).

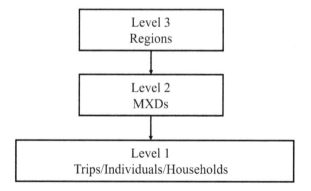

FIGURE 7.1   Hierarchical data structure

Source: Ewing et al., 2010, p. 255; with permission from ASCE

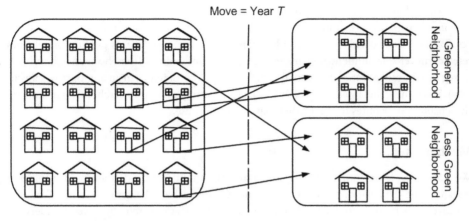

Residents move to greener or less green areas between years (*T*–0) and (*T*+1). Five repeated measures of the GHQ are then nested within individuals.

FIGURE 7.2   Research design and nesting structure

Source: Based on Alcock et al., 2014, p. 1248

The authors of both studies used MLM as a way to account for the nested structure of their data. Repeated measures may exhibit growth or decay over time, which MLM can also handle.

In this chapter, we only consider simple hierarchical data structures, but other forms of nesting do exist. Cross-classified, partial, and incomplete nesting also appears in planning research. Meta-analysis, a nuanced form of literature review, has benefited greatly from MLM. For examples of how planning researchers use these forms of nesting, see Ewing, King, Raudenbush, and Clemente (2005), and Bartholomew and Ewing (2008). Clearly, multilevel models can help us answer a wide range of planning research questions.

History

The origins of multilevel modeling trace back to the nineteenth century, when sociologists began researching contextual effects on individual behavior. Marx explored this idea through political economy, and Durkheim examined how community characteristics can lead to suicide. However, modern mathematical techniques used to analyze contextual questions did not exist until the mid-twentieth century (Larzarsfeld, 1959; Blau, 1960; James & Stein, 1961; Larzarsfeld & Menzel, 1961). By the 1980s, MLM techniques were used in a variety of social science fields, but perhaps no application became as iconic as education research.

Bryk and Raudenbush (1992) greatly extended the use of modern computer science for MLM analysis and provided us with many examples from education research. Education presents a classic case of nesting, with students nested within classrooms and classrooms nested within schools. Student achievement depends on characteristics at all three levels: the individual student (e.g., parents' education), classroom (e.g., student–teacher ratio), and school (e.g., school size). There is obvious dependence of students in the same classroom and of classrooms in the same school.

The first application of MLM in community planning research was not published until relatively recently. Ewing, Schmid, Killingsworth, Zlot, and Raudenbush (2003) explored the relationship between urban form and various physical health metrics. The study found that individuals living in more compact counties exhibited slightly lower body mass indices (BMIs) than individuals living in less compact counties. Before its publication, planning research never split influential characteristics among individuals, households, neighborhoods, or regions. In other words, contextual effects were not considered (in an appropriate statistical way). Since then, the application of MLM has grown in planning research. It is our hope that this chapter contributes to the further expansion of its use.

Mechanics

We now provide an introduction to the way basic multilevel models are used in planning research. The explanations that follow are not meant to be exhaustive. As with all research endeavors, we must continually refine our methods to meet research objectives. Readers who want to learn only how to apply MLM may skip to the next session.

In Chapter 12 of *Basic Quantitative Research Methods for Urban Planners*, you learned about linear regression (ordinary least squares, or OLS). The use of these regression models depends on satisfying basic assumptions of independence and homoscedasticity. The residual error and the independent variables must be independent of one another.

MLM offers a workaround in scenarios where the data fail to meet these assumptions.

OLS Assumptions of Independence

Suppose we want to analyze the impacts of residential environment on BMI, as in Doyle, Kelly-Schwartz, Schlossberg, and Stockard (2006). In a traditional OLS model, we might include a range of individual- and county-level characteristics as independent variables and set BMI as the dependent variable. However, the outputs of our model would tell a biased story. We may see false (e.g., too small) OLS estimates of the standard errors for our county predictors' values. Artificially low standard errors can lead to Type 1 errors, where we incorrectly reject a true null hypothesis (Cheah, 2009). Moreover, OLS estimates will be inefficient. Why does this happen?

Individuals who live in the same county share all the county-level characteristics, which means they are not independent. In other words, residents within the same county are more similar to one another than to residents of different counties. The nature of group dynamics can create a significant influence on the characteristics of individuals. In this case, MLM techniques model the hierarchical data structure (e.g., individuals nested within counties) and thereby remove the source of nonindependence in error components.

Bias Using OLS Work-Arounds

Prior to the advent of modern mathematical techniques used in MLM, researchers would attempt to manipulate hierarchical data to analyze them as single-level problems. However, manipulating nested data to satisfy OLS assumptions has drawbacks (de Leeuw & Kreft, 1986).

Aggregation bias, or up-sampling, refers to the aggregation of data at lower levels up to the higher level of analysis. An individual characteristic, such as BMI, can be aggregated up to the neighborhood level by assigning to a neighborhood the average BMI of its residents.

Disaggregation bias, or down-sampling, refers to the disaggregation of data at higher levels down to the lower level of analysis. A neighborhood characteristic, such as whether it is high density or low density, can be disaggregated to the individual level by assigning to each resident the density classification of the neighborhood.

In either case, it may seem that our traditional, unilevel regression techniques would suffice. But aggregation and disaggregation present methodological and statistical issues. First, doing either changes the meaning of our variable. Second, by aggregating data, we lose all within-neighborhood variation, which can lead to the Robinson effect or ecological fallacy. The Robinson effect refers to a significant increase in correlation among variables following aggregation. The ecological fallacy refers to unjustified claims that correlations between aggregated variables are representative of the correlations between variables measured at the individual level (de Leeuw & Kreft, 1986). MLM techniques enable us to preserve methodological and statistical accuracy.

You can both aggregate and disaggregate data using the household dataset provided with this book, which will help you identify the problems with each. Level-1 data provide individual household travel records and associated predictor variables, and level-2 data provide place characteristics, those specific to the region. As a class exercise, using SPSS, you can aggregate and compute the means of level-1 variables and then merge the mean values into the level-2 dataset. Using linear regression, you can then model mean VMT per household (the variable is actually the natural logarithm of VMT) in terms of mean household characteristics from level-1 and regional characteristics from level-2. You have averaged out most of the variance in the level-1 dataset. You will find that the R-squared is low, the regression coefficients make no sense, and the t-statistics are not significant due to the large standard errors, which, in turn, are due to small sample size.

Alternatively, as a class exercise, you can merge your level-2 place characteristics into your level-1 household characteristics, so that every household from the same region has the same values of the regional characteristics. Inspecting the dataset, you will see repeat values of the regional characteristics. It looks odd since you are used to datasets where observations are independent. Using linear regression, you can then model household-level VMT against individual household characteristics from level 1 and regional characteristics from level 2. Because there is so little variance in the regional characteristics, linear regression will produce very small standard errors for the coefficients of regional characteristics, and very high t-statistics and significance levels. From the regional level, regional population (a proxy for region size) and regional compactness have the expected signs, but fuel price does not. Again, the regression results cannot be trusted.

Additional Benefits of MLM

Multilevel modeling allows us to partition variance between lower levels of data (e.g., individuals) and higher levels of data (e.g., counties). Neither OLS nor any other regression technique partitions variance in this way. MLM enables an analyst to explain the variance at each level using variables specific to that level. In MLM, some of the total variance will be associated with lower-level units such as individuals, and some will be associated with higher-level units such as counties (Doyle et al., 2006). The individual variance will often be at least partly explained by individual sociodemographic variables, while county-level variance will be at least partly explained by county characteristics such as size or wealth.

Another distinguishing characteristic of MLM is its ability to handle unbalanced data. This refers to situations where your higher levels (e.g., counties) contain varying lower-level (e.g., individual) sample sizes. Other regression techniques, such as repeated measures analysis of variance (ANOVA), cannot handle unbalanced data, and any case with missing data is either dropped from the analysis or imputed. Using iterative model estimation techniques, such as maximum and restricted maximum likelihood estimation, MLM can use all of the available data. As in Doyle et al. (2006), it is not a problem that the number of BMI scores collected differs across counties. Counties that provide only a small number of BMI scores still contribute information that is used in model estimation (though less information than counties with large numbers of BMI scores). It is easy to see why MLM has become a widely used statistical method.

Mathematics of Multilevel Modeling

MLM software generates an intercept (constant) and two types of estimates for regression coefficients (slopes). The software first fits a regression equation for each group of individuals at the lowest level. Thus, for each group, we obtain an estimate of the intercept and estimates of regression coefficients for each of the level-1 independent variables. The intercept estimates are usually considered a random variable, whereas the coefficient estimates can be either fixed or random effects.

It is common practice to first estimate the coefficients as though they were random and then, if the variance among coefficients across groups is not statistically significant, to treat the coefficients as fixed. A fixed effect is the overall average estimate of a given parameter across all groups. A random effect, on the other hand, is the difference between the coefficient for a group and the grand mean coefficient. As such, the random effects terms take on different values for each group. In this manner, the characteristics of groups help to explain variance in the group-level parameters and thus allow for the testing of fixed effects, random effects, and interactions within and between levels.

While the following is a simplification, it will make MLM more understandable to the reader. This is the way Raudenbush and Bryk (2002), the leaders in the field, teach MLM. The multilevel models can be characterized as pairs of linked statistical models. At the first level (level 1), outcomes are modeled within each second-level (level 2) group as a function of respondent characteristics plus a random error. Thus, each group has a group-specific regression equation that describes the association between level-1 outcomes and level-1 independent variables. At level 2, the place-specific intercept and coefficients are conceived as outcomes and are modeled in terms of group characteristics plus random effects.

In some MLM models, only the place-specific intercepts vary across places, while all of the place-specific regression coefficients are fixed (invariant) across places. These are often termed *random intercept* models, to denote that only the intercept randomly varies. In other MLM models, the place-specific regression coefficients randomly vary as well. These are often termed *random coefficient* models.

Baseline Model

In the interest of clarity, we introduce the MLM equations using a simplified research design from Ewing et al. (2010): We have a cross-section of data on individual trips (level 1) starting and ending in mixed-use developments (level 2). For now, we'll ignore the effects of regional variables (level 3). We want to measure the impact that mixed-use developments (MXDs) have on travel behavior. Before adding a single predictor variable, we can see the basic structure of a multilevel model.

The level-1 equation takes the following form:

$$Y_{ij} = \beta_{0j} + r_{ij}$$

where

Y_{ij} is the vehicle miles traveled (VMT) for trip i, which begins and ends within an MXD j,
β_{0j} is the mean VMT for all trips in MXD j, and
r_{ij} is the *individual effect*, that is, the deviation of individual trip i from the MXD mean VMT. These random effects are assumed normally distributed with mean 0 and variance σ^2.

The level-2 model, also known as the group equation, takes the following form:

$$\beta_{0j} = \gamma_{00} + \mu_{0j}$$

where

γ_{00} is the grand (overall) mean VMT across all trips in all MXDs, and
u_{0j} is the *group effect*, that is, the deviation of MXD j from the grand mean VMT.

Substituting the level-2 equation into the level-1 equation yields the mixed model.

$$Y_{ij} = \gamma_{00} + u_{0j} + r_{ij}$$

You may recognize that our mixed model takes the same form as the one-way random-effects ANOVA model, with grand mean γ_{00} (fixed effect), group effect u_{0j} (random effect), and individual effect r_{ij} (random effect). In the absence of predictor variables, this mixed model is also known as a fully unconditional random-intercept model. The fully unconditional model is essential for showing us how much variance in VMT exists within and across MXDs.

With that in mind, we seek to explain the variance at each level through measured variables specific to individual trips and MXDs. Adding predictor variables at any level helps to further explain differences among the slopes and intercepts and hence explain variance in VMT. Broadly speaking, more complex models allow us to look at random intercepts (intercepts as outcomes), random coefficients (slopes as outcomes), and intercepts and slopes as outcomes. Additionally, we may choose to include cross-level interactions, nonlinearities, or other nuanced elements.

Random-Intercept Model

In the *random-intercept model*, we introduce one or more level-2 predictors to explain variance in group intercepts (mean VMT per MXD). From Ewing et al. (2010), we want to see if MXD land area (square miles) and intersection density (intersections per squares mile) impact VMT at the group level. Our level-1 model stays the same, but our level-2 model becomes:

$$\beta_{0j} = \gamma_{00} + \gamma_{01} AREA_j + \gamma_{02} INTDEN_j + u_{0j}$$

Substituting this equation into the level-1 equation yields the following mixed model:

$$Y_{ij} = \gamma_{00} + \gamma_{01} AREA_j + \gamma_{02} INTDEN_j + u_{0j} + r_{ij}$$

The random intercept model helps to explain variance at both levels of nesting. Again, γ_{00} represents the grand mean of VMT across all trips. The term u_{0j} indicates the residual variability of a group's (MXD) mean VMT about the value predicted by AREA and INTDEN. The term r_{ij} indicates the variability of an individual trip's VMT about the group (MXD) mean. A significant γ_{01} represents the effect of land area on an individual trip's VMT within the given MXD. If γ_{01} is positive, the data suggest that, as MXD area increases, so does VMT. Conversely, if γ_{01} is negative, the data suggest the opposite is true: As MXD area increases, VMT decreases. The parameter that represents a relationship between intersection density and VMT (γ_{02}) can be interpreted in the same way.

Random-Coefficients Model

In the *random-coefficients model*, we introduce a single level-1 predictor as a covariate and allow it to vary across MXDs. From Ewing et al. (2010), we select household size (number of members in household) as a level-1 predictor of travel behavior. The new level-1 model becomes:

$$Y_{ij} = \beta_{0j} + \beta_{1j} HHSIZE_{ij} + r_{ij}$$

The new level-2 model becomes:

$$\beta_{0j} = \gamma_{00} + u_{0j}$$
$$\beta_{1j} = \gamma_{10} + u_{1j}$$

The mixed model becomes:

$$Y_{ij} = \gamma_{00} + \gamma_{10} + u_{0j} + u_{1j} HHSIZE_{ij} + r_{ij}$$

As before, we interpret γ_{00} as the grand mean intercept, u_{0j} as deviations of MXD intercepts about the grand mean intercept, and r_{ij} as the deviations of individual trips about MXD means controlling for household size. In this model, γ_{10} represents the grand mean slope or average linear relationship between household size and VMT, and u_{1j} indicates the difference between the slope for group j and the grand mean slope. We can then compare the relative amounts of variance explained by the random-intercept model and the random-coefficients model.

Intercepts- and Slopes-as-Outcomes Model

In the random-intercept model, we allowed the level-1 *intercept* to vary randomly across MXDs. In the random-coefficients model, we allowed the level-1 *slopes* to vary randomly across MXDs. In the intercepts- and slopes-as-outcomes model, we include predictors at level-1 and level 2 and allow both the level-1 intercept and the level-1 slope to vary. This model is also sometimes referred to as a *random-coefficients model*.

Treating HHSIZE as a predictor of household travel behavior, the level-1 model becomes:

$$Y_{ij} = \beta_{0j} + \beta_{1j}HHSIZE_{ij} + r_{ij}$$

Including AREA and INTDEN as predictors of household travel behavior, the level-2 model becomes:

$$\beta_{0j} = \gamma_{00} + \gamma_{01}AREA_j + \gamma_{02}INTDEN_j + u_{0j}$$

$$\beta_{1j} = \gamma_{10} + \gamma_{11}AREA_j + \gamma_{12}INTDEN_j + u_{1j}$$

The mixed model becomes:

$$Y_{ij} = \gamma_{00} + \gamma_{01}AREA_j + \gamma_{02}INTDEN_j + u_{0j} + \gamma_{10}HHSIZE_{ij} + \gamma_{11}AREA_jHHSIZE_{ij} +$$
$$\gamma_{12}INTDEN_jHHSIZE_{ij} + u_{1j}HHSIZE_{ij} + r_{ij}$$

Notice that when we have predictors at both levels, we introduce cross-level interactions. Here, the cross-level interactions are between household size and area and between household size and intersection density. In plain language, this says that the coefficient of household size in the level-1 model will vary with both the area and the intersection density of the MXD. This means that VMT will vary with both, due to effects on both the intercept and the coefficients. It may be, for example, that VMT is more sensitive to household size in larger MXDs due to known variations in mode shares with household size.

"In general, hierarchical linear models may involve multiple level-1 predictors where any combination of random, nonrandomly varying, and fixed slopes can be specified" (Raudenbush & Bryk, 2002, p. 28). This speaks to the flexibility of MLM.

Step by Step

MLM analysis can be performed in multiple software including HLM, SPSS, R, Stata, and Mplus. Hierarchical linear and nonlinear modeling (HLM) (Raudenbush et al., 2011) is a convenient choice for its ease of use. You can download its student edition for free.

To download the most recent version of the student edition HLM, go to www.ssicentral. com/hlm/student.html. This exercise uses HLM 7.03. Note that the student version limits the sample sizes to 8,000 (level 1) and 350 (level 2). For a level-3 model, the maximum number of observations at levels 1, 2, and 3 is approximately 8,000, 1,700 and 60, respectively. Also, no more than five independent variables at each level of the model can be included. Also, note that the HLM works only for Windows. At the end of this Step-by-Step section, we also present an R script to run MLM, which works for both Windows and Mac OS.

In this exercise, we model household travel, especially household VMT. As previously introduced, it depends not only on characteristics of the household, such as size and income level, but on characteristics of the region. We use two files: "HTS.household.10regions.sav" and "HTS.region.10regions."

Treating household size (*hhsize*) and household income (*lnhhincome*) as predictors of household VMT (*lnvmt*), the level-1 model becomes:

$$lnvmt_{ij} = \beta_{0j} + \beta_{1j}hhsize_{ij} + \beta_{2j}lnhhincome_{ij} + r_{ij}$$

Including regional population (*regpop*) and compactness index (*compact*) as predictors of VMT, the level-2 model becomes:

$$\beta_{0j} = \gamma_{00} + \gamma_{01} regpop_j + \gamma_{02} compact_j + u_{0j}$$

Due to the limitation of the student edition, we first need to reduce the size of the household dataset. In SPSS, open "HTS.household.10regions.sav" and go to "Data" → "Select Cases." (See Figure 7.3.)

Click on the "Sample" button under "Random sample of cases," and then enter "50" to select 50% of all cases (Figure 7.4). Then select "Copy selected cases to a new dataset," enter a dataset name (e.g., "HTS.household.sample"), and click on "OK."

About half of the original households will appear in a new dataset. Save the dataset as a separate SPSS file (e.g., "HTS.household.sample.sav").

Now we are ready to run multilevel modeling in HLM. Open HLM—whatever version you have; in this example, we use HLM 7.03 student version. (See Figure 7.5.)

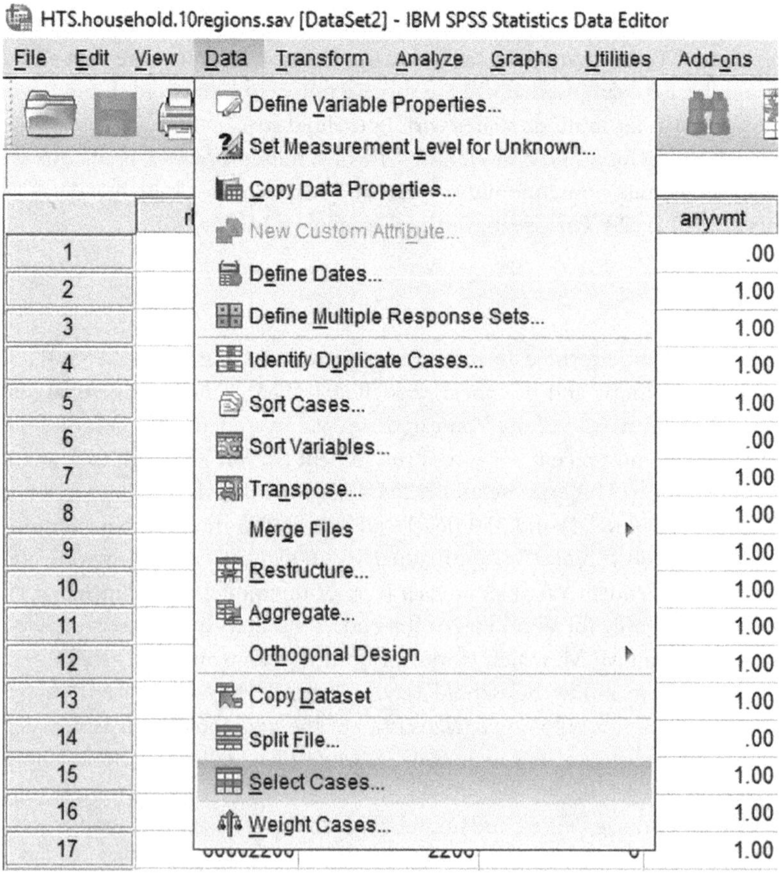

FIGURE 7.3 Go to "Select Cases" menu to reduce the sample size

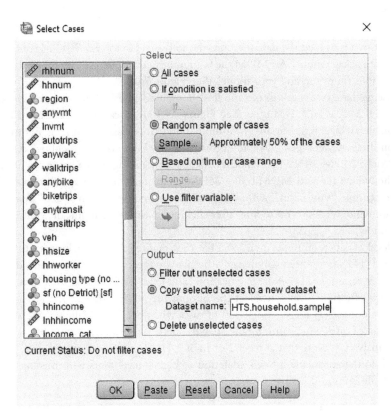

FIGURE 7.4 "Select Cases" window

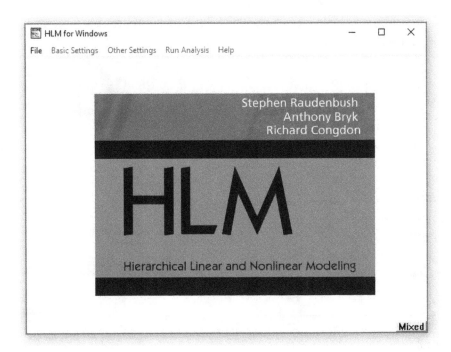

FIGURE 7.5 "HLM for Windows" screen

The first step is to load the data files into the software. Go to "File" → "Make new MDM file" → "Stat package input." An MDM file is an intermediate file used by HLM that contains the instructions for estimating your model. (See Figure 7.6.)

Because we have two levels in our model—household at level 1 and region at level 2—— we select "HLM2" as an MDM type. (See Figure 7.7.) HLM can analyze three or four levels of nesting, hierarchical multivariate linear models, and cross-classified models. For more information on these model types, please refer to the HLMv7 manual (Raudenbush et al., 2011).

The "Make MDM—HLM2" window will appear. (See Figure 7.8.) First of all, we need to save the MDM file and MDMT file (MDM template). Enter an appropriate MDM file name, for example, "vmt.mdm," within "MDM File Name (use. mdm suffix)" box (top right of the main window) and "vmt.mdmt" after clicking on the "Save mdmt file" button (top left of the window).

Each level of data requires its own SPSS file. (See Figure 7.9.) By clicking on the "Browse" button, load "HTS.household.sample.sav" (the file you created when you reduced the original data by 50%) under "Level-1 Specification" and load "HTS.region.10regions.sav" under "Level-2 Specification." You can select the options for missing data in the level-1 file. Two available options are (1) list-wise deletion of cases when the MDM file is made and (2) list-wise deletion of cases when running the analysis. Here, we select the latter option ("Yes" and "running analyses"). Note that at level 2 or higher, HLM assumes complete data. Otherwise, HLM will do the automatic list-wise deletion of higher-level units with missing data when the MDM file is created.

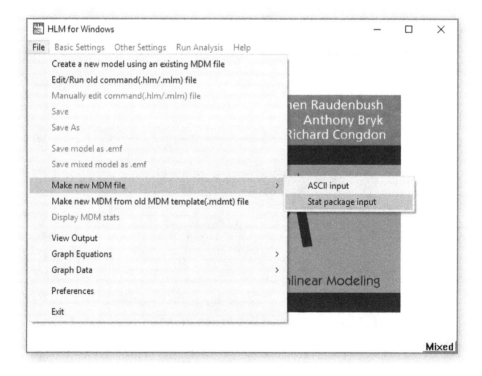

FIGURE 7.6   Reading SPSS data in HLM

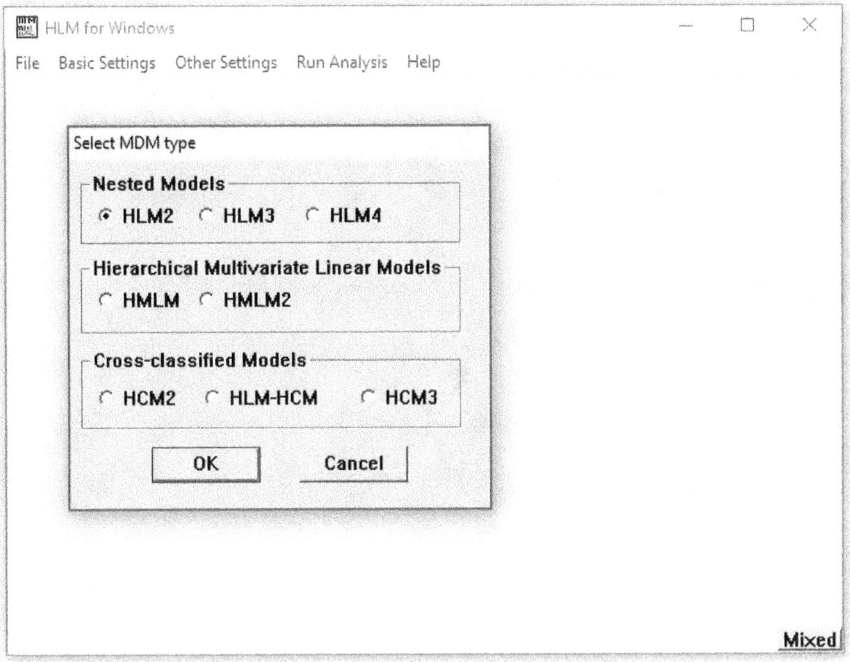

FIGURE 7.7 Select HLM2 as a modeling type

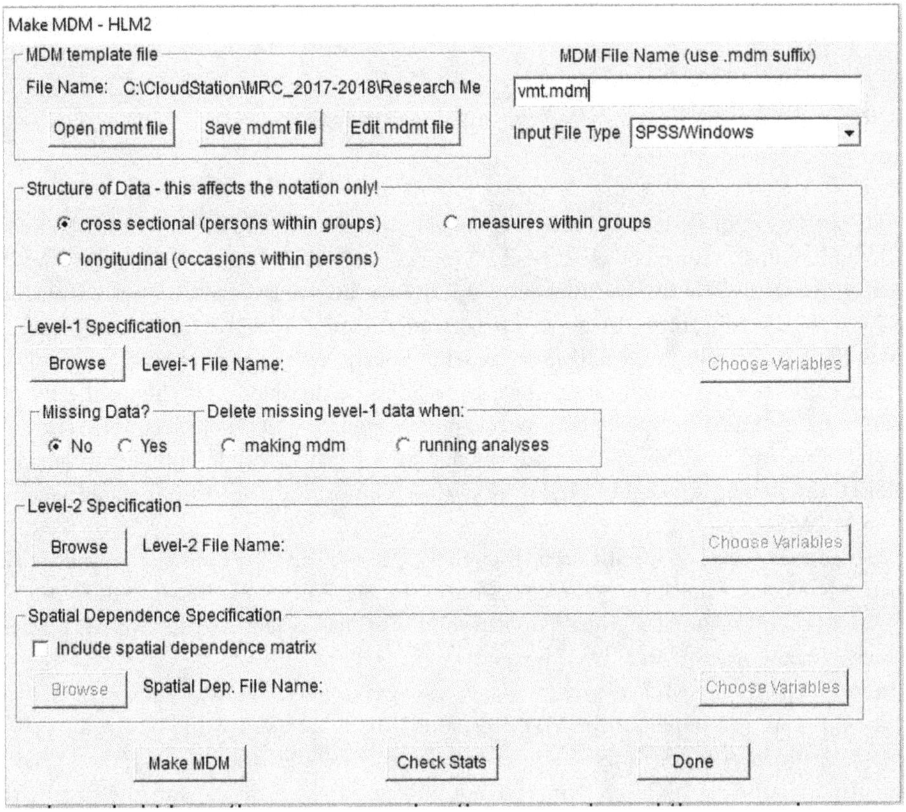

FIGURE 7.8 Saving MDM and MDMT files in "Make MDM" window

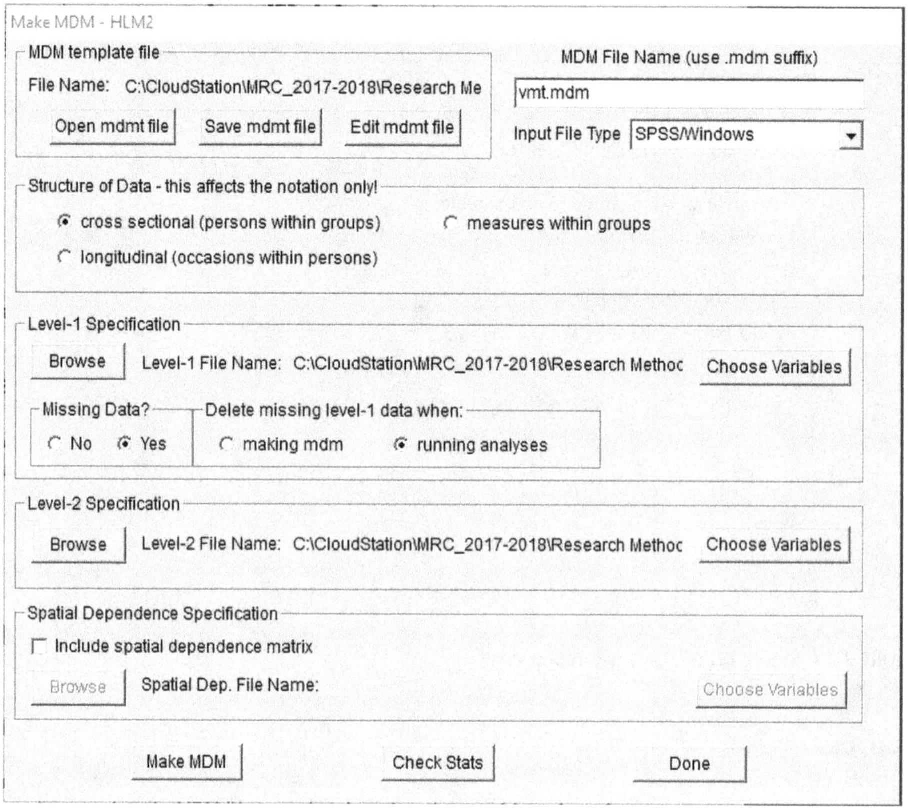

FIGURE 7.9 Loading SPSS data and selecting missing data options

The last step in this window is selecting variables included in the model at each level .

Both files must be sorted by the level-2 ID (if it's a three-level model, all three files must be sorted by the level-3 ID first and then level-2 ID). Two files are linked by a level-2 ID, which is REGION in our example. To assure this assumption, sort the level-1 file by the level-2 ID field in SPSS before you run HLM (our dataset is already sorted appropriately).

Under the "Level-1 Specification" box, click "Choose Variables" and choose the ID and variables by clicking the appropriate check boxes (Figure 7.10). We select REGION for the "ID" box and LNVMT (log-transformed value of VMT), VEH (number of vehicles), HHSIZE (household size), and LNHHINCO (log-transformed value of household income) for "in MDM" boxes.

Then, under "Level-2 Specification" box, click "Choose Variables" and choose the ID and variables by clicking the appropriate check boxes (Figure 7.11). We select REGION for the "ID" and REGPOP (total regional population), FUEL (gas price), and COMPACT (compactness index score) for "in MDM" boxes.

In the main "Make MDM" window, click the "Make MDM" button. A screen displaying the prompts and responses for MDM creation will appear. When the screen disappears, the level-1 and level-2 descriptive statistics will automatically be displayed (Figure 7.12). Pay particular attention to the N column. It is not uncommon to forget to sort the data by the

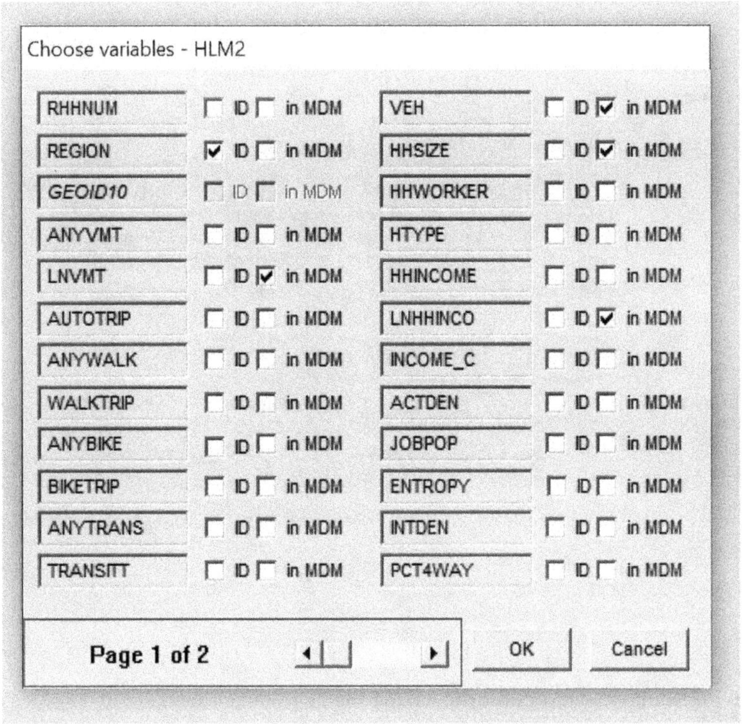

FIGURE 7.10 Choosing variables at level 1

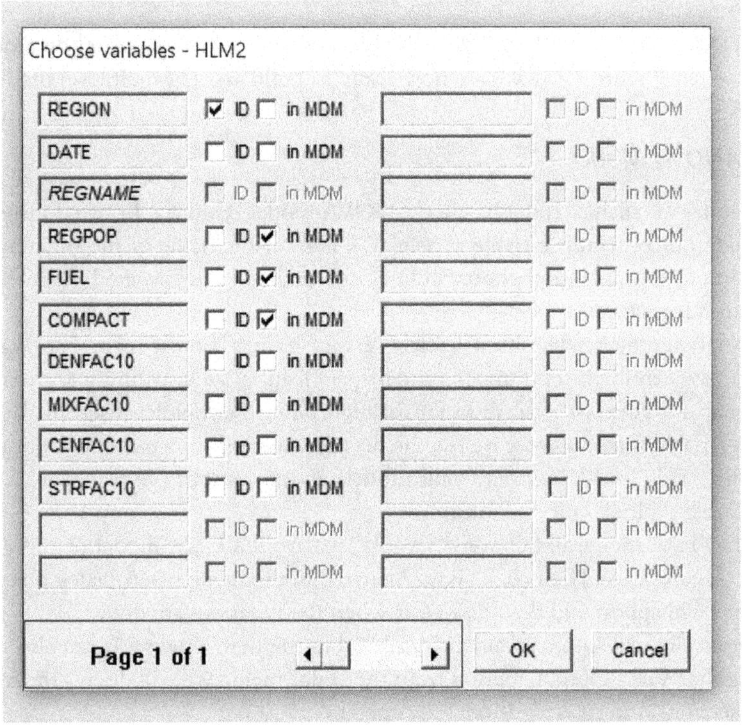

FIGURE 7.11 Choosing variables at level 2

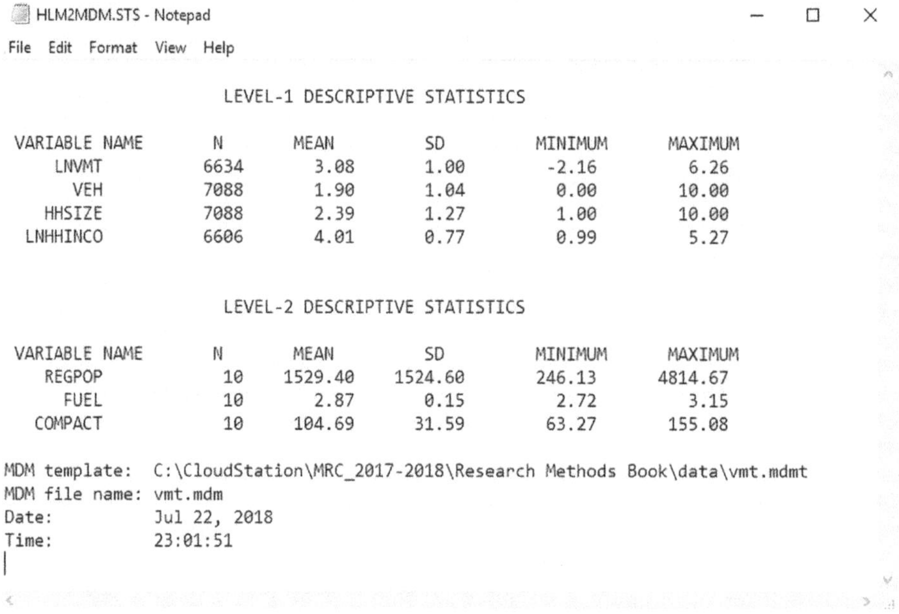

HLM2MDM.STS - Notepad — □ ✕

File   Edit   Format   View   Help

```
              LEVEL-1 DESCRIPTIVE STATISTICS

VARIABLE NAME      N      MEAN       SD      MINIMUM     MAXIMUM
    LNVMT         6634    3.08      1.00     -2.16        6.26
      VEH         7088    1.90      1.04      0.00       10.00
   HHSIZE         7088    2.39      1.27      1.00       10.00
 LNHHINCO         6606    4.01      0.77      0.99        5.27


              LEVEL-2 DESCRIPTIVE STATISTICS

VARIABLE NAME      N      MEAN        SD      MINIMUM     MAXIMUM
   REGPOP         10    1529.40   1524.60    246.13     4814.67
     FUEL         10       2.87      0.15      2.72        3.15
  COMPACT         10     104.69     31.59     63.27      155.08
```

MDM template: C:\CloudStation\MRC_2017-2018\Research Methods Book\data\vmt.mdmt
MDM file name: vmt.mdm
Date: Jul 22, 2018
Time: 23:01:51

FIGURE 7.12   Descriptive statistics for the MDM file

ID variable, which can lead to lots of missing data. The descriptive statistics are automatically saved as "HLM2MDM.STS," but you can also save it with a different file name (e.g., "vmt_descriptive.txt").

Click "Done," and the HLM window displays the variables at each level on a drop-down menu on the left (Figure 7.13). We are now ready to build and test multilevel models.

Baseline ANOVA Model

The first model we analyze is the baseline ANOVA model (Figure 7.14). To do this, we must first designate our outcome variable at level 1. Click on the name of the outcome variable (LNVMT in our example), and choose "Outcome variable." The specified model will appear in an equation format.

After specifying the baseline model, select "Basic Settings" on the menu bar (Figure 7.15). This menu gives multiple options of model specification such as linear regression, logistic regression, and Poisson/negative binomial regression in a multilevel setting. Because our dependent variable is continuous, we use the default selection "Normal (Continuous)." Enter a title in the "Title" field (e.g., vmt-null model) and an output file name in "Output file name" field (e.g., "hlm2_vmt_null.html").

Open the "File" menu, and choose "Save As" to save the HLM model (e.g., "hlm2_vmt_null.hlm") (Figure 7.16). Then click "Run Analysis" in the menu bar. A dialog box displaying the iterations will appear and then disappear when the iterations are done.

The output file will automatically be displayed in the new window. It can also be opened by selecting the "View Output" option from the "File" menu. We will discuss the model output in the section, "Interpreting Model Parameters."

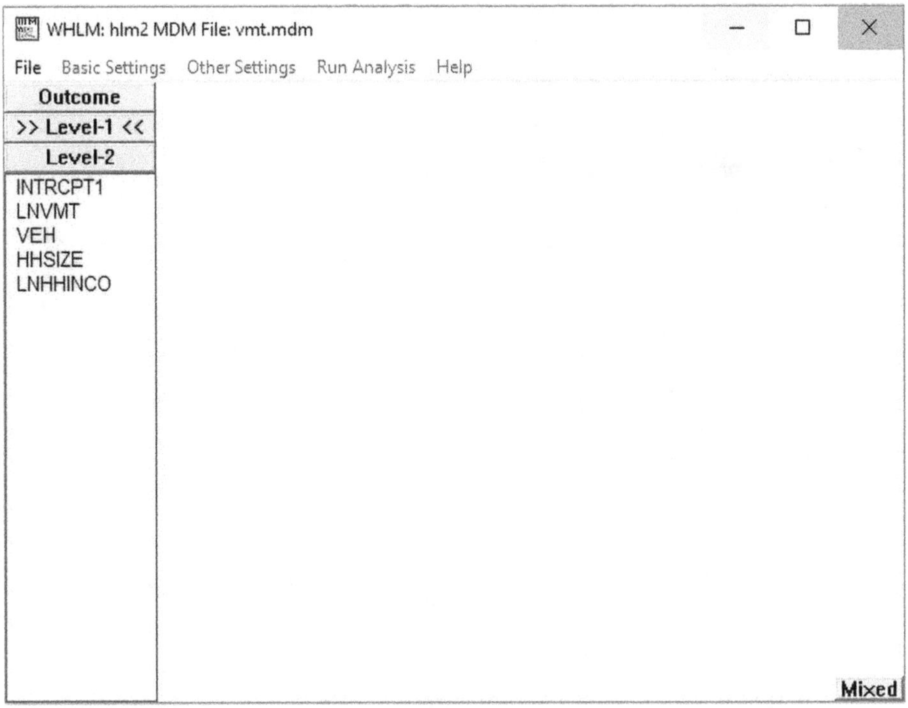

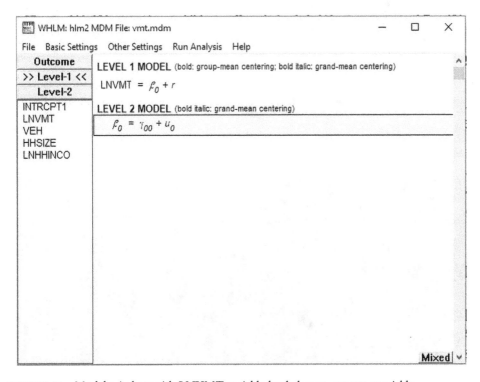

FIGURE 7.13   WHLM window with variables loaded

FIGURE 7.14   Model window with LNVMT variable loaded as an outcome variable

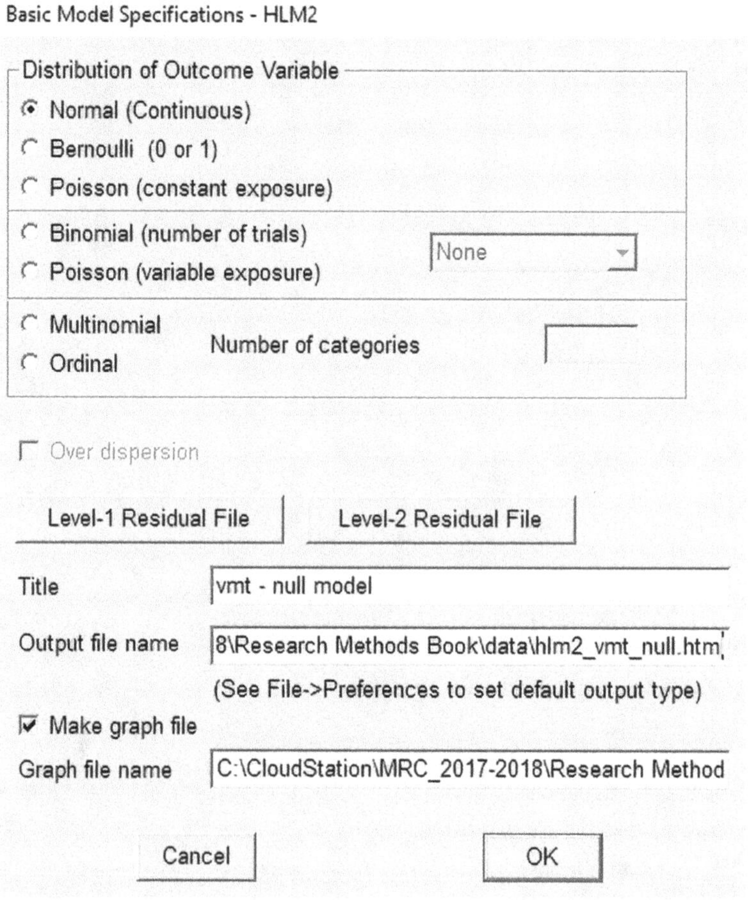

Basic Model Specifications - HLM2

Distribution of Outcome Variable

⊙ Normal (Continuous)

○ Bernoulli (0 or 1)

○ Poisson (constant exposure)

○ Binomial (number of trials)

○ Poisson (variable exposure)   None ▼

○ Multinomial

○ Ordinal   Number of categories ____

☐ Over dispersion

| Level-1 Residual File | Level-2 Residual File |

Title   vmt - null model

Output file name   8\Research Methods Book\data\hlm2_vmt_null.htm

(See File->Preferences to set default output type)

☑ Make graph file

Graph file name   C:\CloudStation\MRC_2017-2018\Research Method

| Cancel | | OK |

FIGURE 7.15   Basic model specification: "HLM2" dialog box for the baseline VMT model

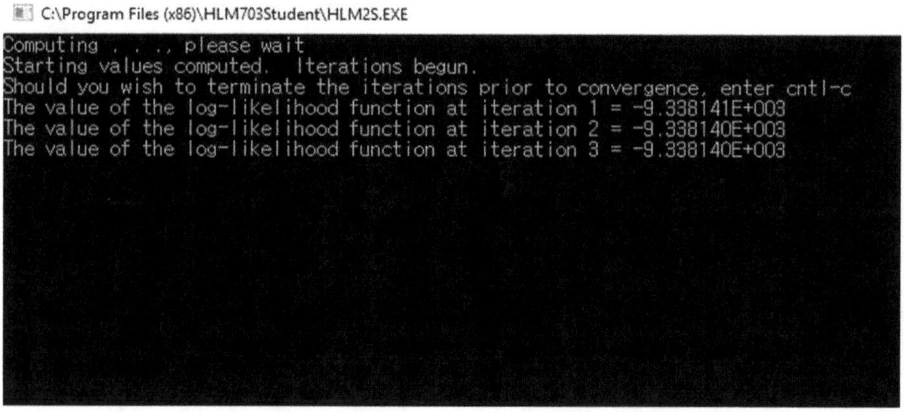

C:\Program Files (x86)\HLM703Student\HLM2S.EXE

```
Computing . . ., please wait
Starting values computed.  Iterations begun.
Should you wish to terminate the iterations prior to convergence, enter cntl-c
The value of the log-likelihood function at iteration 1 = -9.338141E+003
The value of the log-likelihood function at iteration 2 = -9.338140E+003
The value of the log-likelihood function at iteration 3 = -9.338140E+003
```

FIGURE 7.16   Iteration screen

Random-Intercept Model

Once we create the MDM file, it is simple to modify the models. To create the means-as-outcomes model from the baseline ANOVA model, we add predictor variables. Click on the "Level 2" button, then click on the name of a predictor variable, and click the type of centering. Here, we use "add variable uncentered." For additional details on centering and its influence on model interpretation, see Hofmann and Gavin (1998) and Enders and Tofighi (2007).

Click on the "Level 1" button to add VEH, HHSIZE, and LNHHINCO variables at level 1, and then click on the "Level 2" button to add REGPOP, FUEL, and COMPACT variables at level 2. The specified model will look like the image in Figure 7.17.

Before running the random-intercept model, make sure that you change the title and output file name (in the "Basic Settings" menu) and save the model (in the "Save As" menu).

Interpreting Model Parameters

In this section, we turn to the goal of statistical analysis: interpreting model parameters. We refer to the model outputs produced by HLM for our baseline ANOVA and random-intercept models. We introduce the concepts of the Intraclass Correlation Coefficient (ICC), fixed effects, and random effects.

Let's look at the model output we just ran with six predictor variables. The first part of the printout summarizes the model specifications (e.g., file names, number of units, and model equations). (See Figure 7.18.)

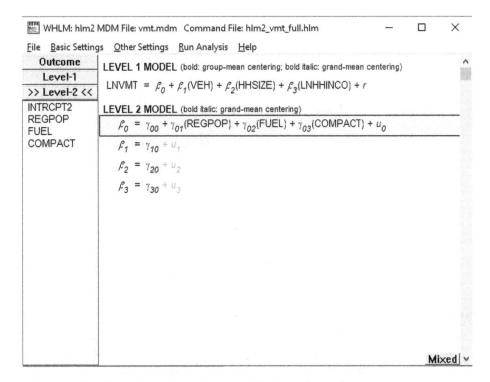

FIGURE 7.17   Model window with predictor variables loaded at both levels

Specifications for this HLM2 run

Problem Title: vmt - full model

The data source for this run = vmt2.mdm
The command file for this run = C:\CloudStation\MRC_2017-2018\Research Methods Book\data\HLM\hlm2_vmt_full.hlm
Output file name = C:\CloudStation\MRC_2017-2018\Research Methods Book\data\HLM\hlm2_vmt_full.html
The maximum number of level-1 units = 7088
The maximum number of level-2 units = 10
The maximum number of iterations = 100

Method of estimation: restricted maximum likelihood

The outcome variable is LNVMT

Summary of the model specified

Level-1 Model

$$LNVMT_{ij} = \beta_{0j} + \beta_{1j}*(VEH_{ij}) + \beta_{2j}*(HHSIZE_{ij}) + \beta_{3j}*(LNHHINCO_{ij}) + r_{ij}$$

Level-2 Model

$$\beta_{0j} = \gamma_{00} + \gamma_{01}*(REGPOP_j) + \gamma_{02}*(FUEL_j) + \gamma_{03}*(COMPACT_j) + u_{0j}$$
$$\beta_{1j} = \gamma_{10}$$
$$\beta_{2j} = \gamma_{20}$$
$$\beta_{3j} = \gamma_{30}$$

Mixed Model

$$LNVMT_{ij} = \gamma_{00} + \gamma_{01}*REGPOP_j + \gamma_{02}*FUEL_j + \gamma_{03}*COMPACT_j$$
$$+ \gamma_{10}*VEH_{ij}$$
$$+ \gamma_{20}*HHSIZE_{ij}$$
$$+ \gamma_{30}*LNHHINCO_{ij}$$
$$+ u_{0j} + r_{ij}$$

Run-time deletion has reduced the number of level-1 records to 6196

FIGURE 7.18   HLM output: model specifications

Final Results - Iteration 8

Iterations stopped due to small change in likelihood function

$$\sigma^2 = 0.78824$$

τ
INTRCPT1,β_0 0.03176

Random level-1 coefficient	Reliability estimate
INTRCPT1,β_0	0.918

The value of the log-likelihood function at iteration 8 = -8.091094E+003

FIGURE 7.19   HLM output: final model statistics

Figure 7.19 shows the estimates of the variance and covariance components from the final iteration and selected statistics based on them. σ^2 is a level-1 variance component, or an estimate of the unexplained level-1 variance (error). Tau, or τ, is a level-2 variance–covariance component, or an estimate of the variance of group means about the grand mean. The reliability estimate indicates the extent to which there are large, reliable differences among group means that might be explained by level-2 predictors (Raudenbush & Bryk, 2002). The deviance statistic provides a relative measure of model fit, where values closer to 0 indicate better model fit. It is calculated using the log-likelihood value of the maximum likelihood estimate of the model. As in OLS regression, models are often compared based on model fit. Using likelihood ratio tests that provide chi-squared values, researchers can determine the significance of improvements in model fit due to the inclusion or exclusion of predictor variables (Garson, 2013).

Deviance $= -2 *$ Log-likelihood

Whereas reliability is the proportion of variance among group means that is true-score variance (tau) and might be explained by group-level characteristics, the intraclass correlation coefficient (ICC) is the proportion of variance among level-1 outcome scores that might be explained by group-level characteristics. As you can see from the following equation, we divide the group-level variance by the total variance. In our example, we calculate an ICC value of 0.039, which equals $0.0318/(0.0318 + 0.7882)$. This indicates that 3.9% of the variation in household VMT can be attributed to regional characteristics. Further specification of the model is, in effect, an attempt to explain the level-1 within-region (σ^2) and level-2 between-region (τ) variances through measured variables.

$$ICC = \tau_{00} / (\tau_{00} + \sigma^2)$$

The tables in Figure 7.20 present the final estimates for the fixed effects with GLS (generalized least squares) and robust standard errors, respectively. With large sample sizes, we recommend using the second table with robust standard errors—the standard errors are the same, but the t-ratios and associated p-values are different between the two tables. Among the regional-level variables, only COMPACT is marginally significant at $p < .1$ level. The more compact a region is, the fewer VMT a household might generate. Among the household-level variables, all three variables are significant the at $p < .001$ level and have expected positive signs. The household VMT increases with the number of cars, the number of household members, and household income. As fixed effects, we could expect these relationships to hold across the 10 regions.

The last part (Figure 7.21) presents variance components at level 1 and level 2 and related test statistics. A pseudo-R2 can be computed by summing the variance components for the fitted model and comparing it to the variance components of the null model with intercepts (baseline ANOVA model) only.

Further Understanding of Random Effects

Multiple random effects, represented by u in the series of equations, can be included at any and all levels. We can interpret random effects based on the level in which they appear and the terms in which they appear. A level-1 random effect is conceptually similar to the residual error term in OLS models in that it represents the deviation of the predicted score for each data point, $\hat{Y}_{ij}$, from the observed score for each data point, Y_{ij}. At higher levels, each random effect is the difference between a group mean and grand mean of a given effect. Our baseline ANOVA model includes a random effect u_0 on the intercept.

Final estimation of fixed effects:

Fixed Effect	Coefficient	Standard error	t-ratio	Approx. $d.f.$	p-value
For INTRCPT1, β_0					
INTRCPT2, γ_{00}	1.571828	1.446562	1.087	6	0.319
REGPOP, γ_{01}	0.000065	0.000050	1.301	6	0.241
FUEL, γ_{02}	0.006615	0.577727	0.011	6	0.991
COMPACT, γ_{03}	-0.003219	0.002849	-1.130	6	0.302
For VEH slope, β_1					
INTRCPT2, γ_{10}	0.186056	0.013097	14.206	6183	<0.001
For HHSIZE slope, β_2					
INTRCPT2, γ_{20}	0.171610	0.009681	17.726	6183	<0.001
For LNHHINCO slope, β_3					
INTRCPT2, γ_{30}	0.243746	0.017411	14.000	6183	<0.001

Final estimation of fixed effects (with robust standard errors)

Fixed Effect	Coefficient	Standard error	t-ratio	Approx. $d.f.$	p-value
For INTRCPT1, β_0					
INTRCPT2, γ_{00}	1.571828	1.105589	1.422	6	0.205
REGPOP, γ_{01}	0.000065	0.000040	1.652	6	0.150
FUEL, γ_{02}	0.006615	0.384814	0.017	6	0.987
COMPACT, γ_{03}	-0.003219	0.001446	-2.226	6	0.068
For VEH slope, β_1					
INTRCPT2, γ_{10}	0.186056	0.011478	16.210	6183	<0.001
For HHSIZE slope, β_2					
INTRCPT2, γ_{20}	0.171610	0.011375	15.086	6183	<0.001
For LNHHINCO slope, β_3					
INTRCPT2, γ_{30}	0.243746	0.031912	7.638	6183	<0.001

FIGURE 7.20 HLM output: final model estimates

Final estimation of variance components

Random Effect	Standard Deviation	Variance Component	$d.f.$	χ^2	p-value
INTRCPT1, u_0	0.17821	0.03176	6	199.35756	<0.001
level-1, r	0.88783	0.78824			

Statistics for current covariance components model

Deviance = 16182.188451
Number of estimated parameters = 2

FIGURE 7.21 HLM output: variance components and associated statistics

Conceptually, this random effect means that in addition to estimating an overall average household VMT (log-transformed value), γ_{00}, we also estimate the variability of each region's average VMT about that grand mean. The magnitude of this variance estimate is reported in the "Final estimation of variance components" table (Figure 7.21) along with a statistical test of whether the amount of variance is significantly different from 0. In our example, the magnitude of the variance component is 0.03176 with a corresponding $\chi^2(4) = 199.358$, $p < .001$. These statistics indicate that there is significant variability in the estimated group-level averages about the overall average. Our ability to model and test the variability of group-level averages about the overall average is a powerful attribute of MLM. In our example, we found there was significant variability in the estimates of regional VMT averages. In an attempt to explain some of this variability, we created the means-as-outcomes model, which included regional population, compactness, and gas price as region-level predictors.

In R

Figures 7.22 through 7.24 show an R script to run a multilevel modeling for household VMT. Because the data are given as two SPSS files, we need to read both and merge them using *left_join* function (*dplyr* package; Figure 7.22). The *regname* column is used as a common field to join region dataset into household dataset. Note that in this R script, we don't need to

```
# MULTILEVEL MODELING
library(foreign)
hts<-read.spss("HTS.household.10regions.sav",to.data.frame=TRUE)
region<-read.spss("HTS.region.10regions.sav",to.data.frame=TRUE)
region$regname<-trimws(region$regname)
hts$regname<-as.character(hts$region)

library(dplyr)
hts.mlm<-left_join(hts,region,by="regname")
names(hts.mlm)
```

```
## [1] "rhhnum"        "hhnum"         "region.x"      "anyvmt"
## [5] "lnvmt"         "autotrips"     "anywalk"       "walktrips"
## [9] "anybike"       "biketrips"     "anytransit"    "transittrips"
## [13] "veh"          "hhsize"        "hhworker"      "htype"
## [17] "sf"           "hhincome"      "lnhhincome"    "income_cat"
## [21] "actden"       "jobpop"        "entropy"       "intden"
## [25] "pct4way"      "stopden"       "emp10a"        "emp20a"
## [29] "emp30a"       "emp30t"        "statefp10"     "countyfp10"
## [33] "tractce10"    "blkgrpce10"    "geoid10"       "intptlat10"
## [37] "intptlon10"   "veh_cat"       "regname"       "region.y"
## [41] "date"         "regpop"        "fuel"          "compact"
## [45] "denfac10"     "mixfac10"      "cenfac10"      "strfac10"
```

FIGURE 7.22 Reading two SPSS data (household travel survey and region data) and joining them using *dplyr* package: R script and outputs

```
library(lme4)
library(lmerTest)
mlm.base<-lmer(lnvmt~(1|regname),data=hts.mlm)
summary(mlm.base)

## Linear mixed model fit by REML. t-tests use Satterthwaite's method [
## lmerModLmerTest]
## Formula: lnvmt ~ (1 | regname)
##    Data: hts.mlm
##
## REML criterion at convergence: 37759.3
##
## Scaled residuals:
##      Min      1Q  Median      3Q     Max
## -7.2566 -0.5478  0.1388  0.6939  3.0157
##
## Random effects:
##  Groups    Name        Variance Std.Dev.
##  regname   (Intercept) 0.04293  0.2072
##  Residual              1.00141  1.0007
## Number of obs: 13285, groups:  regname, 10
##
## Fixed effects:
##              Estimate Std. Error      df t value Pr(>|t|)
## (Intercept)   3.12574    0.06689 9.29640   46.73 2.39e-12 ***
## ---
## Signif. codes:  0 '***' 0.001 '**' 0.01 '*' 0.05 '.' 0.1 ' ' 1
```

FIGURE 7.23   Running a multilevel regression model—a variance component model: R script and outputs

Note: lmerTest package provides *p*-values to multilevel model outputs.

reduce the sample size from the level-1 data, unlike the SPSS exercise where we sampled 50% of the data. The *lmer* function in *lm4* package allows to run a multilevel model with a continuous variable. We first run a variance component model (Figure 7.23) and a full model with three household-level predictors and three region-level predictors (Figure 7.24). The *lmerTest* package in Figure 7.23 allows us to see *p*-values associated with the independent variables in the summary table of a multilevel model.

Planning Examples

Quality of Life

Many built environment professionals claim that compact and mixed-use development fosters a higher quality of life (Leccess & McCormick, 2000; Smart Growth Network, 2006). Yang (2008) took aim at this conclusion by examining the relationship between urban form and an operationalized definition of quality of life—neighborhood satisfaction. Her objective was to determine if a well established theory holds up against empirical evidence.

Two questions motivated the research. First, do people who live in more compact and mixed-use environments express a higher level of satisfaction with their neighborhoods, all else being equal? And, second, do the associations between physical form characteristics and neighborhood satisfaction vary across spatial scales?

```
mlm1<-
lmer(lnvmt~veh+hhsize+lnhhincome+regpop+fuel+compact+(1|regname),data=hts.mlm
)
summary(mlm1)

## Linear mixed model fit by REML. t-tests use Satterthwaite's method [
## lmerModLmerTest]
## Formula: lnvmt ~ veh + hhsize + lnhhincome + regpop + fuel + compact +
##     (1 | regname)
##    Data: hts.mlm
##
## REML criterion at convergence: 32690.5
##
## Scaled residuals:
##     Min      1Q  Median      3Q     Max
## -7.4886 -0.5342  0.1147  0.6665  3.1710
##
## Random effects:
##  Groups   Name        Variance Std.Dev.
##  regname  (Intercept) 0.03913  0.1978
##  Residual             0.81020  0.9001
## Number of obs: 12410, groups:  regname, 10
##
## Fixed effects:
##               Estimate Std. Error         df t value Pr(>|t|)
## (Intercept)  1.674e+00  1.566e+00  6.082e+00   1.069   0.326
## veh          1.854e-01  9.480e-03  1.240e+04  19.552  <2e-16 ***
## hhsize       1.688e-01  7.006e-03  1.240e+04  24.087  <2e-16 ***
## lnhhincome   2.642e-01  1.236e-02  1.240e+04  21.374  <2e-16 ***
## regpop       6.778e-05  5.486e-05  5.942e+00   1.235   0.263
## fuel        -8.738e-02  6.239e-01  6.145e+00  -0.140   0.893
## compact     -2.313e-03  3.041e-03  6.438e+00  -0.761   0.474
## ---
## Signif. codes:  0 '***' 0.001 '**' 0.01 '*' 0.05 '.' 0.1 ' ' 1
##
## Correlation of Fixed Effects:
##            (Intr) veh    hhsize lnhhnc regpop fuel
## veh         0.001
## hhsize     -0.012 -0.328
## lnhhincome -0.017 -0.346 -0.105
## regpop      0.426  0.017 -0.014 -0.003
## fuel       -0.984 -0.001  0.009 -0.006 -0.519
## compact     0.522  0.006 -0.003 -0.009  0.567 -0.659
## fit warnings:
## Some predictor variables are on very different scales: consider rescaling
```

FIGURE 7.24 Running a multilevel regression model—a full model: R script and outputs

Note: lmerTest package provides p-values of multilevel model outputs.

To answer these questions, Yang (2008) set up hierarchical linear models using the SAS PROC MIXED procedure (Singer, 1998). Multilevel modeling was necessary in this case because OLS assumptions of independence were violated by the data structure. Individuals share block-level attributes, and blocks share neighborhood level attributes. Secondary benefits of this approach included controlling for spatial autocorrelation, where spatial clustering of sample points may have existed. For an extended discussion of spatial autocorrelation, see Chapter 9.

Yang (2008) compared neighborhood satisfaction scores of households throughout Portland, Oregon, and Charlotte, North Carolina. These metropolitan statistical areas (MSAs) have similar population, demographic, and housing type mixes but exhibit divergent land use policies and development patterns. Portland receives wide acclaim for its compact development, sometimes termed smart growth, whereas Charlotte is commonly cited as one of the least compact, or most sprawling, MSAs. Similarly, mixed-use development, a concept related to sprawl, varies across neighborhoods irrespective of their MSA.

Yang estimated two distinct models for each MSA. One set of models associated neighborhood-level physical form with average (pooled) neighborhood satisfaction. This highlighted the influence of neighborhood-level characteristics only. A second set of models associated neighborhood-level and block-level physical forms with individual reports of neighborhood satisfaction.

We present the outcomes (see Figure 7.25) and interpretations of the second set of models here and refer you to Yang (2008) for the outcomes and interpretations of the first set. The results may shed light on Yang's opening question: Does empirical evidence support the oft claimed positive association between built form and quality of life? At the neighborhood level, housing mix was the only attribute that significantly and positively correlated with neighborhood satisfaction, and then only in Charlotte. Model results for both MSAs indicated that a small increase in density from the baseline was significantly and negatively associated with neighborhood satisfaction. The Charlotte model suggested that open space within a block was positively associated with neighborhood satisfaction.

Homeownership and Poverty

Research on families in poverty indicates that both individual and community characteristics influence the way various challenges are experienced (Brooks–Gunn, Duncan, & Aber, 1997; Coulton & Pandey, 1992). In this study, Brisson and Usher (2007) operationalized the concept of social capital as informal neighborhood bonding and analyzed its relationship to homeownership in low-income neighborhoods.

Brisson and Usher hypothesized that informal neighborhood bonding could predict homeownership above and beyond other contextual characteristics such as income and duration of residence. The research design nested individuals (level 1) within low-income neighborhoods (level 2). Census block groups defined neighborhood boundaries, and 800 individual data points were extracted from a 2002–2003 survey titled "Making Connections," sponsored by the Annie E. Casey Foundation (AECF). The model included 410 neighborhoods from 10 cities with a mean of 14 individual respondents per neighborhood. As in the previous case study, city was not used as a level of nesting because just 10 units would have been insufficient for modeling the effects of city-level variables.

Informal neighborhood bonding social capital was a weighted composite score based on five distinct indicators. For a fuller explanation of the score, see Brisson and Usher (2007). Other independent variables included race, ethnicity, gender, and median income and duration of residence in the neighborhood. Homeownership, a dichotomous variable where 1 indicated ownership and 0 indicated something other than ownership, served as the dependent variable in this study. A multilevel model was needed to account for the nested data structure and to distinguish between individual and neighborhood sources of variability. The authors employed a random intercepts model so that neighborhoods could vary based on contextual characteristics affecting homeownership.

			Model A for Charlotte MSA, NC–SC		Model A for Portland–Vancouver MSA, OR–WA	
			Coeffic.	Std. error	Coeffic.	Std. error
Intercept			3.068	0.396**	4.386	6.485
Level 2: Neighborhood attributes						
Physical form variables	Density	Housing units per acre	–0.096	0.052	0.030	0.018[b]
	Land use mix	Jobs per resident	–0.042	0.031	0.025	0.017
	Street patterns	Factor score derived from other street pattern variables	0.050	0.044	–0.079	0.058
	Housing mix	Index of qualitative variation for housing structure types	0.438	0.209*	–0.029	0.128
Control variables	Socio-demographic	% White	0.004	0.002*	0.011	0.004**
		% age 25 and over with bachelor's degree or more	0.010	0.002**	0.011	0.002**
	Turnover	% of residents moved in between 1995 and 2000	–0.011	0.005**	–0.011	0.005*
	Housing	Median year structure built	0.000	0.002	0.000	0.003
Level 1: Individual and block attributes						
Physical form variables	Density/housing mix	Low density				
		Medium low density	–0.246	0.101*	–0.218	0.071**
		Medium high density	n/a	n/a	n/a	n/a
		High density	n/a	n/a	n/a	n/a
	Land use mix measures	Commercial and business land use within a block	–0.057	0.077	0.094	0.066
		Open space within a block	0.151	0.059*	0.076	0.059
		Recreational facilities in neighborhood	0.046	0.067	0.092	0.090
		Neighborhood stores within a mile	0.022	0.065	0.092	0.057
Control variables	Socio-demographic	Age of householder	0.007	0.002**	0.004	0.002*
		Married couple with children	0.110	0.059	0.133	0.064*
		Race of householder	0.067	0.064	–0.004	0.155
		Householder with high school education and above	0.141	0.072*	0.058	0.080
		Family income (log)	0.014	0.030	0.024	0.028
	Turnover	Length of residence (months)	0.000	0.000	0.000	0.000
	Neighborhood perception	Neighborhood crime	–0.545	0.076**	–0.410	0.064**
		Appearance index	–0.290	0.033**	–0.300	0.029**
		Bothersome situation exists	–0.725	0.077**	–0.591	0.063**
		Gated community	–0.073	0.176	0.292	0.139*
	Housing conditions	Owner occupied	–0.196	0.082*	–0.188	0.082*
		Single family detached unit	–0.071	0.122	–0.004	0.094
		Personal rating of housing unit quality	0.571	0.017**	0.483	0.017**
Random coefficient variance			0.035	0.021*	0.030	0.019
Residual			1.801	0.052**	1.719	0.049**
N			2,898		2,776	
PRE from intercept-only model		Neighborhood level	0.92		0.92	
		Residual	0.42		0.37	

Note:
Entries showing "n/a" mean that coefficients were not released for publication for these categorical variables with small sample sizes (<75). Coefficients for these two density variables were both negative in the two models, and t values for these variables show that they are not statistically significant.

$^0p < 0.1$ $^*p < 0.05$ $^{**}p < 0.01$

FIGURE 7.25 Hierarchical regression of neighborhood satisfaction on both neighborhood-level (level-2) and block-level (level-1) variables

Source: Yang, Yizhao. (2008). A tale of two cities: Physical form and neighborhood satisfaction in metropolitan Portland and Charlotte. Journal of the American Planning Association, 74(3), 307–323. copyright © The American Planning Association, www.planning.org, reprinted by permission of Taylor & Francis Ltd, http://www.tandfonline.com on behalf of The American Planning Association.

As with OLS regression, MLM is useful for hypothesis testing. Figure 7.26 shows the results for a series of model tests on homeownership. The results provided support for Brisson and Usher's hypothesis—informal neighborhood bonding social capital helped to explain

	Fully unconditional	Bonding only	Neighborhood only	Bonding and neighborhood
Individual level				
Bonding SC		1.36* (0.04)		1.36* (0.04)
Race: White[a]		2.96* (0.09)	2.89* (0.09)	3.01* (0.09)
Hispanic		1.61* (0.08)	1.47* (0.08)	1.48* (0.08)
Asian		2.22* (0.13)	2.21* (0.13)	2.24* (0.14)
Other Race		1.65* (0.13)	1.57* (0.15)	1.60* (0.14)
Gender (Female)		0.85* (0.05)	0.81* (0.06)	0.83* (0.06)
Neighborhood level				
Intercept (grand mean)	0.66* (0.05)	0.15* (0.16)	0.12* (0.16)	0.04* (0.21)
Income			1.03* (0.01)	1.02* (0.01)
Duration of residence			1.11* (0.01)	1.11* (0.01)
Random effects (variance)				
Neighborhood	0.90*	0.75*	0.43*	0.42*

*$p < 0.05$.
[a]The reference category for race/ethnicity is "Black" because the highest percentage of respondents in the sample is Black.

FIGURE 7.26 Odds ratios with standard errors in parentheses for random intercept models testing the effects of bonding social capital and neighborhood context on homeownership in low-income neighborhoods

Source: copyright © The American Planning Association, www.planning.org, reprinted by permission of Taylor & Francis Ltd, http://www.tandfonline.com on behalf of The American Planning Association.

variability in homeownership status more than neighborhood income and duration of residence alone.

The ICC for the baseline (unconditional) model, indicated that neighborhood context explained 21% of the variation in homeownership and individual-level characteristics explained *at most* 79% of the variation in homeownership. A dichotomous outcome variable means that we can interpret the coefficients as "likelihood ratios." According to the Bonding and Neighborhood model, a one-unit increase in a respondent's informal bonding social capital was associated with a 36% increase in the likelihood of homeownership.

Conclusion

This chapter focused on multilevel modeling (MLM), which is built on the theory and procedures of linear regression. We discussed the need for MLM, the benefits, and the structural equations that underlie the model. Then we presented the history, mechanics, and a step-by-step guide to perform MLM. There are various names for MLM (e.g., mixed-effects modeling, random-effects modeling), which can be conducted in various software packages (e.g. MLwiN, MPlus, R, SAS). We used HLM (v7) because of its representation of the structural equations at different levels, which made it possible to illustrate important concepts and R because of its flexibility and non-limitation of the model specification.

To recapitulate, MLM is ideally suited to analyze data that are hierarchically organized. Multilevel models attribute variance in the outcome variable to characteristics of the individual and to characteristics of the broader context in which the individual is nested. MLM provides unbiased estimates of the effects of independent variables at multiple levels as well as their interactions. To introduce MLM, we considered only simple hierarchical data structures, but other forms of nesting do exist. We refer you to the references section for more in-depth discussions MLM and these topics.

Works Cited

Alcock, I., White, M. P., Wheeler, B. W., Fleming, L. E., & Depledge, M. H. (2014). Longitudinal effects on mental health of moving to greener and less green urban areas. *Environmental Science & Technology, 48*(2), 1247–1255. https://doi.org/10.1021/es403688w

Anselin, L. (1988). *Spatial econometrics: Methods and models (studies in operational regional science).* The Netherlands: Springer.

Bartholomew, K., & Ewing, R. (2008). Land use—Transportation scenarios and future vehicle travel and land consumption: A meta-analysis. *Journal of the American Planning Association, 75*(1), 13–27. https://doi.org/10.1080/01944360802508726

Blau, P. M. (1960). Structural effects. *American Sociological Review, 25*, 178–193. https://doi.org/10.2307/2092624

Brisson, D. S., & Usher, C. L. (2007). Social capital in low-income neighborhoods. *Family Relations, 54*(5), 644–653. https://doi.org/10.1300/J079v34n01_01

Brooks-Gunn, J., Duncan, G. J., & Aber, J. L. (1997). *Neighborhood poverty: Context and consequences for children.* New York, NY: Russell Sage Foundation.

Bryk, A. S., & Raudenbush, S. W. (1992). *Hierarchical linear models: Applications and data analysis methods.* Newbury Park, CA: Sage Publications.

Cheah, B. C. (2009). *Clustering standard errors or modeling multilevel data.* New York, NY: Columbia University.

Coulton, C. J., & Pandey, S. (1992). Geographic concentration of poverty and risk to children in urban neighborhoods. *American Behavioral Scientist, 35*(3), 238–257. https://doi.org/10.1177/0002764 292035003004

de Leeuw, J., & Kreft, I. (1986). Random coefficient models for multilevel analysis. *Journal of Educational Statistics, 11*(1), 57–85. https://doi.org/10.3102/10769986011001057

de Leeuw, J., Meijer, E., & Goldstein, H. (2008). *Handbook of multilevel analysis.* New York, NY: Springer Science & Business Media.

Doyle, S., Kelly-Schwartz, A., Schlossberg, M., & Stockard, J. (2006). Active community environments and health: The relationship of walkable and safe communities to individual health. *Journal of the American Planning Association, 72*(1), 19–31. https://doi.org/10.1080/01944360608976721

Enders, C. K. (2010). *Applied missing data analysis.* New York, NY: Guilford Press.

Enders, C. K., & Tofighi, D. (2007). Centering predictor variables in cross-sectional multilevel models: A new look at an old issue. *Psychological Methods, 12*, 121–138. http://dx.doi.org/10.1037/1082-989X.12.2.121

Ewing, R., Greenwald, M., Zhang, M., Walters, J., Feldman, M., Cervero, R., . . . Thomas, J. (2010). Traffic generated by mixed-use developments—Six region study using consistent built environmental measures. *Journal of Urban Planning and Development, 137*(3), 248–261. https://doi.org/10.1061/(ASCE)UP.1943-5444.0000068

Ewing, R., King, M. R., Raudenbush, S., & Clemente, O. J. (2005). Turning highways into main streets: Two innovations in planning methodology. *Journal of the American Planning Association, 71*(3), 269–282. https://doi.org/10.1080/01944360508976698

Ewing, R., Pendall, R., & Chen, D. (2002). *Measuring sprawl and its impact: The character & consequences of metropolitan expansion.* Washington, DC: Smart Growth America.

Ewing, R., Schmid, T., Killingsworth, R., Zlot, A., & Raudenbush, S. (2008). Relationship between urban sprawl and physical activity, obesity, and morbidity. *American Journal of Health Promotion, 18*(1), 47–57. https://doi.org/10.1007/978-0-387-73412-5_37

Garson, D. (2013). *Hierarchical linear modeling: Guide and applications.* Thousand Oaks, CA: Sage Publications.

Hofmann, D. A., & Gavin, M. B. (1998). Centering decisions in hierarchical linear models: Implications for research in organizations. *Journal of Management*, *24*(5), 623–641. https://doi.org/10.1177%2F014920639802400504

Hox, J., & Roberts, J. K. (2011). *Handbook of advanced multilevel analysis*. New York, NY: Routledge.

James, W., & Stein, C. (1961). Estimation with quadratic loss. In J. Neyman (Ed.), *Proceedings of the fourth Berkeley symposium on mathematical statistics and probability* (Vol. 1, pp. 361–379). Berkeley and Los Angeles, CA: University of California Press.

Kreft, I. G. G., de Leeuw, J., & Aiken, L. S. (1995). The effect of different forms of centering in hierarchical linear models. *Multivariate Behavioral Research*, *30*(1), 1–21. https://doi.org/10.1207/s15327906mbr3001_1

Larzarsfeld, P. F. (1959). Problems in methodology. In R. K. Merton, L. Broom, & L. S. Cattrell (Eds.), *Sociology today*. New York, NY: Basic Books.

Larzarsfeld, P. F., & Menzel, H. (1961). On the relations between individual and collective properties. In A. Etzioni (Ed.), *Complex organizations*. New York, NY: Holt, Rinehart & Winston.

Leccess, M., & McCormick, K. (2000). *Charter of the new urbanism*. New York, NY: McGraw-Hill.

Maas, C. J. M., & Hox, J. (2005). Sufficient sample sizes for multilevel modeling. *Methodology*, *1*(3), 86–92.

Raudenbush, S. W., & Bryk, A. S. (2002). *Hierarchical linear models: Applications and data analysis methods* (2nd ed.). Thousand Oaks, CA: Sage Publications.

Raudenbush, S. W., Bryk, A. S., & Congdon, R. (2011). *HLM 7 for Windows [Computer software]*. Skokie, IL: Scientific Software International, Inc.

Schweitzer, L., & Zhou, J. (2010). Neighborhood air quality, respiratory health, and vulnerable populations in compact and sprawled regions. *Journal of the American Planning Association*, *76*(3), 363–371. https://doi.org/10.1080/01944363.2010.486623

Singer, J. (1998). Using SAS PROC MIXED to fit multilevel models, hierarchical models, and individual growth models. *Journal of Educational and Behavioral Statistics*, *24*(4), 323–355. https://doi.org/10.3102/10769986023004323

Singer, J., & Willet, J. (2003). *Applied longitudinal data analysis: Modeling change and event occurrence*. New York, NY: Oxford University Press.

Smart Growth Network. (2006). *This is smart growth*. Retrieved from www.smartgrowthonlineaudio.org/pdf/TISG_2006_8-5x11.pdf

Yang, Y. (2008). A tale of two cities: Physical form and neighborhood satisfaction in metropolitan Portland and Charlotte. *Journal of the American Planning Association*, *74*(3), 307–323. https://doi.org/10.1080/01944360802215546

8

STRUCTURAL EQUATION MODELING

Matt Miller, Ivana Tasic, Torrey Lyons, Reid Ewing, and James B. Grace

Overview

This chapter first introduces some background and historical information on how structural equation modeling (SEM) came to be developed. Then the main differences between SEM and earlier multivariate methods are explained. The chapter describes three main applications of SEM:

1. Path analysis
2. Factor analysis
3. Hybrid models

Computer programs are recommended for these applications. The chapter concludes with two example applications of SEM within the planning field.

Structural equation modeling is a *model-centered*, or *a priori hypothesis*, methodology that seeks to evaluate theoretically justified models against data (Grace et al., 2012). The SEM approach is based on the modern statistical view that theoretically based models, when they can be justified on scientific grounds, provide more useful interpretations than conventional methods that simply seek to reject the *null hypothesis* of no effect. An equation is said to be *structural* if there exists sufficient evidence from all available sources to support the interpretation that one variable has a causal effect on another variable.

SEM has several related and distinctive features (Grace, 2006). In SEM:

- Hypothesized path models are developed based on a priori knowledge about the processes under investigation using all available information.
- The investigator tests the degree to which the data relationships implied by one or more models are consistent with the observed relations in the data. Many models that might be envisioned are rejected because they are inconsistent with the data.
- Probability statements about the model are reversed from those associated with null hypotheses. Probability values (p-values) used in statistics are measures of the degree to

which the data are unexpected, given the hypothesis being tested. In null hypothesis testing, a finding of a p-value $< .05$ indicates that we can reject the null hypothesis (typically of no effect) because the data are very unlikely to come from a random process. In SEM, we seek a model goodness-of-fit test statistic that has a large p-value ($>>.05$) as that indicates that the data are consistent with the model).

- Different processes operating in systems are identified by decomposing relationships into direct and indirect pathways. Pathways can thus be either simple or compound, depending on whether they pass through other variables or not. The total effect of one factor on another is the cumulative impact summed over all the pathways (direct and indirect).

The estimation of structural equation models involves solving a set of interconnected equations. There is an equation for each *response* or endogenous variable in the network. Variables that are solely predictors of other variables are termed *exogenous* variables. Solution procedures for SEM most commonly focus on the observed versus model-implied correlations/covariances. The unstandardized correlations or covariances are the raw material for such analyses. Overall model fit is judged in comparison to a *saturated* model (one that allows all variables to intercorrelate), and this comparison permits the analysis to discover missing linkages and thereby the rejection of inconsistent models.

Purpose

In this book and in *Basic Quantitative Research Methods for Urban Planners*, the focus has been on statistical methods in which the researcher is striving to explain or predict a single dependent variable with one or more independent variables. The focus shifts in this chapter. James Grace, a coauthor of this chapter and international expert on SEM, has opined:

> It is not widely understood that the univariate model, and especially ANOVA, is not well suited for studying systems, but rather, is designed for studying individual processes, net effects, or for identifying predictors. The dominance of the univariate statistical model in the natural sciences has, in my personal view, retarded (greatly) the progress of science.

The power of SEM is perhaps easiest to convey by comparing it to conventional regression analysis. A primary distinction of great significance is that regression models are based on the formula $Y = f(X)$, where Y is a response of interest and X is some list (vector) of potential predictors. A key enterprise in regression is finding ways to decide which combination of X variables (which are typically intercorrelated) should be included in the model. Most important from a scientific standpoint is that regression analysis provides no way to include information about why various X variables are correlated. This limitation generally precludes the development of causal hypotheses because there is no capacity to make a statement about the causal connections among predictors.

SE models, in contrast, are based on the formula $Y = f(X, Y)$. This permits the development of hypothesis in the form of causal networks (e.g., Figure 8.1). Causal networks provide serious support for scientific interpretations but also permit opportunities for the discovery of new, unanticipated connections, as well as for the rejection of a hypothesized network based on data patterns.

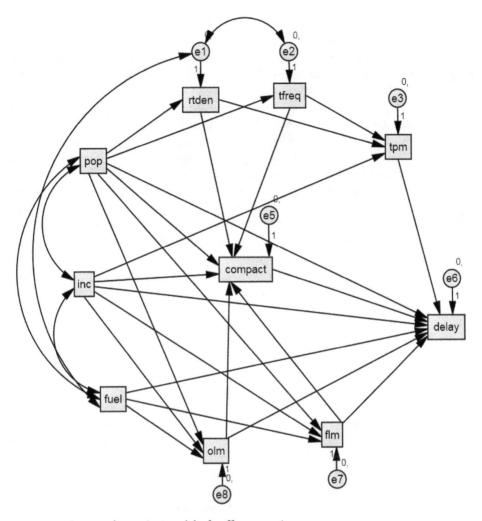

FIGURE 8.1 Structural equation model of traffic congestion

Source: Reprinted from Ewing, R., Tian, G, & Lyons, T. (2018). Does Compact Development Increase or Reduce Traffic Congestion? *Cities, 72,* 94–101.with permission from Elsevier

SEM is also intended to address the problem of endogeneity, as a statistical issue where one or more of the predictors are affected by other predictors. Built environment-transportation studies provide the classic case for SEM (Ewing, Bartholomew, Winkelman, Walters, & Chen, 2008; Ewing, Hamidi, Gallivan, Nelson, & Grace, 2014; Ewing, Tian, & Lyons, 2018), where development density is treated as endogenous.

Three main applications for SEM are path analysis, confirmatory factor analysis (CFA), and hybrid models.

Path analysis is a special case of SEM that focuses on hypotheses involving directional relationships among observed variables. It is most appropriate when the theoretical concepts of interest can be directly measured. For example, in a recent article using SEM, urbanized area size (pop) and per capita income (inc) were linked to area compactness (compact), which in turn was hypothesized to affect traffic congestion (delay). Area size and per capita income appeared to affect traffic congestion both directly and indirectly through effects on area compactness (Ewing et al., 2018). There are many situations in which observed variable path models could represent our understanding of problems. The biggest exception is when dealing with psychological concepts and other situations where only indirect measurement using multiple indicators is seen as adequate. This situation is addressed in SEM using the next two model types.

Confirmatory factor analysis (CFA) focuses on hypotheses about unseen processes. The CFA is a constrained factor analysis representing hypotheses about underlying influences that are not directly measurable. The archetypal application of CFA involves the study of intellectual abilities and tendencies through examinations of correlations among responses to test questions. This same methodology can be used to address the imperfect measurement of less abstract concepts via multiple indicators. In CFA, variables representing underlying processes, termed latent variables, can be included in models, along with a representation of their hypothesized influences on observed variables. Latent variables can be used to represent abstract concepts that are unobservable, as well as variables that are hypothetically measurable, but for which we have no measurements in hand. For example, measurements of personal income and home values may be used to infer household wealth, even when no direct measure of household wealth can be obtained.

Hybrid models represent a more complex hypothesis that specifies causal path relations between latent variables, with observed variables serving as reflective indicators of the latent variables. SEM analysis of hybrid models is usually conducted in two stages. First, the hybrid model is converted into a CFA by replacing directed links among latent variables with exogenous correlations. The evaluation of this model seeks to ascertain whether the data are consistent with the assignment of observed measures to latent concepts. It is common that some indicators are more highly correlated than can be explained by simply the latent influences hypothesized. This creates the need to consider additional elements of the measurement model, which can be in the form of either error correlations representing omitted factors or cross-linkages representing the joint action of multiple latent factors. Lack of fit can even lead to a reconsideration of the number of latent variables or of the appropriateness of observed indicators. Once the factor structure is consistent with data relations, there is a return to the full model including directed relationships among latent variables to be evaluated. This two-step process separates questions of measurement from those of the latent process, providing a more complete evaluation of the hybrid model.

History

SEM owes its modern development to Jöreskog (1970), who created a conceptual framework for viewing path analysis (Wright, 1921), factor analysis (Spearman, 1904), ANOVA (Fisher, 1925), and multiple regression (Fisher, 1922) as special cases of a more general representation of causal hypotheses. He further popularized SEM through the development of the LISREL software. Both the technical capabilities and range of applications of SEM continue to expand to the present day. The modern evolution of SEM has been chronicled in Grace et al. (2012). At present, there are a number of different estimation approaches for SE models, including those involving the global analysis of covariance relations, as well as local estimation methods using either likelihood or Bayesian techniques. In this chapter, we describe and illustrate the classic implementation of SEM based on covariance relations and commonly used software in social science applications.

Mechanics

Software

Perhaps the most popular software for SEM estimation is AMOS. AMOS is available as a stand-alone program or within SPSS. It runs in two modes: AMOS Graphics and AMOS Text (for users familiar with its programming language). While SPSS AMOS is used for this chapter, other SEM software exists. Other commercial packages include Stata, MPlus, LISREL, and STATISTICA. Stata is another very increasingly popular option for SEM, with the capability of including generalized linear model specifications for data violating normality assumptions. MPlus supports many advanced procedures and can estimate multilevel SEM models, for example. R provides an open-source alternative, lavaan. Older or less well-known packages include EQS, SAS-CALIS, SYSTAT-EzPath, Mx, and STATISTICA-SEPATH. In addition to approaches that rely on covariances to represent the data, SE models can be evaluated using local estimation techniques, which is more time-consuming and requires more advanced knowledge but which allows for more complex specifications (e.g., nonlinear relations) and Bayesian estimation (Grace et al., 2012). Some of these possibilities are now automated in newer R packages (blavaan and piecewiseSEM).

Symbols of SEM

SEM is a form of graphical modeling and therefore a system in which relationships are represented in both graphical and equational form. The graphical representation is a key component of any SE model and helps to clarify causal assumptions as well as interpretations.

Certain standards have been established on how to draw SEM causal path diagrams, using specific symbols for variables and relationships. Some researchers go beyond the basic symbols and incorporate additional variable types (c.f., Grace et al., 2012). The symbols given in Figure 8.2 have the broadest use.

Model Development, Specification, and Evaluation

There are two major components of SEM: the representation of the hypothesis of interest (the SE model) and the work flow process that explains and justifies the logical steps leading to strong inferences (the SE modeling). In SEM, the general form of the model is specified

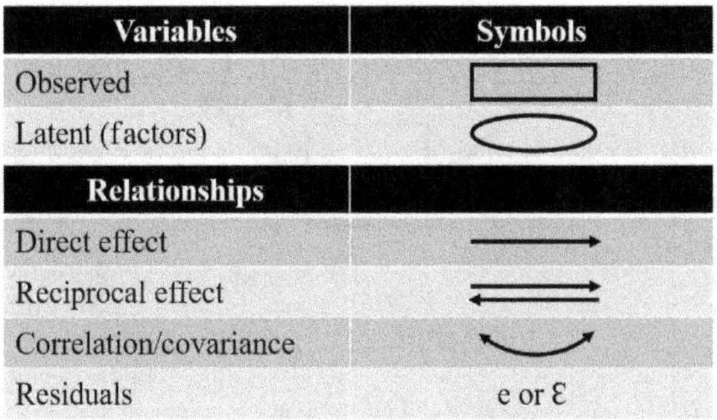

Variables	Symbols
Observed	▭
Latent (factors)	⬭
Relationships	
Direct effect	→
Reciprocal effect	⇄
Correlation/covariance	⌣
Residuals	e or ε

FIGURE 8.2 Symbols for SEM graphical representation

before the details of statistical specifications are added. The purpose of the work flow is to test the hypothesis/hypotheses in as confirmatory a manner as possible. This approach is quite different from exploratory methods that look at relationships in the data until some plausible description of the data is found. It is also different from the narrow application of null hypothesis testing where one simply seeks to reject or accept an initial position of *no effect*.

A common way to begin is with the development of a conceptual framework relating concepts to one another based on theoretical knowledge (see Chapter 5 of *Basic Quantitative Research Methods for Urban Planners*). This conceptual *meta-model* is then used to develop a specific path diagram that includes observed variables, latent variables, directed/causal paths, correlations, and disturbance terms (unspecified sources of variation). In terms of their place in the model, variables are defined as exogenous or endogenous. An example submodel (showing only three variables from a larger model) is presented in Figure 8.3.

After creating the conceptual framework and path diagram, SEM users develop corresponding equations based on the diagram and the details of the data, such as the nature of the responses (e.g., continuous or binary), dependencies in the data (e.g., are data nested/hierarchical or longitudinal). For Figure 8.3, the associated equations are as follows:

$$y_1 = \gamma_{11}x_1 + \zeta_1$$
$$y_2 = \gamma_{21}x_1 + \beta_{21}y_1 + \zeta_2$$

Once the model is fully specified, the investigator proceeds to the estimation step, followed by the model evaluation process. In this chapter, we assume that one is working with a software package. Each package has its own built-in techniques for accommodating data complexities. Model evaluation is also supported in various ways by different software packages. Later in the chapter, we illustrate estimation and evaluation techniques in the context of two of these packages, AMOS and R.

Figure 8.3 shows some terminology specific to SEM. This will aid in understanding rules specific to path coefficients between variables in SEM. The linear equations that comprise

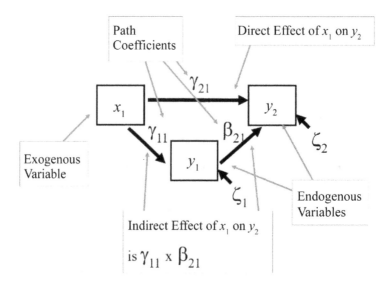

FIGURE 8.3   SEM terminology

our example SEM are simply linear regression equations (see Chapter 12 of *Basic Quantitative Research Methods for Urban Planners*). If you understand linear regression, you are halfway there to understanding SEM. Once we have a network of relationships, however, some guidance is needed to interpret the implied causal effects. A few basic rules provide interpretive guidance for models. To understand these rules, we need first to recognize the two different types of pathways that can produce a causal connection between two variables. The first and most obvious is a *causal chain* relationship. Each pair of variables in Figure 8.3 is connected by a causal chain relationship $(x_1 \rightarrow y_1; x_1 \rightarrow y_2; y_1 \rightarrow y_2)$. The second type of causal connection is the *common cause*. In Figure 8.3, y_1 and y_2 are additionally related by having a common cause, which is x_1. The total association between y_1 and y_2 is the combined influence of the causal chain plus the (backdoor) common cause.

- **First Rule of Path Coefficients**: The path coefficients for unanalyzed relationships (curved arrows) between exogenous variables are simply the observed correlations (standardized form) or covariances (unstandardized form).
- **Second Rule of Path Coefficients**: When two variables are connected by a single causal pathway, the path coefficient relating the two is the simple regression coefficient.
- **Third Rule of Path Coefficients**: The strength of a compound path is the product of the coefficients along the path.
- **Fourth Rule of Path Coefficients**: When two variables are connected by more than one causal pathway, the path coefficient connecting them is a *partial* regression coefficient (i.e., the effect controlling for the influence of the common cause).
- **Fifth Rule of Path Coefficients**: The total effect one variable has on another equals the sum of its direct and indirect effects.

If an SE model has links connecting all variables, then the model is said to be *saturated*; if not, the model is *unsaturated*. If reciprocal relationships between variables are present, the SEM model is said to be nonrecursive. Otherwise, the model is recursive (flow of cause–effect is unidirectional throughout the entire model).

One additional term is central to SEM, *identification*. For the model parameters to be estimated with unique values, they must be identified (i.e., have only one unique solution). As in linear algebra, we have a requirement that we need as many known pieces of information as we do unknown parameters. Several circumstances can prevent identification of all parameters in a model, including:

- Too many paths specified in the model,
- Multicollinearity (nonunique information), and
- Combination of a complex model and a small sample.

The good news is that most SEM software checks for identification and lets you know which, if any, parameters are not identified.

Interpreting Results

Being a *model-centric* methodology, the first results of interest are those that quantify overall goodness of fit (GOF). A reasonably good overall fit between model-implied and observed covariances is needed before the individual coefficients reported are to be trusted. When important linkages are left out of a model, it creates discrepancies between the model-implied and observed covariance matrices. These discrepancies are our primary signal that the scientific hypothesis needs to be reconsidered.

Our rules of path coefficients help us to understand how model-implied covariances can differ from those observed. Imagine a variant of the model in Figure 8.3 of the form $x_1 \rightarrow y_1 \rightarrow y_2$ (the link between x_1 and y_2 is omitted). According to the Third Rule of Path Coefficients, the model-implied standardized covariance between x_1 and y_2 will equal γ_{11} times β_{21}. If x_1 actually influences y_2, the observed standardized covariance will deviate from the model-implied one. The individual discrepancies are summed up over the entire model, producing an overall discrepancy metric.

Conveniently, the discrepancy metric, generally known as the *model fit statistic*, follows a chi-square distribution. This allows for an overall fit test to determine whether the data are significantly discrepant from model expectations. This GOF test often referred to as the *overall model chi-square test*. In contrast to null hypothesis tests where the investigator is typically seeking to reject the null by finding p-values $< .05$, for the overall model chi-square test we require a nonsignificant result (p-values $> .05$) in order to have confidence in the model. Frequently, investigators may have to propose slightly modified models to achieve this outcome.

The model chi-square statistic tends to be highly sensitive to large sample sizes (> 200). For this reason, other measures that are less sensitive to sample size are often reported. These measures include the root mean squared error (RMSE) and variants such as %RMSE (percent mean squared error) and RMSEA (root mean squared error of approximation). Methods that completely ignore sample size are also often reported. For these, goodness of fit is summarized in terms of the percentage of total possible discrepancy that is explained (and thus range from 0.0 to 1.0). Examples are the Comparative Fit Index (CFI) and the Normed Fit Index (NFI). The suggested cutoff values are CFI > 0.9 and NFI > 0.95. AMOS provides suggested cutoff values for all goodness-of-fit measures produced by the software.

When it is determined that there is a major model–data discrepancy, the investigator will seek insights by consulting the reported Modification Indices. These provide information on the reduction in a discrepancy that would occur if an additional linkage was added to the model. Including new links requires theoretical justification to insure that these additions are interpretable. Tests of overall model fit continue until a defensible correspondence between model and data is obtained. The reader should be aware that obtaining an adequate overall GOF value does not guarantee that there are no omitted linkages that are important, only that the summed discrepancies over the whole model are modest. This finer issue can be addressed when individual links are considered.

Once omitted linkages have been considered, then the process of model simplification is addressed. Model chi-square tests do not indicate whether the included links are supported by the data (i.e., coefficients are significantly different from zero). For this phase of testing, we consult the t-statistics and p-values reported for the individual parameters included in the model.

A table similar to a regression table will be presented in the estimates page of the SEM output. You will be presented with the path name on the left of the table, followed by the path coefficient estimate. The estimate is similar to an unstandardized or standardized coefficient from a regression table, depending on which output is requested. The next two columns to the right will be the SE for standard error, just as in regression, and the CR for the critical ratio. The critical ratio can be interpreted like a t-statistic in linear regression analysis. Large critical ratio values indicate that relationships are real and not included due to chance. *p*-values presented on the far right of the table identify whether path coefficients are statistically significant at conventional levels (<.01, <.05, or <.10).

Now we are using *p*-values in a conventional way. If individual parameters have high *p*-values (>.05), we may wish to consider whether links can be removed without impacting overall model fit. Simplification is usually tested one link at a time, beginning with the weakest paths first. Comparing models where a link has been removed is traditionally done using a single-degree-of-freedom chi-square test (chi-square increases more than 3.84 when a single link is removed). Investigators may instead prefer to use information methods, such as the Akaike Information Criterion (AIC) to evaluate model parsimony. Increasingly, the final selection of models is supported by AIC tables that report the information differences among models. For models with AIC differences less than 2.0 units, the researcher may use his or her scientific judgment to decide which model is most consistent with the known information.

Step by Step

This section describes the steps associated with estimating a structural equation model, specifically a path analysis, with AMOS and R. An illustration using latent variable models can be found in Byrne (2016).

SEM analysis can be performed using various software packages, including AMOS, Mplus, LISREL, R, and Stata. IBM SPSS AMOS is a convenient and popular choice as the modeling can be implemented by drawing path diagrams, allowing the investigator to focus on science. You can download its 30-day trial edition for free. To download the most recent version of AMOS, go to www.ibm.com/us-en/marketplace/structural-equation-modeling-sem. This exercise uses AMOS 25. Note that AMOS works only for the Microsoft Windows operating system while R works for both Windows and Mac OS.

In this exercise, we model vehicle miles traveled (VMT) per capita in urbanized areas, a key indicator of land use and transportation system performance. Using SEM, Ewing et al. (2014) built two models of VMT in urbanized areas: one using cross-sectional data and the other one using longitudinal data. They found that population, income, and freeway capacity are positively related to VMT, while gasoline prices, development density, and transit service levels are negatively associated. This exercise replicates their study with a smaller dataset: 157 UZAs in "UZA.sav" versus 315 UZAs in their study.

The variables used in our SEM exercise fall into three groups: an outcome variable, exogenous explanatory variables, and endogenous explanatory variables. All variables are log-transformed, following Ewing et al. (2014). Our focal outcome variable is daily VMT per capita in 2010 (*lnvmt*). The exogenous variables are regional population in thousands (*lnpop*), annual per capita income in thousands (*lninc*), average fuel price per gallon (*lnfuel*), freeway lane mile per 1,000 population (*lnflm*), other highway lane miles per 1,000 population (*lnolm*), directional route miles of heavy rail per 100,000 population (*lnhrt*), and directional route miles of light rail per 100,000 population (*lnlrt*), as they are the results of long-lived policy decisions. 1.0 was added to the rail values so that urbanized areas with no rail mileage would have a zero value when log-transformed.

The endogenous mediating variables are functions of exogenous variables and may also influence one another. These were also log-transformed. They are gross population density

TABLE 8.1 Descriptive statistics of the variables included in the SEM by variable type

	N	Mean	Standard Deviation
Dependent variable			
lnvmt	157	3.15	0.23
Exogenous variables			
lnpop	157	6.40	0.96
lninc	157	3.27	0.19
lnfuel	157	1.02	0.06
lnflm	157	−0.49	0.42
lnolm	157	0.85	0.28
lnhrt	157	0.16	0.75
lnlrt	157	0.37	1.07
Endogenous mediating variables			
lnpopden	157	7.44	0.43
lnrtden	157	0.60	0.75
lntfreq	157	8.68	0.55
lntpm	157	4.00	1.15

in persons per square mile (*lnpopden*), transit route density in route miles per square mile (*lnrtden*), transit service frequency in annual vehicle revenue miles per route mile (*lntfreq*), and annual transit passenger miles per capita (*lntpm*). They depend on real estate market forces and regional and policy decisions: whether to increase transit revenue service, whether to zone for higher densities. Table 8.1 shows descriptive statistics for the various variable types.

Step 1: Open AMOS (Figure 8.4)

Step 2: Read the data file ("UZA.sav") by clicking "File" and "Data files." Or you can click the "Select data file(s)" icon ▦ on the left side of the screen (Figure 8.5)

In the "Data Files" window, you can load the dataset by clicking the "File Name" button, selecting the "UZA.sav" file, and click "OK" (Figure 8.6). In the same window, the "View Data" button shows you the data in a table view. You can come back to this window whenever you wish to view the data or read a different data file.

Step 3: Add variables

There are at least two ways to add a variable in the path diagram window. First, you can click a box called "Draw observed variables" (▦) and name the variable. Or you can call a variable list in the dataset and select variables to include in the model. We will use the second approach here.

Click "Variables in Dataset" icon (▦) on the left side of the screen, or go to the "View" menu and select "Variables in Dataset" option (note that as many other functions in AMOS do, this option has a keyboard shortcut, Ctrl + Shift + D).

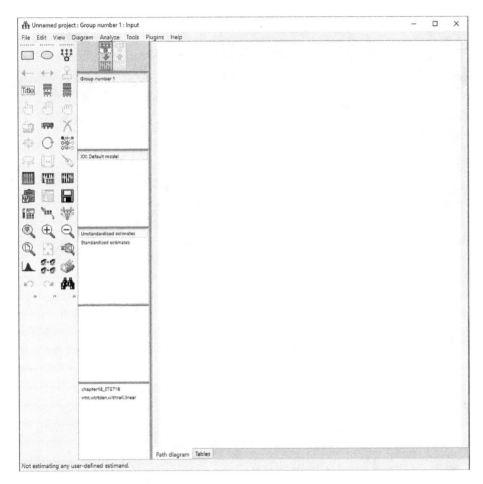

FIGURE 8.4   IBM SPSS AMOS window

A variable list window will pop up (Figure 8.7). You can add any variable to the model by drag-and-dropping the variable name into the blank path diagram section (the right side of the screen) .

Variables are first dragged into the window and arranged logically, often with exogenous variables on the left side of the window, mediating variables in the middle, and the outcome variable on the right. Add the following 12 variables and arrange them as in the image in Figure 8.8: *lnvmt, lnpop, lninc, lnfuel, lnflm, lnolm, lnhrt, lnlrt, lnpopden, lnrtden, lntfreq, lntpm*. If you want to move a variable box, use "Move object" tool ( ).

Step 4: Specify linkages

The next step is adding the hypothesized causal paths between variables. Using "Draw paths (single-headed arrows)" icon (←) (or F5 key), we add all directed relationships displayed in the Ewing et al. (2014) paper. If you want to remove a variable or a path, there is the "Erase objects" tool (✗).

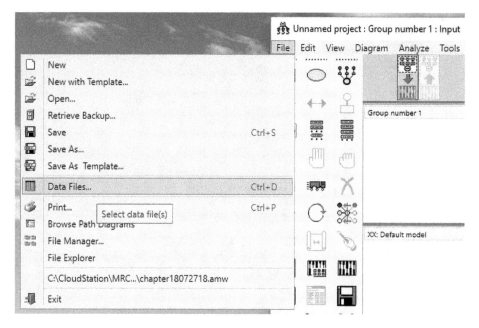

FIGURE 8.5   Open the dataset in AMOS

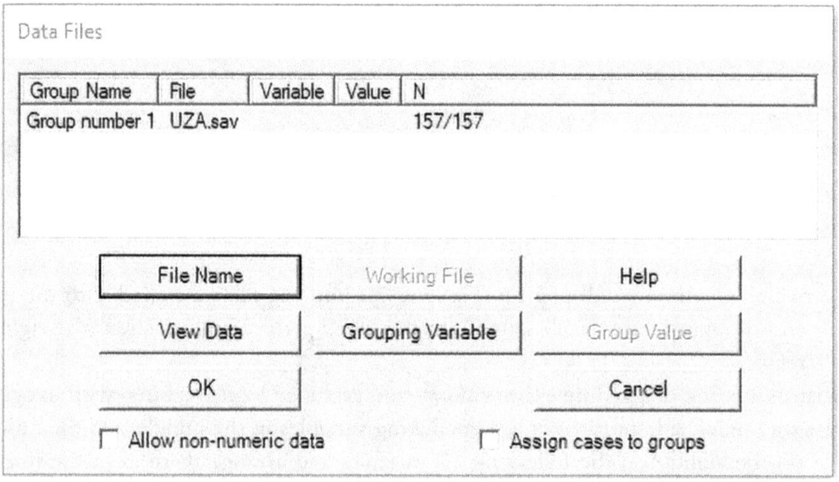

FIGURE 8.6   Reading "UZA.sav" file

The normal procedure is to add covariances/correlations between all exogenous variables (unless there is a theoretical reason to do otherwise). How this is done is described later in the chapter. For purposes of illustration, we here run the model without including the exogenous covariances, guaranteeing poor model fit and providing an opportunity to show how to detect and add omitted links. (See Figure 8.9.)

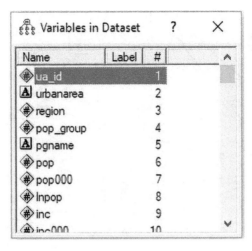

FIGURE 8.7 Variable list window

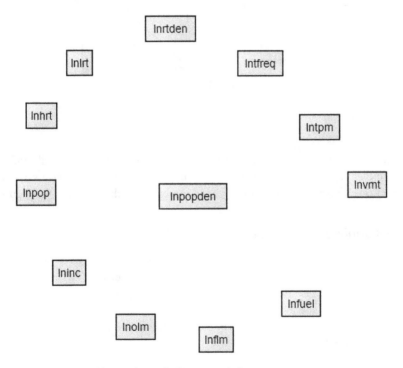

FIGURE 8.8 Locating variables in the path diagram window

Step 5: Add error variables

Each endogenous variable (and our focal outcome variable) must have a disturbance or residual term that is attached to the variable. These represent the other, unspecified influences contributing to the variations in responses. A model cannot be estimated without them. The exogenous variables have no residuals. You can add a residual term by clicking "Add a unique

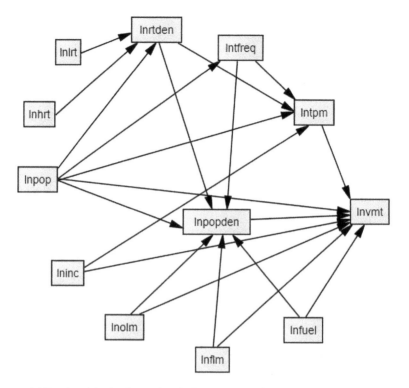

FIGURE 8.9   Adding hypothesized causal paths between variables

variable" icon (⊕) and then clicking the target variable box. After adding all residual term boxes, name them appropriately (e.g., e1, e2, ... and e5). To name or change a variable name, click "Select one object at a time" icon (🖑) and double-click the variable. (See Figure 8.10.)

Step 6: Set analysis properties and output options

Click the "Analyses properties" icon (▦) or go to the "Analyze" menu → "Analyses proper-ties." In the "Estimation" tab, select "Maximum likelihood" (a default) (Figure 8.11). "Estimate means and intercepts" is also typically checked, as AMOS requires this in order to estimate an SEM when variables in the model have missing values.

Then, go to the "Output" tab and select "Indirect, direct & total effects" and "Modification indices." (See Figure 8.12.)

Step 7: Run model

Run the model by clicking the "Calculate estimates" icon (▦) or pressing Ctrl + F9 keys. In this case, an "AMOS Warnings" window will pop up because we failed to add covari-ances/correlations among exogenous variables (Figure 8.13). You will be given two options—proceed or cancel. As previously mentioned, normally exogenous variables are allowed to be correlated before running an SEM. If exogenous variables are actually correlated, adding double-headed arrows between two exogenous variables will be required. This is analogous

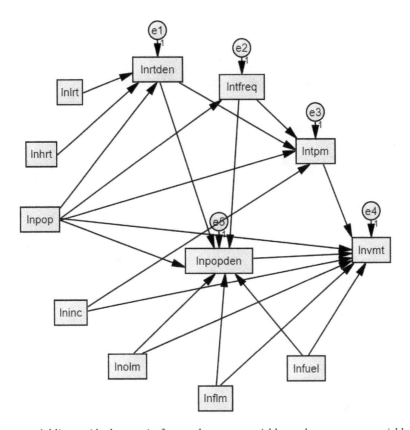

FIGURE 8.10 Adding residual terms in four endogenous variables and an outcome variable

to linear regression, where independent variables are allowed to be correlated. We will come back to the correlation issue later. Now, click the "Proceed with the analysis" button. (See Figure 8.13.)

Step 8: Examine the model fit

The modeling results can be seen by clicking the "View Text" icon (▦) or by going to the "View" → "Text Output" menu or pressing F10 key (Figure 8.14). The first screen shows the chi-square statistic for the model, its degrees of freedom, and probability level. Remember that in SEM, we seek a model chi-square statistic that has a large p-value ($>.05$ or greater) as it indicates that the data are reasonably consistent with the model. In this case, the low p-value shows that the model is not consistent with the data. We need to modify the model to resolve the discrepancy.

As the model does not meet the chi-square criterion of $p > .05$ as a goodness–of–fit test, it has to be further refined typically by adding causal and correlational arrows suggested by modification indices.

Particularly if the chi-square goodness-of-fit criterion is not met, the researcher may also look at other goodness-of-fit measures in the "Model Fit" output (Figure 8.15). It provides

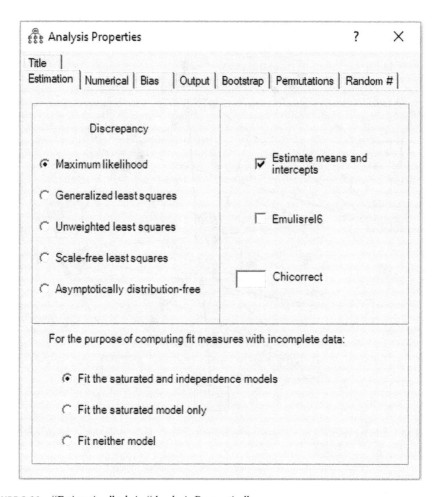

FIGURE 8.11 "Estimation" tab in "Analysis Properties" menu

various indices. The authors of this chapter and other SEM modelers pay particular attention of the CFI and RMSEA. The CFI is scaled as a goodness of fit index, with 1.0 indicating perfect fit. The RMSEA, in contrast, is scaled as a badness-of-fit statistic, with perfect fit indicated by the value 0.0. Kline (2016) suggests the following rule of thumb for RMSEA. RMSEA value ≤ 0.05 indicates a close approximate fit, values between 0.05 and 0.08 suggest reasonable error of approximation, and RMSEA ≥ 0.10 suggests a poor fit. A p-value for the RMSEA is also provided to aid with interpretation. Also, Kline (2016) indicates that CFI values greater than 0.90 may indicate a reasonably good fit of the model. The current model does not meet rules of thumb for of the indices.

If the model fit leaves something to be desired, modification indices are provided in the AMOS output (Figure 8.16). They can be computed as long as the SPSS dataset has no missing values for the variables in the model. While an SEM can be estimated when missing values exist, the absence of modification indices makes it much more difficult and time-consuming to optimize a model. The model developer is effectively "flying blind." For this reason, the authors of this chapter typically limit their samples to cases without missing values in order to obtain modification indices. Note that AMOS has options for estimating values for missing data, which provide an advanced approach to the problem.

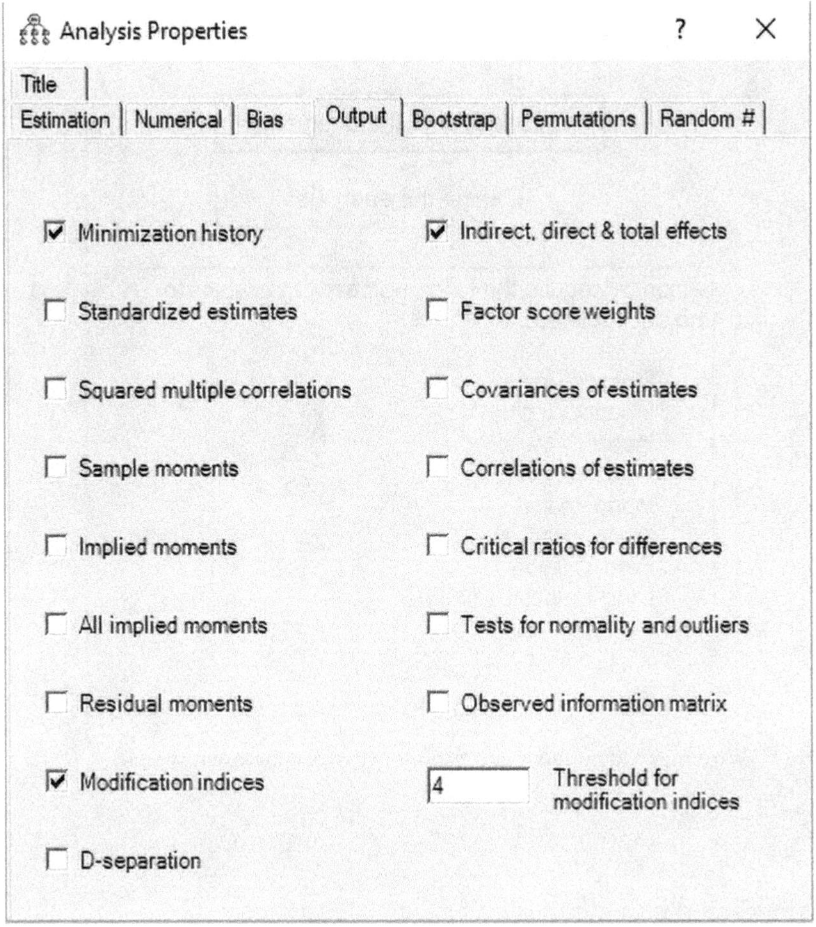

FIGURE 8.12   "Output" tab in "Analysis Properties" menu

Step 9: Respecify and rerun model

If the modification indices for certain pairs of variables are greater than 3.8, then causal or correlational paths should be drawn for those pairs of variables in the SEM diagram (after considering theoretical interpretability), and the model should be estimated again. The chi-square values will be reduced and the associated *p*-value increased, indicating a better model fit. This process of checking modification indices and adding pathways typically continues until overall GOF is deemed to be adequate. A caveat here is that a researcher should not modify (or re-specify) the model solely based on modification indices; you must make sure that the modification is consistent with the theoretical explanation of the model.

To specify a correlation between two exogenous variables, use "Draw covariances (double-headed arrows)" icon (↔) (or the F6 key) and connect two variables of interest (Figure 8.17). Here, we connect the following 14 sets of exogenous variables and run the model again:

- *lnpop*   <-->   *lnhrt*
- *lnlrt*   <-->   *lnpop*

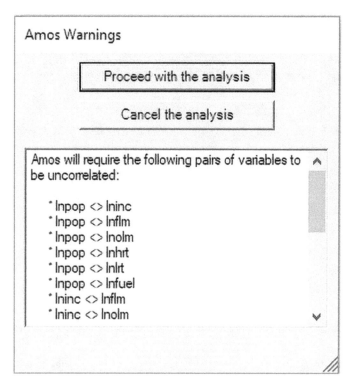

FIGURE 8.13　Warning window about correlations between exogenous variables

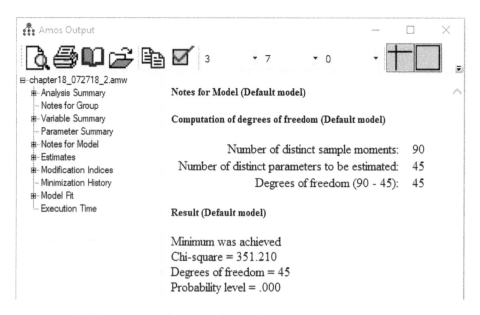

FIGURE 8.14　AMOS output window: notes for model

Amos Output — □ ×

⬚ 3 ▾ 7 ▾ 0 ▾

□-chapter18_072718_2.amw
- ⊞-Analysis Summary
- ⋯ Notes for Group
- ⊞-Variable Summary
- ⋯ Parameter Summary
- ⊞-Notes for Model
- ⊞-Estimates
- ⊞-Modification Indices
- ⋯ Minimization History
- ⋯ Model Fit
- ⋯ Execution Time

Model Fit Summary

CMIN

Model	NPAR	CMIN	DF	P	CMIN/DF
Default model	45	351.210	45	.000	7.805
Saturated model	90	.000	0		
Independence model	24	1011.454	66	.000	15.325

Baseline Comparisons

Model	NFI Delta1	RFI rho1	IFI Delta2	TLI rho2	CFI
Default model	.653	.491	.683	.525	.676
Saturated model	1.000		1.000		1.000
Independence model	.000	.000	.000	.000	.000

FIGURE 8.15   AMOS output window: model fit

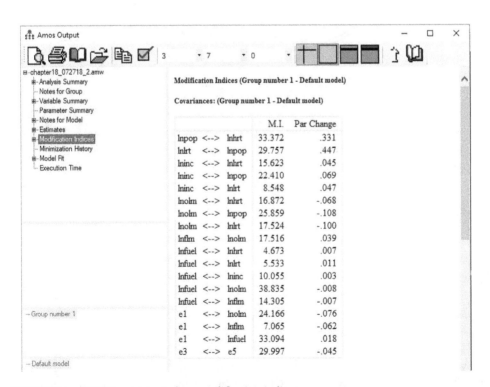

FIGURE 8.16   AMOS output window: modification indices

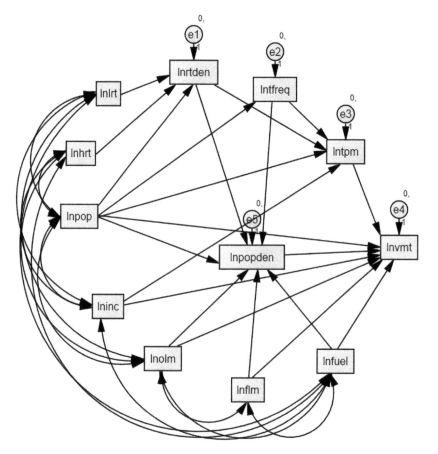

FIGURE 8.17   Adding covariance paths in the path diagram

- *lninc*   <-->   *lnhrt*
- *lninc*   <-->   *lnpop*
- *lninc*   <-->   *lnlrt*
- *lnolm*   <-->   *lnhrt*
- *lnolm*   <-->   *lnpop*
- *lnolm*   <-->   *lnlrt*
- *lnflm*   <-->   *lnolm*
- *lnfuel*   <-->   *lnhrt*
- *lnfuel*   <-->   *lnlrt*
- *lnfuel*   <-->   *lninc*
- *lnfuel*   <-->   *lnolm*
- *lnfuel*   <-->   *lnflm*

With these additional paths, the chi-square statistic is reduced to 126.941, but the p-value is still lower than 0.05. However, the CFI value almost meets the 0.9 rule of thumb. For economy of the presentation, we stop checking GOF at this point and turn our attention to model simplification.

Step 10: Consider model simplification

The researcher also needs to check the path coefficients in the "Estimates" output for the direct relationships between all variables hypothesized to be causally related to one another. As in linear regression, coefficient interpretation focuses on coefficient signs and statistical significance. These are comparable to linear regression equations, and the same standards apply. Links are often omitted when path coefficients are not statistically significant unless the relationship is of theoretical significance. Note that including nonsignificant links has only a minor influence on model fit and on the other parameters (unlike the omission of significant links).

Step 11: Present and interpret results

The model results in this abbreviated analysis are mostly similar to those in the full study (Ewing et al., 2014) (Figure 8.18). Estimated VMT per capita in a UZA (*lnvmt*) increases with a regional population (*lnpop*), income (*lninc*), and freeway capacity (*lnflm*). Also, it decreases with gasoline prices (*lnfuel*), development density (*lnpopden*), and transit service levels (*lntpm*). But unlike in the full study, *lnfuel* and *lntpm* are not statistically significant at the $p = .05$ level here (due to the reduced sample).

The "Estimates" output also displays estimated means and intercepts of the variables (Figure 8.19).

Regression Weights: (Group number 1 - Default model)

			Estimate	S.E.	C.R.	P	Label
lnrtden	<---	lnlrt	.158	.058	2.749	.006	
lntfreq	<---	lnpop	.308	.040	7.783	***	
lnrtden	<---	lnpop	.111	.072	1.545	.122	
lnrtden	<---	lnhrt	.133	.083	1.589	.112	
lntpm	<---	lnrtden	.916	.065	14.096	***	
lntpm	<---	lntfreq	.900	.101	8.883	***	
lnpopden	<---	lnrtden	.263	.020	13.139	***	
lnpopden	<---	lntfreq	.180	.031	5.776	***	
lnpopden	<---	lnfuel	.399	.297	1.344	.179	
lnpopden	<---	lnflm	-.132	.036	-3.639	***	
lnpopden	<---	lnolm	-.481	.065	-7.350	***	
lntpm	<---	lninc	1.325	.262	5.056	***	
lntpm	<---	lnpop	.048	.063	.765	.444	
lnpopden	<---	lnpop	.059	.020	3.025	.002	
lnvmt	<---	lntpm	-.027	.018	-1.527	.127	
lnvmt	<---	lnpopden	-.179	.063	-2.841	.004	
lnvmt	<---	lnfuel	-.459	.304	-1.511	.131	
lnvmt	<---	lnolm	.039	.072	.543	.587	
lnvmt	<---	lnflm	.172	.036	4.778	***	
lnvmt	<---	lninc	.329	.086	3.818	***	
lnvmt	<---	lnpop	.060	.020	3.045	.002	

FIGURE 8.18 AMOS output window: regression coefficients

Means: (Group number 1 - Default model)

	Estimate	S.E.	C.R.	P	Label
lnpop	6.399	.074	86.180	***	
lnhrt	.160	.059	2.687	.007	
lnlrt	.371	.085	4.365	***	
lninc	3.274	.015	218.455	***	
lnflm	-.490	.034	-14.498	***	
lnolm	.851	.022	39.502	***	
lnfuel	1.023	.004	227.979	***	

Intercepts: (Group number 1 - Default model)

	Estimate	S.E.	C.R.	P	Label
lnrtden	-.190	.451	-.422	.673	
lntfreq	6.707	.256	26.239	***	
lnpopden	5.278	.423	12.479	***	
lntpm	-9.006	1.064	-8.465	***	
lnvmt	3.650	.572	6.379	***	

FIGURE 8.19 AMOS output window: means and intercepts

The "Estimates" output also provides tables of direct, indirect, and total effects among the variables in the model (Figure 8.20). These tables, with the graphical representation of the model and direct path coefficients, are the main results to be presented. They show how each variable changes directly and indirectly with respect to other exogenous or endogenous variables via causal paths drawn in AMOS. The authors of this chapter always report direct, indirect, and total effects for the main outcome variable vis-à-vis each of the other variables in the model (see Ewing et al., 2016). For example, the direct effect of income (*lninc*) on VMT (*lnvmt*) is 0.329, while the indirect effect through *lntpm* is −0.036. As a result, the total effect of income on VMT is 0.294, the sum of direct effect and indirect effect.

Step 12: Present interpretational caveats

It is important when presenting SEM methodology and results to distinguish between hypothesis and findings. Causal interpretations do not come from the data, but from the scientific knowledge of the system under investigation. SEM is a particularly stringent hypothesis testing system because many of the initial assumptions are falsifiable given appropriate data. Achieving good fit between model and data provides support for a causal interpretation, but those interpretations must be defended by the investigators on mechanistic grounds.

In R

Figures 8.21 through 8.23 show an R script to run a structural equation modeling for regional VMT. While there are several packages to run SEM, we use *sem* function in *lavaan* package in this exercise. First, we need to code a model formula for every endogenous variable—*lnrtden*, *lntfreq*, *lntpm*, *lnpopden*, and *lnvmt*, based on Figure 8.10 (see Figure 8.21). Figure 8.22 shows

Total Effects (Group number 1 - Default model)

	lnhrt	lnpop	lnlrt	lninc	lnolm	lnflm	lnfuel	lntfreq	lnrtden	lnpopden	lntpm
lntfreq	.000	.308	.000	.000	.000	.000	.000	.000	.000	.000	.000
lnrtden	.133	.111	.158	.000	.000	.000	.000	.000	.000	.000	.000
lnpopden	.035	.144	.042	.000	-.481	-.132	.399	.180	.263	.000	.000
lntpm	.121	.427	.145	1.325	.000	.000	.000	.900	.916	.000	.000
lnvmt	-.010	.022	-.011	.294	.125	.195	-.531	-.057	-.072	-.179	-.027

Direct Effects (Group number 1 - Default model)

	lnhrt	lnpop	lnlrt	lninc	lnolm	lnflm	lnfuel	lntfreq	lnrtden	lnpopden	lntpm
lntfreq	.000	.308	.000	.000	.000	.000	.000	.000	.000	.000	.000
lnrtden	.133	.111	.158	.000	.000	.000	.000	.000	.000	.000	.000
lnpopden	.000	.059	.000	.000	-.481	-.132	.399	.180	.263	.000	.000
lntpm	.000	.048	.000	1.325	.000	.000	.000	.900	.916	.000	.000
lnvmt	.000	.060	.000	.329	.039	.172	-.459	.000	.000	-.179	-.027

Indirect Effects (Group number 1 - Default model)

	lnhrt	lnpop	lnlrt	lninc	lnolm	lnflm	lnfuel	lntfreq	lnrtden	lnpopden	lntpm
lntfreq	.000	.000	.000	.000	.000	.000	.000	.000	.000	.000	.000
lnrtden	.000	.000	.000	.000	.000	.000	.000	.000	.000	.000	.000
lnpopden	.035	.085	.042	.000	.000	.000	.000	.000	.000	.000	.000
lntpm	.121	.379	.145	.000	.000	.000	.000	.000	.000	.000	.000
lnvmt	-.010	-.037	-.011	-.036	.086	.024	-.072	-.057	-.072	.000	.000

FIGURE 8.20 AMOS output window: indirect, direct, and total effects

```
#STRUCTURAL EQUATION MODELING (SEM)
library("foreign")
uza<-read.spss("UZA.sav",to.data.frame=TRUE)

library(lavaan)
model<-'
lnrtden ~ lnlrt + lnhrt + lnpop000
lntfreq ~ lnpop000
lntpm ~ lntfreq + lnrtden + lnpop000 + lninc000
lnpopden ~ lnpop000 + lnrtden + lntfreq + lnolm + lnflm + lnfuel
lnvmt ~ lntpm + lnpop000 + lnpopden + lninc000 + lnolm + lnflm + lnfuel
'

results<-sem(model,data=uza)
summary(results,standardized=T,fit=T)
```

FIGURE 8.21 Reading SPSS data ("UZA.sav") and specifying SEM model in *lavaan* package: R script

```
## lavaan 0.6-5 ended normally after 55 iterations
##
##    Estimator                                         ML
##    Optimization method                           NLMINB
##    Number of free parameters                         26
##
##    Number of observations                           157
##
## Model Test User Model:
##
##    Test statistic                               117.687
##    Degrees of freedom                                24
##    P-value (Chi-square)                           0.000
##
## Model Test Baseline Model:
##
##    Test statistic                               782.162
##    Degrees of freedom                                45
##    P-value                                        0.000
##
## User Model versus Baseline Model:
##
##    Comparative Fit Index (CFI)                    0.873
##    Tucker-Lewis Index (TLI)                       0.762
##
## Loglikelihood and Information Criteria:
##
##    Loglikelihood user model (H0)               -300.902
##    Loglikelihood unrestricted model (H1)       -242.059
##
##    Akaike (AIC)                                 653.804
##    Bayesian (BIC)                               733.267
##    Sample-size adjusted Bayesian (BIC)          650.967
##
## Root Mean Square Error of Approximation:
##
##    RMSEA                                          0.158
##    90 Percent confidence interval - lower         0.130
##    90 Percent confidence interval - upper         0.187
##    P-value RMSEA <= 0.05                           0.000
##
## Standardized Root Mean Square Residual:
##
##    SRMR                                           0.099
##
## Parameter Estimates:
##
##    Information                                 Expected
##    Information saturated (h1) model          Structured
##    Standard errors                             Standard
```

FIGURE 8.22 R output of an SEM model—Part I: model fit measures

```
## Regressions:
##                  Estimate  Std.Err  z-value   P(>|z|)   Std.lv   Std.all
##    lnrtden ~
##       lnlrt        0.158    0.058    2.737     0.006     0.158    0.225
##       lnhrt        0.133    0.084    1.585     0.113     0.133    0.132
##       lnpop000     0.111    0.072    1.545     0.122     0.111    0.142
##    lntfreq ~
##       lnpop000     0.308    0.038    8.052     0.000     0.308    0.541
##    lntpm ~
##       lntfreq      0.900    0.101    8.912     0.000     0.900    0.418
##       lnrtden      0.916    0.065   14.163     0.000     0.916    0.586
##       lnpop000     0.048    0.063    0.770     0.441     0.048    0.039
##       lninc000     1.325    0.264    5.011     0.000     1.325    0.214
##    lnpopden ~
##       lnpop000     0.059    0.019    3.046     0.002     0.059    0.143
##       lnrtden      0.263    0.020   13.201     0.000     0.263    0.499
##       lntfreq      0.180    0.031    5.795     0.000     0.180    0.247
##       lnolm       -0.481    0.067   -7.220     0.000    -0.481   -0.337
##       lnflm       -0.132    0.036   -3.641     0.000    -0.132   -0.141
##       lnfuel       0.399    0.297    1.344     0.179     0.399    0.057
##    lnvmt ~
##       lntpm       -0.027    0.018   -1.532     0.125    -0.027   -0.142
##       lnpop000     0.060    0.019    3.056     0.002     0.060    0.254
##       lnpopden    -0.179    0.063   -2.851     0.004    -0.179   -0.316
##       lninc000     0.329    0.087    3.798     0.000     0.329    0.278
##       lnolm        0.039    0.072    0.543     0.587     0.039    0.049
##       lnflm        0.172    0.036    4.729     0.000     0.172    0.323
##       lnfuel      -0.459    0.304   -1.513     0.130    -0.459   -0.115
##
## Variances:
##                  Estimate  Std.Err  z-value   P(>|z|)   Std.lv   Std.all
##     .lnrtden      0.483    0.055    8.860     0.000     0.483    0.857
##     .lntfreq      0.210    0.024    8.860     0.000     0.210    0.708
##     .lntpm        0.336    0.038    8.860     0.000     0.336    0.244
##     .lnpopden     0.032    0.004    8.860     0.000     0.032    0.203
##     .lnvmt        0.029    0.003    8.860     0.000     0.029    0.586
```

FIGURE 8.23   R output of an SEM model—Part II: regression model output

Note: The coefficients and p-values are identical to those from AMOS.

the SEM model-fit statistics (e.g., CFI, RMSEA), and Figure 8.23 shows regression coefficients, p-values, etc., which are identical to the AMOS results.

Planning Examples

Built Environment and VMT

An article by Cervero and Murakami (2010) used SEM to explore the relationship between built environment characteristics and vehicle miles traveled (VMT). This is not unlike our example. SEM was used to evaluate the potential traffic-moderating effects of a more complete street network and greater retail availability. The authors justified their use of SEM by saying, "SEM is particularly useful for teasing out complex multivariate data structures and, in particular, for tracing through the relative direct and indirect effects of variables on each other."

This study set out to determine if *sustainable urbanism* can reduce greenhouse gas (GHG) emissions. Sustainable urbanism calls for redesigning cities to reduce the need to drive and to reduce the lengths of necessary automobile trips. This is accomplished by consolidating trips inside mixed-use centers and through the use of alternative modes. GHG emissions were modeled as a combination of gas mileage (gallons/mile), carbon content (carbon/gallon), and activity (VMT).

Increased densities were expected to reduce VMT, with elasticities of magnitudes of −0.30. Elasticities for dense urban centers that include rail transit were predicted to be even higher.

SEM was selected as an analytical tool because past studies had been criticized based on self-selection bias. Studies that did control for such endogeneity found little or no link between VMT and density. Using SEM made it possible to statistically control for two-way relationships between variables.

Issues related to the way in which density is measured were of particular concern. Specifically, density is sometimes correlated with a wide variety of urban form factors such as land use diversity, transit access, and street connectivity. Using a single variable (average population density) to measure urban form misrepresents urban form in this case. As a result, multiple density and destination accessibility measures were included in the SEM analysis.

The data used for the analysis were cross-sectional and included VMT obtained from the Federal Highway Administration (FHWA). The analyzed dataset included 370 of 391 urban areas where the geographies were consistent across all data sources. (See Figure 8.24.)

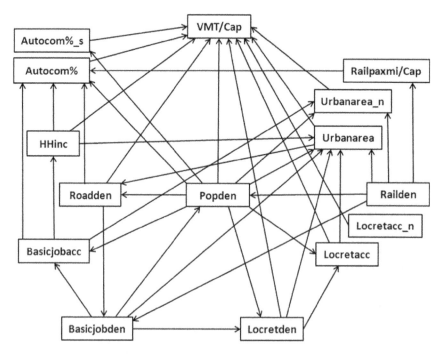

FIGURE 8.24 Path diagram of factors influencing vehicle miles traveled (VMT) per capita among 370 U.S. urbanized areas, 2003

After presenting a table with variable names, variable descriptions, data sources, and descriptive statistics about the variables, the path diagram was presented by the authors. The outcome variable (VMT/CAP) is at the top of the model and can be identified by having no arrows leading away from it. *Locretacc_n* (local retail accessibility number) and *railden* (rail density) are the only exogenous factors. Both represent region-specific factors that improve regression quality. Also included in the model are additional measures of accessibility to basic jobs and local retail.

It is useful to note that while destination accessibility is a construct that is generally thought to affect VMT, the variables used to represent that construct tended to differ from analysis to analysis, and thus so did the factor values. It is critical to note exact measures and data sources when performing any sort of statistical modeling.

IBM AMOS 7.00 was used by the authors to analyze two different models: a linear model and a model with log-transformed variables. The output of the log model is reproduced in Table 8.2.

As can be seen, the table presents both the direct effects of each variable on each other but also the indirect effects of variables upon each other through mediating (intermediary)

TABLE 8.2 Structural equation model, log–log estimation: model summary dependent variable, VMT/Cap

Independent Variables	Direct Coefficient	Indirect Coefficient	Total Coefficient
Direct			
Popden	−0.604	0.233	−0.381
Roadden	0.419	−0.005	0.415
Autocom%	0.602	0.000	0.602
Hhinc	0.260	−0.052	0.209
Locretden	0.097	0.024	0.121
Locretacc	0.079	0.013	0.091
Urbanarea	0.036	−0.019	0.017
Interaction			
Locretacc_n	−0.140	0.000	−0.140
Urbanarea_n	0.121	0.000	0.121
Autocom%_s	0.027	0.000	0.027
Indirect			
Basicjobden		−0.075	−0.075
Basicjobacc		0.018	0.018
Railpaxmi/cap		−0.002	−0.002
Railden		−0.003	−0.003
Summary statistics			
N	370		
x^2	263.038		
Degrees of freedom (df)	56		
x^2/df	4.697		
CFI (>0.900)	0.969		
NFI (>0.950)	0.961		
NNFI (>0.900)	0.942		
RMSE (≈ 0.05)	0.100		

Note: CFI—comparative fix index; NFI—normed fit index; NNFI—non-normed fit index; RMSEA—root mean square error of approximation.

variables. The total effect is also provided. Following convention regression terminology, the variables are broken into direct, indirect, and interaction terms.

The model evaluation metrics presented include the Comparative Fit Index (CFI), Normed Fit Index (NFI), as well as RMSEA. The suggested cutoff values of CFI > 0.9, NFI > 0.95, and RMSEA of about 0.05 are given, as suggested in Fan, Thompson, and Wang (1999).

The model evaluation indicated that "the strongest predictors are population densities, automobile commuting modal shares, and roadway density, followed by household income." The dummy variable for being located in the *Southern* region was also highly significant, which makes sense given the region's low average density and low compactness index scores (Ewing & Hamidi, 2014). Clusters of retail density, such as malls, were also associated with high VMT per capita. Public transit affected VMT, both directly and indirectly.

The comparison of direct and indirect effects makes it possible to establish how certain factors moderate other factors and are confounded by others. In the former case, the high VMT/Cap expected for high population density are moderated by the share of auto commuters. In the latter, Job accessibility is mediated by urbanized area size: Small urban areas have better accessibility by being small.

For clarity, the article presents portions of the actual SEM model to show the most important relationships between variables. An example of this is shown in Figure 8.25. This makes it possible to discuss the results sections without reproducing the entire SEM path model and without the distractions of coefficients and error terms, making it possible to focus the reader's attention on one piece at a time.

Sprawl and Upward Mobility

In April 2016, the fourth and fifth authors of this chapter published an article in *Landscape and Urban Planning*, utilizing SEM to account for the complex relationship between urban sprawl and upward social and economic mobility (Ewing, Hamidi, Grace, & Wei, 2016).

According to the authors, upward mobility, sometimes interchangeably used with intergenerational mobility, is a broader term that refers to one's ability to move to a higher income bracket and social status and is often tied to one's opportunities. Contrary to the general

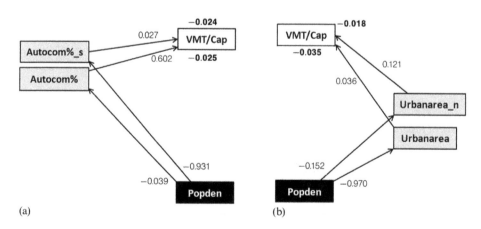

(a) (b)

FIGURE 8.25 SEM model of variable relationships

perception, the United States has a much more class-bound society than other wealthy countries. Literature shows that the chance of upward mobility for Americans is just half that of the citizens of Denmark and many other European countries (Isaacs et al., 2008; Jäntii et al., 2006).

Previous studies have found sociodemographic factors related to better upward mobility to include (1) less residential segregation, (2) less income inequality, (3) better primary schools, (4) greater social capital, and (5) greater family stability (Chetty, Hendren, Kline, & Saez, 2013; Chetty, Hendren, Kline, & Saez, 2014; Chetty, Hendren, Kline, Saez, & Turner, 2014). In addition to other influences, the built environment may contribute to the low rate of upward mobility in the United States.

This paper used structural equation modeling to partition direct and indirect effects of sprawl on upward mobility for 122 commuting zones in the United States (Figure 8.26). The compactness index developed by Ewing and Hamidi (shown as "index") was used to represent the effects of sprawl. Based on the literature review, the authors hypothesized the effects of sprawl on upward mobility to operate directly (in the model) through influences on job inaccessibility (i.e., poor and minority populations left in central cities are distant from

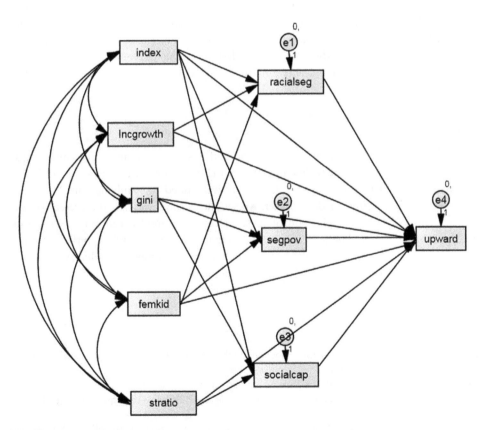

FIGURE 8.26 Causal path diagram for upward mobility in terms of metropolitan/commuting zone compactness and other variables

Source: Ewing et al., 2016; Reprinted from Ewing, R., Hamidi, S., Grace, J. B., & Wei, Y. D., (2016). Does urban sprawl hold down upward mobility? Landscape and Urban Planning, 148, 80–88. with permission from Elsevier

and poorly connected to major centers of employment in suburban areas). The authors also hypothesized sprawl affects mobility indirectly through influences on three mediating factors: weak social capital, racial segregation, and income segregation. Other exogenous variables found to be directly related to upward mobility were the rate of income growth, the share of families with kids having a female head of household and no husband, and the average student–teacher ratio in public schools, as suggested by the literature.

In this study, SEM evaluation was based on four factors: (1) theoretical soundness, (2) chi-square tests of absolute model fit, (3) root-mean-square errors of approximation (RMSEA), which unlike the chi-square, corrects for sample size, and (4) the comparative fit index (CFI). To obtain the best possible fit of the model to the data, the authors added links suggested by large modification indices. The resulting model is shown in Figure 8.26.

This study found that upward mobility is significantly higher in compact areas than in sprawling areas. The direct effect of sprawl, which is attributed to better job accessibility in more compact commuting zones, is stronger than the indirect effects. Of the indirect effects, only one, through the mediating variable income segregation, is significant.

These findings shed light on the built-environmental dimension of upward mobility. Higher density/mixed-use development has been shown to generate incrementally more jobs, higher wages, economic resilience, and lower unemployment rates, all of which advance upward mobility. Such efforts would be particularly important in some planning practice, such as affordable housing allocation and transportation investments. This study ends with a call for a subsequent international study: "Urgently needed are also international comparative studies, given the rapid urbanization and emerging trend of urban sprawl in developing countries" (Ewing et al., 2016, p. 87).

Conclusion

Univariate models, such as multiple regression and ANOVA, continue to dominate most analysis. We feel that it is not widely understood that these approaches are reductionist and descriptive, two attributes that make them not well suited for studying causal/scientific hypotheses about systems. In this chapter, we sought to show through the presentation of simple examples that the application of structural equation models can enhance scientific understanding and should be used more commonly in planning research than they currently are. Of course, care must be taken to achieve proper interpretations. Nonetheless, ultimately SEM can take us further in our understanding than can univariate analyses, and we encourage more investigators to try them to make their own determinations.

Works Cited

Byrne, B. M. (2016). Structural equation modeling with AMOS: Basic concepts, applications, and pro-gramming (3rd ed.). New York, NY: Routledge Press.

Cervero, R., & Murakami, J. (2010). Effects of built environments on vehicle miles traveled: Evidence from 370 US urbanized areas. *Environment and Planning A, 42*(2), 400–418. https://doi.org/10.1068/a4236

Chetty, R., Hendren, N., Kline, P., & Saez, E. (2013). *Economic impacts of tax expenditures: Evidence from spatial variation across the U.S.* The Equality of Opportunity Project, Retrieved September 12, 2014, from http://obs.rc.fas.harvard.edu/chetty/tax_expenditure_soi_whitepaper.pdf

Chetty, R., Hendren, N., Kline, P., & Saez, E. (2014). Where is the land of opportunity? The geography of intergenerational mobility in the United States. *National Bureau of Economic Research, 129*(4), 1553–1623.

Chetty, R., Hendren, N., Kline, P., Saez, E., & Turner, N. (2014). Is the United States still a land of opportunity? Recent trends in intergenerational mobility. *National Bureau of Economic Research, 104*(5), 141–147.

Ewing, R. (2014, Fall). *Quantitative methods.* Class Notes, University of Utah.

Ewing, R., Bartholomew, K., Winkelman, S., Walters, J., & Chen, D. (2008). *Growing cooler: The evidence on urban development and climate change.* Washington, DC: Urban Land Institute, Chapter 8.

Ewing, R., & Hamidi, S. (2014). *Measuring sprawl.* Retrieved from www.smart growthamerica.org/measuring-sprawl

Ewing, R., Hamidi, S., Gallivan, F., Nelson, A. C., & Grace, J. B. (2014). Structural equation models of VMT growth in US urbanised areas. *Urban Studies, 51*(14), 3079–3096.

Ewing, R., Hamidi, S., Grace, J. B., & Wei, Y. D. (2016). Does urban sprawl hold down upward mobility? *Landscape and Urban Planning, 148*, 80–88. https://doi.org/10.1016/j.landurbplan.2015.11.012

Ewing, R., Tian, G., & Lyons, T. (2018). Does compact development increase or reduce traffic congestion? *Cities, 72*, 94–101.

Fan, X., Thompson, B., & Wang, L. (1999). Effects of sample size, estimation method, and model specification on structural equation modeling fit indexes. *Structural Equation Modeling: A Multidisciplinary Journal, 6*(1), 56–83. https://doi.org/10.1080/10705519909540119

Fisher, R. A. (1922). The goodness of fit of regression formulae, and the distribution of regression coefficients. *Journal of the Royal Statistical Society, 85*(4), 597–612.

Fisher, R. A. (1925). *Statistical methods for research workers.* Edinburgh: Oliver and Boyd.

Grace, J. B. (2006). *Structural equation modeling and natural systems.* Cambridge, UK: Cambridge University Press.

Grace, J. B., & Bollen, K. A. (2005). Interpreting the results from multiple regression and structural equation models. *The Bulletin of the Ecological Society of America, 86*(4), 283–295.

Grace, J. B., Schoolmaster, D. R., Guntenspergen, G. R., Little, A. M., Mitchell, B. R., Miller, K. M., & Schweiger, E. W. (2012). Guidelines for a graph-theoretic implementation of structural equation modeling. *Ecosphere, 3*(8), 1–44. http://dx.doi.org/10.1890/ES12-00048.1

Isaacs, J. B., Sawhill, I. V., & Haskins, R. (2008). *Getting ahead or losing ground: Economic mobility in America.* Washington, DC: Brookings Institution.

Jäntti, M., Bratsberg, B., Røed, K., Raaum, O., Naylor, R., Osterbacka, E., Bjorklund, A., & Eriksson, T. (2006). *American exceptionalism in a new light: A comparison of intergenerational earnings mobility in the Nordic countries, the United Kingdom and the United States.* IZA Discussion Paper No. 1938.

Jöreskog, K. G. (1970). Simultaneous factor analysis in several populations. *ETS Research Report Series* (2).

Kline, R. B. (2016). *Principles and practice of structural equation modeling* (4th ed.). New York, NY: The Guilford Press.

Spearman, C. (1904). "General Intelligence," objectively determined and measured. *The American Journal of Psychology, 15*(2), 201–292.

Wright, S. (1921). Correlation and causation. *Journal of Agricultural Research, 20*(7), 557–585.

9

SPATIAL ECONOMETRICS

Keuntae Kim and Simon C. Brewer

Overview

Assume that there is a neighborhood with a high crime rate. From a rational standpoint, we may expect that adjacent neighborhoods have a greater chance of having similarly high crime rates. We can further this expectation to state that the crime rates of nearby neighborhoods may vary in similarity according to the distance from the neighborhood we defined as a reference.

In a broad sense, spatial statistics is a set of statistical techniques that use data that are georeferenced, i.e., have coordinates in space from which we can derive relative distances between observations. Spatial data are generally subject to some, usually unidentified spatial process. This process results in nonrandom spatial distributions, also termed *spatial autocorrelation* or *dependency*; observations located close to one another may have similar values or, less frequently, have highly dissimilar values (Tobler, 1970). Unlike the classical regression models discussed in Chapters 12 of *Basic Quantitative Research Methods for Urban Planners*, underlying assumptions of linear regression models cannot be guaranteed here: (1) that observations are independent from one another and (2) that the sum of residuals (or errors) between predictions of a regression model and observation values is zero to obtain an unbiased estimator. Several methods have been proposed to extend linear models to account for this, and while including spatial dependence among observations in the model may increase the complexity of our analysis, spatial analysis provides us with an explicit understanding of various phenomena in reality.

In this chapter, we split the methods and techniques for spatial data into two major parts: spatial data analysis and spatial econometrics. Spatial data analysis largely focuses on the identification and quantification of spatial patterns, which may be subsequently integrated into regression models. This avoids the violation of regression assumptions previously described and can help identify the spatial processes at play (Arbia, 2006; Anselin, 1988a, 2010; Paelinck & Klaassen, 1979). Through the integration of spatial analysis with classical econometrics, spatial econometrics is used to test whether changes in the space affect spatial structure or organizations of our domains of interest in urban planning.

We structure the chapter as follows. The first section introduces spatial data types, coordinate systems, and provides a brief historical background. The "Mechanics" section is split into a first part detailing spatial analysis techniques, including basic visualization and tools to explore spatial association, including Moran's Index, Getis-Ord's G-statistics, and Ripley's K. The second part explains spatial econometrics methods commonly used in planning research, including spatial lag and error models for global regression models based on spatial data, and geographically weighted regression (GWR), a model for local spatial regression analysis. A final section introduces spatial filtering, a recent and more generalizable method. Each section will be accompanied by worked examples using the free open-source software R. The chapter ends with two planning research cases—one using spatial analysis and the other using spatial econometrics—and concludes with the outlook of spatial analysis and spatial econometrics in future planning research.

Purpose

The purpose of all analytical methods based on spatial data is to explore and ultimately account for spatial dependency in the variable(s) of interest (Goodchild, Anselin, Appelbaum, & Harthorn, 2000). In spatial analysis, the outcomes are visualizations of the spatial patterns and a summary of the degree of dependency, which, together with established inference tests, allow researchers to judge the extent to which their analysis may be affected by spatial autocorrelation. In spatial econometrics, the goals are to build similar regression models to classical methods but to correct for the influence of the spatial dependency. The dependency itself can be considered in one of two ways, either as a variable of interest in the model or as an extra error term (a *spatially random* field). Ignoring this dependency can impact both the estimate of coefficients and their standard errors, leading to both incorrect inference and interpretation.

It is worth noting at this point that the methods presented here are designed to work with what may be described as continuous spatial dependency, that is, where similarity in values changes in a continuous way with distance. Other methods may be preferred where this is not the case. For example, where there is a strong regional effect on the response, mixed-effects models (also referred to as multilevel models; see Chapter 7) may provide a better structure. However, this will fail to account for any subregional spatial dependency. If no spatial dependency is found in the variables, then simple regression models or other methods are preferred for efficiency and simplicity of research.

Spatial Data

Spatial data can be considered a series of observations at locations $s = (s_1, s_2, \ldots, s_n)$, generally occurring in a two-dimensional plane or three-dimensional space. Each location is associated with a set of coordinates ($s(x,y)$) and one or more variables ($s(z)$) recorded at that location. The data often have associated metadata, providing information about the system of coordinates, and so on. Cressie (1992) defines three types of spatial data for analysis:

1. **Point pattern data**: The observations represent some events occurring in space, for example, plants, ore deposits, individuals with a given disease. The main interest is in exploring whether the locations of these events are random and, if not, whether the events cluster or occur randomly. From this, models can be built to help explore what factors may contribute to the spatial nonrandomness.

2. **Geostatistical data**: Here, observations are taken from point locations but represent samples of a larger spatial continuous process. These are most frequently used with environmental data, for example, air quality variables, pollution levels, climatic variables. The main goal is usually to capture the underlying spatial dependency to allow predictions at new locations.
3. **Areal data**: These represent any spatial data where information is aggregated to a larger spatial region, for example, average house price by census tract, school funding by state, GDP per country. Most socioeconomic variables used in land-use planning take this form, and the methods presented here will focus largely on this data type.

History

Spatial analysis has been developed simultaneously across a diverse set of research areas, including geography, economics, regional science, urban planning, transportation engineering, geology, epidemiology (Fischer & Getis, 2010). One of the earliest examples of spatial analysis dates back to the mid-nineteenth century, during a cholera outbreak in London, England. Dr. John Snow recorded the number of people who had died at different addresses, then plotted these numbers on a map of the area (Figure 9.1). The resulting map showed that

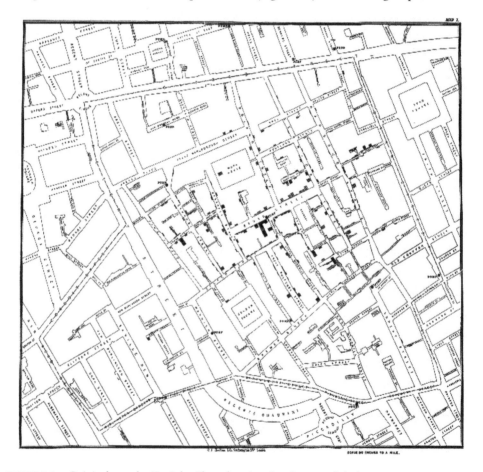

FIGURE 9.1 Original map by Dr. John Slow showing the clusters of cholera cases

Source: Wikipedia, "1854 Broad Street Cholera Outbreak"

these cases were *clustered* near a specific water pump on Broad Street, subsequently identified as the source of the disease, and ultimately resulting in a reconsideration of the method of disease transmission. While not based on formal tests, this work demonstrated several of the characteristics of modern spatial analysis, including the use of visualization and the concept of an underlying spatial process.

Development of the modern form of spatial analysis began in the 1950s. Notably, scan statistics—a particular case and antecedent of spatial econometrics that suggests selecting subsamples close to one another and performing regressions—was developed by Fisher in 1959. Later in spatial econometrics, this idea became a part of processes in geographically weighted regression (GWR) models (Arbia, 2014). Also, fundamental principles of spatial autocorrelation—a set of techniques that measure the correlations of a variable with changes in locations of observation units in space—were established during this period. As a part of spatial autocorrelation techniques, Moran's index (or Moran's I) was first introduced by P.A.P. Moran in his 1950 article and helped researchers quantify the degree to which similar values of a variable cluster within a particular spatial boundary (see discussion in the "Mechanics" section). Getis and Ord (1992) subsequently developed the G-statistic as an alternative measure of spatial autocorrelation. Two influential books on *Spatial Autocorrelation and Spatial Process* by Cliff and Ord contributed to outlining the fundamental principles of spatial analysis in modern form (Cliff & Ord, 1973, 1981).

The term "spatial econometrics" was first introduced in 1974, followed by two highly influential books in 1979 and 1988 that played a significant role in establishing the principles and formulation of spatial econometrics as distinct from spatial analysis (Anselin, 2010): The narrow definition of spatial econometrics is the collection of standard econometrics methods or techniques that take georeferenced data and regression modeling approaches into account in the analysis. Particularly, in the regional science context, Anselin's book in 1988 focused on delineating spatial econometrics as "the collection of techniques that deal with the peculiarities caused by space in the statistical analysis of regional science models" (Anselin, 1988a, p. 7).

A new analytical approach to spatial econometrics was introduced in the early 2000s—geographically weighted regression (GWR). Unlike a standard global econometric regression model, GWR allows regression parameters to vary over space so that coefficient values are based on local variations in the data. This allowed the modeling of spatial heterogeneity, that is, the nonstationary effects between covariates and a response (Fotheringham, Brunsdon, & Charlton, 2002). The 2000s also saw the development of spatial filtering (Griffith, 2003), a more easily generalizable approach to spatial regression models, in which a set of proxy variables are found to represent spatial processes. Once accounted for, this allows observations to be considered as independent and a wide range of traditional regression methods to be employed. These more recent developments underscore the fact that, as a separate statistics field, spatial econometrics is still in a developmental phase, and integration of spatial econometrics with other statistical methods will continue to progress in the future.

Mechanics

Spatial analysis starts with exploratory analysis, like all regression methods. However, the presence of georeferenced information means that there are several extra considerations during the analysis. Strictly speaking, spatial analysis includes steps from processing, visualizing, and summarizing spatial data to testing spatial dependence by using several different tests. Spatial econometrics, on the other hand, includes steps for modeling approaches such as spatial regression models and identifying spatial patterns in the data (Anselin, 2010).

The first two subsections explain spatial analysis for exploratory spatial data analysis purposes, such as handling different types of spatial data (points, lines, and polygons) and plotting spatial data on a map. Then, the next subsections explain three spatial autocorrelation techniques commonly used by researchers: Moran's I, G-statistics, and Ripley's K-function. These four subsections cover basic principles and practices of exploratory spatial data analysis often used in research. The last two subsections build on this to explain the spatial econometrics models widely used in planning research: spatial error, spatial lag, and geographically weighted regression (GWR) models.

Handling Spatial Data

Like other traditional statistical models, the first step of spatial analysis starts with data management and preprocessing. This applies not only to the recorded variables but to the locational information taken for each observation ($s(x, y)$). Spatial data are most easily managed within a geographic information system (e.g., ESRI ArcGIS, QGIS, GeoDa, GRASS GIS, etc.), which contain a wide array of functions for spatial data management. The data are stored either as *vector* or *raster* data; vector data can be used to store information from spatial objects that can have arbitrary and irregular form, whereas raster data are stored on a regular grid. As vector data comprise the large majority of spatial data for urban studies, we focus on those here.

In general, three types of vector data are commonly used:

1. **Spatial points**: Used to represent objects where the area is unimportant, for example, fire hydrants, utility poles, manhole covers. Represented by a single set of coordinates.
2. **Spatial lines**: Used to represent elements of a network, for example, roads, streams, utility lines. Represented by a set of segments, each with coordinates representing the start and end of the segment.
3. **Spatial polygons**: Used to represent areas, for example, lots, census tracts, counties. Represented by a polygon, with a set of coordinates making up the vertices and with an implicit closure between the last and first coordinates.

Vector data may also include information on the topological relationships among individual objects, used to define connectivity. For example, by defining the connections between individual polygons, it is possible to represent shared boundaries between housing lots, or administrative units, making it simple to query neighborhood relationships.

In R (the software utilized in this chapter), all of these are represented by a hierarchical data object, which may include coordinates, data values, and metadata. At the highest level, the object contains the minimum spatial extent or bounding box (*bbox*) and the projection system (*proj4string*), discussed later in the chapter. The next level stores the coordinates of each object, and the final level stores the variables recorded for each object. This structure allows fairly simple queries to be made, for example, finding the first census tract or all census tracts where the median income is greater than a certain value. An example is shown in Figure 9.2 for spatial point data.

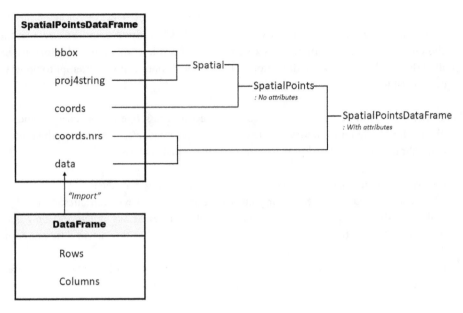

FIGURE 9.2   Structure of spatial point data

Source: Bivand, Pebesma, & Gómez–Rubio, 2013

Georeferencing

In order to identify any spatial dependency in a set of data, we need an accurate representation of the relative proximity of observations and so require that the coordinates of each observation reflect their real-world location as accurately as possible. These are subject to two main sources of uncertainty: measurement errors and georeferencing errors. The former arise from GPS uncertainty, data rounding, or transcription errors and will not be covered here. The second are more important to be aware of as they may arise during analysis, particularly when integrating data from different sources, so a brief description of the process is given here.

In short, georeferencing is the process of locating objects on the surface of an approximate sphere (the Earth) and transforming them into a Cartesian plane to allow visualization and estimates of distance. We start with locations recorded as angular coordinates from some reference point; latitude is the angle away from the equator, and longitude is the angle from a meridian. To fully transform these, a series of choices need to be made:

1. **What ellipsoid is used?** The Earth is not a perfect sphere and is best described as an ellipsoid, which requires the radius at the equator to be specified and the degree of flattening.
2. **Which datum is used?** This defines the reference points for both horizontal and vertical coordinates. Different data may be used in different regions to improve the fit of the ellipsoid to the actual surface of the Earth.

3. **What projection is used?** A projection is a mathematical transformation of angular coordinates to a two-dimensional Cartesian plane. While these take into account the chosen ellipsoid and datum, there is a wide range of possible projections. Unfortunately, all of these will involve some distortion of the locations, but most will attempt to preserve one spatial feature, either distance, direction, or area.

A full discussion of the georeferencing process is beyond the scope of this chapter, and we refer the reader to any introductory GIS textbook (e.g., Bolstad, 2016). However, the following points should be considered prior to carrying out spatial analysis:

- Be aware of which parameters were used in georeferencing your dataset.
- Choose appropriate projections for your region of interest or research question.
- Make sure the same parameters are used for all datasets, especially when obtaining georeferenced datasets from multiple sources. Reproject any data that are in different coordinate systems to the same system.
- For some types of analysis, Euclidean distance measurements can be replaced with great circle distances that account for the curvature of the Earth when estimating distances.

Defining Spatial Associations

At the heart of spatial analysis methods is the concept of a *neighborhood*. This provides a representation of the interaction between different locations, that is, for any observation, the set of other observations that may be considered to influence the value of a variable at that location. This is analogous to the use of lags in time-series analysis, and the neighbors of a given location may be referred to as spatial lags. The construction of this is important, as subsequent analyses then quantify any spatial dependency by looking at the similarity of values across sets of neighboring points. There are three main approaches to defining neighbors: contiguity, distance, and graph-based methods.

Contiguity methods are designed for use with polygon and grid-based data. Polygons are considered to be neighbors if their boundaries touch. Neighbors are assigned using one of two methods: Rook's or Queen's case, named for the corresponding movement of chess pieces (see Figure 9.3). In Rook's case, two adjacent geographic objects are considered to be neighbors if they share a boundary over some distance. Queen's case extends this to allow

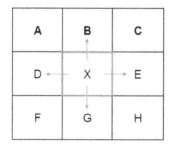 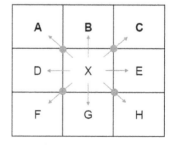

FIGURE 9.3 Defining the concept of neighborhood: Rook's (left) and Queen's (right) cases

Source: With permission from Lee, J., & Wong, D. W. S. (2001). Statistical analysis with Arcview GIS. Toronto, CA: John Wiley & Sons.

objects to be neighbors if at least one point is shared on a boundary, which allows links across touching corners (Lee & Wong, 2001). Neighborhood links formed by these methods are symmetric; if location a is a neighbor of location b, then the reverse is true.

Distance methods consider two objects to be neighbors if the distance in between is less than some specified cutoff and so are most suitable for use with point data. This method works well when the objects are relatively regularly located in the study region. The method results in symmetric neighbors, but if the locations are very irregularly distributed, the choice of cutoff distance is nontrivial. If the cutoff is too short, some distant objects may be isolated. Too long and objects in densely packed regions will have a much larger number of neighbors and carry more weight in any analysis. An extension of this method simply links each observation to its n nearest neighbors, which avoids the problem of a varying number of neighbors. However, this can often result in quite distant locations being linked, especially if n is large, and may cause asymmetric links between locations.

Graph-based methods are also designed to work with point locations. Possibly the most widely known of these is Delauney triangulation, which links sets of three locations into triangles, with the constraint that no link between any two points can cross another link. This usually results in a well structured neighborhood structure but can include some unrealistic links around the border of the region, particularly with island and peninsula geographies. A solution here is to trim the Delauney triangulation using a sphere of influence (Avis & Horton, 1985). Triangulation methods do not work well with spatial data that have regular geometry, as more than one solution can be found.

Although the last two methods are designed for use with point data, they may also be used with polygons by converting these to spatial points representing centroids of each spatial polygon object (Figure 9.4). In general, the geographical centroid is used, but other centroids can be used, for example, the population center of a region.

A final point to consider is that all these methods ignore real-world features that might alter the connectivity between two locations. For example, two locations may be close to each other but separated by a highway or river, which would limit the interaction between them. Other locations may be far apart but connected by rail services or other fast connections. Islands may be connected to the mainland only at certain points where boat services or bridges exist. It is important, then, to consider these methods as tools that provide an initial neighborhood structure to work with. Subsequent visualization and editing are important to obtain a final network.

The final step prior to analysis is to convert the neighborhood structure into a spatial weight matrix (W). This is a square matrix with n rows and columns, where $W_{i,j} > 0$ if location j is a neighbor of location i, and $W_{i,j} = 0$ otherwise. There are several choices for $W_{i,j}$ for neighboring locations. The simplest is a binary matrix with $W_{i,j} = 1$. Where the number of neighbors varies between locations,

a row-standardized matrix can be used $W_{i,j} = 1/k$, where k is the count of numbers for location i. Sometimes, complex weights are used to reflect different degrees of connectedness, for example inverse distances between locations.

Plotting Spatial Data

One significant advantage of spatial data for exploratory analysis purpose is that we can present the attributes of data on a map, that is, *geovisualization* (Fischer & Getis, 2010). Among

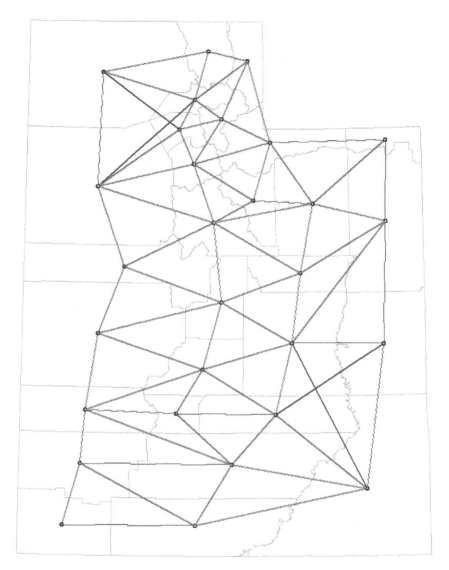

FIGURE 9.4   Example of converting spatial polygons (census tracts) into spatial points (centroids) and calculating neighbors

Note: Additional solid lines are produced by the Queen's case of neighborhoods.

geovisualization techniques, *choropleth mapping* is commonly used to explore spatial data and present the spatial analysis results. Choropleth mapping is a thematic mapping technique in which areas or points are colored in proportion to values of a variable in the spatial data table. With a single variable, choropleth maps visualize how the value of that variable varies across geographical areas of interest. With multiple variables, choropleth mapping produces a set of maps that explore possible relationships between variables. By plotting spatial data

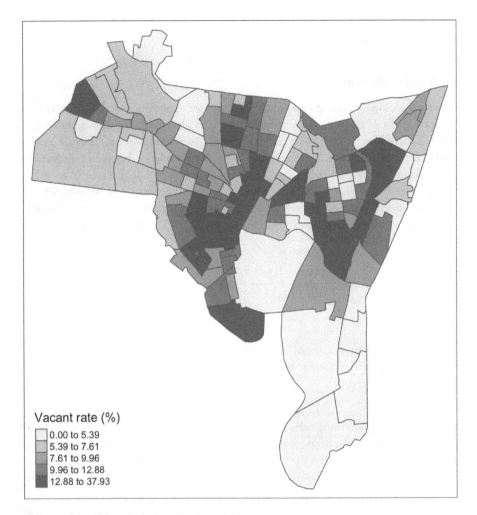

Vacant rate (%)

	0.00 to 5.39
	5.39 to 7.61
	7.61 to 9.96
	9.96 to 12.88
	12.88 to 37.93

FIGURE 9.5 Choropleth map for a single variable

Source: Brunsdon & Comber, 2015

on a map, researchers can intuitively identify overall spatial patterns, identify potential outliers, and use knowledge of the region to start to generate hypotheses concerning the spatial process.

Figure 9.5 shows an example of a choropleth map for exploratory spatial data analysis in the New Haven Crime Log data (www.newhavencrimelog.org), which is publicly available in R as base data. In a choropleth map of the vacant rate, we see that the vacant rates tend to be high south and east of the downtown area.

While geovisualization and choropleth mapping techniques help researchers explore overall patterns of variables in space, the next step is to quantify the strength of these patterns. Doing so, we need spatial econometrics methods to model the data, which can also be used to identify subregions of the study area with particularly marked patterns. We explore here three commonly used methods: Moran's *I*, Getis *G*, and Ripley's *K*.

Moran's Index (Moran's I)

Moran's *I* is the oldest and most commonly used tool for exploring spatial data, developed by P.A.P. Moran in 1950, and is designed to measure spatial autocorrelation as a modified version of Pearson's correlation. We start with the expectation that if values of a variable are randomly distributed across the study area, there should be no autocorrelation between values at neighboring locations. If there is spatial dependency, then we expect higher values to neighbor high values and lower values to neighbor low values, resulting in a positive autocorrelation between neighbors. Similarly, for negative autocorrelation, high (low) values would neighbor low (high) values. Moran's *I* is given by:

$$I = \frac{n}{\sum_i \sum_j W_{ij}} \cdot \frac{\sum_i \sum_j W_{ij}\left(z_i - \bar{z}\right)\left(z_j - \bar{z}\right)}{\sum_i \left(z_i - \bar{z}\right)^2}$$

where
W_{ij} is the (i,j)th element of a spatial weight matrix W,
n is number of spatial objects in the data, and
z is the variable of interest.

The numerator gives the spatial autocovariance: the summed cross-product of deviation from the mean of a variable at the location of interest and all other locations and the spatial weight matrix. The inclusion of the weight matrix ensures that the contribution to this sum of all non-neighbors is set to zero. This is then divided by the variance to provide an autocorrelation term.

Moran's *I* varies between approximately +1.0 and −1.0, and can be interpreted in a similar way to a correlation coefficient. Positive values indicate positive spatial autocorrelation: Similar values of a variable tend to cluster together. Negative values indicate negative spatial autocorrelation: The values at neighboring locations tend to be dissimilar. A value close to 0 indicates a lack of spatial autocorrelation. Figure 9.6 shows a simple illustration of spatial patterns based on Moran's Index values

Moran's I

Dispersed   Clustered
(-1.0)   (+1.0)

FIGURE 9.6   An illustration of spatial patterns based on the Moran's *I*

Source: From the online guide to ArcGIS, Esri

As we cannot infer from the value of Moran's I if the autocorrelation is significantly different from random, we then convert this to a z-score. This may then be compared to a standard normal distribution, allowing a p-value to be derived:

$$Z(I) = \frac{I_{obs} - E(I)}{\sqrt{\sigma_I^2}}$$

where
I_{obs} is the observed Moran's I for variable z,
$E(I)$ is the expected value of Moran's I for no autocorrelation, and
σ_I^2 the expected variance of Moran's I for variable z.

The expected value of Moran's I is given by:

$$E(I) = \frac{-1}{(n-1)}$$

where
n is the number of units in the study area.

To estimate the variance of Moran's I, we use either an assumption of normality, if the data are assumed to have been drawn from some larger normally distributed spatial pattern, or randomization, if not. The second of these introduces a correction for kurtosis of the data (Bivand, Pebesma, & Gómez-Rubio, 2013).

A local version of Moran's I was established by Anselin (1995), which decomposes the global Moran's I just described into an estimate of autocorrelation for each spatial object. It can be used to examine whether autocorrelation is relatively constant or if the global values are driven by locations that exhibit particularly strong autocorrelation.

$$I_i = \frac{n(z_i - \bar{z})}{\sum_n^{i=1}(z_i - \bar{z})^2} \cdot \sum_j \frac{W_{i,j}}{z_j - \bar{z}}$$

Like the global Moran's I, the local results can be transformed to z-scores for inference. As the local Moran's I evaluates correlations for all individual spatial objects, the summed local Moran's I estimate gives the global Moran's I estimate (Anselin, 1995, 2005).

The local autocorrelation can be visualized in a *Moran scatterplot*, where the x-axis gives the value of z at location i, and the y-axis the average value of the neighboring locations (Figure 9.7). The plot is divided into four quadrants using the mean of z. Locations falling in the bottom-left or top-right quadrants are positively autocorrelated, and those in the top left and bottom right are negatively autocorrelated. Locations situated at the extreme ends of these quadrants exhibit marked autocorrelation patterns. The slope of a regression line's fit to the scatterplot is equal to the global Moran's I.

Values on the x-axis represent the value at a given location. Values on the y-axis represent the mean value for all neighbors of that location.

Getis-Ord G-statistics

Developed by Getis and Ord (1992), the *Getis-Ord General (G) statistic* provides a complementary approach to exploring spatial dependency. Rather than using the correlation between

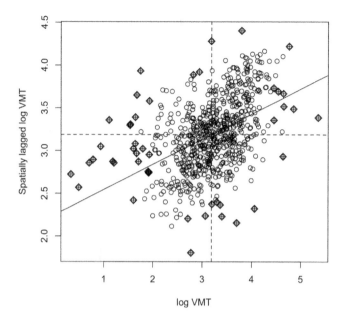

FIGURE 9.7   Example of Moran's scatterplot showing the degree of autocorrelation for the log vehicle mile traveled in the travel survey dataset: values on the x-axis = the value at a given location; values on the y-axis = the mean value for all neighbors of that location (the spatially lagged value)

neighboring values to identify areas of similarity, the G-statistic is used to identify clusters of high or low values, termed *hotspots* and *coldspots*, respectively. These can be used, for example, to find locations that provide particular high or low numbers of users of a transit system or other feature. The global G-statistic is given by:

$$G = \frac{\sum_i \sum_j w_{ij} z_i z_j}{\sum_i \sum_j z_i z_j} \quad (i \neq j)$$

where
w_{ij} is the (i,j)th element of a spatial weight matrix W,
z_i is the variable value for spatial object i, and
z_j is the variable value for spatial object j.

The value of G therefore reflects the proportion of the total sum of values that are linked to a given location. If relatively high, then there are hotspots of high value in the region, and if relatively low, there are coldspots of negative values. Inference of the G-statistic follows the same steps as Moran's *I*, by converting to a *z*-score and comparing to a standard normal distribution:

$$Z(G) = \frac{G_{obs} - E(G)}{\sqrt{\sigma_G^2}}$$

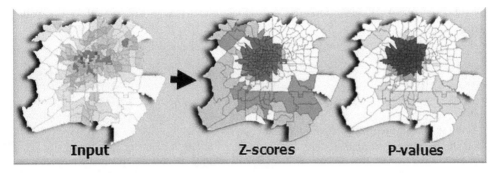

FIGURE 9.8   Example of hotspot analysis using the z-scores of the local G-statistics

Source: From the online guide to ArcGIS, Esri

where the expected value is given by:

$$E(G) = \frac{W}{n(n-1)}$$

As with Moran's I, the local version of Getis G can be used to visualize the location of the hot- or coldspots (Figure 9.8).

Spatial Econometrics

The methods described in the previous section allow the detection of autocorrelation in a spatially distributed variable. We now turn to methods to model variables in the presence of autocorrelation. First developed by Anselin (1988a) and advanced by LeSage and Pace (2009), *spatial econometrics* is a statistical approach that considers spatial interaction and effects among observations in models. Anselin proposed a framework of spatial autoregressive models, extending the general linear model to include spatial autocorrelation, either as a separate regression term (spatial lag models) or as an extended error term (spatial error models). The standard general linear model formula is defined as:

$$y = \beta X + \varepsilon$$
$$\varepsilon \sim N(0, \sigma^2)$$

where
y is a response observation variable $(y_1, y_2, \ldots, y_n)$,
X is a set of covariates $(x_1, x_2, \ldots, x_n)$,
β is a set of coefficients $(\beta_1, \beta_2, \ldots, \beta_n)$, and
ε is the error term, assumed to be independent and constant.

Spatial lag models consider that the autocorrelation arises from a diffusive process between locations, such as resource flow or *spillover*. For example, if crime rates are high in a given location, this may spill over into neighboring locations, as criminal activity is not constrained by administrative boundaries. As such, it is considered to be a process of interest and is modeled explicitly by including spatially lagged values of y for each location (the value of y at all the neighbors of i) and a single autoregressive coefficient that reflects the strength of the spatial dependency.

$$y = \rho Wy + \beta X + \varepsilon$$
$$\varepsilon \sim N\left(0, \sigma^2\right)$$

where
ρ is the spatial autoregressive coefficient, and
W is the spatial weight matrix.

The **spatial Durbin model** provides an extension to this, which includes lagged covariates in addition to the autoregressive term. This provides a method to include the diffusive effects of a covariate, for example, if house prices in a census tract are affected by crime rates in adjoining tracts. The model is defined as:

$$y = \rho Wy + \beta X + \gamma WX + \varepsilon$$
$$\varepsilon \sim N\left(0, \sigma^2\right)$$

where
γ is the set of coefficients for the spatially lagged covariates,
W is the spatial weight matrix, and
WX is the set of spatially lagged covariates, where the spatial weight matrix W defines the neighbors.

Spatial error models, in contrast, consider the autocorrelation to be a nuisance parameter that affects the independence of the error term. As such, this is more difficult to interpret but is usually attributed to missing covariates, particularly those that are not easily quantified, for example, culture, social capital, locational prestige. The standard error term is then decomposed into a spatially random part (Wu) and a noise term:

$$y = \beta X + \varepsilon$$
$$\varepsilon = \lambda Wu + v$$
$$v \sim N\left(0, \sigma^2\right)$$

where
λ is the coefficient for the spatially correlated errors, and
W is the spatial weight matrix.

For all the spatial autoregressive models, coefficients are estimated using maximum likelihood, with likelihood functions developed for normally distributed response variables (Anselin, 1988a). Nonzero values of the spatial autoregressive coefficients (ρ, γ, λ) indicate the presence of autocorrelation in the associated terms.

Spatial error and spatial lag models are used to account for a spatial autocorrelated process, either as a variable of interest or as a nuisance term. However, determining which SAR model is required is often difficult. The most commonly used statistical technique to solve this problem is the *Lagrange multiplier (LM) test* (Anselin, 1988b). Separate tests exist for the lag term and for the error term, but both test the null hypothesis that no spatial dependency exists in that term. So for the LM lag test, the null hypothesis is $\rho = 0$, and for the LM error test, $\lambda = 0$. It has been shown that false positives may be obtained for either test if there is strong enough dependency in the other term (i.e., a positive LM lag test due to strong autocorrelation of error terms). Robust versions of these tests were then introduced by Anselin, Bera, Florax, and Yoon (1996) to correct for this and enable robust discrimination between the two sources of dependency. Details of LM tests will be shown in the "Step by Step" section).

Spatial Filtering

More recently, an alternative specification of SAR models has been developed that isolate the spatial dependency using spatial filtering (Griffith, 2008). This approach is based on the same concept of differencing in time-series ARIMA models, in which the value of the response variable at any time point is replaced with the difference between the value at that time point and the preceding time. In a two-dimensional spatial field, this is implemented by replacing the value of y at a given location with the average difference to its spatial neighbors. If we take the equation for the SLM just given:

$$y = \rho W y + \beta X + \varepsilon, \ \varepsilon \sim N\left(0, \sigma^2\right)$$

and move the lagged y term to the left-hand side:

$$y - \rho W y = \beta X + \varepsilon$$

giving:

$$y\left(I - \rho W\right) = \beta X + \varepsilon$$

Where $1 - \rho W$ is the spatial filter and represents spatial dependency in the response variable. A spatial filter can also be derived for SEM models, where it is applied to the error term:

$$y = \beta X + \varepsilon\left(I - \rho W\right)^{-1}$$

While this filter is implicit in the SAR models just described, several methods exist to identify and isolate this. Among these, two convert the spatial dependency into *spatially independent variables* (Getis & Griffith, 2002), allowing the use of traditional linear models, including OLS and generalized linear models (GLMs). We concentrate here on the Moran eigenvector approach described by Griffith (2000), based on an eigen decomposition of the following matrix:

$$\left(I - 11^T / n\right) \cdot W \cdot \left(I - 11^T / n\right)$$

where
I is a $n \times n$ identity matrix,
1 is a vector of ones of length n, and
W is the spatial weight matrix.

Decomposition of this matrix yields a set of *n* orthogonal eigenvectors, called Moran eigenvectors (ME). Each eigenvector represents a possible spatial pattern, where the first eigenvector represents the pattern with the strongest positive autocorrelation and highest Moran's *I* value. The second then represents the next strongest pattern, which is uncorrelated with the first, and so on. The *n*th eigenvector represents the pattern with the strongest negative autocorrelation and is uncorrelated with all other eigenvectors. The different eigenvectors therefore represent spatial pattern at different scales, from landscape to regional to local.

The top row of Figure 9.9 shows the first and fourth ME, both of which show strong spatial patterns. The bottom left represents ME 265 where the pattern is random, and the bottom right is ME 670 which shows strong negative autocorrelation. Spatial filtering consists of choosing a set of these patterns to represent the unknown spatial process. The Moran's *I* value for each pattern is given in the bottom left corner.

Each eigenvector obtained is a simple vector of length *n* and may be then used as a covariate in the regression model. As the observed spatial pattern is usually more complex than any

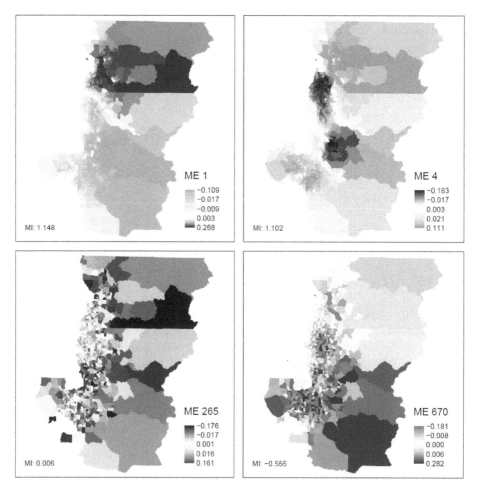

FIGURE 9.9   Four examples of hypothetical ME patterns obtained from the eigen decomposition of the spatial weight matrix for Washington

single component, a set of eigenvectors is selected using a stepwise method. Starting with the observed Moran's I value, each eigenvector is added to the model, and the value of I is recalculated. The vector that results in the largest reduction in I is retained, and the process is repeated until the reduction is less than some threshold value.

One of the main advantages of this approach is that it may be easily used with GLMs, allowing the modeling of binomial and Poisson variables in a spatial context. For a spatial GLM, Griffith and Peres-Neto (2006) recommend including the full design matrix X in the matrix used in the decomposition, as the orthogonality of the eigenvectors can be corrupted during the estimation of the GLM coefficients:

$$\left[I - X\left(X^T X\right)^{-1} X^T\right] \cdot W \cdot \left[I - X\left(X^T X\right)^{-1} X^T\right]$$

where
X is the design matrix with p covariates and a vector of n ones.

Geographically Weighted Regression Model

Geographically weighted regression (GWR) is another spatial econometrics technique that has been recently used in planning research, attempts to account for spatial dependency and spatial heterogeneity, and allows that model coefficients may vary across space. In contrast to the other methods considered here, which define a global model for the study area, GWR consists of a set of local regression models, usually estimated at each observed location (Fotheringham et al., 2002).

For geographically weighted OLS regression, a model is fit for each location i, as follows:

$$y_i = \beta_i X_i + \varepsilon_i, \varepsilon_i \sim N\left(0, \sigma_i^2\right)$$

where
y_i is the set of response values,
X_i is the set of covariates,
β_i is a set of coefficients for location i, and
ε_i is the error term for location i.

The model is fit using weighted least squares, where weights are based on the distance between each observation in the dataset and location i. Weights are assigned using a two-dimensional kernel centered at location i. There are several options for the form of the kernel, including box, Gaussian, tricubic, and exponential. The method also requires a bandwidth, which controls the size of the kernel, and is usually chosen by cross-validation. Bandwidth may be set to fixed or adaptive. Fixed bandwidths use the same size for all locations and are suitable for data that are fairly regularly distributed in space. Adaptive bandwidths vary according to data density, with smaller values in data-rich regions and larger values in data-sparse areas. This second method is more suitable for irregularly distributed observations, as it ensures that all local models are built using the same number of neighboring observations. It is worth noting that the choice of bandwidth can be quite time-consuming, especially with large datasets.

Once chosen, models are then estimated for each location. The results can be presented as a table or map showing the spatial variation in model coefficients and standard goodness-of-fit measures (Figure 9.10). Large variations in coefficients can be taken as evidence of spatial heterogeneity of the modeled relationship, whereas variation in goodness-of-fit may indicate misspecification in regions where the values are low.

Once the whole procedure is done, regression coefficients of each spatial object are estimated as a range. Using these ranges of regression coefficient estimates for each spatial object, we can draw a choropleth map of the regression coefficient. A choropleth map helps researchers identify spatial heteroscedasticity of the distribution of regression coefficients and local outliers across the study region for covariates being evaluated.

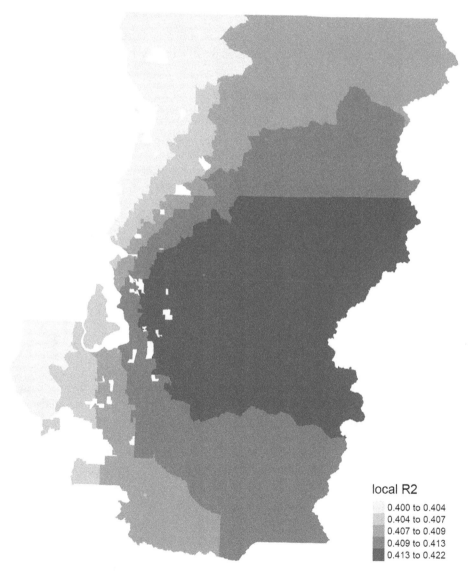

local R2
- 0.400 to 0.404
- 0.404 to 0.407
- 0.407 to 0.409
- 0.409 to 0.413
- 0.413 to 0.422

FIGURE 9.10 This is taken from a GWR model developed for vehicle miles traveled for Washington State. See the step-by-step examples for more details.

While GWR performs well as an exploratory tool to identify local relationships within a large spatial dataset, several studies have criticized it as a modeling approach. Simulation studies have shown it to be particularly affected by collinearity, which can result in apparent spatial patterns in coefficients, even when the mean spatial process is constant (Páez, Farber, & Wheeler, 2011), while applications with smaller datasets can result in counterintuitive coefficients and correlations between variables (Wheeler & Tiefelsdorf, 2005). Páez et al. (2011) recommend caution in the application of GWR, with particular attention to potential collinearity, the choices of bandwidth and sample size, with over 160 samples recommended.

Point Pattern Analysis

While the majority of spatial studies in urban planning have used the econometric methods just described, some recent studies have used point pattern analysis to examine the location of households or pedestrians, and we give a brief introduction to these methods in this section.

In contrast to the econometric methods, in which we wish to model the variation in some variable at a set of georeferenced locations, the goal of point pattern analysis is to study the spatial distribution of a set of features on a landscape, for example, animals, plants, pedestrians, disease cases. In particular, we wish to know if the features exhibit a nonrandom distribution, either clustered or regular. If the spatial distribution is nonrandom, we can infer that there is some underlying spatial process that results in the observed distribution. As our interest is in the location of observations, point pattern analysis is not applicable to all spatial data, only those that can exhibit some level of self-organization.

We define a point pattern dataset as a set of objects or *points* occurring at locations $s = (s_1, s_2, \ldots, s_n)$ within a study window W. The point pattern may be summarized by its *intensity* (λ), giving the expected number of points for a given areal unit:

$$\lambda = \frac{n}{A}$$

where
λ is the intensity of the spatial point process,
n is the number of spatial points, and
A is the area of the study window.

The intensity may then be used to define a null model of complete spatial randomness (CSR), giving the expected distribution of points with no organization. The basic model used is a homogenous Poisson process, which states that the expected number of points in any unit area is taken from a Poisson distribution with mean equal to λ. The locations of points are assumed to be independent from each other; that is, the occurrence of a point does not change the probability of the occurrence of any other point (Diggle, 2013) and cannot be exactly colocated. An extension to this, inhomogeneous Poisson processes allow for the study of point patterns where the intensity is nonstationary. Other spatially distributed variables can then be used to model the spatial variations in this intensity.

Ripley's K

While several measures of the organization of point patterns have been proposed, the most commonly used is Ripley's K (Ripley, 1976). Unlike the Moran's I and the Getis-Ord

G-statistics, Ripley's K is a function of distance and describes the total number of points that would be found within a certain distance of any randomly chosen point in the study area. It is defined as:

$$K(d) = \lambda^{-1} \cdot E(N_d)$$

where $E(N_d)$ is the expected number of points within a distance d from any point in the study area, and λ is the intensity of the spatial point process.

The estimated value of Ripley's K is derived from the set of all interpoint distances in the dataset. For any distance d, this is derived as:

$$\hat{K}(d) = \lambda^{-1} \cdot \sum_{i}^{n} \sum_{j}^{n} \frac{\delta_{ij}(d_{ij}, d)}{n}, i \neq j$$

where
d_{ij} is the distance between any two points i and j, and
δ_{ij} is an indicator function equal to 1 if $d_{ij} < d$, and 0 otherwise.

In practice, Ripley's K is calculated for a set of distances, and the resulting values of K are visualized as a function of distance d. Thus one of the advantages of this approach is that it provides a measure of spatial organization at different spatial scales.
    Under the hypothesis of CSR, Ripley's K takes the following values:

$$K_{CSR}(d) = \pi d^2$$

The observed value of K may then be compared to this to look for evidence of clustering or ordering of the spatial points. For example, if $\hat{K}(d) > K_{CSR}$, then more points are located within d of one another than would be expected. If d is low, this is generally evidence of clustering. Examples are given in Figure 9.11.
    Significant departures from CSR are generally tested using a Monte Carlo approach. Here, a large number of spatial point patterns are generated that have equivalent intensity but follow the assumptions of CSR. For each pattern, Ripley's K is estimated, and upper and lower confidence intervals are calculated from the envelope of resulting values. If $\hat{K}(d)$ falls outside these limits, this is taken as evidence for significant organization at that distance.
    The L-function is often used as an extension to Ripley's K to help in visualization and to stabilize the variance of K. This is simply the square root of K divided by π:

$$\hat{L}(d) = \sqrt{\frac{\hat{K}(d)}{\pi}}$$

And the expected value under CSR is:

$$L_{CSR}(d) = \sqrt{\frac{\pi d^2}{\pi}} = d$$

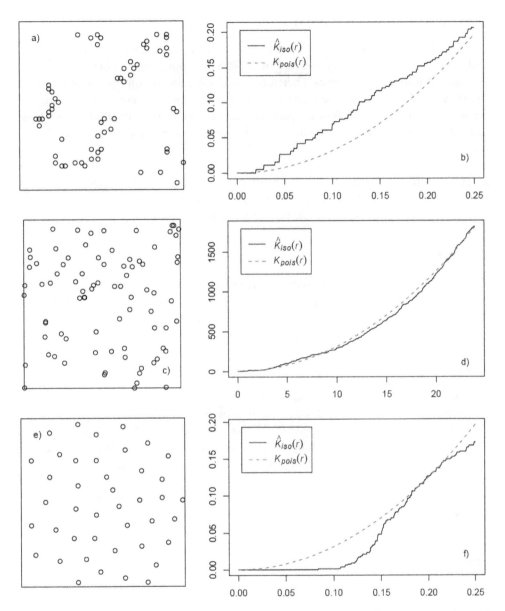

FIGURE 9.11 Examples of point patterns and the corresponding K-function: top row: clustered pattern; middle row: random pattern; bottom row: ordered pattern

Ripley's K may be extended to the bivariate case, where we consider the possible spatial interaction between two different point patterns. From this, we can ask whether one type of point attracts or repulses another, for example, if certain features of a landscape or street cause pedestrians to cluster or disperse. This is referred to as Ripley's K-cross and is calculated by replacing the interpoint distances in the Ripley's K equation with distances between points from the two types and calculating the number of points of type B that fall within distance d of points of type A. The value for K-cross under CSR and inference testing proceeds in the same way as previously described.

Step by Step 1: Spatial Data Analysis

The previous chapters of this book use both SPSS and R to conduct various statistical analyses Unfortunately, the current version of SPSS does not provide functions for spatial analysis and spatial econometrics. Therefore, this chapter focuses on the use of R, which has several add-on packages designed for spatial analysis and regression. In this chapter, we will make use of the following packages, so we start then by installing these. Note that you will only have to install these once, but the packages must be loaded each time you restart R.

```
install.packages(c("sp", "spdep", "spatialreg", "spgwr",
                "rgdal", "tmap", "RColorBrewer"))
```
To load a given package, use the **library()** function:

```
library(sp)
```

For more detailed introduction to R, the CRAN project website provides a free manual of using R (https://cran.r-project.org/manuals.html). Otherwise, out of a number of introductory R books, we recommend *R in Action* (2nd edition, 2015) by Robert Kobacoff and *R in a Nutshell: A Desktop Quick Reference* (2015) by Joseph Adler.

Reading the Data

We start by loading the household survey data file (HTS.household.10regions.sav). As this is an SPSS file, we use the **read.spss()** function from the foreign library. The data are loaded and stored as a data frame object (**hts**), the default data type. This represents data as a set of variables (columns) recorded for a series of observations (rows). Other types of object exist, and the **class()** function can be used to examine the current type.

```
hts = foreign::read.spss("HTS.household.10regions.sav",
to.data.frame = TRUE)

## re-encoding from CP1252

class(hts)

## [1] "data.frame"
```

The following functions can be used to generate information about the structure of any R object (**str()**) and summary statistics:

```
str(hts)      # Identifying variables and their types
summary(hts)  # Summary statistics
```

The dollar notation is used in R to access individual variables from a data frame. The variable of interest is **lnvmt** (vehicle miles traveled on a log scale); so to extract just this, type:

```
hts$lnvmt
```

This notation can then be used to calculate various statistics, for example, to get the mean value of **lnvmt**:

```
mean(hts$lnvmt) # Mean
```

This returns an **NA** as there are missing values in the variable. To exclude these, we add the argument **na.rm = TRUE** to the function:

```
mean(hts$lnvmt, na.rm=TRUE) # Mean
```

Some other summary statistics:

```
sd(hts$lnvmt, na.rm=TRUE) # Standard deviation
var(hts$lnvmt, na.rm=TRUE) # Variance
median(hts$lnvmt, na.rm=TRUE) # Median
quantile(hts$lnvmt, na.rm=TRUE, c(0.25, 0.75)) # Quantiles
         (25 and 75%tile)
```

Documentation describing any R function can be obtained using the **help()** function or by prepending a question mark to any function name. For example:

```
help(mean)
?mean
```

Spatial Data in R

The *sp* package provides a series of classes for spatial data, which are largely analogous to the data objects used by most standard GIS software. Here, we convert the data frame read in the previous section to a SpatialPointsDataFrame. This object keeps all the information in the original table by adding metadata (or "slots") with information relevant to georeferencing.

To convert a data frame to a SpatialPointsDataFrame, we need simply to specify which columns contain the coordinates. We start by selecting the subset of observations with coordinates by excluding any missing values. This will result in 3,904 households in Seattle, Washington. Next we specify which variables contain the coordinates, automatically converting this to a spatial object in R:

```
hts.sp <- subset(hts, !is.na(intptlon10))
coordinates(hts.sp) <- ~intptlon10+intptlat10
class(hts.sp)
str(hts.sp)
```

Using **str()** now shows that a new set of information has been added, including the coordinates, bounding box, and the projection (**proj4string**). The projection string is defined using the PROJ4 library (http://proj4.org), which uses a set of standard parameters to define a projection. In this case, it is currently undefined ("NA"), so we will now set it to a standard longitude/latitude projection based on the WGS1984 datum. Here we use one of the EPSG numeric codes to set the projection. More information about these codes can be found at the EPSG website (http://spatialreference.org/ref/epsg/).

```
proj4string(hts.sp) = CRS("+init=epsg:4326")
proj4string(hts.sp)
```

```
## [1] "+init=epsg:4326 +proj=longlat +datum=WGS84 +no_defs
+ellps=WGS84 +towgs84=0,0,0"
```

If we recheck the projection string, you will see that this has added information about the projection datum, ellipsoid, and so on.

We now make a simple map showing the location of the households. We first modify the figure margins, then plot simple circles, where the color is specified by the **col** parameter as an RGB triplet, with each color specified as a value between 0 and 1. Note that the fourth number in the **rgb()** function specifies the transparency level.

```
plot(hts.sp, pch=16, cex=.5, col=rgb(1, 0.55, 0, 0.2),
      axes=TRUE)
```

To improve this map, we can overlay other spatial layers. We first import an existing shape-file of census tract boundaries (*tract10.shp; a shapefile for Washington state available from the online resource page of this book*), using the **readOGR()** function from the *rgdal* package. In contrast to the point data, this is a set of polygons describing the tracts and is stored in R as a SpatialPolygonsDataFrame:

```
library(rgdal)
ct.sp <- readOGR("./tract10/tract10.shp")
class(ct.sp)
proj4string(ct.sp)
```

The projection details for this shapefile are different from our data. The shapefile has been projected to Lambert Conic Conformal (**+proj=lcc**). We will therefore need to reproject our household data to match using the **spTransform()**. This requires the object to be reprojected and a description of the new projection (we just use the **proj4string** from the census tract data):

```
hts.sp <- spTransform(hts.sp, CRS(proj4string(ct.sp)))
proj4string(hts.sp)
```

```
## [1] "+proj=lcc +lat_1=45.83333333333334
+lat_2=47.33333333333334 +lat_0=45.33333333333334 +lon_0=-
120.5 +x_0=500000.0000000001 +y_0=0 +ellps=GRS80 +units=us-
ft +no_defs"
```

And we now remake the figure, starting with the census tract boundaries, then adding the household locations (Figure 9.12; note that this plots the entire state):

```
plot(ct.sp, lwd=1, lty=6, border="gray", axes=TRUE)
plot(hts.sp, pch=16, cex=.5, col=rgb(1, 0.55, 0, 0.2),
add=TRUE)
```

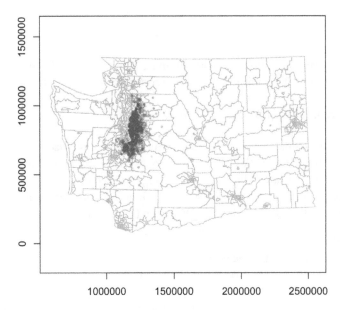

FIGURE 9.12   Projected map of household data in Seattle, Washington

As a final step, we show how to export the SpatialPointDataFrame as an Esri shapefile using the **writeOGR()** function from the *rgdal* package. Note that we need to specify the file name (**layer**), the directory where this will be written (**dsn**), and the type of file to write (**driver**).

```
writeOGR(hts.sp, layer="hts_loc",
         dsn="./shapefiles/",
         driver="ESRI Shapefile",
         overwrite_layer=TRUE)
## Warning in writeOGR(hts.sp, layer = "hts.sp", dsn =
"./shapefiles",
## driver = "ESRI Shapefile", : Field names abbreviated for
ESRI Shapefile
## driver
```

Creating Spatially Aggregate Variables

For the modeling examples given here, we will be interested in exploring the variation in the logged median vehicle miles traveled (**lnvmt**) per census tract following the study by Ewing et al. (2015). In order to do this, we need to aggregate the variables from the household dataset to the census tract polygons. We use the **aggregate()** function in the *sp* package, which allows the aggregation of values from one spatial dataset to another, to calculate the mean value of **lnvmt** in each census tract.

```
ct.sp$lnvmt = aggregate(hts.sp["lnvmt"], ct.sp, mean,
na.rm=TRUE)$lnvmt
summary(ct.sp$lnvmt)
```

```
## Min. 1st Qu. Median Mean 3rd Qu. Max. NA's
## 0.3195 2.7996 3.2171 3.1879 3.6304 5.3577 770
```

Prior to any analysis, we do a little data cleaning. The **summary()** function shows that five of the census tracts have missing values for **lnvmt**, so we will delete these:

```
ct.sp = ct.sp[!is.na(ct.sp$lnvmt),]
```

We can use these results to plot out the median income per census tract to make a choropleth or thematic map (Figure 9.13). We will make use of functions from the *tmap* package to make the map, so we start by loading this package. The *tmap* package builds maps as a series of layers by adding a set of functions together. We start by making a simple map, with just the shapefile (**tm_shape()**) and polygon borders (**tm_border()**), then add a fill to color the polygons.

```
library(tmap)
tm_shape(ct.sp) + tm_borders()
tm_shape(ct.sp) + tm_borders() + tm_fill("darkorange")
```

Next, we replace the single color in **tm_fill()** with a variable name to create the choropleth map. Note that we also specify the name of the color palette to use and an argument (**style()**), which specifies how the intervals of the color palette are formed (try replacing **"pretty"** with **"quantile"** or **"order"**).

```
tm_shape(ct.sp) +
  tm_fill(col = "lnvmt", palette = "Greens", style = "pretty",
title = "log VMT")
```

Spatial Data Analysis

We now want to explore the dataset for spatial autocorrelation in vehicle miles traveled using the add-on package *spdep*.

```
library(spdep)
```

We start by creating and visualizing two example neighborhood structures using the **poly2nb()** function.

```
Queens case
```

```
ct.nb.q <- poly2nb(ct.sp)
ct.nb.q
plot(ct.sp, border="darkgrey")
plot(ct.nb.q, coordinates(ct.sp), add=TRUE, col="blue",
lwd=2)
```

```
  Rook's case (queen=FALSE)
```

```
ct.nb.r <- poly2nb(ct.sp, queen=FALSE)
plot(ct.sp, border="darkgrey")
```

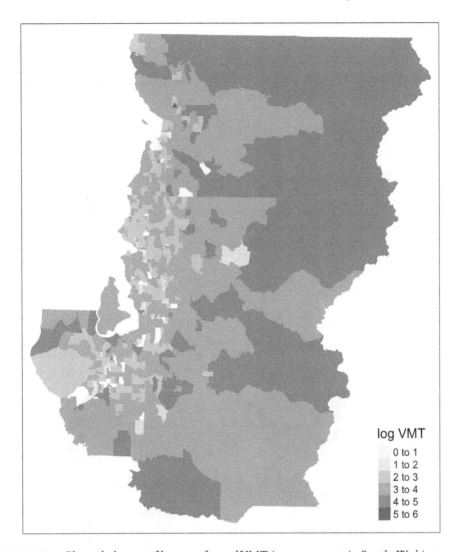

FIGURE 9.13 Choropleth map of log-transformed VMT in census tracts in Seattle, Washington

```
plot(ct.nb.r, coordinates(ct.sp), add=TRUE, col="green",
lwd=2)
```

Moran's I

We now will use Moran's *I* to test for autocorrelation, using the function **moran.test()**. This function requires two inputs: the variable to be tested for autocorrelation and the spatial weight matrix. We therefore start by converting the Queen's case neighborhood structure to a spatial weight matrix, then run Moran's *I*:

```
ct.lw = nb2listw(ct.nb.q)
moran.test(ct.sp$lnvmt, ct.lw)
```

The results give a Moran's *I* value of 0.294, a *z*-score of 12.882, and a *p*-value of 0, allowing us to reject the null hypothesis of no spatial autocorrelation. Note that by default the test is under the assumption of randomization. We now investigate the pattern of autocorrelation by estimating local values of Moran's *I*, using the **localmoran()** function and the same data as in the previous example.

```
ct.locm <- localmoran(ct.sp$lnvmt, ct.lw)
head(ct.locm)
```

The output is a set of values for each census tract giving the value of Moran's *I* (**Ii**), the expected value and variance (**E.Ii** and **Var.Ii**), and the *z*-score and *p*-value. High *z*-scores and low *p*-value indicate that a particular tract is highly correlated with its neighbors. To visualize the output, we make choropleth maps of the *z*-score and the associated *p*-value (Figure 9.14). Evidence for significant positive autocorrelation is found to the east, as well as some areas of downtown Seattle.

```
ct.sp$locmi = ct.locm[,"Z.Ii"]
map1 = tm_shape(ct.sp) +
  tm_fill(col = "locmi", palette = "RdBu", style = "order")
ct.sp$locmip = ct.locm[,"Pr(z > 0)"]
```

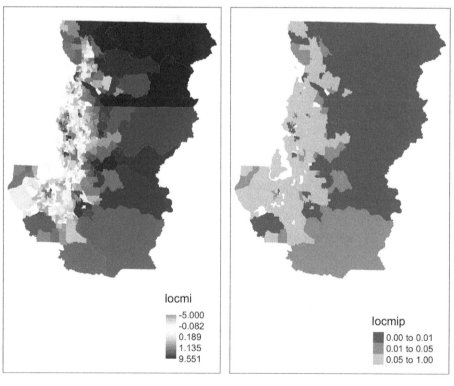

FIGURE 9.14   Maps of local Moran's *I* values of log VMT (left) and *p*-values (right) in census tracts in Seattle, Washington

```
breaks = c(0, 0.01, 0.05, 1)
map2 = tm_shape(ct.sp) +
  tm_fill(col = "locmip", palette = "-Reds", breaks = breaks)
tmap_arrange(map1, map2)
```

The Getis-Ord Index

The Getis-Ord index can be calculated using the **localG()** function, which again takes the variable to be tested and the weight matrix.

```
ct.locg <- localG(ct.sp$lnvmt, ct.lw)
```

We now map the results (Figure 9.15). As the values of G are in standard deviations of a standard normal distribution, we look for areas that exceed −1.96 or 1.96 as evidence for

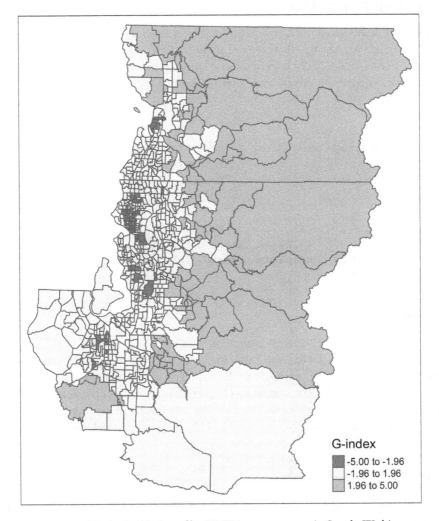

G-index

- -5.00 to -1.96
- -1.96 to 1.96
- 1.96 to 5.00

FIGURE 9.15   Map of Getis-Ord Index of log VMT in census tracts in Seattle, Washington

significant cold- or hotspots, respectively. A notable hotspot occurs, not too surprisingly, out to the east, where vehicle travel is elevated in many tracts. The patch of positive autocorrelation in the downtown area is shown here to be a coldspot, that is, lower than expected values.

```
ct.sp$locg = ct.locg
summary(ct.locg)
breaks = c(-5,-1.96, 1.96, 5)
map2 = tm_shape(ct.sp) +
  tm_fill(col = "locmip", palette = "-Reds", breaks = breaks)
tm_shape(ct.sp) + tm_borders() +
  tm_fill(col = "locg", palette = "-RdBu", breaks = breaks,
title = "G-index") +
  tm_legend(bg.color = "white")
```

Step by Step 2: Spatial Econometrics

We now turn to modeling the variation in the vehicle miles traveled. We start by making a new spatial object (**cthh.sp**) that contains all the variables used in the model presented in Table 5 of Ewing et al. (2015). Note that, in contrast to that paper using household-based approach, we aggregate to census tract level to illustrate the process of building a spatial regression model.

```
library(spatialreg)
cthh.sp = aggregate(hts.sp[c("lnvmt", "hhsize",
                             "hhworker", "hhincome",
                             "emp10a", "emp30t",
                             "jobpop", "actden",
                             "entropy", "intden",
                             "pct4way")],
                    ct.sp, mean, na.rm=TRUE)
cthh.sp = cthh.sp[complete.cases(cthh.sp@data),]
summary(ct.sp$lnvmt)
```

OLS Regression

Next, we fit an OLS model to these data to provide a baseline model. The R function for building a linear model is **lm()**, which uses the formula syntax with the dependent variable on the left-hand side and the covariates on the right. The second argument is the data object that contains these variables. The **summary()** function provides summary diagnostics for the model, showing here that several of the variables have a significant relationship with the vehicle miles traveled, including household size, household income, entropy, and intersection density.

```
lnvmt.lm = lm(lnvmt ~., cthh.sp)
summary(lnvmt.lm)
```

From the previous section, we know that the dependent variable is autocorrelated. However, as it is possible that this is fully accounted for by one of the covariates, we make a quick test for residual spatial autocorrelation before proceeding. We first remake the neighborhood structure and weight matrix. Residuals are extracted from the model object with **residuals()** and added back to the spatial object. Finally, we use these to run the test:

```
cthh.nb = poly2nb(cthh.sp)
cthh.lw = nb2listw(cthh.nb)
cthh.sp$lmres = residuals(lnvmt.lm)
moran.test(cthh.sp$lmres, cthh.lw)
```

The high z-score (and associated low p-value) suggest that the residuals are autocorrelated and violate the assumption of independence. Visualizing the residuals shows that the problem stems largely from the set of positive residuals in the east:

```
tm_shape(cthh.sp) +
  tm_fill(col = "lmres", palette = "PRGn", style = "quantile",
title = "LM residuals") +
  tm_legend(bg.color = "white")
```

Before proceeding, we drop the residuals from the spatial object.

```
cthh.sp = cthh.sp[,-12]
```

Lagrange Multiplier Test

The previous test shows that the residuals are autocorrelated. We now turn to the development of a spatial model. We start by performing the Lagrange multiplier test to help with the choice of model.

```
summary(lm.LMtests(lnvmt.lm, cthh.lw,
test=c("LMerr","LMlag")))
```

As the Lagrange diagnostic value is slightly higher for the spatial lag model, we will use this. However, there is little practical difference between them, and ultimately a more complex model structure may be required.

Spatial Lag Model

We start by building the spatial lag model. This uses the function **lagsarlm()** and takes the same arguments as the linear model with the addition of the spatial weight matrix.

```
lnvmt.splag <- lagsarlm(lnvmt ~.,
                        data=cthh.sp@data, listw=cthh.lw)
summary(lnvmt.splag)
##
## Call:lagsarlm(formula = lnvmt ~., data = cthh.sp@data,
    listw = cthh.lw)
##
## Residuals:
##          Min           1Q     Median           3Q          Max
```

```
## -2.818887  -0.256273  0.027966  0.280896  2.287921
##
## Type: lag
## Coefficients: (asymptotic standard errors)
##                 Estimate     Std. Error   z value    Pr(>|z|)
## (Intercept)     2.25007780   0.21215445   10.6058    < 2.2e-16
## hhsize          0.18622097   0.03186442    5.8442    5.091e-09
## hhworker        0.15335838   0.05007209    3.0628    0.002193
## hhincome        0.00371490   0.00081212    4.5743    4.777e-06
## emp10a         -0.00014693   0.00721065   -0.0204    0.983743
## emp30t         -0.01147278   0.00314387   -3.6492    0.000263
## jobpop         -0.15976421   0.09853428   -1.6214    0.104930
## actden          0.00018367   0.00191488    0.0959    0.923588
## entropy        -0.20350414   0.10985004   -1.8526    0.063945
## intden         -0.00137934   0.00044324   -3.1119    0.001859
## pct4way        -0.00083781   0.00137933   -0.6074    0.543584
##
## Rho: 0.16791, LR test value: 10.217, p-value: 0.0013915
## Asymptotic standard error: 0.052031
##      z-value: 3.227, p-value: 0.0012509
## Wald statistic: 10.414, p-value: 0.0012509
##
## Log likelihood: -485.5168 for lag model
## ML residual variance (sigma squared): 0.24497, (sigma:
    0.49494)
## Number of observations: 676
## Number of parameters estimated: 13
## AIC: 997.03, (AIC for lm: 1005.3)
## LM test for residual autocorrelation
## test value: 3.5047, p-value: 0.061196
```

The **summary()** function again produces a large quantity of model diagnostics, including updated model coefficients and inference tests. The parameter **Rho** is the autoregressive coefficient, here equal to 0.168, providing a measure of the strength of the autocorrelation, that is, how the vehicle miles traveled in any given location is influenced by the VMT in neighboring locations. Now let's check to see whether this has accounted for the residual autocorrelation:

```
moran.test(residuals(lnvmt.splag), listw = cthh.lw)
```

The test is no longer significant, indicating that the residuals for this new model are now independent and that the autocorrelation has been accounted for.

Spatial Error Model

A spatial error model can be built using the **errorsarlm()** function, and the same parameters as the lag model:

```
lnvmt.sperr <- errorsarlm(lnvmt ~.,
                    data=cthh.sp@data, listw=cthh.lw)
summary(lnvmt.sperr)
```

Now the parameter of interest is **Lambda**, the coefficient measuring the error autoregression, here equal to 0.135.

Spatial Filtering

For spatial filtering, two steps are required. In the first, the function **SpatialFiltering()** performs the eigen decomposition of the spatial weight and design matrices, then undergoes a stepwise selection of the resulting eigenvectors, based on the change in Moran's I calculated on the residuals when the eigenvector is included. Two criteria can be used for selection:

> **tol**: Stop when no eigenvector reduces Moran's I by more than this value
> **alpha**: Stop when the p-value of the Moran's I z-score is greater than this value

Here, we run this for the VMT dataset, using an **alpha** value of 0.25. Note that the function requires the original neighborhood structure rather than the spatial weight matrix, which is calculated internally:

```
lnvmt.ev = SpatialFiltering(lnvmt ~.,
                            data=cthh.sp, nb=cthh.nb,
                            style="W",
                            alpha = 0.25, ExactEV = FALSE)
lnvmt.ev
```

The output tells us that two eigenvectors were selected. These eigenvectors are extracted and then used in the **lm()** function as additional regressors in a new model:

```
ev.sel <- fitted(lnvmt.ev)
lnvmt.sf = lm(lnvmt ~. + ev.sel, cthh.sp)
summary(lnvmt.sf)
```

The spatially filtered model shows an improvement in the R^2 compared to the original OLS model. As the spatial lag and error models are fit by maximum likelihood, we can use the AIC scores to compare them, shown in the following table. This value can be found in the summary diagnostics of the models or can be extracted for each model using the **AIC()** function.

Model	AIC
Linear model	1005.2506
Spatial lag	997.0336
Spatial error	1002.8819
Spatial filter	983.3518

In this case, the filtered model offers the best overall model fit. We finish this section by estimating Moran's I for the residuals of this model, which shows that the autocorrelation has been well accounted for:

```
moran.test(residuals(lnvmt.sf), cthh.lw)

##
## Moran I test under randomisation
```

```
##
## data: residuals(lnvmt.sf)
## weights: cthh.lw
##
## Moran I statistic standard deviate = 0.65125,
##   p-value = 0.2574
## alternative hypothesis: greater
## sample estimates:
## Moran I statistic      Expectation          Variance
##     0.0137159854    -0.0014814815     0.0005445667
```

Geographically Weighted Regression

We now use GWR to explore spatial heterogeneity in the model. We use the add-on library *spgwr* to perform GWR (an alternative is *GWmodel*). This also requires two steps: the selection of the model parameters and then fitting the chosen model. The parameters to be chosen relate to the size of the window used for the individual, local regressions. The window size can be fixed or adaptive, in which case the number of observation used is constant across windows. Here we choose an adaptive window and Gaussian weights.

```
library(spgwr)
lnvmt.bw <- gwr.sel(lnvmt ~.,
                    data = cthh.sp, adapt = TRUE,
gweight = gwr.Gauss,
                    longlat = TRUE, method = "cv",
verbose=TRUE)
lnvmt.bw
```

The value returned is the proportion of observations (**q**) chosen by cross-validation. We now include this in the **gwr ()** function to build the final model.

```
lnvmt.gwr <- gwr(lnvmt ~., data = cthh.sp,
                 adapt = lnvmt.bw, gweight = gwr.Gauss,
hatmatrix = TRUE)
lnvmt.gwr
```

The summary output now shows the range of coefficients obtained for the individual local models. This information can be retrieved and mapped out using choropleth maps to explore the variation in model fit (Figure 9.16). We start by mapping the local R^2, which shows a generally lower model performance in the center of the study area.

```
tm_shape(lnvmt.gwr$SDF) +
  tm_fill(col = "localR2", palette = "Reds", style =
"quantile", title = "local R2")

## quartz_off_screen
##                  2
```

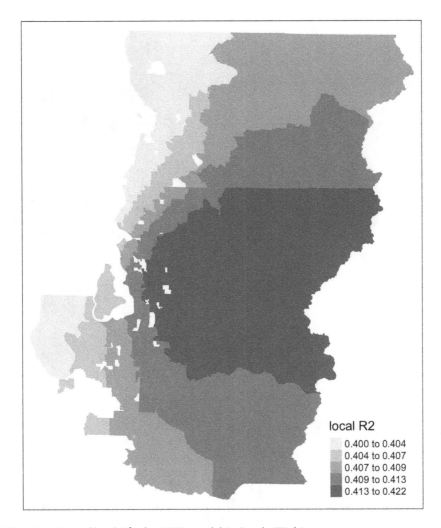

local R2
0.400 to 0.404
0.404 to 0.407
0.407 to 0.409
0.409 to 0.413
0.413 to 0.422

FIGURE 9.16   Map of local R^2 of a GWR model in Seattle, Washington

We then go on to map the coefficients for each tract, showing an approximate east–west split in the relative importance of the coefficients (Figure 9.17):

```
map1 = tm_shape(lnvmt.gwr$SDF) +
  tm_fill(col = "hhsize", palette = "Reds", style =
"quantile")
map2 = tm_shape(lnvmt.gwr$SDF) +
  tm_fill(col = "hhincome", palette = "Reds", style =
"quantile")
map3 = tm_shape(lnvmt.gwr$SDF) +
  tm_fill(col = "entropy", palette = "Reds", style =
"quantile")
```

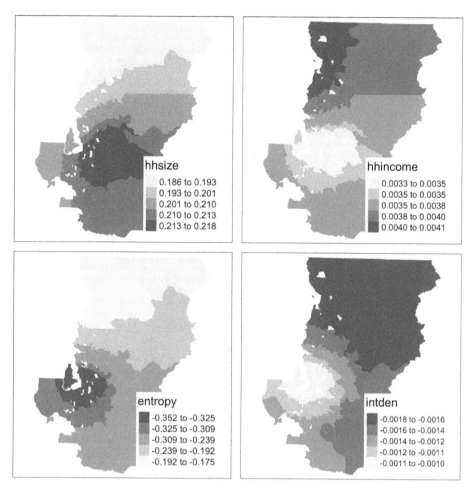

FIGURE 9.17 Map of coefficients of four independent variables in a GWR model in Seattle, Washington

```
map4 = tm_shape(lnvmt.gwr$SDF) +
  tm_fill(col = "intden", palette = "Reds", style =
"quantile")
tmap_arrange(map1, map2, map3, map4)
```

Planning Examples

Quantifying Urban Form: Compactness Versus Sprawl

In 2005, Yu-Hsin Tsai collected the 1995 Census Transport Planning Package (CTPP) Urban Element data for 219 metropolitan areas with a population of less than 3 million in the United States. The main purpose of the paper is to identify characteristics of metropolitan form in general—especially understanding the difference between compactness and sprawling cities.

Also, the author attempted to figure out whether the polycentric metropolitan form can be considered compact or sprawling.

To address research questions, he defined four dimensions of metropolitan forms—metropolitan size, density, the degree of equal distribution, and degree of clustering. Quantitative variables to measure these four dimensions were suggested, but in the case of the degree of clustering, the author estimated Moran's I to find out the extent to which high-density Census tracts within metropolitan areas are clustered or randomly dispersed. The author used the global Moran's I formula to measure the degree of clustering for all Census tracts within metropolitan areas, based on two variables: population and employment.

However, the Moran's I estimates themselves do not tell us the spatial pattern of the Census tracts, only that they are clustered or dispersed. To interpret the estimates, the author defined three archetypes of metropolitan forms based on the Moran's I estimates: monocentric form, polycentric form, and decentralized sprawl. In Figure 9.18, the Moran's I values are used as threshold values for identifying the types of metropolitan form for 219 metropolitan area samples in the study; for example, if Moran's Index estimates of population or employment for a metropolitan area in the sample data exceeds 0.13, that metropolitan area has a monocentric metropolitan form regarding degree of clustering of population or employment.

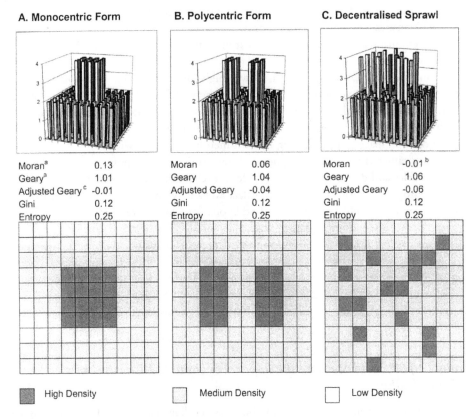

FIGURE 9.18 Moran's I formula in the article

Source: Tsai, 2005

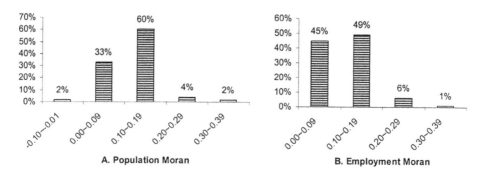

FIGURE 9.19 Histograms of Moran's Index distribution by population and employment

Source: Tsai, 2005

As a result, the author found that the population Moran's *I* ranges between −0.1 and 0.4 with an average of 0.11, which suggests that metropolitan areas in the data are relatively compact regarding the degree of clustering of the population within Census tracts. In terms of employment, an average of the Moran's Index estimates is similar to that of population (Figure 9.19). However, looking at the distribution of the Moran's *I* estimates (B in Figure 9.19), the clustering patterns of employment seems quite split: Slightly more than half the number of metropolitan areas show the compact form.

Choropleth maps support his argument that metropolitan areas with high Moran's *I* tend to have monocentric and compact patterns of population and employment and vice versa. For example, in Figure 9.20, Athens, Georgia, shows a high employment concentration within the metropolitan boundary, whereas Kokomo, Indiana, shows dispersed patterns of employment.

This article is a typical example of how we can use spatial autocorrelation measures in research. The author uses a typical measure of spatial autocorrelation (Moran's *I*) to describe the form of a real space or place and argues that metropolitan areas with either high Moran's *I* estimates of either variable reflect compact characteristics of metropolitan urban form.

The variables and data used in this study do not reflect the four commonly used dimensions of metropolitan forms due to lack of data availability, and the author admits that the Moran's *I* estimates could be improved if additional variables were used in the Moran's *I* formula. Due to advances in spatial, demographic, social, economic, and environmental data management, recent articles on measuring the degree of urban compactness reflect actual development patterns within urban areas (Hamidi & Ewing, 2014). By combining current compactness measures with the spatial analysis used in this article, it would be interesting to look at how different clustering patterns of census tracts with high compactness index or low compactness index values are within each current Metropolitan Statistical Area (MSA) boundary.

Spatial Lag Model to Measure the Impacts of Light Rail Transit (LRT) on Gentrification

In the 2017 article examining the relationship between light rail transit (LRT) stations and changes in neighborhood characteristics associated with gentrification, Baker and Lee provided an example of how planners can apply spatial autoregressive (SAR) models to planning issues.

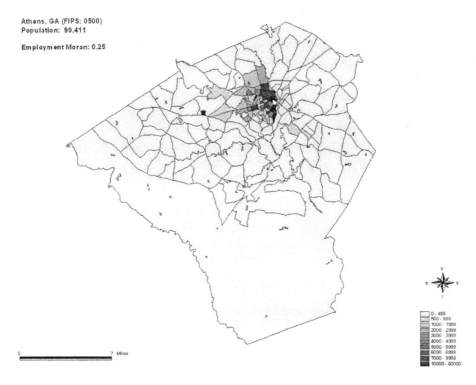

Athens, GA (FIPS: 0500)
Population: 99,411

Employment Moran: 0.25

0   7 Miles

0 - 499
500 - 999
1000 - 1999
2000 - 2999
3000 - 3999
4000 - 4999
5000 - 5999
6000 - 6999
7000 - 9999
10000 - 60000

Kokomo, IN (FIPS: 3850)
Population: 80,827

Employment Moran: 0.02

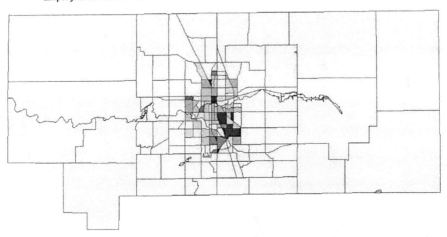

FIGURE 9.20   Comparison of Moran's coefficients and spatial patterns of employment: top: Athens, Georgia; bottom: Kokomo, Indiana

Source: Tsai, 2005

Based on studies that attempted to identify the relationship between enhanced location desirability and neighborhood change, the authors hypothesized that the presence of LRT stations is related to the possible presence of gentrification, while increasing public transit use and population density. To test this hypothesis, the authors developed a *Neighborhood Change Index (NCI)* as a composite index variable of neighborhood change at the census tract level by using residential socioeconomic characteristics through principal component analysis (PCA). Then, by collecting longitudinal (1980–2010) socioeconomic data at the census tract level, they set up seven dependent variables known to measure gentrification in past studies—race, education, income, poverty, population density, public transit commute, and nonprivately owned vehicle (POV) commute. Among these eight dependent variables, the authors defined the first five variables including the NCI as indicators for measuring gentrification, whereas the other three variables are used as indicators related to transit-oriented development (TOD) of LRT stations.

Spatial polygons of census tract areas were converted into centroids to create a binary (dummy) variable of LRT station buffer; the value 1 is assigned if a census tract's centroid falls within a 0.5-mile station buffer, and the value 0 is assigned otherwise. Using this dummy variable, the interaction term variable (*UALRTs*: LRT station buffer × each of 14 UA dummy variables) was drawn to identify the extent to which the presence of LRT station influences gentrification and changes related to TOD in neighborhoods near the station for a given urbanized area. Other socioeconomic and housing characteristics variables were included as control variables and were stored in the attribute tables of either census tract centroid spatial data or LRT station spatial data.

In investigating the relationship between the presence of an LRT station and potential gentrification, the authors thought that spatial dependence would exist between values of sociodemographic variables within any given census tract and values within its neighboring census tracts. It suggests that the simple ordinary least square (OLS) linear regression model without correcting spatial autocorrelation problems produces biased results. Therefore, they chose the spatial autoregressive modeling approach and used spatial lag models to estimate the possibility that dependent variables at any given census tract are correlated with values of the same variable in its neighboring census tracts.

To identify spatial effects between the presence of an LRT station and gentrification and neighborhood change, two separate SAR models were implemented: an SAR model using full census tracts across 14 UAs and a model using census tracts that have more possibilities of being gentrified by falling within the bottom two quantiles in each UA in the NCI. The full sample SAR model found that changes in race were the most significant factor for gentrification, but signs and magnitude of coefficients of the other seven dependent variables showed mixed results. For example, in Figure 9.21, the NCI score of neighborhoods near LRT stations in Portland decreased over time (a 27.7% relative decrease compared to non-LRT-station neighborhoods), but public transit commute increased (a 3.8% relative increase compared to non-LRT-station neighborhoods). On the other hand, in the case of St. Louis, one gentrification-related variable (Education) increased (a 4.5% relative increase compared to non-LRT-station neighborhoods in St. Louis), whereas the TOD-related variable (the percentage of public transit commute) decreased (a 3.2% relative decrease compared to non-LRT-station neighborhoods). The second SAR model using gentrifiable census tract samples showed similar coefficient patterns as the first SAR model, but overall magnitude of the coefficient of the eight dependent variables increased. Due to mixed results of impacts of LRT

	NCI		Race		Education		Income		Poverty		PD		PT		Non-POV	
	Coeff.	P Value	Coeff.	P Value	Coeff.	P Value	Coeff.	P Value	Coeff.	P Value	Coeff.	P Value	Coeff.	P Value	Coeff.	P Value
1980 data set																
San Francisco	0.0911	0.0888*	0.0426	0.0002***	0.0147	0.1772	0.3074	0.002***	-0.0284	0.0005***	0.277	0***	0.0377	0.0002***	0.0693	0***
Cleveland	-0.0923	0.3166	-0.0865	0***	-0.0042	0.8243	-0.1199	0.4846	-0.0081	0.5646	-0.1082	0.3521	0.0589	0.0008***	0.0281	0.3128
San Diego	-0.012	0.8725	-0.0307	0.0575*	-0.013	0.3942	0.0037	0.9789	0.0228	0.0463**	-0.0461	0.6254	0.009	0.5266	-0.0098	0.6653
Pittsburgh	-0.1424	0.1177	-0.0016	0.9369	-0.016	0.3894	-0.4312	0.0109**	0.0037	0.7926	-0.0726	0.5272	-0.0345	0.0457**	-0.0644	0.019**
Buffalo	-0.0121	0.9233	-0.0506	0.0618*	0.0324	0.2053	-0.391	0.0943*	0.002	0.9166	0.0095	0.9522	-0.0282	0.238	-0.212	0***
Portland	-0.2766	0.0011***	-0.0295	0.1053	-0.0229	0.1836	-0.0728	0.6439	0.0397	0.0021***	0.1617	0.1298	0.0378	0.0187**	0.0083	0.745
Sacramento	-0.0528	0.5883	0.0355	0.0911*	0.0031	0.8754	-0.0688	0.7041	0.0028	0.8506	-0.3471	0.0048***	0.0246	0.1845	0.0223	0.4487
San Jose	-0.0213	0.8008	0.0248	0.1742	0	0.9987	0.1596	0.3101	-0.0128	0.3208	-0.0741	0.4874	0.0063	0.6954	0.0233	0.3618
Rho	0.558		0.7771		0.5882		0.1713		0.3766		0.4623		0.4249		0.3751	
Log likelihood	-2676.45		3141.469		3506.339		-4978.198		4723.878		-3537.477		3857.855		2069.278	
AIC (SAR)	5414.9		-6220.9		-6950.7		10018		-9385.8		7137		-7653.7		-4076.6	
AIC (OLS)	6357.9		-3358.1		-5949.9		10123		-9080.5		7939.2		-7234.4		-3767.7	
1990 data set																
Los Angeles	-0.0502	0.2634	-0.0308	0.0057***	-0.0221	0.0357**	-0.1465	0.1724	0.0161	0.058*	-0.0329	0.6469	0.0027	0.6809	0.0089	0.364
Baltimore	0.0491	0.4487	0.0313	0.0516*	0.0163	0.2812	-0.2714	0.0799*	0.0156	0.2004	-0.0799	0.4403	-0.0061	0.526	-0.0175	0.219
St. Louis	0.0874	0.3792	-0.014	0.5706	0.0454	0.0512*	0.3075	0.1958	0.0354	0.059*	0.0368	0.817	-0.0322	0.029**	-0.0392	0.0727*
Denver	0.2554	0.0086***	0.0432	0.0732*	0.0254	0.2628	0.1342	0.5634	-0.0175	0.3408	-0.2111	0.1738	-0.0116	0.421	-0.0251	0.2383
Dallas	-0.0748	0.3619	0.0046	0.8198	0.0109	0.5711	0.0649	0.7405	-0.0285	0.0653*	-0.1111	0.3965	-0.0185	0.1272	-0.052	0.0039***
Salt Lake City	-0.117	0.2627	0.0217	0.4023	-0.0322	0.1878	0.2702	0.2791	0.0434	0.0276**	-0.2498	0.1344	-0.0124	0.4232	-0.0379	0.0984*
Rho	0.5388		0.7387		0.5064		0.1156		0.2495		0.4466		0.2961		0.2807	
Log likelihood	-2595.398		5276.421		5827.39		-7477.225		7186.533		-5248.621		8563.747		6299.979	
AIC (SAR)	5244.8		-10499		-11601		15008		-14319		10551		-17073		-12546	
AIC (OLS)	6448.4		-7132.4		-10649		15039		-14140		11394		-16831		-12321	

Note: This table only presents the coefficients of interaction terms between LRT station dummy and UA dummy variables. Full results including control variables are reported in Table A3. AIC = Akaike information criterion; LRT = light rail transit; OLS = ordinary least squares; PD = Population Density; Non-POV = Non-Privately Owned Vehicle; PT = Public Transit; SAR = spatial autoregressive lag model; UA = urbanized area.
*p < .10. **p < .05. ***p < .01.

FIGURE 9.21 Summary SAR model results for (a) the full sample and (b) the gentrifiable sample

	NCI		Race		Education		Income		Poverty		PD		PT		Non-POV	
	Coeff.	P Value	Coeff.	P Value	Coeff.	P Value	Coeff.	P Value	Coeff.	P Value	Coeff.	P Value	Coeff.	P Value	Coeff.	P Value
1980 data set																
San Francisco	0.0612	0.4607	0.0814	0***	0.0285	0.0853^b	0.4699	0.0056***	-0.034	0.0133**	0.3718	0.0005***	0.0379	0.0392***	0.069	0.0166**
Cleveland	0.0688	0.6548	-0.0217	0.5332	0.0113	0.7129	-0.2002	0.5237	-0.044	0.0846*	-0.2735	0.1659	0.0786	0.0209**	0.0611	0.2514
San Diego	-0.0603	0.5428	-0.0309	0.1676	-0.0209	0.2893	0.0491	0.8081	0.0406	0.0113**	-0.0242	0.8494	0.0099	0.6523	-0.0165	0.6303
Pittsburgh	0.1124	0.5921	-0.0132	0.7817	-0.0141	0.7351	-0.425	0.3211	-0.0161	0.6426	-0.2843	0.2917	-0.0391	0.399	0.0052	0.9428
Buffalo	0.1782	0.3582	-0.0633	0.1486	0.0854	0.027**	-0.5693	0.1502	-0.0433	0.177	-0.1305	0.5997	-0.0762	0.0755*	-0.3522	0***
Portland	-0.3714	0.0035***	-0.046	0.1097	-0.0279	0.2697	-0.0718	0.7818	0.0427	0.0424**	0.2247	0.1681	0.054	0.0549*	0.0004	0.9931
Sacramento	-0.1369	0.3426	0.049	0.1324	-0.015	0.6014	-0.1449	0.6222	0.0102	0.669	-0.485	0.0089***	0.0276	0.3858	0.0023	0.9627
San Jose	0.0399	0.7226	0.0316	0.2137	0.0181	0.4185	0.1661	0.4685	-0.0063	0.7354	-0.0424	0.7684	0.0044	0.8608	0.0154	0.6928
Rho		0.4452		0.4891		0.4562		0.1542		0.2182		0.3389		0.3427		0.2365
Log likelihood		-1391.752		1105.158		1326.075		-2552.985		1677.664		-1790.672		1173.108		430.03
AIC		2845.5		-2148.3		-2590.2		5168		-3293.3		3643.3		-2284.2		-798.06
1990 data set																
Los Angeles	-0.0235	0.6675	-0.0056	0.6726	-0.0099	0.3725	0.1171	0.391	0.0257	0.0381**	0.1113	0.1418	-0.001	0.9288	0.0099	0.5372
Baltimore	0.0181	0.8542	0.0127	0.5984	0.0225	0.262	0.114	0.6439	0.0478	0.0324**	0.0208	0.8793	0.0107	0.6105	0.0159	0.5821
St. Louis	0.099	0.4814	0.0415	0.2271	0.0495	0.0833*	0.5898	0.0932*	0.0473	0.1376	0.1982	0.3094	-0.0788	0.0084***	-0.1043	0.0112**
Denver	0.394	0.0009***	0.108	0.0002***	0.0409	0.0891*	0.0864	0.7702	-0.018	0.5018	-0.1644	0.3164	-0.0179	0.4764	-0.0346	0.3164
Dallas	-0.0302	0.7963	0.0046	0.8198	0.0002	0.992	-0.2289	0.4331	-0.0001	0.9961	-0.1111	0.3965	-0.0185	0.1272	-0.1165	0.0007***
Salt Lake City	-0.0269	0.8376	0.0217	0.4023	-0.0396	0.1378	0.2431	0.4582	0.0542	0.0682*	-0.2498	0.1344	-0.0124	0.4232	-0.0379	0.0984*
Rho		0.3216		0.4433		0.3612		0.0965		0.1310		0.2893		0.1674		0.1840
Log likelihood		-944.5905		1726.129		2098.39		-2674.921		1918.968		-1565.392		2038.219		1426.629
AIC		1943.2		-3398.3		-4142.8		5403.8		-3783.9		3184.8		-4022.4		-2799.3

Note: This table only presents the coefficients of interaction terms between LRT station dummy and dummy variables. Full results including control variables are reported in Table A4. AIC = Akaike information criterion; LRT = light rail transit; OLS = ordinary least squares; PD = Population Density; Non-POV = Non-Privately Owned Vehicle; PT = Public Transit; SAR = spatial autoregressive lag model; UA = urbanized area.
*p < .10, **p < .05, ***p < .01.

FIGURE 9.21 (Continued)

station on gentrification and TOD effects in spatial analysis, the author concluded that there is no clear evidence of prevalent gentrification in LRT station areas.

This study shows that spatial econometrics models can identify spatial patterns of observations and model a spatial autocorrelated process hidden behind observations. By taking spatial effects among census tracts into account, this study successfully shows the relationship between the presence of LRT stations and gentrification based on the actual spatial patterns of dependent variables across 14 urbanized areas.

Conclusion

This chapter explained the purpose, history, and mechanics of spatial analysis and spatial econometrics with a practical demonstration in R. As a distinctive statistics field, spatial econometrics is still in development so this chapter focused only on techniques commonly used in planning literature. There is an increasing awareness of the issues when using spatial data in planning studies, and this chapter aims to provide a starting point familiarize themselves with these methods, their application and interpretation.

Works Cited

Anselin, L. (1988a). Lagrange multiplier test diagnostics for spatial dependence and spatial heterogeneity. *Geographical Analysis, 20*(1), 1–17. https://doi.org/10.1111/j.1538-4632.1988.tb00159.x

Anselin, L. (1988b). *Spatial econometrics: Methods and models.* Norwell, MA: Kluwer Academic Publishers.

Anselin, L. (1995). Local indicators for spatial association—LISA. *Geographical Analysis, 27*(2), 93–115. https://doi.org/ 10.1111/j.1538-4632.1995.tb00338.x

Anselin, L. (2005). *Spatial regression analysis in R: A workbook.* Center for Spatially Integrated Social Science. Retrieved from www.csiss.org/gispopsci/workshops/2011/PSU/readings/W15_Anselin 2007.pdf

Anselin, L. (2010). Thirty years of spatial econometrics. *Papers in Regional Science, 89*(1), 3–25. https://doi.org/10.1111/j.1435-5957.2010.00279.x

Anselin, L., Bera, A. K., Florax, R., & Yoon, M. J. (1996). Simple diagnostic tests for spatial dependence. *Regional Science and Urban Economics, 26*(1), 77–104.

Arbia, G. (2006). *Spatial econometrics: Statistical foundations and applications to regional convergence.* Berlin, Germany: Springer Science & Business Media.

Arbia, G. (2014). *A primer for spatial econometrics with applications in R.* Berlin, Germany: Springer.

Avis, D., & Horton, J. (1985). Remarks on the sphere of influence graph. *Annals of the New York Academy of Sciences, 440*(1), 323–327.

Baker, D. M., & Lee, B. (2017). How does light rail transit (LRT) impact gentrification? Evidence from fourteen US urbanized areas. *Journal of Planning Education and Research.* https://doi.org/10.1177%2 F0739456X17713619

Bivand, R. S., Pebesma, E., & Gómez-Rubio, V. (2013). *Applied spatial data analysis with R.* New York, NY: Springer.

Bolstad, P. (2016). *GIS fundamentals: A first text on geographic information systems* (5th ed.). Ann Arbor, MI: XanEdu Publishing.

Brunsdon, C., & Comber, L. (2015). *An introduction to R for spatial analysis and mapping.* London: Sage Publications.

Cliff, A. D., & Ord, J. K. (1973). *Spatial autocorrelation.* London: Pion.

Cliff, A. D., & Ord, J. K. (1981). *Spatial process: Models and applications.* London: Pion.

Cressie, N. (1992). Statistics for spatial data. *Terra Nova, 4*(5), 613–617.

Diggle, P. J. (2013). Statistical analysis of spatial and spatio-temporal point patterns (3rd ed.). Boca Raton, FL: CRC Press.

Ewing, R., Tian, G., Goates, J. P., Zhang, M., Greenwald, M. J., Joyce, A., . . . Greene, W. (2015). Varying influences of the built environment on household travel in 15 diverse regions of the United States. *Urban Studies, 52*(13), 2330–2348.

Fischer, M. M., & Getis, A. (2010). *Handbook of applied spatial analysis: Software tools, methods and applications*. New York, NY: Springer.

Fotheringham, A. S., Brunsdon, C., & Charlton, M. (2002). *Geographically weighted regression: The analysis of spatially varying relationships*. New York, NY: Wiley.

Getis, A., & Griffith, D. A. (2002). Comparative spatial filtering in regression analysis. *Geographical Analysis, 34*(2), 130–140.

Getis, A., & Ord, J. K. (1992). The analysis of spatial association by use of distance statistics. *Geographical Analysis, 24*(3), 189–206. https://doi.org/10.1111/j.1538-4632.1992.tb00261.x

Goodchild, M. F., Anselin, L., Appelbaum, R. P., & Harthorn, B. H. (2000). Toward spatially integrated social science. *International Regional Science Review, 23*(2), 139–159. https://doi.org/10.1177%2F016001760002300201

Griffith, D. A. (2000). A linear regression solution to the spatial autocorrelation problem. *Journal of Geographical Systems, 2*(2), 141–156.

Griffith, D. A. (2003). *Spatial autocorrelation and spatial filtering: gaining understanding through theory and scientific visualization*. Berlin, DE: Springer Science & Business Media.

Griffith, D. A. (2008). Spatial-filtering-based contributions to a critique of geographically weighted regression (GWR). *Environment and Planning A, 40*(11), 2751–2769.

Griffith, D. A. (2013). *Spatial autocorrelation and spatial filtering: Gaining understanding through theory and scientific visualization*. Berlin, DE: Springer Science & Business Media.

Griffith, D. A., & Peres-Neto, P. R. (2006). Spatial modeling in ecology: The flexibility of eigenfunction spatial analyses. *Ecology, 87*(10), 2603–2613.

Hamidi, S., & Ewing, R. (2014). A longitudinal study of changes in urban sprawl between 2000 and 2010 in the United States. *Landscape and Urban Planning, 128*, 72–82.

Lee, J., & Wong, D. W. S. (2001). *Statistical analysis with ArcView GIS*. Toronto, CA: John Wiley & Sons.

LeSage, J., & Pace, R. K. (2009). *Introduction to spatial econometrics* (1st ed.). Boca Raton, FL: Chapman and Hall/CRC.

Moran, P. A. P. (1950). Notes on continuous stochastic phenomena. *Biometrika, 37*(1), 17–23. https://doi.org/10.2307/2332142

Paelinck, J. H. P., & Klaassen, L. H. (1979). *Spatial econometrics*. Hants, UK: Saxon House.

Páez, A., Farber, S., & Wheeler, D. (2011). A simulation-based study of geographically weighted regression as a method for investigating spatially varying relationships. *Environment and Planning A, 43*(12), 2992–3010.

Ripley, B. D. (1976). The second-order analysis of stationary point processes. *Journal of Applied Probability, 13*(2), 255–266. https://doi.org/10.2307/3212829

Tobler, W. R. (1970). A computer movie simulating urban growth in the Detroit region. *Economic Geography, 46*(supp 1), 234–240.

Tsai, Y. H. (2005). Quantifying urban form: Compactness versus sprawl. *Urban Studies, 42*(1), 141–161. https://doi.org/10.1080%2F0042098042000309748

Wheeler, D., & Tiefelsdorf, M. (2005). Multicollinearity and correlation among local regression coefficients in geographically weighted regression. *Journal of Geographical Systems, 7*(2), 161–187.

10

META-ANALYSIS AND META-REGRESSION

Mark Stevens, Torrey Lyons, and Reid Ewing

Overview

Planning academics and practitioners have one research practice in common: conducting literature reviews. You may think of this as an inherently academic exercise (nearly all academic articles include a literature review right after (or within) the introduction). But we would wager that most technical memos written by planners begin with Google searches aimed at finding relevant literature.

Every planning research article should include a well written literature review. A good literature review helps to establish authors' credibility by demonstrating their familiarity with the relevant literature and helps to justify the research presented in the article by summarizing what is already known about the topic of the article and identifying the important knowledge gaps that the article seeks to fill. One planning journal—the *Journal of Planning Literature* (*JPL*)—exclusively publishes literature review articles that synthesize previous research findings on various planning topics. With two reviews per issue and four issues per year, there is no shortage of review articles on planning topics. An October 2013 column in *Planning* magazine, by the third author of this chapter, reviewed the publication criteria used by *JPL* in the areas of style, scope, accuracy, analysis, and connection to planning. They provide a good roadmap for planning academics and practitioners alike.

In contrast, there have been comparatively few *meta-analyses* of planning literature. What is a meta-analysis? A meta-analysis is a study of studies: it uses the statistical results from several individual studies to express an overall average result. The typical literature review is strictly qualitative: "Jackson found this, and Williams found that." Meta-analyses are quantitative: "Studies by Jackson, Williams, and others, found that the average effect of A on B is C." Meta-analyses are very common in fields such as economics, psychology, and medicine. Those headline-grabbing articles about cancer risks or drug effectiveness are likely to be meta-analyses of several previous studies on those topics.

A 2010 study identified the academic journals that planning researchers read the most (Goldstein & Maier, 2010). A cursory review shows that these journals have published only a small number of meta-analyses. Nijkamp and Pepping (1998) analyzed factors critical to the success of sustainable city initiatives. Stamps (1999) applied meta-analysis to the visual preference literature. Cervero (2002) reviewed different types of studies on the issue of induced travel demand. Lauria and Wagner (2006) reviewed empirical studies in planning theory. Debrezion, Pels, and Rietveld (2007) summarized the impact of railway stations on residential and commercial property values. Bartholomew and Ewing (2008) analyzed scenario planning studies to assess the impacts of compact growth scenarios on reducing vehicular travel. Berke ,and Godschalk (2009) computed average plan quality scores across several plan evaluation studies. Ewing and Cervero (2010) synthesized findings regarding the influence of the built environment on travel behavior. A Google Scholar search of keywords "meta analysis" and "urban planning" suggests that there is only a handful of additional meta-analyses in our field.

Most recently, Stevens (2017) used a variation on meta-analysis (known as meta-regression analysis) to update part of the Ewing and Cervero (2010) study. To our knowledge, this is only the second application of meta-regression to the planning field.

History

The earliest application of a method vaguely resembling today's meta-analysis goes as far back as the seventeenth century, when it was used to synthesize the growing body of knowledge in astronomy. Pearson (1904) was the first to use an approach like meta-analysis to aggregate the findings of clinical studies (O'Rourke, 2007).

In the early 1970s, Light and Smith developed what they referred to as the *cluster approach* to pool data from all related studies in order to find a single, conclusive result. This approach had the obvious limitation of requiring easy and unlimited access to data, which is typically not the case. A subsequent solution that did not require access to original study data was known as the *vote-counting method*. This method placed existing studies into three categories: studies with positive significant results, studies with negative significant results, and studies with no significant results. This way of synthesizing research, however, was inadequate for situations in which there was a small sample of studies or the reported effects were of small magnitude (Hedges & Olkin, 1980).

Therefore, later in the 1970s, Glass suggested that the magnitude of the effects reported in studies was more important than statistical significance. He coined the term "meta-analysis" and recommended that *effect size*, defined as the difference between the experimental and control group means divided by the control group standard deviation, become the common currency of meta-analysis. After first defining and advocating the method in 1976, Smith and Glass (1977) were the first to apply it, specifically to studies on the effects of psychotherapy. Controversy surrounded the initial development and application of meta-analysis, but it has gained widespread support and ubiquitous application in subsequent decades, becoming standard practice for the synthesis of quantitative research (Lipsey & Wilson, 2001).

Meta-regression analysis is a variation on conventional meta-analysis that was developed by economists Tom Stanley and Stephen B. Jarrell and introduced to the literature in 1989 (Stanley & Jarrell, 1989). Stanley and his colleagues have continued to enhance the metaregression methodology since that time, and it is now widely used for synthesizing economic research. Stanley et al. (2013) estimate, for example, that as many as 200 meta-regression analyses are conducted on economic topics each year.

Stanley and colleagues have written a book with detailed guidance for how to conduct meta-regression analysis (Stanley & Doucouliagos, 2012) and an article with guidelines for researchers to follow in reporting their own meta-regression analysis methods (Stanley et al., 2013).

Purpose and Mechanics

Conventional Meta-Analysis

A meta-analysis is different from a traditional research study. Whereas traditional studies collect primary data to analyze, a meta-analysis uses summary statistics from past studies on a given topic as the data points in a new analysis. This approach has both advantages and disadvantages for validity and reliability, as every standard textbook on meta-analysis explains (Lipsey & Wilson, 2001; Hunter & Schmidt, 2004; Schulze, 2004; Littell, Corcoran, & Pillai, 2008; Borenstein, Hedges, Higgins, & Rothstein, 2009).

The primary advantage of meta-analysis is that it synthesizes all available (quantitative) findings on a topic, allowing common threads to emerge. The pooling of samples in a carefully constructed meta-analysis also makes its results more generalizable than those of the smaller primary studies on which it is based. But conventional meta-analysis has drawbacks too. Combining stronger studies with weaker ones may contaminate the results of the former. Further, meta-analysis often mixes *apples and oranges* due to variation among studies in modeling techniques, independent and dependent variables, and sampling units. Yet if we choose instead to compare only very similar studies, sample sizes can become small, threatening statistical reliability. Lastly, the studies for a meta-analysis are often chosen only from the published literature. This can result in publication bias, since studies that show statistical significance are more likely to be published than those that don't (Borenstein, Rothstein, & Sutton, 2005). Publication bias may inflate the absolute size of the effects estimated with a meta-analysis. As we explain shortly, meta-regression analysis can be used to address each of these limitations of conventional meta-analysis.

By far the most highly cited application of meta-analysis to planning is the article by Ewing and Cervero (2010), titled "Travel and the Built Environment: A Meta-Analysis." It is the second most highly cited article in the 80-year history of the *Journal of the American Planning Association*. Ewing and Cervero identified studies linking the built environment to travel using the Academic Search Premier, Google, Google Scholar, MEDLINE, PAIS International, PUBMED, Scopus, TRIS Online, TRANweb, Web of Science, and ISI Web of Knowledge databases, using the key words "built environment," "urban form," and "development," coupled with keywords "travel," "transit," and "walking." They inspected more than 200 studies that quantitatively relate characteristics of the built environment to measures of travel. From the universe of built environment/travel studies, they computed effect sizes for more than 50 studies.

To combine results from different studies, a meta-analysis requires a common measure of effect size. The common metric used by Ewing and Cervero was the elasticity of a travel outcome—VMT, walking, or transit use—with respect to one of the D variables—development density, land use diversity, street network design, destination accessibility, and distance to transit. An *elasticity* is the ratio of the percentage change in one variable associated with the percentage change in another variable (a point elasticity is the ratio when these changes are infinitely small). Elasticities are dimensionless (unit-free) measures of the associations between pairs of variables and are the most widely used measures of effect size in economic and planning research.

Ewing and Cervero used individual elasticities from primary studies to compute weighted average elasticities for several pairs of dependent/independent variables representing travel outcomes and built environment attributes. They summarized their results this way: "For all variable pairs, the relationships between travel variables and built environmental variables are inelastic. The weighted average elasticity with the greatest absolute magnitude is 0.39, and most elasticities are much smaller. Still, the combined effect of several built environmental variables on travel could be quite large" (p. 275).

They used sample size as a weighting factor because they lacked consistent standard error estimates from the primary studies. Weighting by sample size is by far the most common approach in meta-analyses, since sample sizes are nearly always known (Shadish & Haddock, 1994, p. 264). However, no weighting factor except standard error allows judging whether the resulting weighted averages are statistically different from zero. Since they combined significant and insignificant individual effect sizes and did not have the data necessary to test for significance, Ewing and Cervero did not report statistical confidence for any of their results. They advised readers to exercise caution in using weighted average elasticities when the primary elasticities upon which they are based are statistically insignificant.

Meta-Regression Analysis

Meta-regression analysis, a special type of meta-analysis, uses effect size estimates reported in previous studies as the dependent variable in a new regression model that computes a single, representative effect size estimate across the studies. In cases where there is a lot of variation in the magnitude and/or direction of the reported effect size estimates, meta-regression analysis can be used to help explain why different studies on the same topic report different (and sometimes conflicting) results. Independent variables in the meta-regression model measure features of the effect size estimates themselves and the studies from which they were drawn, including (for example) measures of how precise the estimates are and whether the studies followed best practices. Analysts can use the equation produced by this regression model to calculate a representative effect size estimate that is adjusted for different types of bias and other factors, as explained later in this chapter.

Like meta-analysis, meta-regression analysis has both pros and cons. Starting with the cons, meta-regression is more complex to carry out than conventional meta-analysis and generally requires more data. Meta-regression requires that the researcher possess at least basic knowledge of regression modeling and that the researcher be able to access information from the primary studies (such as standard errors for the elasticity estimates) that are not always readily available.

Yet these challenges are not insurmountable, and, when employed strategically, meta-regression can be used to address many of the limitations of conventional meta-analysis. First, a researcher using meta-regression analysis can effectively distinguish between stronger and weaker studies by including an independent variable in the meta-regression model that measures the author's subjective assessment of each study's quality, whether on a continuous scale or as a dummy variable equal to 1 for studies considered to be strong and equal to 0 for weak studies. This type of procedure enables the researcher to determine whether stronger studies report different effect sizes than weaker studies. Alternatively, Stanley and Doucouliagos (2012) recommend that researchers use a more objective approach that weights each estimate by the inverse of its variance. This places more weight in the regression model on estimates with smaller variances, which are considered to be higher-quality estimates because they were measured with greater precision. The value of the representative elasticity produced by the regression model would therefore lean more in the direction of the higher-quality estimates than the lower-quality estimates.

Second, meta-regression analysis can help to resolve the apples and oranges problem that can pose a significant challenge to conventional meta-analyses. Whereas researchers might have to conduct separate meta-analyses for studies on a given topic that nevertheless differ in some important way(s), they can include those studies in a single meta-regression analysis and then make adjustments for the relevant differences. By coding and including independent variables in the meta-regression model to measure differences in primary studies that might contribute to variation in reported effect size estimates, planning researchers can test whether there is a statistically significant difference in the reported effect sizes in the literature for studies that use one type of modeling technique versus another, studies that use one type of variable measurement versus another, studies that were conducted in urban versus suburban areas, and so on. The ability of the meta-regression model to make such distinctions is technically limited only by the ability of the researcher to measure the distinctions and to include the measurements as independent variables in the model, though sample size (and degrees of freedom) considerations are likely to dictate just how many independent variables the researcher can feasibly include in the model.

Third, planning researchers can use meta-regression analysis to evaluate whether and to what extent a literature is affected by publication bias and to correct the set of reported findings for that bias if it is found to be present. In order to understand publication bias and the problems it can cause, it is important for planning researchers to first consider that the research findings that are publicly reported inevitably represent only a sample of all research findings that are produced behind the scenes. Researchers commonly test many different regression model specifications before arriving at the final version of the model that produces the findings they choose to report. The selection of the final model is ultimately subjective: there is generally no such thing as an objectively *correct* model, other than in trivial cases that are not of interest to researchers.

Publication bias becomes a problem when the sample of findings that researchers choose to report are consistently biased in one direction. This type of bias is common in academic literatures because researchers often have strongly held beliefs about how one variable affects another (e.g., planning researchers might tend to believe that as cities become more compact, residents of the city will walk more and drive less). These types of beliefs can influence a researcher's selection of which findings to report, as researchers are more likely (other things being equal) to report those findings that best coincide with their own expectations and their own understanding of how the world works (Stanley & Doucouliagos, 2012). The more that researchers in a discipline choose to report findings that lean in one direction over another, the more distorted the discipline's understanding of the research issue will become over time.

Researchers using conventional meta-analysis have sometimes sought to address publication bias by combining findings from both published and unpublished studies, in hopes that the unpublished findings would be less biased and help to offset bias in the published findings. While it is generally a good idea for planning researchers to include both published and unpublished studies in a meta-analysis, this practice alone is not enough to address the problem of publication bias because even authors of unpublished studies tend to follow the same process of reporting only a (potentially-biased) sample of their findings. Indeed, so-called publication bias has been detected even in unpublished studies, leading some researchers to suggest that the term "publication bias" is a bit of a misnomer and that it would be more accurate to use the term "selective reporting bias" instead (Stanley & Doucouliagos, 2012).

In order to know whether the findings that have been reported on a given topic are a biased sample of all findings that have been produced on the topic, it seems intuitive to assume that we would need to be able to compare the reported findings to the unreported findings. But how can we possibly know what the unreported findings look like if they have (by definition) not been reported? This is where the power of meta-regression analysis is fully revealed.

Researchers have developed a suite of creative and powerful techniques in meta-regression analysis for dealing with publication bias. The first technique is graphical and involves creating a scatterplot of each estimate in the dataset against the inverse of its standard error. In a literature without publication bias, the points in the scatterplot will generally form the shape of a symmetrical, upside-down funnel; an asymmetrical funnel that is more heavily weighted on one side than on the other is compelling evidence that the sample of estimates that has been reported is biased in that direction and that estimates in the other direction have generally been underreported. This type of scatterplot is referred to as a *funnel graph* because of the funnel shape that is expected to emerge in an unbiased plot of estimates. The key insight behind the funnel graph is that we do not in fact need access to the unreported estimates in order to compare them to the set of reported estimates: we can rely instead on sampling theory and our knowledge of what an unbiased distribution of estimates should look like to help us make a visual assessment of how biased any given distribution of reported estimates is in relation to the theoretical, unbiased distribution of all estimates.

The second technique for dealing with publication bias in a literature is statistical and involves testing whether the reported estimates are correlated with their standard errors. We can perform this test by including the standard error of each estimate as an independent variable in the meta-regression model. This procedure provides a test for publication bias because, as Stanley and Doucouliagos (2012, p. 60) note, "When publication selection is present, the reported effect is positively correlated with its standard error, *ceteris paribus*; otherwise, estimates and their standard errors will be independent, as required by the conventional *t*-test and guaranteed by random sampling theory." This test procedure has been named the *funnel asymmetry test* (FAT) because it essentially tests whether or not the estimates in the funnel graph form a symmetrical funnel shape (Stanley & Doucouliagos, 2012). The FAT is performed by estimating the following simple meta-regression model:

$$t_i = \beta_1 + \beta_0(1/SE_i) + v_i$$

where
t_i is the *t*-statistic associated with the effect size estimate from a primary study, and
SE_i is the standard error of the effect size estimate.

The FAT involves testing the null hypothesis that $\beta_1 = 0$. If β_1 is found to be greater than 0, that is taken as evidence of positive publication bias; if β_1 is found to be less than 0, that is taken as evidence of negative publication bias. If the null hypothesis is not rejected, then there is no evidence of publication bias (though it might still be present. The FAT is known to have low statistical power, such that a failure to reject the null hypothesis does not necessarily mean that the literature being tested is free from publication bias).

We can perform a *precision-effect test* (*PET*) to determine whether the effect size estimate is different from zero in a statistical sense, by testing the null hypothesis that $\beta_0 = 0$. A failure to reject this hypothesis is taken as evidence that the effect size estimate is not significantly different from zero, that, in other words, there is no underlying relationship between the variables of interest that were the focus of the primary studies, and that any relationship that was previously detected was a result of publication bias and/or sampling error.

In cases where the null hypothesis is rejected and a genuine underlying relationship apparently exists, researchers can use the *precision-effect estimate with standard error* (or *PEESE*) as the best available effect size estimate that is corrected for the effects of publication bias. The PEESE is estimated using the following simple meta-regression model, assuming that the effect size estimates included in the model (as the dependent variable) have been weighted by the inverse of their variance:

$$effect_i = \beta_0 + \beta_1 SE^2_i + \varepsilon_i$$

where
$effect_i$ is the effect size estimate from a primary study, and
SE^2_i is its variance.
The PEESE is equal to the constant term (β_0) from the equation.

It is common in meta-analysis to imagine that there is a single, *true* underlying effect size and that variation in effect sizes reported across studies is only a result of sampling error (and/or publication selection on the part of researchers). However, there is not always a single true value of the effect size that holds across all contexts. A problem of *excess heterogeneity* can arise when the expected value of the effect size depends on time, space, or other factors (Stanley & Doucouliagos, 2012, p. 81). In other words, for some phenomena of interest to planners, the size (or even direction) of the effect of one variable on another (such as the effect of density on travel behavior) might be different in City A than in City B. When this type of heterogeneity is not accounted for, the effect size estimates produced from a meta-analysis or a meta-regression analysis are likely to be biased. (This is a form of the familiar omitted-variable bias that is common in all regression analysis.)

Statistical tests have been developed to determine whether the level of observed heterogeneity in a particular set of estimates exceeds what would be expected from sampling error alone. However, meta-regression experts report, "In our experience, all areas of research contain excess heterogeneity" (Stanley & Doucouliagos, 2012, p. 82), and they advise that researchers skip the statistical tests, simply assume that excess heterogeneity does exist in their dataset, and then proceed to address the heterogeneity.

Heterogeneity in reported effect size estimates can be addressed by modeling it, that is, by including additional independent variables in the meta-regression model that measure features of the studies that are believed to contribute to the heterogeneity. By controlling for the effects of these other factors, the meta-regression model can produce less-biased and more accurate representative elasticity estimates that can be tailored to the specific scenario of interest. For example, by including an independent variable in the model that measures whether the primary study was conducted in the United States or elsewhere, the researcher could use the model to produce one representative elasticity estimate for the United States and a separate one for non-U.S. locations. Of course, the researcher could also test the effects of location at a much finer scale, depending on the goals of the research and data availability. The level of detail included in the model is constrained only by the data available to the researcher.

In planning, one of the earliest applications of meta-regression analysis was in 2017 by Stevens (2017), who synthesized findings from multiple studies of compact development's influence on driving. The effect size estimates he used were coefficients from regression models with VMT as the dependent variable and measures of compact development as independent variables.

Stevens constructed his dataset by first collecting all of the relevant papers included in the Ewing and Cervero (2010) meta-analysis. He then conducted an Internet database search in summer 2015 to locate more papers on the topic, searching thousands of online records for English-language studies conducted between 1996 and 2015 that examined compact development and driving.

Stevens's final meta-regression models used data from the 37 studies in his sample to tell us what the average elasticity would be for each D-variable if residential self-selection is controlled for and the effects of selective reporting bias were removed. He included a variable in his meta-regression models that measured whether each of the elasticity estimates was derived from a study that controls for residential self-selection. This variable helped to indicate the difference (if any exists) in the size of reported elasticities for studies that controlled for residential self-selection versus those that did not. He tested for and removed the effects of publication (or selective reporting) bias from his elasticities by following the procedures described by Stanley and Doucouliagos (2012).

His synthesis of research findings suggests that people do tend to drive less when D-variables change in the direction of compact development. (See Figure 10.1.) Whether the effects are large or small depends on what you consider large and small (Ewing & Cervero, 2017; Stevens, 2017). Figure 10.1 compares weighted average elasticities from Ewing and Cervero's original analysis, weighted average elasticities from an updated analysis using Stevens' expanded sample, plus two meta-regression results from Stevens. For a list of pros and cons associated with Stevens' meta-regression versus conventional meta-analysis, see Ewing (2017) and Ewing and Cervero (2017).

Planning Examples

Scenario Planning

An analysis using multiple scenarios—a scenario planning process—can be properly understood as one that provides a series of stories about the future that collectively define a range of possible outcomes. The roots of scenario analysis lay within the broader topic of adaptive response technique, the military applications of which can be traced back centuries. More modern applications include those done by the RAND Corporation, where, during the 1950s, scenario analysis was used to anticipate and prepare for possible Soviet nuclear attack strategies (Kahn, 1962). The apocryphal business application was Royal Dutch/Shell's use of scenario analysis to effectively anticipate the OPEC Oil Embargo of 1973 (Schwartz, 1991). Since then, scenario analysis has become fairly common in business circles, and the business-based literature is well developed.

Scenario analysis came to transportation planning comparatively late. It was preceded by a similar, though much more limited technique called *alternatives analysis*, which arose in

Findings from two *JAPA*-published studies that sought to determine how compact development impacts driving rates show how different samples and different methods can lead to very different results. The takeaway for planners: Methodology matters.

WEIGHTED AVERAGE ELASTICITIES—EWING AND CERVERO

WEIGHTED AVERAGE ELASTICITIES—STEVENS

META-REGRESSION ELASTICITIES—STEVENS

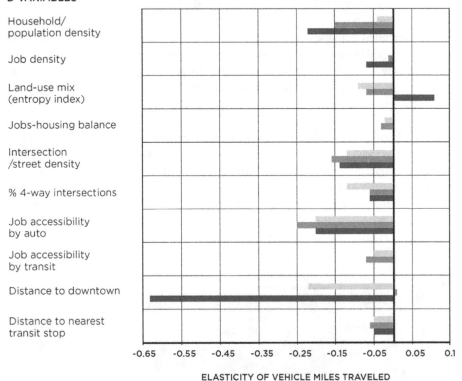

FIGURE 10.1 Elasticities of VMT with respect to D variables

Source: Ewing, 2017; with permission from The American Planning Association

the early 1960s in response to the Federal Aid Highway Act's mandate that metropolitan regions conduct *3C* (continuing, cooperative, comprehensive) planning. By the 1970s, alternatives analysis had become a standard component of most project-level environmental studies, thanks largely to the passage of the National Environmental Policy Act in 1969 (Weiner, 1999). Alternatives analysis bears some obvious similarities to scenario planning, chiefly in the consideration of alternative responses to an identified problem. Its practice, however, has in most cases been highly constrained, allowing consideration of alternate transportation improvements but excluding other possible variables, such as land use patterns and economic conditions and policies.

Scenario planning has become a best practice in regional transportation planning (Ewing & Bartholomew, 2018). The conventional practice is to test future alternative transportation investments against a fixed future land use forecast in order to see how well the former meets the travel demands generated by the latter. In conventional practice, future land use patterns are taken as a given that cannot be modified by an MPO or its constituent governments.

An alternative approach, exemplified by RTPs of Baltimore, Boise, Boston, Colorado Springs, Lansing, Portland, Sacramento, Salt Lake City, and other leading regions, assumes that future development patterns can take various forms, just as future transportation investments can take various forms. These various forms are run through the regional travel demand model to see how well they perform with respect to VMT, congestion, and other transportation outcomes. The main conclusion from these scenario plan studies is that transportation outcomes depend as much on development patterns as they do on transportation system improvements.

Bartholomew (2007) used meta-analysis to summarize 80 scenario planning projects from 48 U.S. metropolitan areas. The typical scenario planning process compares a *trend* development pattern, usually a continuation of urban sprawl, to one or more compact alternatives. The alternatives usually have higher gross densities, involve mixed land uses to a greater extent, and channel more development into urban centers. They invest more in transit, less in highways. His results were not impressive: For 31 studies, Bartholomew reports a median VMT reduction relative to a trend of 2.3%, and a median reduction of NO_x emissions of 2.1%.

But that's not the end of the story. Bartholomew also reported a big difference in VMT from study to study, ranging from an increase of 7% over a 20-year span for plans involving more dispersed development to a decrease of 17% for plans doing everything possible to contain VMT. (See Figure 10.2.)

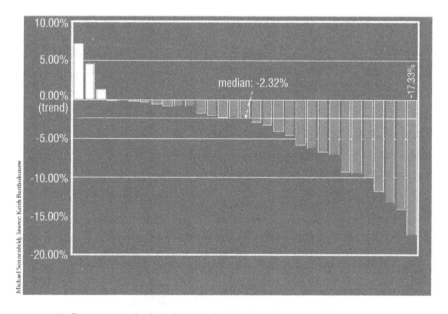

FIGURE 10.2   Difference in vehicle miles traveled over a 20-year period

Source: Bartholomew, 2007; Reprinted by permission from: Springer, Transportation, Land use-transportation scenario planning: promise and reality, Keith Bartholomew, Copyright: Springer Science+Business Media B.V. 2006

Plan Quality

Despite the centrality of comprehensive plans to the profession of city and regional planning, there is a gap in knowledge about the quality of plans because they are not routinely evaluated against best practice standards. Our second example of meta-analysis in a planning context appeared in the February 2009 issue of the *Journal of Planning Literature* and was titled "Searching for the Good Plan: A Meta-Analysis of Plan Quality Studies" (Berke & Godschalk, 2009).

Berke and Godschalk provided a comparative meta-analytic analysis of the findings from published plan quality evaluations, ranging from research studies in the United States to national planning policy applications in Holland and New Zealand, and offered recommendations about future directions in improving the content analysis of plan documents and research design in plan quality evaluation.

Their meta-analysis synthesized 16 studies of plan quality, followed by a critique of the methodology used in these studies. They followed the standard meta-analytic procedure

EVALUATION CRITERIA

Internal Characteristics
- Issue identification and vision: community needs, assets, trends
- Goals: future land use and development patterns
- Facts: current and future conditions
- Policies: principles guiding land use decisions
- Implementation: commitments to carry out actions
- Evaluation: provisions for tracking change
- Consistency: all mutually reinforcing

External Characteristics
- Organization and presentation: provisions to enhance understanding
- Coordination: integration with other plans, policies
- Compliance: consistent with plan mandates

FIGURE 10.3   Evaluation criteria for internal and external characteristics

Source: Ewing, 2009; with permission from The American Planning Association

of transforming the study statistics (e.g., means and standard deviations) into standardized scores. Using mean scores weighted by sample size, Berke and Godschalk found that the plans identify issues clearly but are weak in specifying community goals, establishing policies to achieve those goals, and providing the data needed for goal setting and policy formulation. They concluded that state-mandated plans are consistently of higher quality than optional plans.

Overall, they found that the mean scores for implementation were moderate while the scores for monitoring and evaluation were somewhat lower. Some plans clearly specified timelines for implementation and monitoring, but many did not. Compliance with plan mandates was high, though it appears that the plans often followed the letter of the law rather than the spirit. The plans received a relatively low mean score for interorganizational coordination and a still lower score for overall organization and presentation.

The article ended with recommendations for improving plan quality, which should be useful for practitioners. For researchers, it's the boost authors give to meta-analysis that is most valuable. "Planning research has expanded to the point where we are witnessing a critical need for this approach," they write. The message for literature reviewers is clear: Think big, become meta-analysts. (See Figure 10.3.)

Conclusion

In this chapter, we introduce two methods for the study of studies. Meta-analysis is a tool that researchers in the social sciences have used for decades to synthesize the available quantitative findings on a topic. Meta-analysis uses the findings from multiple studies to produce a single, authoritative effect size or elasticity of an outcome variable with respect to other independent variables. In planning, this method has been employed to combine the reported effects from large bodies of literature in a subfield in order to arrive at a figure that can more easily be utilized by planning academics and practitioners. The most famous application of meta-analysis in planning was the seminal work by Ewing and Cervero entitled "Travel and the Built Environment: A Meta-analysis." The ability to perform, or even just interpret a meta-analysis is helpful for planners, as our practical example has shown. Planners can use the results of meta-analyses in scenario planning when elasticities are applied to the predicted outcomes of estimated changes in conditions.

A more sophisticated method for creating a single figure from multiple studies of a topic has since been developed. Meta-regression is, in some part, a response to the problems of "publication bias" in creating skewed results in a meta-analysis. Meta-regression allows researchers to control for factors that might influence the findings of a study such as a study design or the inclusion of a specific important variable, publication bias, and excess heterogeneity, among others. This method was originally pioneered in the late 1980s by economists but has only recently made its way into the planning literature. The use of meta-regression in the planning field represents a step forward in the rigor of research synthesis, allowing us to feel even more confident with our figures representing well-studied relationships.

Works Cited

Bartholomew, K. (2007). Land use-transportation scenario planning: Promise and reality. *Transportation, 34*(4), 397–412. https://doi.org/10.1007/s11116-006-9108-2

Bartholomew, K., & Ewing, R. (2008). Land use—Transportation scenarios and future vehicle travel and land consumption: A meta-analysis. *Journal of the American Planning Association, 75*(1), 13–27. https://doi.org/10.1080/01944360802508726

Berke, P., & Godschalk, D. (2009). Searching for the good plan: A meta-analysis of plan quality studies. *Journal of Planning Literature, 23*(3), 227–240. https://doi.org/10.1177/0885412208327014

Borenstein, M., Hedges, L.V., Higgins, J., & Rothstein, H. R. (2009). *References* (pp. 409–414). Hoboken, NJ: John Wiley & Sons.

Borenstein, M., Rothstein, H., & Sutton, A. J. (Eds.). (2005). *Publication bias in meta-analysis: Prevention, assessment and adjustments.* Hoboken, NJ: Wiley.

Cervero, R. (2002). Induced travel demand: Research design, empirical evidence, and normative policies. *Journal of Planning Literature, 17*(1), 3–20.

Debrezion, G., Pels, E., & Rietveld, P. (2007). The impact of railway stations on residential and commercial property value: A meta-analysis. *The Journal of Real Estate Finance and Economics, 35*(2), 161–180.

Ewing, R. (2007, March). Regional scenario plans and meta-analysis. *Planning,* 38.

Ewing, R. (2009, March). Meta-analysis of plan quality—More than a literature review. *Planning,* 42.

Ewing, R. (2017, January). Making sense of different results: Is meta-regression necessarily best? *Planning,* 58–59.

Ewing, R., & Bartholomew, B. (2018). *Best practices in metropolitan transportation planning.* New York, NY: Routledge.

Ewing, R., & Cervero, R. (2010). Travel and the built environment: A meta-analysis. *Journal of the American Planning Association, 76*(3), 265–294.

Ewing, R., & Cervero, R. (2017). "Does compact development make people drive less?" The answer is yes. *Journal of the American Planning Association, 83*(1), 19–25.

Goldstein, H., & Maier, G. (2010). The use and valuation of journals in planning scholarship: Peer assessment versus impact factors. *Journal of Planning Education and Research, 30*(1), 66–75. https://doi.org/10.1080/0042098042000309748

Hedges, L. V., & Olkin, I. (1980). Vote-counting methods in research synthesis. *Psychological Bulletin, 88*(2), 359–369.

Hunter, J. E., & Schmidt, F. L. (2004). *Methods of meta-analysis: Correcting error and bias in research findings.* Thousand Oaks, CA: Sage Publications.

Kahn, A. B. (1962). Topological sorting of large networks. *Communications of the ACM, 5*(11), 558–562.

Lauria, M., & Wagner, J. A. (2006). What can we learn from empirical studies of planning theory? A comparative case analysis of extant literature. *Journal of Planning Education and Research, 25*(4), 364–381.

Lipsey, M. W., & Wilson, D. B. (2001). *Practical meta-analysis.* Thousand Oaks, CA: Sage Publications.

Littell, J. H., Corcoran, J., & Pillai, V. (2008). *Systematic reviews and meta-analysis.* Oxford: Oxford University Press.

Nijkamp, P., & Pepping, G. (1998). Meta-analysis for explaining the variance in public transport demand elasticities in Europe. *Journal of Transportation and Statistics, 1*(1), 1–14.

O'Rourke, K. (2007). An historical perspective on meta-analysis: Dealing quantitatively with varying study results. *Journal of the Royal Society of Medicine, 100*(12), 579–582.

Pearson, K. (1904). Report on certain enteric fever inoculation statistics. *British Medical Journal, 2*(2288), 1243–1246.

Schulze, R. (2004). *Meta-analysis-A comparison of approaches.* Boston, MA: Hogrefe Publishing.

Schwartz, P. (1991). *The art of the long view.* New York: Bantam Books.

Shadish, W. R., & Haddock, C. K. (1994). Combining estimates of effect size. In H. Cooper & L. V. Hedges (Eds.), *The handbook of research synthesis* (pp. 261–284). New York: Russell Sage.

Smith, M. L., & Glass, G. V. (1977). Meta-analysis of psychotherapy outcome studies. *American Psychologist, 32*(9), 752–760.

Stamps III, A. E. (1999). Demographic effects in environmental aesthetics: A meta-analysis. *Journal of Planning Literature, 14*(2), 155–175.

Stanley, T. D., & Doucouliagos, H. (2012). *Meta-regression analysis in economics and business.* London: Routledge.

Stanley, T. D., Doucouliagos, H., Giles, M., Heckemeyer, J. H., Johnston, R. J., Laroche, P., . . . Rost, K. (2013). Meta-analysis of economics research reporting guidelines. *Journal of Economic Surveys, 27*(2), 390–394. https://doi.org/10.1111/joes.12008

Stanley, T. D., & Jarrell, S. B. (1989). Meta-regression analysis: A quantitative method of literature surveys. *Journal of Economic Surveys, 3*(2), 161–170. https://doi.org/10.1111/j.1467-6419.1989.tb00064.x

Stevens, M. R. (2017). Does compact development make people drive less? *Journal of the American Planning Association, 83*(1), 7–18.

Weiner, E. (1999). *Urban transportation planning in the United States: An historical overview,* Westport, CT: Praeger.

11

MIXED-METHODS RESEARCH

Adam Millard-Ball and Keuntae Kim

Overview

Historically, planning researchers have been divided into qualitative and quantitative camps. They differed in their underlying theories of what constituted valid research (their epistemology), and their choice of methods oriented either toward interviews, ethnographies, and other qualitative approaches or toward the types of quantitative methods discussed throughout this two-volume book set.

In line with other disciplines, however, planners are increasingly turning to mixed methods as a pragmatic approach to explore different facets of a research question and to increase the validity of their findings. Mixed-methods research is defined as an approach "where the researcher mixes or combines quantitative and qualitative data, research techniques, concepts, or language into a single study" (Johnson & Onwuegbuzie, 2004).[1]

While Chapter 3 ("Types of Research") in *Basic Quantitative Research Methods for Urban Planners* briefly discussed mixed methods, this chapter provides a more in-depth explanation of the rationale and application. Two planning studies—one on gentrification and neighborhood change and the other on pedestrian safety—illustrate how mixed methods are used in practice.

Purpose

Quantitative analysis rarely gives a definitive answer. As discussed throughout this book, the quantitative methods typically employed in planning research can illuminate associations between different variables but have significant limitations. In particular, *causal* relationships are difficult to determine through regression analysis (Chapters 12 and 13 in *Basic Quantitative Research Methods for Urban Planners* and Chapter 4 in this volume). Methods such as structural equation modeling (Chapter 8 in this volume) and quasi-experimental analysis (Chapter 14 in *Basic Quantitative Research Methods for Urban Planners*) may be better suited to isolating causal linkages but are not possible to apply in many or most studies.

Qualitative methods, such as in-depth interviews, participant observation, ethnography, and focus groups, have much to commend them. They are particularly useful in understanding motivations and perceptions, in allowing individuals' voices to be heard, and in generating new theories in contexts where the researcher may not have firm prior hypotheses. However, qualitative methods also have weaknesses, such as a lack of generalizability (i.e., the difficulty in extrapolating findings from a small number of interviews or case studies), and entail difficulty in replicating a study where the data represent unique interactions between the researcher and participants.

Mixed-methods research can bridge the often adversarial divide between qualitative and quantitative camps. If we consider the types of research as a continuum stretching from purely quantitative at one end to purely qualitative research at the other end, mixed-methods research lies somewhere in the middle (Trochim & Donnelly, 2008).

Mixed methods aim to harness the different strengths of quantitative and qualitative techniques, through using them in tandem within a single study or research program. Qualitative research deals with the why and how of something, while quantitative research mostly responds to questions of how much. A key assumption is that the two types of methods do not share the same biases (Gaber & Gaber, 1997) and that thus the strengths of one method can compensate for the weaknesses of the other. Often, the qualitative component identifies processes, mechanisms, and perceptions, while the quantitative component estimates the magnitude of any impact or generates conclusions that apply to a wider set of contexts.

Sometimes, mixed methods are seen as a form of *triangulation* (Jick, 1979) in that researchers can compare findings from different methods and check where these results agree. Triangulation can also be used to validate data sources. For example, the study of gentrification by Loukaitou-Sideris, Gonzalez, and Ong (2019) used both parcel assessment data and field observations to identify buildings that had undergone renovations or major improvements—a valuable approach since each source had its own inaccuracies and omissions. The gentrification researchers also used visual surveys and interviews with local stakeholders to identify neighborhood changes that were not captured by other data sources—upscale landscaping or businesses catering to new types of clientele, to give two examples.

However, mixed methods can be equally valuable when the component methods produce contradictory results. Such divergence often becomes an opportunity to enrich an explanation (Jick, 1979). For example, Gaber and Gaber (1997) find two very different pictures of street vending on 14th Street in Manhattan—a neighborhood of white, upper-income residents according to census data—and an intricate social and economic dynamic between lower-income, recent immigrants according to participant observation-based field research. They conclude (p. 96): "If each method were taken independently as a primary source of data, the individual interpretations of street vending on 14th Street would each yield very different insights and thus very different policy recommendations."

Creswell and Plano Clark (2018, pp. 8–12) identify seven situations in which mixed methods are particularly valuable:

1. **To provide more complete and corroborated results**: The study of gentrification by Loukaitou-Sideris et al. (2019), previously discussed, provides a good example of this type of triangulation.
2. **To explain initial results**: For example, Benner and Pastor (2015) use qualitative data to make sense of their econometric findings on the relationship between social inclusion and regional economic prosperity. Their interviews allow different causal pathways to be uncovered in a way that is not possible with regression analysis.

3. **To develop survey instruments**: An initial qualitative study can identify key questions and response options to be incorporated in a questionnaire or other survey instrument.
4. **To enhance an experimental study**: Qualitative methods can provide more nuance on experimental results by interviewing participants.
5. **To provide a more holistic understanding of case studies**: Benner and Pastor (2015) use census data, employment statistics, and other indicators to build quantitative profiles of each of their 11 case study regions that complement their interview-based qualitative work.
6. **To involve participants in the study**: In one study of community gardens in Buffalo, the engagement of local residents helped to shape the scope and findings of the GIS analysis (Knigge & Cope, 2006).
7. **To develop, implement, and evaluate a program**: Particularly in longer-term research programs, qualitative work can be used to design a policy or behavioral intervention, which can then be tested quantitatively in subsequent work.

Mixed methods can be particularly suited for *wicked problems*, which are inherently complex, ill defined, and lacking straightforward solutions. According to Mertens (2018), mixed methods provide a common language, a way to communicate with diverse stakeholders and a more nuanced set of findings that speak to the complexity of the planning problem.

An important downside of mixed-methods research is the greater demand on researchers' time and methodological skills. Using more than one method almost always takes longer than a single-method study. Moreover, multiple methods may require researchers to expand their methodological repertoire or to work in a team where the members have expertise in different research approaches. Teamwork is desirable in this complex world of ours, but it does complicate the research process.

History

The idea of using quantitative and qualitative methods in a single study was already evident in early natural science in the seventeenth century (Maxwell, 2016). Galileo's observation of the moon's craters was a result of both visual observation and mathematical measurement of their shadow lengths. Geologist Charles Lyell, meanwhile, estimated the relative age of different European strata using fieldwork descriptions and also measurements of the proportions of fossil shells (Maxwell, 2016). In earlier years, there was less methodological orthodoxy, and researchers were less specialized, meaning that it was more common to draw on multiple methods (Pinto, 2012).

The quantitative paradigm became dominant in the first half of the twentieth century, as researchers believed that meaningful results could be obtained through experience or direct measurement—that is, positivism (Trochim & Donnelly, 2008). However, some quantitative studies still added interviews or field observations to complement their primary quantitative methods, even though mixed methods were not formalized in the research process (Pinto, 2012).

The 1970s to the late 1980s saw an ardent debate, or *paradigm war*, between quantitative and qualitative researchers. In order to defend the purity of quantitative and qualitative research design and methods, advocates on both research sides argued that quantitative and qualitative research methods could not and should not be combined within a single study—the so-called incompatibility of methods thesis (Johnson & Onwuegbuzie, 2004). Applications of multiple methods belonging to the same research approach were widely used, but the integration of methods from different research paradigms was not accepted in most research practices.

As the paradigm wars declined in salience after 1990, researchers began to believe that compatibility of quantitative and qualitative methods was possible and that mixed methods allowed for more comprehensive answers to broader research questions. Mixed methods emerged from the paradigm war as a third paradigm—pragmatism—that sought to bridge quantitative–qualitative divides and epistemological transitions. Pragmatism sought to sidestep philosophical and epistemological debates over the validity of research, to the extent that these debates did not make a difference in the actual research process (Johnson & Onwuegbuzie, 2004; Creswell & Plano Clark, 2018).

Notably, in the early 2000s, Tashakkori and Teddlie published the *Handbook of Mixed Methods in Social & Behavioral Research*, which provided the first comprehensive overview of mixed methods research; the handbook is now in its second edition (Tashakkori & Teddlie, 2010). In 2007, the *Journal of Mixed Methods Research* was established as a home for articles on both methodological and practical approaches to mixed-methods research. According to the second edition of the Tashakkori and Teddlie handbook, the number of PhD dissertations using mixed methods increased from 23 in 1997 to 718 in 2007.

Mechanics

Mixed methods provide a flexible umbrella for research approaches that combine qualitative and quantitative methods. There is therefore no single recipe for conducting mixed-methods research, and a wide variety of approaches are evident from different studies.

However, mixed-methods work still requires a researcher to uphold the rigor and standards of the individual methods that comprise the study. Mixed methods are not a license for methodological shortcuts. For quantitative methods, the principles discussed in the earlier chapters of this book still apply. For guides to qualitative methods in planning, see Gaber and Gaber (2007) or Silverman and Patterson (2015); for qualitative work in the social sciences more generally, see Hay (2016).

At the simplest level, a mixed methods study might involve a small quantitative or qualitative component added to a study where the opposite approach constitutes the main effort. For example, researchers could conduct formal interviews with stakeholders with whom they may be in contact anyway for the quantitative portion of the research[2] or use qualitative analysis software to code open-ended questions on surveys. Or they may develop quantitative demographic profiles to complement an ethnographic study of neighborhood change.

A more synergistic approach, however, takes greater advantage of the interplay between different methods. One key consideration, discussed in the following subsection, is sequencing: whether one method precedes the other in a study or both are done in tandem. A later subsection discusses the issues that mixed methods raise for data analysis and interpretation.

Sequencing

A useful way to classify and understand mixed-methods research design is through different options for sequencing or the time order in which methods are used. Figure 11.1 shows how sequencing, along with the emphasis given to each method, generates four groupings.

Time Order
Decision

	Concurrent	Sequential
Equal Status	QUAL + QUAN	QUAL → QUAN QUAN → QUAL
Dominant Status	QUAL + quan QUAN + qual	QUAL → quan qual → QUAN QUAN → qual quan → QUAL

Paradigm Emphasis Decision

FIGURE 11.1   Four types of mixed methods research designs: + = concurrent, → = sequential; lowercase letters = low priority or weight in data hierarchy or structure

Source: Johnson & Onwuegbuzie, 2004

Convergent Designs

Qualitative and quantitative methods can be used concurrently, in so-called convergent designs (left column in Figure 11.1). In this type of design, quantitative and qualitative data are brought together in a single stage of the research. Each strand can receive equal emphasis (upper left quadrant in Figure 11.1), or one method can be dominant (lower left quadrant). The primary intent is to compare and synthesize the results from the different methods, for example, through triangulation (Creswell & Plano Clark, 2018).

An example of a convergent design is *Measuring the Unmeasurable: Urban Design Qualities Related to Walkability* (Ewing & Handy, 2009). A panel of 10 urban design and planning experts was shown 48 video clips of streetscapes and asked to both rate the streetscapes on a Likert scale with respect to urban design qualities, such as complexity and transparency, and also to comment on the physical features of each streetscape that caused it to rate high or low on the Likert scale. These *interviews* with panel members helped to qualitatively define urban design qualities of streetscapes and provided the research team with qualitative insights into physical features that influenced their ratings. The panelists' ratings were subsequently modeled quantitatively in terms of the physical features previously identified by the panel to produce metrics used to predict pedestrian activity levels.

Explanatory Sequential Designs

Sequential designs (right column in Figure 11.1) allow one dataset to be built on the results of the other. One variant is the explanatory sequential design (QUAN → QUAL), which uses qualitative methods to explain the initial quantitative results (Creswell & Plano Clark, 2018). Often, such designs use the qualitative component to explain the mechanisms that are driving findings from a regression analysis.

An explanatory sequential design opens up several possible synergies between the qualitative and quantitative parts of the study. For example, in their analysis of the neighborhood impacts of freeway-to-boulevard conversions in San Francisco, Cervero, Kang, and Shively (2009) presented interviewees with the results of regression analysis and asked them to react and elaborate. Yang and O'Neill (2014) and Mouratidis (2018), meanwhile, used household surveys to assess residents' preferences for compact neighborhoods in Eugene, Oregon, and Oslo, Norway, respectively. Each study followed up the survey with qualitative interviews to probe *why* these preferences exist. Mouratidis, for example, ascribed high satisfaction with compact neighborhoods in Oslo to the lack of the disamenities that trouble urban residents in some other cities, such as noise, crime, and lack of greenery.

A similar explanatory sequential design was employed by Benner and Pastor (2015) in their study of equity and economic growth. They used interviews to explore the different causal pathways that might explain their econometric findings, and pointed to the "depth of understanding, particularly of qualitative social processes, that can only be attained with visits to the field."

An explanatory sequential design also enables the use of regression analysis as a systematic way to select case studies for in-depth qualitative study. Purposeful case selection, whether of *typical*, *deviant*, or other types of cases, can maximize the chances that the case studies will reveal useful information and reduce the bias that occurs when researchers select the most well-known cases or those that are convenient to them. [See Seawright & Gerring (2008) and Flyvbjerg (2006) for more guidance on case selection.]

In Millard-Ball's (2013) study of climate planning, discussed in Chapter 3 of *Basic Quantitative Research Methods for Urban Planners*, the chosen case studies were *deviant*; case study cities had either many more or many fewer LEED-certified buildings than would be expected given the city's building activity, environmental preferences, and other variables. The farther a case was from the 45-degree line in Figure 11.2, the worse the prediction was of the regression model, the more deviant the case, and the more likely it was to reveal interesting insights through an in-depth case study. Three case studies were chosen: one overperformer with a climate plan (Suburbiton), one overperformer with no climate plan (Greenacres), and one underperformer with a climate plan (Collegetown).

Benner and Pastor's (2015) study of equity and economic growth, meanwhile, chose 11 metropolitan case studies based on two composite indices measuring growth and equity. By identifying high performers in each geographic region, they selected case studies that were likely to illuminate the processes behind economic and social success. Two of the cases were matched with low performers in the same state, providing paired comparisons that effectively controlled for state-level characteristics.

Exploratory Sequential Designs

In an exploratory sequential design, qualitative data analysis precedes the quantitative phase. Such a design can be used to develop survey instruments or testable hypotheses, to select variables for inclusion in a regression, or to identify the plausibility of a causal process that will then be modeled (Creswell & Plano Clark, 2018). Exploratory sequential designs are particularly useful when there is no guiding framework or theory that can be used to design the quantitative approach.

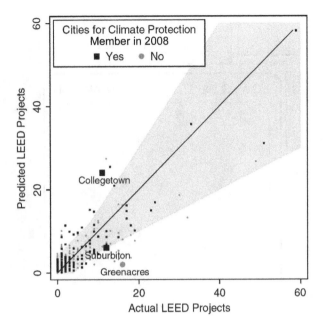

FIGURE 11.2   Case selection: drawn from outside the shaded area, which indicates cities where the predicted number of LEED projects is close to the actual number

Source: Millard-Ball, 2013

Marsden, Kelly, & Nellthorp (2009), for example, analyzed the likely impacts of a new transportation funding scheme in England, under which local governments were rewarded for their performance against targets. Interviews with local government officials helped shape a mail-back survey, which in turn informed a game theoretic model and the design of a laboratory device—a computerized, multiplayer game where players took the role of a local government and responded to different funding allocation rules. The researchers note (p. 66): "None of the methods adopted alone would have provided a picture complete enough for us to draw practical conclusions. Taken together, however, there are some key themes and conclusions arising."

Other Designs

The three designs just discussed—convergent, explanatory sequential, and exploratory sequential—are the most common but by no means the only options for researchers. More complex approaches include *embedded designs*, where one dataset is nested within another dataset; *multiphase designs*, which may be cyclical or recursive as different components of the research inform one another; and *participatory–social justice designs*, where community members are actively involved in the research process (Creswell & Plano Clark, 2018). For example, Knigge and Cope's study of community gardens (Figure 11.3) involved an iterative process as GIS visualizations, interviews, participant observations, and public meetings informed one another but not as part of a linear process (Knigge & Cope, 2006).

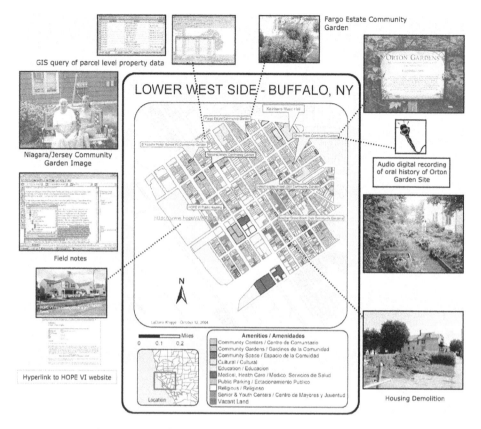

FIGURE 11.3 Visual integration of mixed methods in a recursive design

Source: Knigge & Cope, 2006

Analysis and Interpretation

An important stage in the analysis of most mixed-methods datasets is the triangulation process, where researchers compare findings from the different methods. Loukaitou-Sideris et al. (2019) presented a table and a matrix (shown in Figure 11.4) of the findings of the different quantitative and qualitative indicators of gentrification. The authors argued (p. 239) that "gentrification is a fluid process that cannot be captured by one indicator or one source of data" and thus is best manifested through compiling different empirical indicators. For example, in one of their case study neighborhoods—Mariachi Plaza—they found that census data showed no residential or commercial gentrification, but that visual observations and interviews pointed to early signs of both.

More broadly, a researcher's results might agree (*convergence*), provide complementary information for a comprehensive result (*complementarity*), or contradict each other (*discrepancy* or *dissonance*) (O'Cathain, Murphy, & Nicholl, 2010). In the first two instances—convergence and complementarity—a researcher's confidence in the findings is strengthened, and the depth of analysis can be increased. However, intermethod discrepancies do not necessarily signal a problem with the research but instead are an invitation to return to the data (possibly

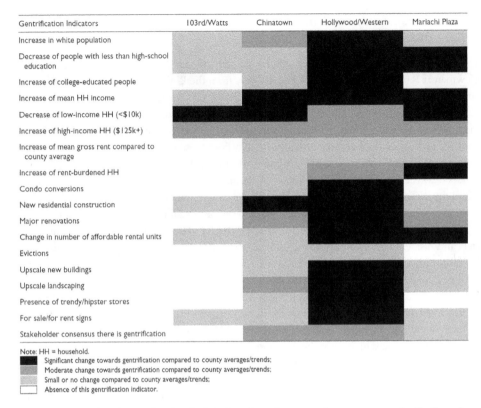

Gentrification Indicators	103rd/Watts	Chinatown	Hollywood/Western	Mariachi Plaza
Increase in white population				
Decrease of people with less than high-school education				
Increase of college-educated people				
Increase of mean HH income				
Decrease of low-income HH (<$10k)				
Increase of high-income HH ($125k+)				
Increase of mean gross rent compared to county average				
Increase of rent-burdened HH				
Condo conversions				
New residential construction				
Major renovations				
Change in number of affordable rental units				
Evictions				
Upscale new buildings				
Upscale landscaping				
Presence of trendy/hipster stores				
For sale/for rent signs				
Stakeholder consensus there is gentrification				

Note: HH = household.
■ Significant change towards gentrification compared to county averages/trends;
▨ Moderate change towards gentrification compared to county averages/trends;
▧ Small or no change compared to county averages/trends;
☐ Absence of this gentrification indicator.

FIGURE 11.4 Study of gentrification in Los Angeles using a matrix to compare the findings from different quantitative and qualitative indicators, allowing the reader to easily identify areas of agreement

Source: Loukaitou-Sideris et al., 2019

collecting more) or to explore the reasons for the diverging findings (Johnson & Onwueg-buzie, 2004; O'Cathain et al., 2010).

Because the analysis, interpretation, and findings of both quantitative and qualitative components are included, journal articles or professional reports using mixed-methods research design tend to be longer than for single-method studies. Furthermore, the traditional styles of writing and ways of delivering information differ widely between quantitative and qualitative research approaches. The use of language and structural writing in mixed-methods research is still under debate among methodologists (Tashakkori & Teddlie, 2010). Therefore, when writing mixed-methods research articles or professional reports, researchers should be cautious with terminology, and they may need to clarify the rationale for and the process of their mixed-methods research design.

Planning Examples

One mixed-methods study, on the effectiveness of climate action planning in California cities (Millard-Ball, 2012, 2013), is discussed in detail in Chapter 3 of *Basic Quantitative Research Methods for Urban Planners.* We provide two other examples.

Mixed-Method Study on Gentrification and Resistance to Displacement in New York City

To address a bigger and more comprehensive picture of gentrification and displacement, Kathe Newman at Rutgers University and Elvin K. Wyly from the University of British Columbia conducted a mixed-methods study (Newman & Wyly, 2006). On the quantitative side, the authors used the longitudinal New York City Housing and Vacancy Survey to measure the change in housing vacancy rates over time and to estimate logistic regression models to identify the extent and neighborhood location of displacement pressures. Results from these regressions showed that households living in lower-cost units were more likely to be displaced. When spatial and time-series data were included in the logistic regression model to identify the role of contextual effects, the authors found significant spatial and localized impacts. For example, renters from the Bronx, Brooklyn, and Queens tended to have a lower probability of displacement than those from Manhattan.

The qualitative element of the study consisted largely of interviews with community organizers and residents in seven sub-borough areas. The interviews sought to assess the catalysts for neighborhood change, the role and internal dynamics of different stakeholder groups, and the effects of neighborhood changes on disadvantaged groups. A key aim was to illuminate the perspectives of the individuals and groups that were experiencing neighborhood change firsthand.

In some respects, the two sets of methods converged in their conclusions. Both interviews and the regression models revealed pressures on displacement due to dramatic changes in the study communities, which disproportionately affected low-income residents.

The interviews, however, also identified practices that did not show up in the quantitative dataset. For example, the displacement figures did not include those forced to double up with other households or people who were made homeless. Moreover, the authors noted that their qualitative work "documents the continued political salience of displacement and reveals an increasingly sophisticated and creative array of methods used to resist displacement."

Combining both quantitative and qualitative results, the authors suggested groups of mechanisms that enable low-income residents to stay in gentrifying neighborhoods—public interventions like the city's rent regulation and affordable housing requirements; and private strategies such as social connections between tenants and landlords, and antidisplacement campaigns by community organizations.

This study represents a good example of how an explanatory sequential mixed-methods design can be implemented within a single study. In the quantitative part, the logistic regression model played a role in measuring the extent of displacement within and across boroughs in New York City. Then, in the qualitative research part, interviews were used to check the validity of the quantitative research and also understand residents' perspectives on displacement and gentrification over time. Policy recommendations at the end of the study came from the findings across the two methods, suggesting that mixed-methods research has the potential to uncover more comprehensive answers to a broader and more complex research question than single-method studies.

Mixed-Method Study of Pedestrian–Automobile Collisions in Los Angeles

Studying the determinants of collisions between pedestrians and automobiles in Los Angeles, Anastasia Loukaitou-Sideris, Robin Liggett, and Hyun-Gun Sung (2007) from UCLA turned to a mixed-methods approach that combined GIS analysis, linear regression, and qualitative case studies. Typically, road safety researchers focus on quantitative tools to model collision risk. But here the researchers complemented this data with field observations of pedestrian activity, pedestrian and motorist visibility, and conflicts at driveways.

In the regression analysis, the authors aggregated collision data to the census tract level, and included independent variables representing four different factors: pedestrian exposure, traffic levels, sociodemographic characteristics, and land use characteristics. The final regression model of collisions showed the strongest associations with population and employment densities (which were treated as proxies for pedestrian exposure), traffic levels, the percentage of Hispanic/Latino residents, and the share of commercial and retail land uses.

However, strong correlations between the different demographic variables—age, gender, ethnicity, poverty, and household size—made it difficult to determine whether income, age structure, or race, or some combination of them, were the most important factors, given that pedestrian collisions occur disproportionately in low-income, minority neighborhoods with a high percentage of children under 15. Moreover, while the extent of commercial and retail land uses had a strong association with collisions, the regression results alone did not indicate whether this is due to greater exposure (more pedestrians are present around retail uses) or an inherent effect of the land use type.

To address some of these limitations, the researchers selected 12 case study street intersections for in-depth field study. Importantly, the quantitative data were used to select the cases. The 12 intersections were drawn from the 20 intersections citywide with the highest collision risk and chosen to reflect geographical and socioeconomic diversity (for example, by avoiding having two case studies in close proximity).

The field surveys collected both quantitative data (e.g., the number of driveways and pedestrian lighting fixtures) and qualitative data (e.g., obstructions to lines of sight) and helped to identify many microlevel characteristics that likely influenced pedestrian safety. For example, almost all the intersections had a large number of driveways, which introduced conflicts between pedestrians and entering and exiting vehicles. Obstructions to vision such as parked cars, stopped buses, and shrubbery and vendors were also observed in every case study, with pedestrians sometimes darting out into the street in front of buses at the stops.

This study is another good example of explanatory sequential mixed methods, where the qualitative data provides more nuance and context to complement the aggregate findings from the regression analysis and GIS mapping. Neither method on its own is conclusive, and, because the qualitative cases are drawn only from high-risk locations, it is difficult to give the findings a causal interpretation. (For example, driveways and visual impairments may also be common at low-risk locations.) However, the strengths and the biases of each method only partially overlap, meaning that the overall conclusions are more robust and lay the groundwork for the authors' policy recommendations, such as annual safety audits, and mitigating the impacts of commercial land uses by consolidating driveways.

Conclusion

Mixed-methods research has a long history, but until recently, the lack of a systematic framework hampered its use and recognition. Since the turn of the century, mixed-methods research has gained in popularity, in planning as well as in the social and health sciences. The approach can yield more comprehensive answers to complicated and broad research questions through blending data, methods, and ways of interpreting results from quantitative and qualitative traditions. Moreover, the synergies between the different methods—such as the ability to take a systematic approach to case selection—allow mixed methods to rise to more than the sum of their component parts.

Because mixed methods can involve many different quantitative and qualitative components, which can be sequenced in various ways, there is no single prescription for mixed-methods data collection and analysis. Various approaches have been used in planning research, including using qualitative data to explain quantitative results and using quantitative methods to generalize exploratory qualitative findings. Regardless, however, researchers should build on best practices for rigor and transparency in each portion of the research.

Mixed-methods research is still in a relatively early phase. As more studies adopt this approach and as the methodological literature progresses, mixed-methods research is likely to enhance its reputation as a distinctive approach and enrich the diversity of both academic and practical research. Historically, planning journals have been methodologically eclectic and open to both qualitative and quantitative ways of knowing, and mixed-methods is a natural extension to an inclusive research tradition.

Notes

1. Note that mixed-methods research should not be confused with mixed models, which are a statistical technique to incorporate fixed and random effects in a regression analysis.
2. Note that approval for human subjects research from a university's Institutional Review Board will often be required for qualitative methods, as well as for surveys and many other quantitative techniques.

Works Cited

Benner, C., & Pastor, M. (2015). *Equity, growth, and community: What the nation can learn from America's metro areas*. Oakland: University of California Press.

Cervero, R., Kang, J., & Shively, K. (2009). From elevated freeways to surface boulevards: Neighborhood and housing price impacts in San Francisco. *Journal of Urbanism: International Research on Placemaking and Urban Sustainability*, 2(1), 31–50.

Creswell, J. W., & Plano Clark, V. L. (2018). *Designing and conducting mixed methods research* (3rd ed.). Thousand Oaks, CA: Sage Publications.

Ewing, R., & Handy, S. (2009). Measuring the unmeasurable: Urban design qualities related to walkability. *Journal of Urban Design*, 14(1), 65–84.

Flyvbjerg, B. (2006). Five misunderstandings about case-study research. *Qualitative Inquiry*, 12(2), 219–245.

Gaber, J., & Gaber, S. L. (1997). Utilizing mixed-method research designs in planning: The case of 14th Street, New York City. *Journal of Planning Education and Research*, 17(2), 95–103.

Gaber, J., & Gaber, S. L. (2007). *Qualitative analysis for planning and policy: Beyond the numbers*. Chicago, IL: American Planning Association.

Hay, I. (Ed.). (2016). *Qualitative research methods in human geography* (4th ed.). Oxford: Oxford University Press.

Jick, T. D. (1979). Mixing qualitative and quantitative methods: Triangulation in action. *Administrative Science Quarterly*, 24(4), 602–611.

Johnson, R. B., & Onwuegbuzie, A. J. (2004). Mixed methods research: A research paradigm whose time has come. *Educational Researcher*, 33(7), 14–26.

Knigge, L., & Cope, M. (2006). Grounded visualization: Integrating the analysis of qualitative and quantitative data through grounded theory and visualization. *Environment and Planning A*, 38(11), 2021–2037.

Loukaitou-Sideris, A., Gonzalez, S., & Ong, P. (2019). Triangulating neighborhood knowledge to understand neighborhood change: Methods to study gentrification. *Journal of Planning Education and Research*, *39*(2), 227–242.

Loukaitou-Sideris, A., Liggett, R., & Sung, H-G. (2007). Death on the crosswalk. *Journal of Planning Education and Research*, *26*(3), 338–351.

Marsden, G., Kelly, C., & Nellthorp, J. (2009). The likely impacts of target setting and performance rewards in local transport. *Transport Policy*, *16*(2), 59–67.

Maxwell, J. A. (2016). Expanding the history and range of mixed methods research. *Journal of Mixed Methods Research*, *10*(1), 12–27.

Mertens, D. M. (2018). *Mixed methods design in evaluation*. Thousand Oaks, CA: Sage Publications.

Millard-Ball, A. (2012). Do city climate plans reduce emissions? *Journal of Urban Economics*, *71*(3), 289–311.

Millard-Ball, A. (2013). The limits to planning: Causal impacts of city climate action plans. *Journal of Planning Education and Research*, *33*(1), 5–19.

Mouratidis, K. (2018). Is compact city livable? The impact of compact versus sprawled neighbourhoods on neighbourhood satisfaction. *Urban Studies*, *55*(11), 2408–2430.

Newman, K., & Wyly, E. K. (2006). The right to stay put, revisited: Gentrification and resistance to displacement in New York City. *Urban Studies*, *43*(1), 23–57.

O'Cathain, A., Murphy, M., & Nicholl, J. (2010). Three techniques for integrating data in mixed methods studies. *The British Medical Journal (BMJ)*, *341*, c4587.

Office of Behavioral and Social Sciences Research. (2010). *Best practices for mixed methods research in the health sciences*. Retrieved from https://obssr.od.nih.gov/wp-content/uploads/2016/02/Best_Practices_for_Mixed_Methods_Research.pdf

Onwuegbuzie, A. J., & Leech, N. L. (2000). Validity and qualitative research: An oxymoron? *Quality & Quantity*, *41*, 233–249.

Pinto, R. M. (2012). Mixed methods design. In N. J. Salkind (Ed.), *Encyclopedia of research design*. Thousand Oaks, CA: Sage Publications.

Seawright, J., & Gerring, J. (2008). Case selection techniques in case study research—A menu of qualitative and quantitative options. *Political Research Quarterly*, *61*(2), 294–308.

Silverman, R. M., & Patterson, K. L. (2015). *Qualitative research methods for community development*. New York, NY: Routledge.

Tashakkori, A., & Teddlie, C. (2010). *Sage handbook of mixed methods in social and behavioral research* (2nd ed.). Thousand Oaks, CA: Sage Publications.

Trochim, W. M. K., & Donnelly, J. P. (2008). *The research methods knowledge base*. Mason, OH: Cengage Learning.

Yang, Y., & O'Neill, K. (2014). Understanding factors affecting people's attitudes toward living in compact and mixed-use environments: A case study of a New Urbanist project in Eugene, Oregon, USA. *Journal of Urbanism: International Research on Placemaking and Urban Sustainability*, *7*(1), 1–22.

CONTRIBUTORS

Brian Baucom, PhD (Chapter 7), is an associate professor in the Department of Psychology at the University of Utah.

Simon C. Brewer, PhD (Chapters 5, 6, and 9), is an associate professor in the Department of Geography at the University of Utah.

Tracey Bushman, (Chapters 5 and 6), is a data technician at Salt Lake City School District.

Divya Chandrasekhar, PhD (Chapter 1), is an assistant professor in the Department of City and Metropolitan Planning at the University of Utah.

Roger Child (Chapter 7) is a PhD candidate in the Department of City and Metropolitan Planning at the University of Utah and the Chair of the Planning Commission for Farmington City, Utah.

Reid Ewing, PhD (editor, Chapters 2–4, 7, 8, and 10) is Distinguished Professor of City and Metropolitan Planning and Distinguished Chair for Resilient Places at the University of Utah and an associate editor of the *Journal of the American Planning Association*.

Andrea Garfinkel-Castro (Chapters 5 and 6) is a PhD candidate in the Department of City and Metropolitan Planning at the University of Utah.

James B. Grace, PhD (Chapter 8), is a Senior Research Scientist at the Wetland and Aquatic Research Center of the United States Geological Survey (USGS).

William H. Greene, PhD (Chapter 4), is an Emeritus Professor in the Department of Economics at New York University Stern School of Business.

Fatemeh Kiani (Chapter 1) is a PhD student in the Department of City and Metropolitan Planning at the University of Utah.

Keuntae Kim (Chapters 9 and 11) is a PhD student in the Department of City and Metropolitan Planning at the University of Utah.

John Kircher, PhD (Chapter 7), is Professor Emeritus in the Department of Educational Psychology at the University of Utah and Chief Scientist on the Converus Science Team.

Zacharia Levine (Chapters 5 and 7) is Community and Economic Development Director of Grand County, Utah, and a PhD student in the Department of City and Metropolitan Planning at the University of Utah.

Torrey Lyons, PhD (Chapters 8 and 10), is postdoctoral scholar at University of North Carolina at Chapel Hill.

Adam Millard-Ball, PhD (Chapter 11), is an associate professor in the Environmental Studies Department at the University of California, Santa Cruz.

Matt Miller (Chapter 8) is Senior Planning Analyst at Metro Analytics and a PhD student in the Department of City and Metropolitan Planning at the University of Utah.

Anusha Musunuru, Ph.D. (Chapter 4), is an engineering associate at Kittelson & Associates, Inc.

Keunhyun Park, Ph.D. (editor, Chapters 1 and 6), is an assistant professor in the Department of Landscape Architecture and Environmental Planning at Utah State University.

David Proffitt (Chapters 3 and 4) is a PhD candidate in the Department of City and Metropolitan Planning at the University of Utah.

Robin Rothfeder, PhD (Chapter 2), is an assistant professor in the Department of Human Dimensions of Natural Resource Management at University of Wisconsin–Stevens Point and a land use specialist with the University of Wisconsin–Madison Division of Extension.

Sadegh Sabouri (Chapters 1 and 6) is a PhD student in the Department of City and Metropolitan Planning at the University of Utah.

Fariba Siddiq (Chapters 1 and 3) is a PhD student in the Department of Urban Planning at UCLA Luskin School of Public Affairs.

Yu Song (Chapter 6) is a former PhD student in the Department of Civil & Environmental Engineering at the University of Utah.

Mark Stevens, PhD (Chapter 10), is an associate professor in the School of Community and Regional Planning at the University of British Columbia.

Ivana Tasic, PhD (Chapter 8), is an assistant professor in the Department of Architecture and Civil Engineering at Chalmers University of Technology.

Kathryn Terzano, PhD (Chapter 3), is a lecturer in College of Integrative Sciences and Arts at Arizona State University.

Matt Wheelwright (Chapter 5) is a PhD candidate in the Department of City and Metropolitan Planning at the University of Utah.

Robert Young, PhD (Chapter 7), is Professor Emeritus in the School of Architecture and a former director of the Historic Preservation Program at the University of Utah.

INDEX

Page numbers in *italics* indicate figures; page numbers in **bold** indicate tables.

Printed in the USA
CPSIA information can be obtained
at www.ICGtesting.com
LVHW072001220224
772581LV00007B/595